IRAN AND IRAQ
AT WAR

IRAN AND IRAQ AT WAR

Shahram Chubin
and
Charles Tripp

WESTVIEW PRESS
Boulder, Colorado.

Published in the United States by
WESTVIEW PRESS
Frederick A. Praeger, Publisher
5500 Central Avenue
Boulder, Colorado 80301

Published in 1988 in London by
I.B.Tauris & Co Ltd
Publishers
3 Henrietta Street
Covent Garden
London WC2E 8PW

This work has been prepared with the generous
assistance of the Fritz Thyssen Stiftung.

Library of Congress Cataloging in Publication Data
Chubin, Shahram.
Iran and Iraq at war / by Shahram Chubin, Charles Tripp.
p.   cm.
Bibliography: p.
ISBN 0–8133–0734–1
1. Iraqi-Iranian Conflict. 1980–   2. Middle East—
Politics and government—1945–   3. Iran—History—1979–
4. Iraq—History—1958–
I. Tripp, Charles. II. Title.
DS318.85.C48   1988
955'.054–dc19   88–5711 CIP

Contents

'After all this, Khomeini comes and calls on the Iraqi people . . . to go out on the rooftops and protest against their government. He said the Shah had gone and someone else had come. It turned out that it was another Shah, but this time wearing a turban': Saddam Hussein, Nineveh, 15 April 1980.

'When a clash is a patriotic and national duty, we shall wage it in all its forms . . . Iraq is once again to assume its leading Arab role. Iraq is once again to serve the Arab nation and defend its honour, dignity and sovereignty. Iraq is destined once again to face the concerted machinations of the forces of darkness . . . This demands sacrifice, but you are not tired of sacrifice': Saddam Hussein, Nineveh, 15 April 1980.

'An Iraqi ruler who bows to Khomeini or to anyone else will be trampled upon by the Iraqis . . . we are not the kind of people to bow to Khomeini. He has wagered to bend us and we have wagered to bend him. We shall see who will bend the other': Saddam Hussein, Baghdad, 20 July 1980.

'We are now forced to fight for peace and to bring the rulers of Iran back to their senses, so that they will establish relations of good-neighbourliness between Iran and the countries of the region': Tariq Aziz, Paris, 25 September 1980.

'Despite our victory, if you ask me now if we should have gone to war, I would say: It would have been better if we had not gone to war. But we had no other choice. If you ask me now: Would you like the war to last a week or six months? I would say: We prefer the war to last a week, provided we regain all our rights . . . But if they think we have not taken a protracted war into consideration, they are mistaken. In this protracted war, we will continue to fight until our enemy says: Yes, we have agreed to your rights': Saddam Hussein, Baghdad, 4 November 1980.

'Khomeini is not a man of religion. Whoever describes him as such is fanatical, stupid and understands nothing of politics. Khomeini is a politician. When he realises he is losing more than he is gaining, he will establish peace': Saddam Hussein, Baghdad, 10 November 1982.

'The rulers of Iran cannot go on with the war without the earnest backing, both in word and deed, of their supporters. Therefore, the need to influence the relationship between the rulers of Iran and their supporters, by creating differences between them on the question of war and peace is a matter of paramount importance': Saddam Hussein, Baghdad, 26 March 1983.

'The damage caused by this criminal is irreparable unless he withdraws his forces and leaves Iraq and abandons his corrupt government; he must leave the Iraqis to decide their own fate. It is not a question of a fight between one government and another; it is a question of an invasion by an Iraqi non-Muslim Ba'thist against an Islamic country, and this is a rebellion by blasphemy against Islam': Ayatollah Rouhollah Khomeini, Tehran, 20 October 1980.

'The day we put, with the grace of God, a victorious end to the imposed war, no other country would dare attack us': Hashemi Rafsanjani, Tehran, 1 February 1985.

'They want to force us to compromise so that tomorrow the reactionaries in the region can speak out against Islam and call it an unsuccessful experiment. They aim to erode the Islamic revolution through an imposed peace and drive it towards destruction': Prime Minister Mir Hussein Musavi, Tehran, 5 June 1985.

'I come from Iran which has been the birthplace of the most acclaimed and, at the same time, the least known revolution of the contemporary period – a revolution based upon the religion of God and in continuation of the path of God's messengers and great divine teachers and a path as long as the whole of human history': President Ali Khamenei, New York, Address to the UN General Assembly, 22 September 1987.

'The Algerian revolution took one million lives out of fourteen million people. We are fifty million. It is still very early for us to put aside our arms and refrain from the holy defence which is one of our mandatory duties . . . We say to the world: we want our rights and justice. Our wish is to see corruption uprooted': Musavi Ardebili (President of the Supreme Judicial Council), Tehran, 9 October 1987.

IRAN-IRAQ LAND FRONTIER

Rawanduz●

Kirkuk●

Panjwin●
Sulaymaniyya● ●Marivan

●Sanandaj

●Paveh

Khanaqin● ●Qasr-e Shirin

●Kermanshah

Ba'qubah● ●Suma
●Mandali

●Baghdad

TIGRIS

Iran

●Mehran

Al Kut●

Shaykh●
Sa'd ●Ali al
      Gharbi

●Andimeshk ●Dezful

Iraq

●Masjed-e
 Soleyman●

Al Amarah●

●Susangird

EUPHRATES

●Ahwaz

- ● - ● - International Boundary
● National Capital
● City or Town

100 50 0 100 km

Basra● ●Khorramshahr
        ●Abadan

Umm Qasr●

Al Fao●

KUWAIT ●Bubiyan PERSIAN GULF

IRAQ-SAUDI ARABIA
NEUTRAL ZONE

Kuwait●

●Mina al Ahmadi

Acknowledgements

This book grew out of a research project initiated by and carried out under the auspices of the Programme for Strategic and International Security Studies, at the Graduate Institute of International Studies in Geneva. The project was generously sponsored by the Fritz Thyssen Stiftung whose funding has also enabled the final report to be published in its present form. The authors would, therefore, like to acknowledge with gratitude the institutional and financial support they have received during the years of the book's gestation.

The authors are also aware of the debt of thanks which they owe to many individuals for the encouragement given to them while they were doing the research. In Europe, the Middle East and North America, colleagues in academic life, government officials and journalists have been unstinting of their time and help. While accepting full responsibility for what follows, the authors acknowledge with thanks the advice of others and hope that the book has benefited accordingly.

1

Introduction

The Iran–Iraq war has been the longest and one of the most impenetrable inter-state conflicts since the Second World War. In some ways it is untypical of wars in the non-industrialized world, both in its duration and in its stakes, which are less material or territorial than they are 'moral' or ideological. In other respects, the war resembles others in the Third World, particularly in the military engagements, and above all in their planning, which has shown a distinctly unprofessional touch. Whether or not this war is a model for future wars in these regions, or registers a trend towards classic inter-state wars rather than towards low-intensity wars or seasonal engagements, cannot be answered definitively.

In certain respects, the Iran–Iraq war is clearly untypical of the sorts of wars one can expect to continue to blight the developing world, since many of its elements are country- and region-specific. For example, the ability to sustain a long and expensive war requires not only allies, but also access to hard currency that few developing states can call upon. In addition, revolutionary Iran's ability to continue the war reflects not only that state's extraordinary political and cultural system, but also the fact that it inherited a very large stock of arms from which it has systematically drawn in over seven years of war, without having had access to any large-scale government supplier for a major weapons system.

One wonders, too, whether the costs of the war in terms of human lives (probably totalling upwards of a million and a half killed and injured – the majority on the Iranian side) could have been sustained by the two belligerents if the stakes had been merely territorial as opposed to ideological. The former are susceptible to compromise, while the latter, at least as Iran has defined them, are not. This brings us to our principal theme: an exploration of the relationship between war and society, and the significant degree to which war, its origins, its conduct and its eventual termination, are closely bound to the nature of the society waging it. As society influences and to some degree determines the reasons for which a state will fight, so a war will make demands on that society and on its political institutions. How a war is fought and the costs which a state accepts in the conduct of war says something not only about the political leadership, but also about the society and politics of that state. Thus how

1

war is waged, the way in which the stakes are defined and perceived, how 'costs' are computed, all are revelatory about the society itself – in some ways perhaps a better indication of society and politics than the routine of peacetime.

The profoundly contrasting nature of the two states and societies involved in the Iran–Iraq war, and their differing responses to it, the authors have chosen to leave implicit. By putting the reactions of the two states side by side, as it were, for the reader to evaluate, they have sought to avoid too formal a comparison. Nonetheless, there is a need at least to note some of the starker contrasts or asymmetries between the two adversaries in summary form, in so far as they affect the conduct of the war. On the most basic level, there is the difference in size, demography and geography, which gives Iran much greater land area, as against Iraq's narrow zone of land in the east, which affords its population an insignificant strategic buffer from the border area neighbouring Iran. Thus, Iraq must act to forestall any Iranian offensive along the thin strip of land (some 60 km) leading from the frontier to Baghdad and Basra. By contrast, Iran has a defence in depth. Its principal cities and capital are beyond the reach of Iraqi ground forces, and though they may be bombed, they cannot be captured. The result is that what for Iran can in theory be a localized or virtual frontier war must, for Iraq, be a total war. Iran's other geographical advantage is its longer coastline and hence its superior access to the Gulf and to the Gulf of Oman. The demographic differences too are significant. They allow Iran greater latitude in conscription and also in accepting human losses. However, this factor is far less relevant in this particular case than Iran's inequality of access to arms which necessitates reliance on foot-soldiers over machinery.

Asymmetries in political relationships significantly affect the conduct of the war. Iran has waged the war as a moral crusade and has been slow to recognize or at least admit the need to gain allies or access to arms. The upshot has been that the Islamic republic has alienated both superpowers at once, as well as important European and Gulf states. It has fought without access to regular supplies of arms from governments and has had to resort to the international arms markets, with their high premiums and financial chicanery. Without rich friends, Iran has had to subsidize its one important regional ally, Syria, in order to rent its support.

Iraq, by contrast, has managed to normalize its relations with both superpowers and to maintain a strong economic and military supply relationship with France, Jordan and Egypt. In addition, it has been able to draw upon the funds and backing of Kuwait, Saudi Arabia and to a lesser degree the other Arab states of the Gulf. In consequence, Iraq, while some $60 billion in debt by the end of 1987, continued to enjoy access to sophisticated and complete weapons systems from the arsenals of the major powers.

One result of this imbalance in access to advanced weaponry in favour of Iraq, versus the numerical advantage that Iran enjoys, is the striking asymmetry in the way in which the war has been conducted. It would be inaccurate to attribute Iraq's reliance on technology and Iran's on manpower principally to the respective ability (and inability) of the two sides to obtain weapons. For in a profound sense, the comparative advantage of either state in the war reflected its internal politics: Saddam Hussein's Iraq was as unable to contemplate high loss of life as a deliberate risk in waging war, as Khomeini's Iran was to consider waging the war efficiently without making a political point. Politically, Iraq could no more imitate Iran in its frontal offensives than Iran could imitate Iraq and admit to reliance on advanced weaponry rather than on 'the new Islamic man'.

The practical results of these technical asymmetries have been striking, but hardly conclusive. Iraq has been unable to convert its superiority of at least 6:1 in aircraft and similar advantages in armour and greater military expenditures into a lever for convincing Iran to sue for peace, let alone into a concrete advantage. Iran, in turn, with its grinding assaults, and its willingness to accept casualties, can neither generate the military momentum necessary to defeat the armies of Iraq in the field, nor to capture a major strategic asset. Unless Iran can do one or the other, or else revise its unlimited war aims to take into account its military limitations, it is destined to continue the war, hoping for an Iraqi collapse from within and willing to settle for it whatever its complexion. As Clausewitz noted, in unlimited wars, where the issues are not territorial and subject to negotiation, but rather the 'overthrow of the enemy', only a complete military victory suffices to achieve the goal.[1]

If Iran has converted to a strategy of attrition, it has been a conversion without much faith. Lacking an alternative strategy, or the resources for continuous warfare, Tehran hopes for a disintegration within Iraq which will leave it with an honourable way out. Iraq's strategy, in turn, is equally bankrupt. Unable to batter sense into its adversary by the use of airpower, or to risk the attrition of its air force, Iraq has sought, since 1984, to internationalize the war. It has taken it into the waters of the Gulf, thereby involving the Gulf states, the United Nations and the superpowers. While it has had some success in this policy during 1987, there is a very real danger for Iraq that the press of other issues, and the superior importance of Iran strategically, will lead to a temporization which will gradually see a refocus of interest on other areas. Once the United Nations is no longer seized of the matter, and the American and European fleets go home, the Gulf states will again be left on their own, only this time without the remotest expectation of further international help. The result could be a crumbling of political will in the region, as well as in Baghdad.

War and society: a preliminary look

The sorts of reasons for which states resort to war, their attitudes towards the use of force, their conduct of operations, their reactions to adversity and crises tell us something about their collective values, as well as their domestic structure. None of these may be susceptible to useful or accurate generalization, or have much value beyond the individual case under examination: variations in regional environment, political configurations, military balances and alliances may tell us more about the likely onset of war, than the study of particular states or types of state structure. But it may equally be the case that emphasis on military capabilities without adequate concern for the structures in which they are rooted, is a fruitless exercise that tends to homogenize and trivialize that very demanding task – the conduct of war – and to understate the distinguishing features that characterize the supreme and ultimate responsibility of the state: the assurance of the security of its citizenry.

War, as an enterprise requiring the commitment of collective resources, as well as attention to the myths which will allow the mobilization of those resources, throws into particularly vivid relief the distinguishing features of the collectivity engaged upon it. These encompass not only the perceived utility of war, but also the organization of its instruments and the rationale underlying their deployment. Consequently, the study of war requires close examination of the political units in question, including the foundations of their power, the definition of their interests and the terrain on which those interests are seen to intersect with the interests of others. In this regard, two particular sets of issues need attention. Firstly, the degree to which the characteristics of the unit in question, and its environment, make war appear to be an appropriate means of pursuing a set of goals, whether internally or externally oriented. Secondly, the degree to which the experience and effects of war can modify the structural and moral balance of the belligerents. Clearly, in wars between states, such considerations demand that the state itself, as the progenitor and target of war, become the proper object of analysis.

War, therefore, can be seen as a phenomenon which both betrays its origins and may transform them. It is particularly important to bear this consideration in mind when focusing on the nature of wars in the Third World. Failure to do so can result in the application of criteria which are culturally specific to the long European traditions of war making and state making. This will limit their utility in an environment where these traditions have been significantly reinterpreted and altered by an indigenous political culture. Whilst it may perforce operate within the given and internationally recognized framework of the state, there will be many areas, possibly crucial to an understanding of the conduct of war, where that culture, and the attitudes and power relations that characterize it, will predominate. It will, however, have been influenced in its turn by the logic of state behaviour. It is precisely this area of competition and adaptation between different political traditions that generates many of the tensions to which such politics are subject and may indeed contribute to the incidence of conflict, as well as determining its nature and laying the foundation for its eventual resolution.

These considerations apply with particular force to the Middle East. The twentieth century has witnessed the emergence of a multitude of independent states in an area which had for centuries been defined politically by the exercise of power based on tribal and communal realities in the name of overarching imperial might, sanctioned solely by the service it could render to Islam. The attempts to come to terms with this legacy and to combine it with the very different principles underlying the foundation of territorial states, have characterized the troubled political history of the area in modern times. The states of the region are still engaged in this process and an understanding of the conflicts it has engendered, as well as of the structural and moral ambiguities it has produced, must underlie any effort to comprehend their nature. Economic and social transformations have occurred largely within the framework of the given states, creating new demands and often fuelling the existing tensions in the states concerned, thereby adding to the problems besetting those who would maintain control.

It is in this context that the distinctive characteristics of war in the Middle East should be assessed, since its incidence brings into focus three interrelated areas of interest. Firstly, there are the peculiarities of the states themselves which have given rise to, and have, in turn, been shaped by, the political structures that now control them. This is the arena in which pressures from within and without have been mediated by regimes or individuals seeking to survive and to protect their interests, using and developing the state machinery at their disposal to carry out an effective response to threat. Whilst such interests may or may not coincide with those of the majority of their subjects, the attempt to appropriate the instruments of the state to this end has necessitated considerable attention to the myths by which such activity can be justified.

The heavy reliance on the coercive apparatus of the state, as well as the justifications employed, have considerable significance for the second area: the emergence of a 'culture' of inter-state relations peculiar to the Middle East, or to a large number of its states. Evolved within the nexus of Arab politics, it owes much to their common legacy and the similar predicaments of many of their regimes. It has been a product of the realities, both normative and structural, which underlie their domestic politics and which, in turn, influence their perceptions of the behaviour of their neighbours. Where the action flowing from such expectations has met a corresponding echo, based on similar premises and on an understanding of the rules thus established, conflict, although severe, has generally been manageable. The most severe breakdowns have occurred in cases, such as those of Israel and Iran, where other foundations for the state have effectively eliminated the expected reciprocity.

This leads to consideration of the third area of interest: the effect upon the states concerned of the experience of war. The mobilization of a community for war, both materially and ideologically, must clearly affect its political organization and the rationale on which certain individuals base their claim to dominate that organization. Equally, the effects of prolonged destruction and collective sacrifice cannot but have an impact on the internal balance of power. Until the outbreak of the war between Iraq and Iran, it has been noteworthy that, in inter-state relations, the periods during which the states have been engaged in violent conflict have been sporadic and, in general, remarkably brief. Yet, at the same time, a number have become involved in prolonged and costly civil wars, and others have maintained an explicit commitment to armed confrontation as a means of resolving the Arab–Israeli conflict. This has tended to emphasize the importance of the role of the military within the politics of the state, while diminishing, in relative terms, the tests to which the armed forces, as an instrument of state power, have been subjected. Indeed, the utilization of the military and of the image of war has been in many cases a means by which governments have sought to mobilize support from their subjects. This has been intended not so much to engage in war itself, as to cement an otherwise precarious polity. It is within this tradition of the experience of war by independent states that assessments concerning the nature, and indeed the utility, of war must be made. In this study of the war between Iraq and Iran, it is the intention to examine some of the implications of the questions raised by the foregoing.

War between Iran and Iraq

In origin the Iran–Iraq war is not unusual. The two neighbouring states have had their normal share of border disputes, have aligned differently on regional and global issues, and have chosen differing paths to development. The immediate antecedents to the war are almost classical in their simplicity and ubiquity. On the one side, a chaotic and revolutionary Iran threatened and provoked its smaller neighbour, while at the same time rejecting the legacy of its monarchical predecessor and stripping itself of its military capabilities. On the other side, there was a centralized regime which felt threatened by its larger neighbour, but which saw an opportunity to seize the leadership of the entire region. While ebullient revolutionary Iran rejected the dictates of prudent statecraft in favour of the propagation of a messianic message, oblivious to the consequences for its neighbours, Iraq, infatuated by its new regional status, decided to seize the military opportunity.

On a more profound level, the causes of the war stemmed from the attitudes of the two states towards the use of force. The Iranian leadership, at that time manifestly plural or decentralized, saw the world through the eyes of their successful revolutionary experience. They rejected the need for standing and professional military forces armed with modern, or culturally contaminating, weapons, in favour of reliance on the people – their faith, their dedication and their unity. For revolutionary Iran, it was axiomatic that power came from the people against which brute military force was useless. It was, therefore, on the people of Iraq and Iran that they relied to remove Saddam Hussein and to spread the Islamic revolution further afield.

Iraq's attitude was very different. It was a compound of ambition and opportunism, with the critical addition of an excessive faith in the efficacy of the resort to force. Saddam Hussein's highly centralized regime, which combined an innocence of traditional military matters with reliance upon force at every opportunity in domestic politics, perhaps accounts for Saddam's belief that in international affairs, as at home, he could cow and repress his foes into submission. It is also possible that Saddam Hussein was the victim of his own conspiratorial training, relying on the winks and nods of various parties in the region, as well as in the West. The Iraqi leadership's belief that the incursion into Iran would be a walkover, leading to a speedy victory, stemmed not only from faulty military intelligence, as well as a profound ignorance of history and of the nature of the foe, but also from an inflated sense of Iraq's capabilities. This is precisely the sort of error associated with highly personalized leadership.

The conduct of the war militarily, and the demands made on the people and the society in its name, acutely reflect the cohesion and integrity of state and nation. In this respect, Iran and Iraq are virtual polar opposites. Iran, by treating the war as a crusade, has identified it as a moral test more than a technical or a material one. It has, therefore, regarded the war as the ultimate challenge, an ennobling ritual to be met and transcended, on the road to a victory that is ideological and moral more than it is military or political. Starting from this perspective, it has been imperative for the Islamic republic to win the war on its own terms and in its own way, if it is to serve as an affirmation of the superiority of its system. The result has been a reversal of traditional ideas about warfare. Rather than seeking methods of defeating the enemy by inflicting losses upon him, the Islamic republic, in the first four years of the war, treated it as an opportunity to demonstrate the dedication of its own people. It sought Iranian martyrs rather than Iraqi casualties. By demonstrating insensitivity to its own losses and an implacable resolve to continue the war, the Iranians hoped to demoralize their less committed and less dedicated foe. Iran thus relied on the zeal and commitment of its rank and file, largely volunteers initially, to overcome the enemy's superiority in technology and firepower.

Iraq, by contrast, did not have such a bank of passion on which to draw.

It had to be very economical with its resources for both domestic political and practical reasons. Whilst there was an official attempt to mobilize mass enthusiasm for what was initially called 'Saddam's War', in reality Iraq tended to rely on high technology and static, heavily fortified and entrenched defences. This emphasis often appeared to verge on an obsession with sophisticated technology as a 'wonder weapon', separate from the skills and knowledge of the men using it. Such was the case in Iraq's much vaunted and scarcely decisive use of the Exocet missile in 1984–7 in the tanker war. This also appeared to be the motivation in its use of chemical weapons from 1984. Saddam Hussein, civilian strategist, appeared to believe in a gleaming, bloodless technological fix to end the war. Politically, Iraq sought to widen the war to the Gulf's waters, to internationalize the conflict and thus to bring pressure on Iran to end it. At the same time, after 1984, Iraq escalated the war to attacks on Iran's cities and economic infrastructure in order to increase the costs. Iran's escalation of the war, on the other hand, was by its prolongation.

Despite the ferocity and the importance of the stakes – national survival for Iraq and 'Islam' itself for Iran – the war has been less than total. It may stretch credulity to argue that it has been characterized by elements of restraint. It has, after all, led to perhaps a million deaths, and has left a similar number of injured or homeless. It has witnessed the use of chemical weapons, the shelling and bombing of civilian areas, and the use of young men in pointless frontal offensives against heavily entrenched and mined defences. Nevertheless, neither antagonist has used all its capabilities at once and each has sought to apply force piecemeal. In part, this is due to the fact that neither party admits to any animosity towards the people of the adversary state, as opposed to the regime ruling the country. For example, Iran only began its shelling of Basra in February 1984, after two years of failing to retaliate for Iraqi missile attacks. The fact that it did so suggested that the Iranian Government no longer entertained expectations of a spontaneous Shi'i revolt against Saddam Hussein in that city. Iraq too has applied its military force incrementally. This has been partly for reasons of prudence and economy. However, it seems also to have been due to an unwillingness to enter into an unlimited war that would further envenom the atmosphere when the time for peacemaking eventually comes. For similar reasons, the two states maintained formal diplomatic representation in each other's capitals, albeit at a low level, for the first seven years of the war, finally ending these in October 1987. Pragmatic considerations have also dictated a minimum of tacit co-operation within the Organization of Petroleum Exporting Countries (OPEC).

The marked contrasts in the political systems of the two adversaries, and in their respective attitudes to the war, should not obscure the similarities or parallels in the views and statements of their respective leaders:

– each believed the other to be domestically unpopular and easily deposed, and appealed over the heads of the government to the people – without result. Both have cultivated opposition forces as 'governments in exile'.

– both sought to universalize the war: Iraq by 'Arabizing' it and Iran by 'Islamicizing' it.

– each calls the conflict 'an imposed war', part of an international conspiracy intended to divert both states from the principal goal of confronting Israel or recovering Islamic territory.

– in both states, the political leaders waged war with a distrust of their own armed forces, and sought to keep control of the war, ceding authority to the professionals only reluctantly.

– in both states, the political leaders waged war with a distrust of their people around a myth of collective identity: in Iraq, the elusive and ambiguous ideas of specifically Iraqi nationalism have been propagated by the regime; in Iran, there has been equal emphasis on the ideas of Islamic community and of Iranian nationalism.

– both states find it easier and more congenial to criticize the United States than the Soviet Union, although the latter has supplied arms to both sides, while the US, to all intents and purposes, has been far less involved.

– in both states the war has become virtually institutionalized, making the contemplation of normalization and of peace difficult.

War is not only a great leveller, it is also a good test for abstract theories and ideologies. Force of circumstance has made the Islamic republic far less doctrinaire over the years of war. The rehabilitation of the professional military and the revival of general officer grades is illustrative of this. So too is Iran's willingness to put its goals into some sort of ranking and to identify specific priorities. This is most evident in foreign affairs, where instead of taking on 'an ocean of Satanic foes' at once, Tehran has sought to establish sound relations with its pro-Western, non-Arab neighbours, Turkey and Pakistan, while attempting to stabilize its volatile relations with its Arab neighbours in the Gulf. The most striking indicator of this pragmatism born of war and adversity has been its willingness to deal with Israel and the United States for arms (without admitting it). This is clearly a sensitive and confusing issue for the Islamic masses who have been told that the liberation of Baghdad is the first step towards the liberation of Jerusalem.

As time has passed, the war which in Iran was depicted as a prelude to an Islamic renaissance, has come to look more and more like a substitute for the building of a model Islamic society. Indeed, as the war has become more total, the fate of the regime, and possibly of the revolution itself, has become inextricably tied to its outcome. At the same time, at least to the outside world, Iran's claim to be fighting only in self-defence and to punish the aggressor in order to ensure a stable peace, has sounded less and less convincing, some five years after it had reclaimed most of its own territory. Observers have watched with horrified, if intermittent, fascination the numbing regularity of Iran's offensives, crediting their motivation to some atavistic or cultural deformation. For the government in Tehran, the issue was more practical. The masses mobilized by the revolution and kept at fever pitch by the Iraqi invasion were the elements which had devoted most to the war and which were most supportive of its continuation 'until victory'. To justify the costs and sacrifices sustained by this constituency, demanded an unambiguous victory. The Islamic republic thus found itself captive' to its own rhetoric: its absolute formulation of war aims could not be negotiable, if it were to maintain domestic political harmony. The costs of anything less than victory, that is, of a compromise peace, came to loom larger than the costs associated with the continuation of the war.

A similar situation obtained in Iraq. There too doctrine and ideology melted in the white heat of war. Iraq now sought to project the image of a 'moderate', in contrast to its 'extremist' foe. It cultivated the pro-Western states of Jordan, Saudi Arabia and Egypt, and modified its claims on Israel and its support for terrorist groups associated with the Arab cause. It now portrayed itself as the bulwark in the defence of the Arab world against a new anti-Arab and reactionary, pseudo-Islamic contagion.

Nevertheless, as the war continued, the original causes receded in importance, and Saddam Hussein's reaction to Iran's provocation appeared more and more flawed and reckless. Any peace hinting at faulty political judgement on the part of Saddam Hussein would be tantamount to political suicide. The costs and privations of the war for the Iraqis, though less than those for Iran, still weighed relatively more heavily on Iraq. The leadership could not rely on any comparable populist or moral revolution among the people, liberating them from dependence on the transitory and ephemeral world. The contrast between the two leaders, between the severe and austere Khomeini and the worldly Saddam Hussein, encapsulates the essence of the two systems. For the Iraqi leadership, only a peace that left the Takritis, the Sunni elite, the Revolutionary Command Council, the Ba'th and Iraq, in that order, intact, could be seriously contemplated.

Iraq's political system has survived more than seven years of war (indeed some believe that it has been strengthened by it), but it has remained a more brittle one than its Iranian counterpart. A serious problem here has been the mobilization of a largely politically inert society whose demands on the leadership would be uncertain in peacetime. In Iraq, too, the military have been rehabilitated and given increasing latitude in the conduct of the war. What their claims on the political leadership will be post-war, in a period of uncertain peace, can only be guessed at. The war unleashed political forces long contained. The management and accommodation of these forces in a period of reconstruction and cold peace will depend in part on the nature of the settlement obtained. This has given Iraq's leaders pause for thought and has accounted for their fluctuations between panic and the belief that they could in fact prevail. For Iraq, too, the war, for all its palpable costs and risks, has had to be balanced against the analogous costs of peace.

It has been said that Iraq cannot win the war and Iran cannot lose it. However, this is an over-simplification at best. If Iraq succeeds in holding out for a return to the *status quo ante bellum*, it will have withstood a siege from a country three times its size. Iran, by contrast, can take little glory from a peace that takes it back to the pre-war settlement. This was available by June 1982. As the Chinese philosopher and strategist, Sun Tzu, reminds us: 'No-one wins in a protracted war'.[2] In fact, the issue for some time has been not who will win the war, but which side will collapse first.

Whilst a study of this kind is explicitly concerned with the attempt to understand both the nature and the consequences of the current conflict between Iraq and Iran, implicit in some of the questions it raises is a framework for the comparative analysis of wars in the Third World. Taking as a base point the observation that wars reflect the major characteristics of the collectivities engaged upon them, the nature of the state outside the European state tradition must come under scrutiny. Although that tradition has been extraordinarily influential in shaping the modern world, it is nevertheless clear that the example it provides is an insufficient, but possibly necessary, condition for an adequate under-standing of the behaviour of the vast majority of contemporary states. Wars between such states can, therefore, illuminate three important areas, increasing our understanding of the ways they work and the ways they interact. Firstly, the commitment of the state and its instruments to war reveals the attitudes of the ruling political elite to the state. Secondly, the effects of war upon society, state and ruling elite add a further dimension to this analysis. In both cases, the crucial and relatively neglected relationship between an indigenous political society and an imported state structure becomes more apparent. Thirdly, the resulting perceived utility of war as a means of achieving regional and domestic objectives within a given international setting, enhances our capacity to assess not only the potential for war in a given region, but also the dynamics that lead to escalation in one direction and to war termination in the other.

Are there lessons to be learned from this war for others? They are not obvious in the domain of military operations. On the Iranian side, they have been characterized by improvization and innovation, stemming, on the one hand, from a refusal to accept or to study traditional tactics, and on the other, from the necessity of adapting weapons systems existing in the pre-war inventory to the needs of a manpower-intensive, supply-deficient, prolonged war. The result has been impressive improvization and ingenuity, the building of a substantial domestic base for light armaments manufacture, but nothing that will make any basic difference to the outcome of the war. The model here is one of solidarity and autarchy, partly from preference, partly from circumstance. The limits to self-reliance are evident in Iran's inability to substitute faith and commitment for access to heavy, modern arms. Iran has, therefore, been unable to achieve the kind of military capability to exploit and sustain breakthroughs deriving from futile acts of extraordinary courage and commitment.

The roles of the superpowers, and of the United Nations in particular, have not been glorious. While unable to concert together to build upon their overlapping interest in preventing an Iranian victory, they have at least managed to limit their competition for unilateral advantage. This has avoided transforming the war into a polarization of East and West. In most wars in developing countries, the superpowers let the fighting fizzle out, or become indirectly involved without risking much of a confrontation. In this unusual case, the capacity of the two states to furnish the blood and treasure needed to sustain a long war, and the potential risks of confrontation, have encouraged a 'hands-off' policy, albeit with nuances. This has been seen as the least dangerous expedient for the superpowers. If the result is a failure in 'conflict management', it is also at least the avoidance of a superpower confrontation.

We have not devoted much space in this study to the role of global factors, the superpowers, the energy balance, the role of external arms suppliers, the United Nations, the Arab League, the Islamic conference etc. etc. These subjects are treated elsewhere and seem at times to be the exclusive concern of students of the war. Instead, we have emphasized the reciprocal effects of war on the two societies and of the societies on the onset and conduct of the war. While in the popular view these states are often viewed as morally equivalent, with little to choose between them, they are, in fact, very different. This has necessitated a somewhat different treatment and emphasizes reliance on different sources. Each author analyses the factors salient to the individual state, rather than attempting to impose a false or strained symmetry. The result is the alternating chapters that follow, which, although not exactly matched, aim to provide a basis for a comparison of the politics of Iran and Iraq at war, 1980–1987.

2

Iraq and the Origins of the Iran–Iraq War

The understanding of war as a social, collective phenomenon demands a prior attempt to understand the community engaged upon it. This requires examination of the cultural, historical legacy shaping its distinctive character and moral universe. Equally important is the study of the distribution of power within the community, producing the particular form of government which is both the product and the manipulator of a historically determined value-system. The dominant leaders who emerge from this process will make the decision to commit the community to war and must seek to conduct the war that follows in accordance not only with the values that they espouse, but also with the demands placed upon them by the structures that maintain their power. In the process, an impression is formed of the moral and structural imperatives determining perceptions of the nature and utility of war, as well as of the instruments required for its prosecution and the proper objectives of its initiation.

Consequently, it is important in seeking to understand the origins of the war between Iraq and Iran that an effort should be made to examine the factors which led to the perception of the Iraqi Government in the autumn of 1980 that war was the most advantageous, and perhaps the only possible, way of reordering Iraq's relations with Iran. This requires analysis of three orders of question, corresponding, firstly, to the nature of the Iraqi state and of the regime by which that state is ruled. The second concerns the perspectives of the regime regarding the justification for war, as well as the instruments appropriate to its prosecution. This involves the leaders' ideas not only of Iraq's moral rights and their own imperatives as rulers, but also of Iraq's structural capacities. Lastly, of course, there is the question of the image formed of Iran and of the utility of war at a particular time to achieve the required objectives.

Nature of the state

In common with many states of the developing world, the territorial and administrative definition of the Iraqi state came about suddenly through the intrusion of European military power. Rather than evolving slowly, if painfully, from the indigenous competition and assimilation which characterized the development of the European states, the state of Iraq was established in the teeth of social rejection. For their own imperial and strategic reasons, the British marked out the boundaries of a collectivity which had never existed before and which lacked the minimal sense of social cohesion thought to be a necessary attribute of statehood. Few, if any, of the communities who found themselves within the territorial confines of the new Iraqi state had thought of their political identity in terms of the alien conception of statehood, let alone in terms of a specifically Iraqi state. On the contrary, two countervailing principles of political identity existed among the people suddenly dubbed 'Iraqis', both of which were inimical to the state as such, and both of which have since exerted considerable influence on its politics.

The first revolved around the local axis of the clan and tribe, focusing on the villages where kinship was the major form of social relationship and identity. This was the chief characteristic of an overwhelmingly rural society, reinforced by the very remoteness of much of the rural hinterland from the few urban centres and by the relative isolation of each local community from the others. In the mountains of Kurdistan and in the marshes of the south this particularism and pronounced localism was most marked. In Kurdistan, it had led to definite linguistic and economic divisions which made communication difficult even among the Kurds themselves; in the south, identity through bloodline and genealogy was undoubtedly more important than common nominal adherence to the Shi'i sect of Islam. Among the Sunni Arab villagers in the geographical centre of the new state, locality and the common kinship which defined the inhabitants of that locality were equally important. It set them apart from other tribes, both settled and nomadic; it gave its members a common identity when they began to migrate into the new and confusing urban environment associated with economic and administrative development; and, crucially for the evolution of the politics of the new state, it provided them with a point of reference and a channel of advancement when it came to mastering the equally confusing state machinery.

The second set of principles involved the urban, educated elites of Sulaymaniyyah, Baghdad, Najaf, Karbala and Basra. In their various ways they had developed ideas of their political identity of equally ancient pedigree which were equally difficult to reconcile with the idea of a modern state. In the north, a coherent sense of Kurdish particularism was emerging in an effort to overcome the Kurds' many divisions – social, economic, linguistic and even religious – and to construct a political entity based on common Kurdish national identity. In the cities of Najaf and Karbala, the spiritual leaders of the Shi'a community, the *Mujtahids*, saw themselves as the guardians of the moral and political destiny of a community of the faithful, recognizing neither territorial boundaries nor temporal rule. In Baghdad and Basra, the Sunni legatees of the Ottoman imperial tradition and privileges, reinforced by the British and assisted by the arrival of the Sherifian elite, sought to maintain their dominant position, while identifying themselves with the Sunni Arab hinterland west and south of them. In all these cases, the community which defined their political identity and commanded their moral attention corresponded with larger and more ancient collectivities than the new state of Iraq. The Kurdish nation, the world of Shi'i Islam, and the domain of the Sunni Arabs represented three civilizations which were contiguous on the terrain of modern Iraq. It was to be the unenviable task of the Government of Iraq to maintain the administrative reality of the state in the absence of collective solidarity.

This characteristic has profoundly shaped the course of Iraqi politics since independence: repeatedly, whether under monarchy or republic, administrative cohesion has taken precedence over the social cohesion that might come from the consent of the population. The latter has never been systematically or genuinely consulted and considerable mistrust has built up between ruler and ruled. The result has been the dubious legitimacy of both the state and the regime. In addition, it has led to a tendency on the part of those who would wield power to rely on the bonds of common origins, rather than of common aims, to create the core cohesion and trust necessary for the seizure and maintenance of power. In this necessarily conspiratorial undertaking two features have become clear in Iraqi politics. Firstly, given the access to the state machinery required for any successful challenge to the existing government, effective rule has remained in the hands of the Sunni Arab minority, despite a number of violent political upheavals. Secondly, because of the requirements of this degree of political control, and of the belief that personal loyalty may be an effective substitute for loyalty to the state, the trend has always been towards autocracy, exercised with varying degrees of ruthlessness. The result has been the emergence within Iraqi politics of an almost hyper-sensitive awareness of who is an 'insider' and who is an 'outsider'. To control so heterogeneous a society without making any concessions to popular consent is only possible through the cohesion of an inner elite around the autocrat, who share common interests and political trust, whatever public show is made of deference to the symbols of popular sovereignty.

The coups d'état which brought the Ba'th back to power in July 1968 were significant on two counts. Firstly, they created a new group of 'insiders', narrowly defined even by Iraqi standards. Although initially having to make concessions to older members of the Ba'th Party, real power was seen to be increasingly in the hands of Saddam Hussein (at that time Deputy Chairman of the Revolutionary Command Council and Assistant General Secretary of the Ba'th Party, Regional Command) and his associates who were mastering the machinery of the state as the path to supreme power. This group was characterized by a similar background

in the conspiratorial and persecuted Ba'th of the late 1950s. Their ability
to survive this period had to some extent been facilitated by the fact that
their underground links depended in some cases on shared tribal or
family backgrounds.[1] Secondly, the Ba'th of 1968 was led by people who
had lived through the disastrous experience of Ba'thist rule in 1963 and
who had drawn a number of lessons from that experience. The chief
lesson, which was put into effect immediately, was the need to exert
complete and thorough-going control over the administrative machinery
of the state. The justification of such a degree of control lay in the
declared mission of the Ba'th as a vanguard leading the Iraqi people into a
new revolutionary era, regardless of their particular wishes.

By the mid-1970s Iraqi politics were characterized by a relatively
cohesive core group within the symbiotic Ba'th-state administrative
structure. The group depended to a large extent upon their contemporary
and champion, Saddam Hussein, but also lent him crucial support in his
struggle to carve out for himself the conditions required for the exercise
of autocracy. For this core group, the maintenance of the closed and
secretive Ba'th at the apex of the administrative structure, as well as the
ruthlessness of its methods, appeared to be justified by the patent
rejection by much of the population of the new society which the Ba'th
claimed to be building in Iraq. Kurdish rebellion in the north and Shi'i
unrest in the towns of the south were plausibly ascribed to forces of
reaction, tribal or sectarian, which sought to counter the revolution led by
the Ba'th.

At the same time, the involvement, real or supposed, of the United
States, Israel and Iran in the internal unrest allowed the Ba'th to project
its own task on to a national stage, linking its endeavours with the unity of
the Iraqi state. Inevitably, this was accompanied by a nascent national
mythology, appropriated by the Ba'th, which sought to convince the Iraqis
that they did indeed share a common past as members of an identifiable
political entity. The suggestion was, of course, that the Ba'th was the
guardian and champion of this national identity. Under this interpretation,
its efforts to re-establish a great Mesopotamian civilization had provoked
the enmity of a number of Iraq's neighbours and justified the massive
expenditure on defence which was so conspicuous a part of the regime's
policies.[2]

Attention was therefore paid to the foundations of legitimacy, it
doubtless being recognized that the state could achieve some form of
permanence only if a sense of collective identity could be inculcated into
the population. But this was to be an operation directed from above in the
service of a burgeoning autocracy. Indeed, there was a clear contradiction
with the ideological tenets of the Ba'th. These held that the particular
states into which the mandatory powers had divided the Arab nation
should be granted no permanence or legitimacy: they were simply
transitory stages on the road to the realization of a greater Arab state,

coterminous with the extent of the Arab nation. For Saddam Hussein, however, this idea of temporary trusteeship did not accord with his ambitions. In addition, to rule Iraq in the name of a pan-Arab ideal ran the risk of alienating a substantial sector of the non-Arab population, as well as of acquiescing in the permeability of Iraqi politics to impulses coming from elsewhere in the Arab world which Saddam Hussein could not control. Evidently, this tallied neither with his views of Iraq's future nor with his idea of his own role in that future.[3]

Once Saddam Hussein achieved a major part of his ambition by becoming President in July 1979, the dual nature of the Iraqi state became increasingly obvious. On the one hand, power was even more tightly concentrated in the hands of Saddam Hussein and a narrowing circle of 'insiders': those who had excluded themselves from this circle by reason of their lukewarm attitude to Saddam Hussein had been in some cases physically liquidated when he came to power. Thus was perpetuated the traditional and autocratic means by which power was exercised in Iraq. On the other hand, efforts were intensified to give the impression that Saddam Hussein was no more than President of a 'modern' state. This involved the election of a National Assembly in June 1980 for the first time since the overthrow of the monarchy in 1958. Although the circumstances of its election and the powers it enjoys make the Assembly wholly a creature of the regime, Saddam Hussein made clear in his opening speech that he intended this gesture to be interpreted as evidence of the necessary link between ruler and people: the former should 'avoid making decisions in dark labyrinths' and political action should thenceforth be 'collective'.[4] It appeared that the logic of nationalism, espoused by the Ba'th as the foundation of its right to rule, had obliged Saddam Hussein to clothe his mastery of the state's administrative machinery with the language of democracy. Voluntary participation by the people in the political process, leading to a sense that the government was answerable to them, might lay the foundations for a future collective identity to underpin the Iraqi state. However, such a course of action would inevitably undermine the present political reality of Saddam Hussein's autocracy. As his actions, rather than his words, demonstrated, he had no intention of permitting such a development.

The danger in this proceeding, so far as the future was concerned, was that, by operating from the basis of highly personalized power and primordial linkages, the ideal of creating a sense of collectivity within Iraq would always elude Saddam Hussein. However, it would at the same time drive him to pay greater attention to the modern state he claimed to lead. This would mean an aggravated sensitivity to the symbols of legitimacy and to the danger of their erosion. It would also induce him to become the demonstrable champion of Iraq's sovereignty and territorial integrity. The trappings of modern statehood were correspondingly more important to Saddam Hussein, the more the reality of his power was founded on a social reality and political perception which antedated the modern state, and in many senses militated against it. However, to admit this beyond the circle of 'insiders', was to invite retribution, not least from the latter, since their support for Saddam Hussein was conditional upon the degree to which he could successfully maintain his position as ruler of the Iraqi state. Consequently, the identification of state and ruler became increasingly part of the regime's propaganda: insults to the ruler were construed as threats to the state. Saddam Hussein tended to encourage the image of a beleaguered Iraq, since this in turn dignified and was believed to legitimize his own claim to dominate the state.[5] It is against this background of precarious identification that the question of the utility of force, and ultimately of war, in the name of the Iraqi state should be examined.

The outward forms of the Iraqi state were nominally those of the collective experience of European political societies. However, the reality of power in effect excluded the mass of the state's population. It was based, instead, on the exclusivity of more private, family bonds. It was scarcely surprising, therefore, that a similar dualism should run through the instruments of coercion at the disposal of the state's rulers, influencing the ways they were used and the justification for their use. Publicly, the armed forces were dedicated to the defence of the state, and to the officially proclaimed Ba'thist vision of the state. However, they were also expected to act in a more traditional guise as the extensions of the autocrat's reach and the defenders of his person. The conscious and unconscious mingling of these roles inevitably determined the way in which the Iraqi regime projected their future use and interpreted the experience of their past deployment. It is through these perspectives that it is possible to interpret the kinds of war for which the Iraqi regime was preparing itself, should regional or domestic circumstances make war seem a necessary or desirable option.

Since the coups of 1968, the Ba'thist leadership had been intent on building up the Iraqi armed forces, although massive expansion and modernization did not occur until the great increase in Iraq's oil revenues made such plans feasible. Perhaps not surprisingly, it was also to occur on an ambitious scale only when the early military leaders of the regime had been displaced by their civilian counterparts. In a regime based on the seizure of power by force and lacking any form of collective consent to the legitimacy of its exercise of power, the question of the position within the state, and above all within the power structure, of the armed forces is clearly a delicate one. While the expansion of the military instrument may be necessary both to strengthen the impression of statehood (with its presumed reinforcement of collective solidarity) and to extend the sphere of the ruler's personal power, within the territorial confines of the state as well as beyond, there remains the problem of control. Clearly, unless the ruler wishes to be at the mercy of those whose command of the means of violence makes them aware that nothing, save superior force, stands between them and the assumption of absolute power, some form of physical or moral counterforce must be devised in order to deter such thoughts from crystallizing.

Well aware of the fate of previous governments in Iraq, the Ba'thist leaders in the 1970s were careful to expand the military within a structure which would give the leaders maximum control. This involved a careful screening of those who sought to be officers by making them apply to become members of the Ba'th and swear allegiance to the party. This did not, of course, guarantee their loyalty. It did, however, provide those who were in control of the Ba'th with the opportunity to scrutinize the social credentials of every officer, as well as to indict that officer in the future, should it become necessary, on the impeccably 'objective' grounds of ideological backsliding. In order to supplement this initial control and to subject the officer corps to continuing scrutiny, the Military Bureau of the Ba'th was formed and placed in charge of organizing surveillance, under the cover of ideological indoctrination, through its network of officials in every military unit.[6]

At the same time, the Ba'th Government was energetic in building up powerful security services outside the military. These not only broke the armed forces' monopoly of the means of coercion, but could also be run on lines more explicitly reflecting the character of organized power, than could an official state instrument. These efforts led to the emergence of the Popular Army (al-Jaish al-Sha'bi): a force of 75,000 Ba'thist volunteers, receiving training in the handling of small arms and acting as a form of party militia. Under the command of Taha Ramadhan, very much one of the 'insiders', closely allied to Saddam Hussein, it was a device to ensure not only that the regime had a means of mobilizing violence outside military control, but also that this particular group of 'insiders' could successfully dominate any rival faction within the Ba'th itself.[7]

This organization of questionable military utility, but of proven political worth, was supplemented by more specialized formations. The Frontier Force, set up after 1975 explicitly to create and patrol the wasteland along the Iran–Iraq border in Kurdistan, was dedicated and formed to address itself to an obviously political task which retained the ambiguity of all such endeavours in Iraq: the demarcation of an Iraqi state in relation to other states, or the extension of Baghdad's centralized and personalized control to all corners of the given state. In addition, the Special Forces and the Republican Guard were expanded, recruited on the basis of confessional allegiance (that is, largely from the Arab, Sunni areas north of Baghdad) and charged with a specific mission to protect the core of the regime. In the process of fitting them for this task, it was noticeable that they were being trained and armed not to deal with civil disturbance but with military revolt. Meanwhile, the battalions of the internal security department were reorganized into the Department of General Intelligence

(Mukhabarat). The premature bid for power by its (Shi'i) Director, Kazzar, in 1973 allowed for the crucial 'insider' takeover of this department, with the result that it was placed in the hands of Saddam Hussein's half-brother, Barzan al-Takriti.[8]

The disposition of power in Iraq can be envisaged as a series of concentric circles emanating from the autocrat, dependent upon him for their animation as well as testifying to his powers by their extent. These specialized organizations and structures have been designed both to defend the inner circle and also to increase the hold over the outer rim of the autocrat's *imperium*. The latter's solidity and reach will form the measure by which his peers will judge him. Thus reinforcing and extending control will be a vital consideration in assuring his political future. Equally, the use of the conscript armies associated with modern statehood to achieve this end will sustain the impression that state interests are being advanced, and that a collective rather than an individual will is being realized. Consequently, the use of the armed forces – quintessentially in their symbolism and outward forms the instruments of state power – is seen to be both a technique to strengthen traditional power relations at the core, and a means of locating that core at the centre of a modern state. The autocrat therefore stands to gain not only in structural terms but also in symbolic resonance, reinforcing his actual as well as moral claim to power.

Justification for war

Indeed, the use made of the Iraqi armed forces prior to the outbreak of war with Iran in 1980 tends to illustrate these themes in the preoccupations of the Iraqi regime. In so doing, it illustrates the regime's conception of war as well as its ideas about how war should be conducted to greatest advantage. Fundamental to this way of thinking was the conviction that the regime was locked in mortal combat with a range of forces intent on loosening its hold on the administration of the Iraqi state, and ultimately on destroying the regime itself. These forces seemed to be interpreted by the Iraqi regime as a series of concentric circles, having their inspiration at a considerable remove from the territory of Iraq, but with the threat brought closer by regional allies. These, in turn, exploited communities within the confines of the Iraqi state to prevent the emergence of Iraq as a collectivity.

It was the task of the Iraqi ruler, therefore, to use force both to thwart their designs within Iraq, by the physical elimination of their agents and to assert the power of the regime and its determination not to be intimidated by the conspiracies which bore down upon it. This was a perception of Iraq and of the region which was itself the product of a conspiratorial organization of power, and which found an apt vehicle in the closed system of the Ba'th as a party and as an ideology. The insecurity of the core group was therefore transferred to the Ba'th party. Through the latter's amplification of the threats posed to the larger ideals it claimed to espouse, a legitimation was sought for the degree of coercion needed to maintain those in power. The revolution was consequently proclaimed to be in danger: the socialist experiment was threatened by imperialism and reaction; the commitment to Arab nationalism was threatened by imperialism, working in alliance with the aggressive forces of Iranian nationalism and Zionism. Throughout the 1970s the language of the Ba'thist regime was the language of struggle – in short, of a revolutionary movement beleaguered and at war with social and regional forces.[9]

The prosecution of this struggle was to be the duty of those who commanded the Iraqi state, using whatever instruments were to hand. Failure to do so would be tantamount to treachery, and would be treated as such, even though it might be little more than a pretext for the removal of a rival for quite other reasons. This was evident in the fate of General Hardan al-Takriti. He had reportedly advised against the use of the Iraqi brigade based in Jordan on the side of the Palestinian factions in their brief war of 1970 against the forces of the Hashemite state. He had done so for the sound military reason that they could not be resupplied in the face of Jordanian hostility, and would therefore probably suffer the ignominy of capture before they could play a militarily decisive role. Nevertheless, his lack of enthusiasm for military action was sufficient grounds for his discrediting and exclusion from the regime. His subsequent death in exile at the hands of associates of Saddam Hussein demonstrated that his downfall was due more to feuding and mistrust within the ruling circle of 'insiders' than to any ideological backsliding. It was clear to those who remained in power that the commitment of the Iraqi armed forces to war, even if questionable in purely military terms, was correct and even necessary from a political point of view: it reduced the vulnerability of elite members to one another and it reinforced a crucial element in the ideology of radical Arab nationalism with reference to which the Ba'thist regime claimed to base its title to rule.[10]

The 1973 war with Israel provided the Iraqi leadership with the opportunity to demonstrate their active commitment to the long-running struggle against Zionism. An Iraqi armoured division was despatched to the Golan front with minimal advance training, no previous co-ordination with either the Syrian or Jordanian forces engaged on that front, little anti-aircraft capability and insufficient transport to ensure that the tanks actually reached the front – all factors which made it a negligible element in the attempt by Syria to recapture the Golan or to prevent the Israeli advance on Damascus. Nevertheless, it was an important symbolic gesture for the rulers, since it indicated their determination to commit the armed instruments of the Iraqi state to the pan-Arab cause, thereby giving reality and identity to the state itself, as well as justifying their control of it. The fact that the pace and outcome of the war were shaped by forces beyond their control and had never been influenced by the Iraqi military contribution, was disguised by the regime's indignant protests to Syria for accepting a cease-fire on the Golan front. This, they indicated, was a surrender in which Iraq would have no part, thereby providing a pretext for the withdrawal of Iraqi troops, among whom there had been gratifyingly few casualties.[11] As a whole, the experience of war in this limited sense had been highly advantageous for the Iraqi regime. However, the fact that participation had been geared almost wholly to achieving internal rather than external aims should alert one to the deep political crisis – the dissociation of regime and state – which coloured perceptions of the use of Iraqi state forces in regional conflicts.

The next significant war in which the Iraqi armed forces were engaged was the explicitly internal war against the Kurds in 1974–75. It nevertheless had considerable regional resonance, especially insofar as it involved Iraq's relations with its neighbour Iran. The assimilation of the Kurds into the Iraqi state, or the failure to do so, posed one of the major challenges to the conception of that state on which successive governments based their claim to rule. When they came to power in 1968 the Ba'thists had attempted sporadically, as had many of their predecessors, to achieve this aim by force. However, it was evident that the forces available to them were simply inadequate to the task. Consequently, a *modus vivendi* was arranged which was testimony to Baghdad's determination not so much to admit the Kurds into the inside circle of power – an inconceivable eventuality – but rather to allow them a measure of autonomy while central government recouped its forces. Indeed, as the build-up, equipment and organization of the rapidly expanding Iraqi armed forces seemed to testify, it was only a matter of time before the figures at the centre of Iraqi politics considered they were sufficiently well equipped to reassert Baghdad's control.

When war broke out in 1974 it was soon clear that the Iraqi Government was fighting more than the Kurds. Not only did American, Israeli and Iranian aid to the Kurdish rebels confirm in the minds of the Iraqi leaders the dire nature of the universal struggle on which they were permanently engaged, but it also made the winning of this war in military terms an extremely daunting prospect. The Iraqi forces suffered heavy casualties but succeeded to a large extent in reducing the areas controlled by the Kurdish rebels. It was when they attempted to deal with the heart of the rebellion that direct Iranian involvement made this militarily impossible in the short term and politically difficult in the long term. However, the rising tension between Iraq and Iran during this period was not beyond Iraq's control. The dictates of internal politics ensured that the Government could not simply abandon its objectives in Kurdistan, but they also ensured that the rhetoric and actions of Iraq brought home to the Iranian Government the possibility that Iraq and Iran might soon be engaged in direct conflict. Fundamentally, it was the desire on both sides to avoid open warfare which led to the Algiers agreement of 1975. This permitted the Iraqi Government to crush the Kurdish rebellion without Iranian interference. However, the price Iraq paid was the abandonment of its claim to full sovereignty over the whole of the Shatt al-Arab waterway and an agreement that the *Thalweg* (or median line of the deepest channel) should thenceforth constitute the boundary between Iran and Iraq. In winning a war against the Kurds, the Iraqi Government had apparently lost an unfought war against Iran.[12]

The memory of the opportunity lost through military weakness, and the humiliation forced upon the Iraqi regime through the Shah's superior coercive power, clearly rankled, in particular with Saddam Hussein who had been in many senses personally responsible for the 1975 agreement. This was the 'bitter reality' Saddam Hussein had been obliged to accept. It was created by Iran's military superiority and by the need to establish a measure of internal unity and armed strength before any attempt could be made to rectify the situation.[13] From this perspective the struggle with Iran would continue, since there was evidently no question of the Iraqi regime accepting in perpetuity an outcome determined by Iranian *force majeure*. As Saddam Hussein stated in December 1980: 'We signed it [the 1975 agreement], but the Iranians gained legal rights under unnatural circumstances and under conditions we could not control . . . the Iranians used military force against us'.[14] Although the relationship between Iraq and Iran after 1975 was no longer one of war, it was one of watchful tension. The Iraqi regime was wary of further attempts by the Shah to extend the circle of his influence, but also kept an eye open for any opportunity that might present itself for the rulers in Baghdad to extend their own influence at his expense. The 1975 agreement was less a peace settlement than a truce in a long-standing personal contest between the rulers in Baghdad and those in Tehran. Its fragility arose from the fact that the concessions made to achieve it tended to be seen as undermining the authority of the man who was ruthlessly determined to become the autocrat of Iraq. Furthermore, he clearly believed that it marked but the first round of a long-running contest with a fellow autocrat in Tehran and also that the chief mechanism by which this contest was to be decided would be through military means. A loudly publicized willingness to commit the armed forces of the Iraqi state to war was to be a means of deterring and intimidating Saddam Hussein's counterpart in Tehran, without necessarily committing those forces to armed conflict. This was the language Saddam Hussein himself had understood in 1975, and it was one he believed the Shah understood as well.[15]

Symbolic deployment of troops and the threatened, although not necessarily manifest, commitment of the Iraqi state to war had been one of the major themes running through the Ba'thist regime's handling of regional issues. Internal issues, such as the Kurdish rebellion, had received more direct but scarcely less traditional treatment. However, what might be called 'the Grand Old Duke of York' attitude was vulnerable in two respects. Firstly, although operating in political terms from the security of a restricted circle of 'insiders' corresponding to a traditional disposition of power, Saddam Hussein was claiming to rule a state. As had been discussed above, a state as a collectivity brings with it a very different set of obligations for those who claim the right to rule from those accompanying the traditional concept of autocracy. While traditional autocracy may have remained the basis of political power and perception in Iraq, it could not be so acknowledged publicly by a regime which founded its claim to legitimacy on its determination to create a genuinely modern community in Iraq. Consequently, the autocrat found himself obliged to assume the defence of such alien concepts as territorial sovereignty, transforming personal outrage into national insult and thereby mobilizing the armed might at his disposal under the guise of national forces eager to fulfil their duty of defending the 'nation's rights'.[16] Under these circumstances, it was unlikely that Saddam Hussein could achieve his own objectives with regard to Iran through largely symbolic means, unless there existed perfect understanding in Tehran of the rules under which this clash of autocratic wills and prestige was to take place.

This feature introduces the second major vulnerability of the theory of warfare based on the assumed universality of autocracy. Common assumptions about the ways in which autocrats behave, the way they control the instruments of their power, the obligations they have taken on in an effort to strengthen their authority and their perceptions of the regional environment – all of these underpin a belief that they are able to read the signals of intent by those parties with whom they are in conflict. A moral universe is thereby created, rooted in the ways in which power itself is viewed, and leading to a series of beliefs about the justification and efficacy of the use of force to express that power. This establishes a sequence or hierarchy of actions, which is little more than a language of escalation, adapted with considerable precision to the presumed similarity of the party or ruler to whom it is addressed. In this lies the danger. Radical political change within the competing entity may alter the rules under which the conflict is prosecuted. However, the probability is that the autocrat who retains power will simply assume that the collapse of his rival has led not to transformation but simply to weakness. Furthermore, he will continue to operate under the old rules of exchange, permitting the exploitation of misfortune by force if necessary, without realizing that his actions are neither understood nor regarded as moves in a limited game by the opposing party. Under these circumstances, a war initiated on the understanding by one belligerent that it is a limited and largely symbolic move in the context of a long-running competition for personal influence, may become something quite different and unexpected as a result of the co-belligerent's rejection of the terms of that understanding.

These were the volatile underpinnings of the relationship between Iraq and Iran during 1978 and 1979 as the Shah was overthrown and the Islamic republic established. Simultaneously, Saddam Hussein was manoeuvring himself into a position in Iraq from which he could make his final move in pursuit of absolute power. This was achieved in July 1979 with his election as President of the Republic and Chairman of the Revolutionary Command Council (the supreme executive and legislative body), as well as his assumption of the post of Commander in Chief of the Iraqi Armed Forces. It was accompanied by purges and executions among the most senior ranks of the RCC, the Ba'th and the government. These confirmed Saddam Hussein's supremacy and narrowed still further the group of 'insiders' who exercised power under his direct control. As his own hold on Iraq tightened, so his ambitions to extend his influence in the region increased. Boosted by the apparent success of the Baghdad Conferences of 1978 and 1979, which seemed to accord Iraq primacy in leading the Arab world in the confrontation with Israel, Saddam Hussein succinctly expressed the implications for the region when the will of the autocrat had at its disposal the resources of the Iraqi state. He told his troops: 'We cannot maintain the nation's honour by defending Iraqi territory only; our duty extends to every part of the Arab homeland and to everywhere our hand reaches to maintain the Arab nation's honour'.[17]

At the same time, it was clear that he would tolerate no attempt to evade his reach within Iraq. The Shi'i cleric, Mohammad Baqr al-Sadr of Najaf, had long been seen by the regime as a focus for ideas of an alternative political order in Iraq. These implicitly challenged the principles exploited by the regime to justify its hold on power, and explicitly challenged that hold when civil disorder erupted in the Shi'i towns of the south during the 1970s. Al-Sadr had consequently been arrested numerous times by the regime. In June 1979, he was arrested once more, just as he was setting out to visit his former colleague, Ayatollah Khomeini, now the effective head of the Islamic Republic of Iran. Violent demonstrations in Najaf and Karbala demanding al-Sadr's release were suppressed with considerable ferocity by the Iraqi security forces, but the authorities made a concession by allowing al-Sadr to return to Najaf, where he was placed under house arrest.[18]

This turmoil had two major results: firstly, by forcing the members of the inner circle of the regime to reveal their attitudes to the ruthless handling of civil disturbance in the Shi'i cities of the south, it allowed Saddam Hussein to identify the doubtful elements of that circle and to rally support against them by labelling them 'outsiders'. If a contemporary report is to be believed, this was achieved by convening an extraordinary meeting of the Ba'th National Command at which the Shi'i Secretary General of the RCC, Abd al-Hussein al-Mashhadi, was publicly compelled to implicate fifty other 'co-conspirators'.[19] Secondly, it encouraged the belief that the disturbances in the Shi'i cities were the work of the new Iranian regime, acting through their local agents. Inevitably, the heated reaction of the Iranian Government and media to the treatment meted out to the Iraqi Shi'a lent further credence to this belief.

Perception of revolutionary Iran

The implications of these developments were that the Iraqi regime began to see Khomeini as a reincarnation of the Shah: that is, as an ambitious Iranian autocrat, intent on using the resources of the Iranian state and the disaffected elements within Iraq to extend his own ambitions at the expense of the interests of the regime in Baghdad. There is no indication that the Iraqi authorities showed any profound understanding of developments in Iranian politics. On the contrary, they clearly persisted in seeing Khomeini as the 'turbanned Shah', acting within the same guidelines and towards much the same end. It was therefore assumed that, like his predecessor, he would be open to much the same means of dissuasion, although, being a newcomer, some forceful demonstration of Iraqi strength might be necessary.[20] The Iranian leaders, for their part, helped to confirm this impression of continuity by enthusiastically portraying the struggle as one between Khomeini and Saddam Hussein for the allegiance of the Iraqi people.[21]

Perception of the continuity of the threat inevitably suggested a similar remedy: the deployment of force to convince the government in Tehran that the regime in Baghdad could no longer be intimidated. Quite apart from the personal memories of 1974–5, it was imperative for Suddam Hussein to assert his authority in this respect. To have failed in this sphere would have been to forfeit the obedience of the 'insider' group he now commanded. It would have indicated to them that he was unable to master the rhetoric and the instrumentalities appropriate to state leadership, putting their future in jeopardy through inattention to the myth and reality of their power. Consequently, from the middle of 1979 the war of words between Tehran and Baghdad intensified, possibly supplemented by unverifiable acts of violence along the common border. In many respects, this was very similar to the old game played against the Shah in the late 1960s and early 1970s.

In April 1980, the Iraqi regime was able to take the conflict one stage further when an assassination attempt was made on the deputy Prime Minister, Tariq Aziz, very much one of the inside figures of the Baghdad regime. He survived, but the fact that his assailant was described as 'an Iraqi of Iranian origin', and that the funeral procession of the victims of the attack was in turn attacked just as it was passing an Iranian school in Baghdad, led to an unambiguous response by Saddam Hussein. Mohammad Baqr al-Sadr and his sister, Amina bint al-Huda, were seized and summarily executed (the first time a senior mujtahid had suffered this fate in modern Iraqi history); membership of the Shi'i-based Al-Da'wa party was made retroactively punishable by death; thousands of Shi'a in Najaf, Karbala and Al-Thawra township in Baghdad were arrested; and a campaign was initiated to expel from Iraq any Iraqi who had even the remotest connection with Iran, by birth, marriage or name. To reinforce the message which he wanted to communicate to Khomeini in Iran, Saddam Hussein spoke defiantly of the Iraqis' refusal to be intimidated even if it meant 'dancing on the wings of death' and 'sacrificing themselves on the field of honour'. As Khomeini urged the Iraqi army to rebel, Saddam Hussein threatened to 'cut off the hand' of anyone trying to interfere in Iraq, stating that 'Iraq is prepared to enter into any kind of battle to defend its honour and sovereignty'.[22]

This cannot be dismissed simply as rhetoric. The images were extravagant, no doubt, but the rhetoric had a specific purpose: it was used to drive home to Tehran the resolve with which the Iraqi regime would act if its security was threatened. In that sense it formed a vital accompaniment to the ruthless suppression of internal dissent. This was a 'war game' analogous to that which had accompanied the suppression of the Kurds in 1974–5, and was meant to be understood as such by the regime in Tehran. Threats of reciprocal action, in the form of Iraqi aid to Iranian minorities, especially those of Arabistan/Khuzestan, had already been made to demonstrate Iraqi capabilities in this regard. The decapitation of the Shi'i activist movement at a stroke further illustrated that the regime would have no hesitation in acting forcefully against perceived agents of Khomeini's influence. At the same time, the repeated vaunting of the prowess of the Iraqi armed forces and the publicity accorded to Saddam Hussein's patronage of them were intended to demonstrate that the Iranian rulers could gain nothing by directly escalating the conflict.

It is at this stage in 1980, however, that one begins to sense a growing belief in the Iraqi leadership that the simulacrum of war in which they had hitherto indulged might profitably be taken one stage further. Direct military engagement, although admittedly of a limited kind, began to seem highly advantageous, and perhaps politically necessary. A number of factors contributed to this trend, although, given the closed and secretive system of Iraqi government, it would be difficult to describe with any accuracy the relative weight of each. Nevertheless, the decisions taken by the Iraqi leadership were taken within a context structured less by their conscious choices than by the logic inherent in their very conception of power: firstly, autocracy exercised in the name of a nation-state imposes its own rules and obligations; secondly, the war on which the autocrat embarks can be limited to the rules by which he wants to play only if his forces are locked in combat with those of an autocrat who is in most important respects a mirror-image of himself.

In 1979–80, Saddam Hussein increasingly adopted the stance of champion of Iraq's rights and sovereignty, as well as of the rights and sovereignty of the Arab nation. Clearly, the contradiction between proclaiming oneself the champion of such attributes of statehood and yet failing to make any moves to give them the territorial reality which statehood demands implies inconsistency, or worse. Consequently, Saddam Hussein found himself obliged to give territorial expression to his otherwise highly personalized claim to authority. On behalf of the Arab nation, this found shape in the demand that Iran relinquish its claims to Abu Musa and the Tunbs (islands of disputed sovereignty near the Strait of Hormuz); it was also reflected in the pretended championing of the 'cause' of the Arab inhabitants of the Iranian province of Khuzestan. On behalf of Iraq, but perhaps especially on behalf of the restoration of Saddam Hussein's prestige, these claims came to focus with increasing regularity on two border areas apparently ceded by Iran in the 1975 agreement, but not yet handed over to Iraq's control, and particularly on the Shatt al-Arab, over which Iraq now claimed full sovereignty. Increasingly, therefore, there was a tangible, territorial concession to be wrung from the Iranian regime, if Saddam Hussein's credibility was to be maintained.[23] This suggested a more offensive or active strategy than had hitherto been deployed by the Iraqi regime to deter Iranian intervention in or intimidation of Iraq.

At the same time, the continuing turmoil in Iran, especially insofar as it involved the Iranian armed forces, suggested that the autocracy which had succeeded the Shah was fundamentally flawed. From the perspective of the Iraqi regime, it now faced an insecure inner circle in Tehran which lacked the means to enforce its will or defend the territory of the state it claimed to rule. It is not improbable that Saddam Hussein saw Khomeini's regime as sharing a predicament similar to that of the Ba'th in the wake of the 1968 coup d'état: beleaguered in the capital by a society at odds with the central authority and racked by communal tensions; an inner circle composed of jealous and competing rivals, presided over by the authority of a single figure whose value was contingent simply on the influence he could continue to exert in the armed forces; the latter so demoralized and hamstrung by purges of the officer corps and by the lack of any regular outside supply to maintain technological credibility that they could at best perform only internal policing duties; and internationally bereft of any significant outside patron who might deter aggression. These were the factors which had heightened the Ba'thist regime's vulnerability and sense of weakness during the early years of its existence. They also seemed to be features shared by Iran in 1980, apparently making Khomeini's regime equally vulnerable.[24]

In these circumstances lie the origins, not of the conflict between Iran and Iraq, but of the war which began in that year: a war for political gain through territorial concession, initiated at a moment of apparent political and military opportunity. In order to wring the kinds of concessions from Iran which Saddam Hussein increasingly seemed to believe were not simply desirable but necessary, war appeared to be the only feasible course. Khomeini had demonstrated during 1979–80 that he was impervious to the various symbolic moves made by the Iraqi leaders. These moves had been intended to indicate their determination not only to resist the expansions of Iranian power but also to extend their own influence. A more explicit and direct use of force was deemed to be the only means of bringing home to him the requirements of the Iraqi leadership. As Saddam Hussein said in July, 1980: 'We do not want war . . . this is for Khomeini to decide'.[25] However, the Iraqi leadership did want land which was occupied by Iranian forces, and furthermore it wanted public Iranian acknowledgement of Iraqi sovereignty over the whole of the Shatt al-Arab, with all the historical, political and regional resonance that such a concession would have brought. These were desiderata which could only be achieved by force, if Khomeini persisted in refusing to acknowledge his own military and political weaknesses – weaknesses which were all too obvious to the leadership in Baghdad.[26]

Accordingly, in late August or early September the Iraqi Government reportedly sent an ultimatum to Tehran demanding the handing over of two areas of land promised in the 1975 agreement but not delivered. When the ultimatum expired, Iraqi forces moved in and began to occupy the disputed 150 square kilometres. Saddam Hussein once again denied that Iraq wanted war, but stated that circumstances required that Iraq use force to regain 'all Iraqi land usurped by the Persians'.[27] In his speech to the National Assembly on 17 September 1980, he reiterated this theme, even as he abrogated the 1975 agreement and claimed Iraqi sovereignty over the whole of the Shatt al-Arab: 'We in no way intend to launch war against Iran or extend the circle of struggle beyond the limits of defending our rights and sovereignty'.[28]

This was not simply dissimulation designed to disguise the fact that Iraq had already prepared to launch a major air and land attack on Iranian territory within the next few days. It was also an indication of the way in which Saddam Hussein visualized the use of force and thus the nature of the war which was about to erupt. The deployment of direct military force by Iraq at a moment of perceived military and political weakness in Iran, was to be a demonstration to the Iranian leadership that the old balance which had existed in the heyday of Iran's military strength under the Shah had now been redressed in Iraq's favour.[29] The Iranian regime, which was assumed to be subject to the same basic laws of political behaviour which governed the regime of the Shah and indeed that of the Ba'th, was supposed to be faced with a choice similar to that which had faced Saddam Hussein in 1975. It could escalate the conflict into general warfare, but, given the Iraqi regime's perceptions of the military strength of the two sides, this was believed to be beyond its capability.

Alternatively, it could negotiate, granting the Iraqi regime crucial legitimacy by acknowledging that the Iraqi use of military force had obliged Iran 'to recognize Iraq's rights and sovereignty'.[30]

Accordingly, on 22 September 1980 Iraq pressed ahead with its demonstrative use of force by invading Iranian territory at four points along their common border and by attacking ten of Iran's military airfields. It was for General Adnan Khayrallah, Minister of Defence and deputy Commander-in-Chief of the Iraqi Armed Forces, to explain a few days later the reasons for the Iraqi attack, using the language of modern statehood and warfare: 'We decided to lay our hands on points vital to Iran's interests inside Iranian territory to deter Iran from striking our national sovereignty and to make it recognize our full sovereignty over the Shatt al-Arab'.[31] This seemed to be a mirror image of the situation in 1975, when an Iranian show of force had both deterred Iraq from retaliating and compelled it to recognize the extent of Iranian sovereignty in the Shatt al-Arab. Khomeini was now expected to enter this rather stylized, albeit bloody, game in the spirit in which it was intended. Ultimately, of course, in the Iraqi view this had less to do with the trappings of territorial sovereignty than with the natural competition between neighbouring autocrats' circles of power. Saddam Hussein had in fact made this abundantly clear at a press conference in 1980, when he stated: 'He [Khomeini] has wagered to bend us and we have wagered to bend him. We will see who will bend the other. The outcome is already clear. Khomeini is fighting at home and has thus saved us the trouble.'[32] Although regarded as an autocrat diminished in strength, Khomeini was still expected to play by the same rules. It was for Saddam Hussein, in the aftermath of 22 September 1980, to ensure that the use of the Iraqi armed forces was geared to the kind of war which he had initiated. It was equally for him, and for the Iraqi leadership, to cope with the consequences when it became evident that their Iranian opponents were not fighting the same kind of war.

3

Iran and the Politics of the War

Introduction

In February 1979 the revolution in Iran brought to power a group of men, by no means monolithic in character, whose outlook on international affairs was conditioned by their revolutionary experience and the lessons they derived from it. In some cases it was their religious faith, however idiosyncratically applied, that framed their world view. Whatever their aims beforehand, once in power they evinced a deep desire to promote their cause far afield and to serve as a source of inspiration and emulation in the Islamic world.

However, while the new leadership seemed to have unbounded regional ambitions, the very success of the revolution appeared to outsiders to have weakened the country's military establishment. The war with Iraq which unfolded shortly thereafter was scarcely a surprise insofar as it contained all the ingredients of the classic formula for inter-state war: on one side, an ambitious regime which threatened its neighbour while at the same time letting its military capabilities languish, and on the other an ambitious neighbour sensing genuine threat from this new regime, but also an opportunity to make political gains by engaging and defeating it. For our purpose it is sufficient to observe here that Iran's political system and society are responsible not only for the onset of the war itself, but for the manner in which it has been conducted, and the way its war aims have been formulated.

None of this should come as a surprise. Historically revolutions have tended to be followed by war, for they blur or change the existing balance of power and/or pose threats – political, ideological, or military – to their neighbours.[1] Revolutions by their very nature are unable to separate their domestic from their foreign affairs. Whether because of the claims they make for the universal applicability of their message and model, or because of their insistence that national or state boundaries should be ignored or revised, they tend to threaten the existing order and take pleasure in doing so. Foreign policy in a revolutionary state seems to demand activism, an affirmation of the vitality of the revolution and of the wider relevance of its example.

Clausewitz emphasized that war reflects the type of society that is waging it:[2]

> The types of war correspond to the types of regime. The strategy suitable to one type (republic, monarchy, despotism) would be contrary to the nature of the other. Choice between types of war is not the outcome of the governing will of one of the belligerents, let alone both. It is the political situation that dictates the main lines of the hostilities, and they are determined in advance by the nature of the relationship between and inside the states.

By its very nature a revolutionary state is less disposed to fight a 'limited war'. Clausewitz observed that in non-revolutionary periods 'communication between enemies based on historical experience contributes moderation to war-like excesses'. By the same token, 'wars approach the absolute form when revolutinary novelty prevents the implicit communication which favours moderation'.[3]

Once started, societies wage the type of war which reflects them and which presumably they find most congenial. An historian of the subject writes: 'The style of war adopted in battle is frequently a telling indicator of the morale of a society'. He also notes the tendency in revolutionary societies for the style of warfare to become 'relentlessly offensive and aggressive'.[4]

Iran is not only a revolutionary society: it is also an Islamic society, perhaps the state most insistent today on thus identifying itself. Historically there has been a strong Muslim military tradition. In Dankwart Rustow's words: 'Islam is the most martial of the world's great religions'. He argues that warfare was an integral part of the Muslim and Ottoman traditions precisely because it served religious, political, and legal ends summed up in the idea of a *jihad* or crusade.[5] It is a striking fact nonetheless that although modern Iran had had no significant experience of warfare in the previous century, in the current conflict extensive use has been made of Islamic symbols and idioms to define issues and motivate the troops. As was the case in the last days of the Ottoman empire (when *jihad* could no longer be said to be the army's main function),[6] religion has been the main source of enthusiasm of the ordinary soldier in the present conflict.

There has been a close and inseparable relationship between the revolutionary regime in Iran, the onset of the war, the way in which the stakes have been defined and the manner in which the war has been conducted. In this chapter we examine some of these relationships from the viewpoint of the influence of the society on the conflict, reversing the perspective in the succeeding chapter to look in turn at how the war has affected the society.

The onset of war

There is nothing inevitable about war: it is the product of human decisions as much as of political or military circumstances. Neighbours can and frequently do live side by side peacefully, with mutual resentments and manifest differences of interest and with no great cordiality. Such was the situation existing between Iran and Iraq in the decades from the end of the Second World War until 1979. What changed this was revolutionary Iran's provocation of Iraq by threatening to take the Islamic revolution to its territory (by indulging in and lending moral sanction to acts of terrorism against Baghdad) *and* the Islamic republic's simultaneous disparagement of the traditional military instrument. Iran proceeded to dismantle the armed forces bequeathed it by the Shah by cancelling military orders, cutting the already reduced military budget by one third, halving conscription to one year, and seeking to return to the United States the 80 F–14 aircraft together with their *Phoenix* missiles. By August 1979 Iran's helicopter force was largely grounded and there were plans to reduce it by one half to economize on spare parts. The Chieftain tanks in the inventory were believed to be only 30 per cent operational. A half-completed tank repair base at Dorud was abandoned and a factory complex for tank parts and ammunition being built outside Isfahan was scheduled to be converted to civilian use.[7]

Apart from the large-scale desertions which were reported to have amounted to 60 per cent of the 171,000-strong army, purges, dismissals, trials and executions had led to the loss of another 12,000 often skilled and trained personnel by the autumn of 1980. Between 30 and 50 per cent of the officers between the rank of major and colonel were removed 'with devastating effect on the army's ability to conduct combat operations'.[8] An official Iranian publication referred to 'an army whose former structure was pulled to pieces in response to the post-revolution necessities and its new structure had not yet taken shape'.[9] If the Iranians had, in their own euphemism, 'reduced the number of the permanent and higher ranking personnel of the armed forces', this could not fail to have adverse consequences for the operational capabilities of the armed forces. After the war began President Bani Sadr referred to the lack of military preparedness thus: 'What had been happening to our armed forces for two years resulted in the fact that the weapons were not regularly checked and they were not ready for use.'[10] Some five years later another President had this to say about the situation in 1980:[11]

> During the early days of the imposed war, some officials on the basis of certain motives played down the role of arms and equipment . . . did not pay sufficient attention to the problem of defence . . . armed with weapons and equipment, a committed believer will not give any chances to the enemy to attack, and all through history, aggressors have attacked those who could not defend themselves.

In addition to the dismantling of the armed forces and the prosecution of a desultory campaign against the Kurds, Iran was almost totally self-absorbed. Despite border incidents and clashes with Iraq since May 1979, and an increasingly strident exchange of rhetoric, Iran remained preoccupied with its revolution. In the autumn of 1979 Iraq raised the issue of the disputed islands in the Gulf. By December, according to a well-placed US official, 'there were reports from Western observers in Iraq that the Iraqis were planning an invasion of Iran's oil-fields and the reports were given credence'[12] by the frequency and tempo of armed clashes. By April 1980, after an attempt on the life of Tariq Aziz (Iraq's deputy Prime Minister), Iran was making explicit threats to unseat the Ba'thist regime in Baghdad. Yet instead of strengthening its forces or reinforcing its frontier defences, it chose to ignore Iraq's diplomatic notes and indicators of military activity (which were subsequently documented by the Iranian Foreign Ministry), including arms purchases, recall of draftees and reservists, dispersal of military aircraft, strengthening of border posts, etc. Iran explained its failure to respond as follows:[13]

> Iran's military and non-military organizations, as well as the Ministry of Foreign Affairs, were too preoccupied with the typically [sic] post-revolutionary problems whereby the Iranian authorities did not lodge any protest against many violations.

Iran's response, or rather lack of it, may well have encouraged Iraq to conclude that, now that Iran was deficient in military organization and equipment, it also lacked the stomach to engage in war.

The reality was somewhat different. Iran was preoccupied not only by internal matters in the post-revolutionary chaos, but by a degree of hubris that rendered it incapable of rational thought. The self-absorption is not untypical of revolutions. Edward Burke observed: 'Nothing is so fatal to a nation as an extreme of self-partiality and the total want of consideration of what others will naturally hope or fear'. The revolution was in a euphoric phase, convinced that it was creating new precedents that set it apart from the constraints of history or the laws of man. Against all the odds, the nation had achieved a revolution; now it was preoccupied with giving that achievement meaning, content and direction. It indulged in its rhetorical attacks on its neighbour with little thought for any possible reaction[14] and with a sense of invulnerability which was soon to be shown to be illusory.

The Iranian leaders' perception of threats, based on their experience in the revolution and certain ideological baggage which they had collected, bore little resemblance to their actual environment. Nevertheless, it was these that motivated them and had first claim on their attention. First among them was the fear of counter-revolutionaries, monarchists and the like. They were busy settling accounts with those they accused of such sentiments, including from time to time the military. But equally to be feared were less tangible threats to the revolution; the intrusion of Western values, the corruption of Islamic ideas and standards, the revival of 'dependence' on the West, all of which would disorient the revolution, empty it of moral content, and sap its pristine integrity. Before the war, Khomeini expressed this clearly: 'We are not afraid of economic sanctions or military intervention. What we are afraid of is Western universities, the training of our youth in the interests of West or East'.[15]

The revolutionaries who controlled Iran after February 1979 were convinced that the regular military forces developed under the Shah were an instrument of oppression, a reflection and a symbol of the country's continued unseemly dependence on the United States, and a source of lavish and unnecessary expenditure. It was only a short step from this to denying the need for such standing forces for territorial defence and to arguing for their replacement by a people's revolutionary militia. The distance was easily traversed by those who continued to see the military as the principal threat to the revolution. Khomeini himself, understandably, continued to distrust them, telling Bani Sadr: 'The military have the Shah in their blood'.[16]

There had indeed been several attempted military coups against the Islamic republic before the war, the last one in July 1980 being the most serious and leading to more purges. On the eve of the war, even after extensive purges and summary executions, the regime still did not trust the military. Prime Minister Rajai expressed the commonly held view: 'A "maktabi" army is preferable to a victorious army'.[17] The regime set about infiltrating political-ideological commissars into the ranks and building up other military and security institutions. Some groups like the *Mojahedin-e Khalq* (People's Resistance), its *Fedayin* (People's Guerrillas) counterpart, and the Iranian Communist (Tudeh) party called for the complete disbanding of the regular forces – a step that Khomeini, understandably, was reluctant to make, and a point which he has consistently emphasized ever since as proof of his commitment to the armed forces. Nevertheless, the military, despite appeals from Khomeini for discipline and the need to maintain the hierarchy, suffered from a post-revolutionary disorder which was difficult to control because it reflected competing ideological and political impulses.

The net effect of the suspicion of the military, and the preoccupation with the course and content of the revolution, was to produce not only a neglect of the regular military forces, but a denial that such forces were needed for external defence or, indeed, that such a concept was worthwhile. Just before the war, Khomeini was obliged to bring back conscription, but he sought to differentiate this from earlier practice by saying: 'This is now a divine matter. This is the defence of the Islamic realm'.[18] Insofar as the leadership in Tehran perceived an Iraqi threat, they viewed it as a species of attrition intended to nibble away at their resources and distract them from building the Islamic republic. There was a pervasive unwillingness to discuss military or security issues except as slogans suffused with ideological overtones. On the eve of the war, Bani Sadr was talking about 'the necessity to free the army from being dependent as regards tactics and strategy . . . culture, military training, weapons . . . Internally we must make the army into a university.'[19]

How then did the Iranian leaders conceive of the military and what role did they envisage for it? It is difficult to answer this precisely because the conceptions were barely thought through. What can be said is that they rejected the view prevailing under the Shah, often simply by taking a diametrically opposite position. If the Shah's armed forces had been configured for external defence, with emphasis on high-technology weapons, staffed by regular military officers (buttressed by some conscripts), a source of prestige for the regime, and acting as the 'implicit coalition' partner in the government of the country,[20] then the revolutionary forces would emphasize their popular component and self-reliance, rank faith and commitment higher than imported equipment, and act as an extension of the revolutionary spirit as well as its mailed fist. While the revolutionary guards (Pasdar) were to be the guardians of the revolution domestically, little attention was paid to the need for defence against external enemies. It was assumed that popular militias infused with revolutionary spirit and Islamic fervour could more than match any putative – and doubtless godless – threat.

When the Iraqi attack came with 10 divisions, Iran could muster only elements of two divisions and some 120 tanks near the frontier. Part of the genuine surprise at the Iraqi attack stemmed from a national arrogance rather than from the characteristics of the regime: a refusal to believe that Iraq would dare launch such an attack on its own. It thus became part of the mythology that the effort to strangle the revolution had been planned by the United States, and Iraq was simply its tool.

The conduct of the war

The Iranian regime and society not only paved the way for the Iraqi attack by provoking Iraq while at the same time weakening their own defence capability and refusing to accept the need for a military with an external defence mission, but Iran's reactions to the war and its conduct were framed by its domestic circumstances. They remained distinctly a product of Iranian society.

For example, the Iraqi invasion did not initially take precedence over domestic politics and unify the ranks of the revolution; on the contrary, the circumstances of domestic politics defined the reaction to the war, which was not given priority. The revolutionary authorities were convinced that Iran's military relationship with the United States had given rise to, rather than reflected, a condition of 'dependency', which in turn constituted 'one of Washington's instruments of hegemonic power'.[21] One might have expected some reconsideration of this view in the light of Iraq's invasion and Iran's palpable need for arms and spare parts. Indeed, during the negotiations over the release of the US hostages, the United States expected that this issue would be raised, and it had, in fact, decided on the authorization of a package of military equipment 'that would be attractive to Tehran while avoiding items that were very sensitive . . . or highly lethal'. This boiled down to $100 million in spare parts for the air force and some $50 million in other equipment.[22] Iran originally raised the issue but never pursued it, despite the crying need once the war had started. This was partly due to continuing distrust of any reconstitution of links with the United States, but it was even more a product of the political rivalry between President Bani Sadr, nominally Commander-in-Chief, and the Islamic Republican Party, who wanted to impose a clerical regime on Iran, and who distrusted the President's obvious cultivation of the regular armed forces.

It is not too much to say that domestic politics continued to take priority over the prosecution of the war, epitomized in the slogan 'Revolution before victory'. Indeed the war became an extension of the domestic power rivalry, to which the arming, structure, strategy and conduct of the military were subordinated. While Bani Sadr insisted that any agreement on the hostages should include the supply of such arms and spare parts as had been paid for, he was simply excluded from the negotiations by the IRP and Prime Minister Rajai. As he put it, they 'simply made it impossible for our armed forces to perform their battle duties effectively and conclusively'.[23] Bani Sadr considered the IRP a 'greater calamity for the country than the war with Iraq'.[24] Khomeini's grandson Hossein reported hearing the IRP say that 'it is preferable to lose half of Iran than for Bani Sadr to become the ruler'.[25] The excuse made by Hashemi Rafsanjani that the nation would not stand for a resumption of arms supplies[26] whatever its validity then, appears hollow in the light of his own attempts to reconstitute these ties after 1985 once his political opponents had been eliminated. Domestic politics affected the conduct of the war not only in the supply of arms for the army from the United States, but in the competition for heavy arms between the army and the Pasdar. And it was domestic pressures that impelled Bani Sadr to order a premature and unsuccessful offensive at Susangird in January 1981.

In short, partisan politics took precedence over any putative national interest, prevented the efficient conduct of the war (we return to this below) and even prevented its settlement. By December 1980, it was already clear to some Iranian officials that the war could have no military solution, but it was also clear that the domestic power struggle made a diplomatic solution impossible.[27]

i)   *The stakes*

Even with the material resources available, the will to fight a war for over seven years – not always in self-defence – requires extraordinary motivation. Khomeini's definition of the stakes involved in the war has more than anything else generated the will and defined the scale of the mobilization. It has been this, and the nature of the Islamic republic, that has enabled the prosecution of a long, costly, and inconclusive war. From the outset, Khomeini defined the war not in territorial or material but in spiritual and even metaphysical terms, making it difficult if not impossible to envisage any diplomatic solution.[28]

> You are fighting to protect Islam and he is fighting to destroy Islam . . . There is absolutely no question of peace or compromise and we shall never have any discussions with them; because they are corrupt and perpetrators of corruption.
>
> The damage caused by this criminal is irreparable unless he withdraws his forces, leaves Iraq and then abandons his corrupt government; he must leave the Iraqi people to decide their own fate. It is not a question of a fight between one government and another; it is a question of an invasion by an Iraqi non-Muslim Ba'thist against an Islamic country; and this is a rebellion by blasphemy against Islam.[29]

Khomeini returned to this theme repeatedly, implying that the stakes could not be comprehended by a conventional analysis of inter-state disputes.[30]

> Those who criticize us say: Why do you not compromise with these corrupt powers? It is because they see things through human eyes and analyse these things with a natural viewpoint. They do not know the views of God and how the prophets dealt with oppressors or else they know but pretend to be blind and deaf. To compromise with oppressors is to oppress. That is contrary to the views of all the prophets.

Again and again the Iranian leadership invoked these apocalyptic themes to justify what appears to be a pointless war.[31]

> Compromise would be tantamount to annihilation. We are now fighting for our religion not for territory. He who relies on God's power . . . will not abandon the arena.

As Rafsanjani put it:

> The fact that we are not making peace stems from the Koran and the honour of Islam and . . . preserving the blood of the martyrs.

Another time, admitting the high cost of the war, he concluded: 'but the war is our existence'.[32] And Prime Minister Musavi:

> This war is against blasphemy. We can achieve nothing other than through

victory over Iraq. This revolution belongs to the whole world . . . If Iran were defeated, all the revolutionary forces would be defeated.

Seven months later, he invoked the fate of the revolution itself as being at stake in the war:

> They want to force us to compromise so that tomorrow the reactionaries in the region can speak out against Islam and call it an unsuccessful experiment. They aim to erode the Islamic Revolution through an imposed peace and drive it towards destruction.[33]

As the Iranians have defined the war not in territorial terms but as a test for Islam, and have equated compromise with defeat, they have left themselves only one course: the continuation of the war until victory. This victory will necessarily have to include the extension of Islam to Iraq, probably as an Islamic republic on the lines of Iran, but in any case a removal of the secular Ba'th. This perspective is deeply rooted in the revolution. Khomeini sees the Iraqis as usurpers, *jahilah*, who must be overthrown. It is Iran's duty to take its model of Islamic activism to its erring brethren, and to assist the Iraqi nation, which has been misled by a usurping regime, to gain power.

In this perspective, Iran is not just a national state (indeed the concept of nation-state is not accepted by Khomeini, who accepts only the 'community of believers' as the appropriate unit of analysis) but a regime of the word of God. Iran *is* Islam, and the war is about the defence of Iran, i.e. Islam. Once this definition-perspective is applied, the regime becomes its prisoner, making the achievement of a pragmatic peace difficult, for peace-making becomes an issue not of Iran's interests but of those of Islam. If Islam is at stake and Islam is the constituency, Iran cannot freely negotiate bilaterally on the basis of some national interest. If Iran is fighting for the vindication of religious principles, it is difficult to stop the war, for even if victory proves impossible of attainment, Iran is duty-bound to continue. Clearly if compromise is a corruption of Islam and defeat a failure of Islam, the issue of the 'costs' in the war is only relative. Iran's definition of the stakes, and how it looks at the war (and the question of negotiation), no less than how it fights it, are a direct outgrowth of the nature of the society, its politics and values.

ii) *Leadership, faith and commitment*

The war started by Iraq in mid-September 1980 came as a surprise to the Iranian leadership, who nonetheless embraced it as a blessing and an opportunity to test the mettle of the nation, and its religious commitment. The sense of embattlement, the cult of martyrdom and ritual, the willingness to 'take on all comers' and the narrow focus that the war gave the somewhat stalled revolution were almost welcomed by the regime.

The war would demonstrate the resilience and vitality of the revolution, and affirm the power of faith, unity and self-sacrifice, and the dominance of the spiritual dimension over the merely material.

Given the importance of motivation in this war, it is essential to understand the role of both leader and ideology (or faith) in mobilizing, maintaining and renewing support for it. Khomeini's unique role has been in representing an image of an upright holy man interested only in the good of the community: stern, demanding, rigorous, but also honest, consistent and implacable; a link with traditional faith, a symbol of moral rectitude, and a source of pride and reassurance for his people. He has defined the stakes in the war that – on their own terms – brook little dispute. It is he who has motivated the many thousands of volunteers and blessed the war effort. The oriental philosopher and strategist Sun Tzu placed the factor of leadership and 'moral influence' in war before those of weather, terrain, command, or doctrine:[34]

> By moral influence, I mean that which causes people to be in harmony with their leaders, so that they will accompany them in life unto death without fear of mortal peril.

Given the stakes at issue in the war, the Iranian leadership has not been shy about the acceptability of the costs:[35]

> Our youth should be trained and be prepared, because in the future we might have longer wars. We must fight for the sake of Islam . . . Despite all our deaths, we have not had as many deaths as in the early days of Islam. We should show self-sacrifice. We should sacrifice all our loved ones for the sake of Islam. This has to be done . . . If we are killed, we have performed our duty, and if we kill, again, we have acted according to our duty.
>
> We regard martyrdom as a great blessing and our nation also welcomes martyrdom with open arms. We are not afraid of war, we are ready for war.

And more recently:[36]

> The nation that comes out ready to be martyred will not be intimidated by the threat of martyrdom.

The same theme that war holds no fears for the nation is often repeated:[37]

> He who has a modest style of living does not fear war. Our Guards who lead a less than normal life do not fear war. Our military men who lead a normal life do not fear war; war would not do them harm. Those who possess palaces and so forth, they should fear war, because they have something to lose.

The apotheosis of this view, in effect the denial of the importance of weapons, was Khomeini's comment to the Revolutionary Guards: 'Victory is not achieved by swords, it can only be achieved by blood . . . it is achieved by strength of faith'.[38]

Again and again Khomeini has sought to instil in his countrymen the importance of a militant stand in the activist tradition of the Prophet, and acceptance of its consequences:

> Anyone who revolted to establish justice, to establish a just rule, has received a slap in the face.
>
>   I say that we have no cause for complaint in that we revolted in order to revive justice, to establish a just rule and Islamic rule for which we received slaps in the face. We should receive more slaps in the face . . . we have to pay the penalty.

He argues that it is very easy to avoid these difficulties by inactivity and following the quietist tradition:[39]

> Therefore, if anyone just sits and prays, he will be left alone . . . no one will bother them. However, this is contradictory to the traditions of the prophets.

In Khomeini's view the attack on the Islamic Republic was not accidental but inevitable, for it was the natural consequence of the threat posed by militant Islam to unbelievers and the corrupt. In his speeches he draws the parallels between the current situation and the experience of the Prophet.[40]

> Had the Prophet come and sat in the Medina mosque all his life just to preach the Koran, then we would have followed him as an example. But he came and from the start of his mission in Mecca he began a struggle.
>
>   He set up a Government; we should do the same. He participated in various wars, we too should fight. He defended [Islam], we too should also defend [it].

The universalization of the conflict with Iraq, in which the war became a metaphor for the Prophet's own earlier struggles, seems to correspond with a need in contemporary Iran stemming perhaps from its Shi'i heritage. Expressed crudely but not without accuracy it appears to say: 'I fight, therefore I am'. While this gives the political leadership ample funds of commitment to draw upon, it gives them little direction as to the acceptable terms for peace short of victory.

Khomeini stressed that the war was a divine duty permitting no room for compromise, and at the same time that Iran was well suited to prosecute it. The war came at an opportune time, rallying the nation and giving the revolution a second wind, a chance to renew itself. From the pronouncements of the leaders, one might well conclude that the nation's opportunity to prove its mettle and live up to its ideals was given priority over the prosecution of the war which become a secondary consideration.

The use of such evocative symbols as blood and martyrdom and the importance of the spiritual over the material in motivating the troops was understandable and effective, but it was but a short step from there to the delusion that weapons, tactics and logistics were inconsequential in warfare.

iii)   *The style of warfare*

If the war was a test of the revolution, and was to be fought to victory for the sake of Islam with little concern for the costs or duration of the conflict, utilizing the assets that the revolution had in plenty (faith, endurance, indomitability), the way it was to be run *militarily* was also to reflect the society. As Khomeini's designated heir, Ayatollah Montazeri, said in mid-1986, the three elements responsible for the victory of the revolution: unity, faith, and decisive leadership, would also determine the outcome of the war.[41] It was perhaps natural for the new leadership to disparage the importance of the traditional elements of warfare since it had attained power not through conflict but through the political collapse of its enemy. Furthermore, it was part of the revolutionaries' experience, as well as ideological baggage, that the power of the people counted for a great deal. It was not very difficult to convert this into a denial of the importance of traditional indicators of military power, and to emphasize the revolution's unique contribution in this area as well. From the outset of the war even those charged with its conduct such as the Defence Minister (and Air Force Commander) Fakhuri argued that the ultimate determinant would be the outcome of the struggle between two systems, 'a war between right and wrong', and that the 'military dimension' was 'secondary'. He foresaw a 'war between two armies in the classical sense as being a very short-term and local war, and as such one that inherently cannot last very long'. More important would be the fact that the 'war will take the form of a people's war . . . a form which may continue for years.[42]

There has been a strong tendency to emphasize tactics and strategy congenial to revolutionary ideology, and to point to the importance of the human element and will in warfare. Witness Rafsanjani:[43]

> We have prepared ourselves for a protracted war and we are not afraid of AWACs and other weapons. We depend on ourselves, our faith and the strength of our people in this war.

The Revolutionary Guards (Pasdar) Commander, Morteza Reza'i, echoed the idea of a long war:[44]

> Only an ideologically motivated army like ours, like the ones which liberated Vietnam and Algeria, are capable of mobilizing the people for a long war of attrition which we plan to wage until the Iraqi regime falls.

Prime Minister Musavi observed that 'the power of faith can outmanoeuvre a complicated war machine used by people bereft of sublime religion'.[45] The case was put most moderately by Colonel Shirazi, Commander of the Ground Forces: 'A war in God's path is not based purely on technology, weapons, science, and expertise'.[46]

The conduct of the war has been strongly influenced by the revolutionary regime's need to demonstrate its vitality, relevance and, above all, uniquely moral superiority. The leadership has repeatedly stressed that Iran is inventing new – Islamic – ways of fighting wars that are the wonder of the world. The head of the Mobilization Unit (Basij), Hojjat el-Eslam Salek, observed in 1982 that Iran's volunteers had succeeded 'in doing away with conventional warfare methods and had introduced a new method called "Islamic warfare" '.[47] President Khamenei told the military in 1984 that it was becoming a 'modern Islamic army', and in 1986 suggested that Iran's military tactics should be documented and given to other states for their instruction.[48]

After over seven years of warfare which have seen an alteration between reliance on traditional military tactics on the one hand and recourse to costly, poorly planned and improvized human wave attacks on the other, there is still a disposition to return to the ideologically congenial and politically reliable standby – people's war. Corps Commander Reza'i suggested in mid-1986 that Iran had still only used 2 per cent of its popular and 12 per cent of its economic forces in the war: 'The war today should be completely transformed into a people's war in accordance with a scheme'. Emphasizing that Iran's 'combatants' (as they are called have shown that they do not need advanced aircraft and tanks to achieve victory, Reza'i said that to win: 'It is sufficient for us to bring into the battlefield four times more infantry forces with light weapons than the Iraqis'.[49]

The armed forces and the Pasdaran

If the revolutionaries did not trust the regular military forces they inherited, or accept the relevance of their professional skills, when the war erupted, they were nonetheless forced to depend upon them and their expertise. The regime has done so without any great pleasure and with little grace, using the regular forces as needed but keeping its special praise for the Revolutionary Guards, which it treats as a privileged group. For political reasons to do with regime security, the Islamic authorities have preferred to conduct the war with two sets of military institutions in parallel rather than risk their integration into one instrument. At the same time they have supervised the rapid expansion of the Pasdaran to match the size of the regular forces.

One should recall the differences in mission of the respective organizations. The regular military are concerned with the defence of the country's borders, and the security of the country against external threats. The Revolutionary Guards (also known as the guardians of the revolution) were conceived as an internal security force. The Revolutionary Guards Commander put this well:[50]

The aim of the Revolution Guards Corps is to protect and preserve the Islamic revolution. Unlike the army ... the Islamic Revolution Guards Corps is in charge of safeguarding the revolution and its gains. As a result it did not recruit or employ individuals but rather 'accepted membership' and unlike the regular military ... we in the Revolution Guards give primary importance to the ideological and political dimensions more than the military ones.

Six years of war later, this mission had not changed appreciably. Mohsen Rafiqdust, the Minister for the Pasdaran, put it thus:[51]

The mission of the army is the preservation of the territorial integrity of the country. The mission of the Guardians of the Revolution is to protect the Islamic revolution, which may be from threats other than those across its frontiers. In short, the army is not to be involved in the struggle against counter-revolution domestically while the Pasdar are.

A critical point from the view of the Islamic authorities has been to ensure that, in the process of using the regular military forces to defend the country, the revolution should not lose control of power or its ideological direction, that it should not lose its way while trying to protect itself. This issue is not unique to Iran and has arisen in comparable cases. It has been well put by John Ellis:[52]

... the more a revolutionary army has to adopt modes of organisation that do not give full play to popular attitudes and aspirations, the more that revolution runs the risk of losing sight of its original vision and the dynamic that gave it birth.

Military success bought at the price of a rigid emphasis upon regularisation and institutional efficiency can be a most ephemeral triumph in terms of the original aims of the revolution.

These considerations were not far from the minds of the Islamic authorities as they supervised the organization of the military. While the regular forces were better trained, the Pasdar were more daring or reckless, giving rise to considerable friction between them as to how the war ought to be fought – quite apart from the issue of war aims, or their relative contributions to the war. Early on, the first civilian Defence Minister, Mostafa Chamran, alluded to these differences:[53]

My view is that the army possesses technical power ... that is, military science, a technology which the guards corps lack, while the guardsmen are endowed with a stronger spirit of faith and devotion.

Chamran noted that this gave rise to very different ideas as to how the war ought to be conducted, and he specifically contrasted Pasdar impetuosity with military reserve:

There is, however, a passionate body of young men who expect the army to fall in with their wishes and miraculously take the enemy by storm in a single moment, an expectation which is unjustified and unrealistic.

Differences of approach regarding the war, and specifically on how it should be conducted militarily, have persisted throughout the conflict. There have been instances when it appeared that the military's skills and the Pasdars' fervour might be combined and made complementary, but these moments were fleeting. Suspicions, resentments, political differences and uncertainty clouded relations throughout. These reflected the larger issue – that of the relationship between the Islamic republic and its military forces.

From the beginning of the war, despite occasional nods in the direction of the professional military designed to reassure them, the Islamic authorities have shown their preference for the Pasdar. They have been referred to by Khomeini as the 'solid pillar' of the revolution, and as playing 'a determining role in the process of revolution' by President Khamenei.[54] Together with the Basij, the Pasdar are singled out for special praise.

Rafsanjani said that the Basij (who are trained by the Pasdar) are a 'blessing from God'; 'If a country wished to carry out the task taken up by the mobilization using only an organized and formal army, they would be unable to do so'. Prime Minister Musavi in turn noted that the country relies on 'the creative, popular and revolutionary forces' and that 'Today we are stronger than ever. We have the Basij and the Corps'.[55]

Although reassuring comments and expressions of gratitude are occasionally extended to the military, these lack conviction and fly in the face of the trends. Since 1980 the Pasdar have quintupled in size to some 350,000,[56] a number that exactly offsets the regular military. More important, the Guards, who have become a praetorian guard for the regime, are accorded numerous privileges, including superior pay and benefits to those enjoyed by the military. They have first call upon arms and spare parts and have better access to the civilian leadership. Both the Guards Commander Reza'i and Minister Rafiqdust are members of the Supreme Defence Council; they have enjoyed a stability of tenure that has not been matched by their military counterparts (although the military are also represented in the council).[57] Since 1982, when a separate Ministry was established for them, the Guards Corps have further expanded their domain. Plans for IRGC naval units were announced in the same year (and launched in May 1986). In September 1985, as a result of a directive from Khomeini[58] demanding the 'forming and strengthening of its (i.e. Guards) ground, air, and naval forces', plans for the formation of all three services for the Guards Corps were accelerated. The Cabinet reviewed these expansion plans shortly thereafter. In March 1986 Minister Rafiqdust spoke of plans to build an IRGC air arm, noting that the budget had already been approved.[59] In May 1986 an IRGC 'Navy' was launched and in September the Guards Corps started an 'advanced artillery training' course and designated a corps for this. These fields had all hitherto been the domain of the professional military.

Despite Khomeini's subsequent attempt to reassure the armed forces of their 'permanence', the suspicion had been kindled that after five years of war the army, which Khomeini's designated successor had said 'people call their own', still was not trusted and, worse, was to be replaced as soon as possible after the war by the pampered Guards.[60] Reza'i, while denying the existence of a rift between the armed forces and the Guards, noted that the IRGC which had been created 'to safeguard the achievements of the revolution' had since grown from a para-military force to a regular army. Khomeini's decree thus 'serves to further strengthen the military power as well as the social standing of the IRGC'.[61]

The Islamic authorities had reason to distrust the military in the light of their plots against the regime in 1980 in particular, and more generally because of their professional ethos which seemed incompatible with that of the Islamic republic. The same was true, for different reasons, of the military, who had reason to be suspicious of the Islamic authorities, offended by their domination of the state, disgusted by their ignorance of military matters, and fearful of their ultimate objectives. Although purged and vilified, the armed forces were reconstituted in 1980 and proved their mettle in the next two years when they succeeded in driving the Iraqis out of Iranian territory, in a number of set-piece and professional military operations.[62] Their reward was to see the leadership of the war passed to the Pasdar in the succeeding two years. These were years of the wasteful and unproductive 'human wave' attacks, costly in lives and of dubious military value. Yet the regime preferred this style of warfare: the cult of the offensive, the crusade involving the masses rather than the coldly efficient technical prosecution of warfare, and the emphasis on commitment over professionalism. As Khomeini put it: 'Equipped with weapons and material devices your enemies come to fight faith and intellect'.[63]

Clearly the style of warfare reflected the social, moral and political nature of the society. If the society wanted 'martyrs not heroes',[64] it was because it was concerned less with outcomes than with processes; less with gaining victory than with affirming certain values and commitments. The military who were trained to consider their offensives in the light of probable costs, estimated returns, the problems of logistics, co-ordination, the achievement of surprise, the neutralization of Iraq's superiority in air and armour and its advantages of interior lines and entrenched defences, had to cope with a leadership that deferred to the Pasdar who, at every opportunity, sought to show that the military lacked their commitment. The upshot was a military that was brought in to substitute for the Pasdar's deficiencies (as happened after 1984) but which was quickly relegated to second position if, once in a while, against all expectation and at a heavy price the Pasdar were able to achieve a success (as happened after the capture of Fao in February 1986).

After the failure of the human wave attacks, the worst excesses associated with the 'Islamic' way of warfare, and specifically the Majnoon offensive of February 1984, the military prevailed upon the authorities to reconsider their approach to the conduct of the war. The upshot was a long hiatus in that year without a major offensive, signs within Iran of a debate on the next step in the war, and indications of deep tension between the military and the Guards. The military reportedly contrasted their treatment and compensation with those of the Pasdaran, objected to gratuitous clerical interference in military affairs, complained about the lack of spare parts for weapons, and sought a change in the conduct of the war in the direction of greater realism.[65] In late 1984, Rafsanjani unmistakably referred to these events and specifically to the differing views of the military and the Pasdar as to how the war should be run.[66]

> Of course, differences of opinion exist on certain matters. It is possible that two brothers, who attack the enemy together, may have differences on tactics, but differences in trenches must be eliminated.

In June 1985, a change in strategy to one of attrition was formally announced as a 'defensive jihad', a shift to limited attacks along the entire length of the frontier rather than to dependence on 'grand final offensives'. By no means incidentally, it was in the wake of this period of palpable military disquiet that Khomeini issued his directive for the build-up of the IRGC in the other services. Yet the period of regular military influence soon proved short-lived; following the Fao operation, run but not planned by the revolutionary guards, the more cautious professionals were again eclipsed. Despite their success at Mehran in June 1986, the more conservative approach to military operations based on planning and more conventional considerations was again superseded by the more daring approach of the Pasdar and Basij, which promised results, albeit at a high price. And in 1986 the regime needed results because economic considerations (see Chapter 5) no longer allowed Iran the luxury of waging a war of attrition. As shown in the new set of offensives at the end of 1986, the frontal grand offensive was back in fashion. The calculation was that politically Iran could afford more casualties than Iraq, and that consequently any offensive that inflicted high costs on the enemy was intrinsically advantageous (no matter the cost) and would lead to ultimate victory.

But the double offensives on the central front on 24 December 1986 and the southern front on 10 January 1987 were unable to repeat the success at Fao. Despite some advance in the south toward Basra, Iran proved unable to break through the Iraqi lines. The cost in terms of manpower – especially trained cadres – was prohibitive in that it reduced the chances of success for any similar offensives in the near future. It also raised questions about Iran's war strategy and the assumptions on which they were based.

It had become an article of faith that Iran would prevail because of the superiority of its fighting men rather than its weapons. This view rested on the assumption that it could dictate the pace and rhythm of the war and that its political system also was more resilient than that of its adversary. These assumptions seemed to have been borne out by experience up to 1986. But it was also evident that Iran was not exempt from war-weariness, particularly when the war was showing no results; and that, for all its evident demographic advantages, it still needed *trained* manpower at the front and this was neither plentiful nor inexhaustible.[67]

Following the offensive on Basra which ended in the spring of 1987, Iran found itself confronting a broader threat, the internationalization of the war provoked and welcomed by Iraq and assisted, in Iran's view, by Kuwait. The net result of the focus on the 'tanker war' and the intervention of the US, the USSR and various European states' navies into the Gulf was to shift attention from the land war in the low season for offensives. Iran compulsively embraced the prospect of confrontation in this much publicized side-show, as if it were a salvation from the difficulties of the grinding war on land. Yet the problems persisted.

In recognition perhaps of the importance of discipline and hierarchy, Khomeini in April 1987 promoted nine officers to general officer rank. The following November, after considerable internal debate, the Supreme Defence Council, supported by Khomeini, announced a new strategy:[68]

> A stage has been reached where, with the continuation of operations and with repeated blows, we should deprive the enemy of respite and bring closer the inevitable . . . defeat.

The strategy of 'repeated blows' was subsequently amplified by Rafsanjani as ushering in 'a totally new phase' based on 'numerous and consecutive' offensives which would wear down the enemy and give him no intervening period for recovery. This required a longer-range programme geared to larger forces-in-being rather than periodic mobilization drives.[69]

The search for a winning formula has thus gone through several phases, from heroic improvized defence (1980–81), to frontal assaults (1982–4), to limited mobile attacks, attrition and 'defensive jihad' (1985) to the return of the grand final offensive (1986–7) and now to the more limited attacks of 'repeated blows' pending what may be a more general permanent mobilization. The Iranian authorities have been unable to devise a strategy which offers a high probability of success not only because of their lack of access to advanced weapons systems on a continuous basis, but also because of the political constraints they have imposed on themselves in the conduct of the war. In late 1987, the Commander of the Pasdaran, Reza'i, still identified the two principal capabilities favouring Iran in the war as i) martyrdom – zeal in attack for which no answer has yet been found; and ii) 'innovation and creativity . . . in the tactics we use in the war against the whole world'.[70]

The organization of the armed forces in war has assumed great importance for the revolutionary authorities. Lacking a reliable military institution of their own at the outset of the war, they relied on the professional military, without extending any trust to them or giving them much leeway in the conduct of military operations. Unwilling to dispense with their expertise, the Iranian leadership has nevertheless been loath to acknowledge it or to entrust the future of the revolution to it. At the same time, the leadership has built up a parallel institution, the Pasdar, an Islamic armed force, which makes up in zeal what it lacks in expertise. The conduct of military operations has thus of necessity been subordinated to political considerations. First, the bifurcation of the forces is not designed to improve co-ordination or efficiency. Second, how are these operations to be conducted – professionally or with an 'Islamic' flavour? Who is to claim the success and who can be made the scapegoat for the failures? Which approach to warfare, to organization, and to commitment is to be vindicated by the war? In microcosm, the war has tested the revolutionaries' pretensions as well as challenging their skills and level of commitment. It should be clear that the prosecution of the war and the attainment of victory cannot be the exclusive aims of the revolutionaries. A victory could, of course, strengthen the revolution. But what about a victory that undermined the revolution, that served to repudiate its populist motivation and fervour, that acted as a tacit rejection of all that it stood for? That victory would be Pyrrhic indeed. Thus, the organization for war, as well as its actual operations, have remained infused with other, non-military, considerations, testifying to the impact of the society on its conduct.

War aims, restraint and termination

The war has lasted so long simply because neither side has had the military capability to impose a decision on the other. At the same time, one of the two parties, Iran, has been unable and unwilling to accept anything less than its original goals. The way the war has been fought, the framing of war aims and the duration of the conflict all testify to the intimate relationship between the way the war is waged and the type of society waging it.

From the start of the war, Khomeini identified the villains as Saddam Hussein and the Ba'th party; he saw the Iraqi people as victims needing help. By ruling out any possibility of discussion or compromise, he committed Iran to wage a war 'until victory' (as the crowds chant in Iran). Such a victory would be sought without resort to attacks on the Iraqi people, and preferably would come as a result of the political collapse of the Ba'th regime, although, if necessary, it could be accomplished by Iranian arms. At the same time, given the nature of Khomeini's authority in Iran, once he had pronounced on them, there could be no discussion of Iran's war aims. The result was to be stalemate; for Iran's political assumptions proved faulty, its military capabilities inadequate, its flexibility non-existent, and its determination unshaken. The longer the war lasted, the more the leader's authority and claim to special wisdom came to be invested in it, and the more difficult extrication became. At the same time, the longer the war continued, the more it came to represent a struggle between two systems of governance, two ways of organizing society.

The Iranian leadership embarked on the war with no intention of harming their neighbour. 'We think of Islam and wish to act according to Islamic teachings', Khomeini said in October 1980. He therefore asked the military to 'do nothing to harm the cities which have no defence . . . Our hands are tied, because we do not wish the ordinary people, the innocent people, to be hurt.' Two years later, he returned to this theme when he noted that the Iranian forces could have inflicted far greater damage

> were it not for their Islamic commitment and their desire to protect the innocent and their fear of destroying property belonging to the brotherly Iraqi nation – a fact which still inhibits them.

Rafsanjani took up the same theme in 1983 when he pointed out that Iran's military operations were guided by a desire to limit casualties on both sides:[71]

> We think that in the future, when an Islamic or people's government is set up in Iraq . . . that will be more useful for the people of Iraq who remain.

In practice, Iran's sensitivity on the matter of casualties was more pronounced when it came to those of Iraq than when it concerned its own: indeed the regime was most generous in its acceptance of casualties, when they were Iranian, particularly in 1982–4. In any case, this view of the Iraqi people did not last. As the hoped-for uprising against the Ba'th regime did not materialize, and as the Iraqis showed every indication of defending themselves and their territory against Iran (and not necessarily for Saddam), the Islamic republic had to shed the illusion of a spontaneous revolt sweeping the Ba'th out and the Islamic revolution in. As if to acknowledge this, in February 1984, Iran dropped its earlier restraint and began the long-range shelling of Basra. From then on Iranian artillery attacks on Basra became commonplace, and they came to be supplemented by missile attacks (*Scud-Bs* of Soviet origin) on Baghdad, especially in early 1985 and late 1986 when the two adversaries indulged in the 'war of the cities'.

In other respects, Iran maintained considerable restraint. It saw no need to imitate Iraq's panicky and cynical use of chemical weapons; it saved its attacks on Iraq's cities as retaliation for Iraqi air strikes on its civilian areas; it had no need or desire to expand the war to the Gulf states, to threaten tanker traffic or the Strait of Hormuz, or otherwise to widen or internationalize the conflict. It was quite content to continue to fight the war on the ground where its soldiers had the advantage of numbers and superior motivation. Iran's policy was to *respond* to Iraq's attacks at sea or on the cities to show that it was capable of doing so, and in order not to relinquish its right to do so or to acquiesce in Iraq's unilateral actions.

Yet if Iran maintained some restraints in the conduct of the war, the lines were becoming increasingly blurred. Where Iraq escalated the conflict by intensifying or widening the war, Iran escalated it by prolonging it. As the 'war of regimes' turned out to be more an issue of nationalisms, Iran was forced to look to a military solution rather than to a convenient political transformation within Iraq. In acknowledging this, it moved to a classic war of conquest in which Iraqi domestic considerations no longer assumed primacy. At the same time, it could not afford to admit that its revolutionary Islamic model had diminished or evoked negligible political resonance in Iraq. For if Iraq (a neighbouring state with some 55 per cent of its 15 million population Shi'i) rejected the Islamic republic, how could Iran possibly claim success for the revolution elsewhere in the region, let alone further afield?

In truth Iran was caught in a quandary, alternating between strategies of attrition based on the belief that Iraq could not sustain a prolonged war and the related belief that the war could be won through the *political collapse* of the enemy, and reliance on a *military victory* through a grand offensive based on the recognition that a prolonged war was a two-edged sword, and that a political collapse might not be forthcoming. The alternation reflects a deep and understandable ambivalence about the conduct of the war, a desire to end it with a smashing affirmation of the revolution's power, and a recognition that past offensives have not demonstrated any Iranian capacity to generate a knock-out blow against the formidable defensive barriers of Iraq. In a war which by its length has de-sensitized outside observers, the cycles of repetition are often missed. Rafsanjani's declarations of 1986 are reminiscent of earlier comments in 1983 and 1984: 'people expect this offensive to be the last military operation that would determine the final destiny of the region'. And 'in the not too distant future we must settle the issue of the war once and for all by means of an appropriate military operation'.[72]

If the difficulties of attaining a military victory are complicated by the regime's refusal to give the regular military complete support, they are made even more problematical by the political inability to formulate war goals that stand some chance of achievement. An insistence on 'no compromise' and ambiguity about Iran's ultimate demands diminish the incentive for any Iraqi opposition to emerge against Saddam Hussein for the duration of the war. Nor is the parallel with the Second World War

Allied position of 'unconditional surrender' (which Foreign Minister Velayati has repeatedly made) any more helpful; such a formula discourages any 'good' Iraqis from emerging, just as the Allies were not prepared to deal with the anti-Hitler elements in Germany.

Perhaps in recognition of the illusory nature of Iran's quest for military victory, and most especially the probable international response in the unlikely event of an Iranian breakthrough, and its experience of the internationalization of the conflict in 1987, Iran's leaders now disavow any intention of invading Iraq: 'We are starting to plan what will happen in Iraq which we do not intend to enter after the victory'.[73]

A decision to end the war rests not with the Parliament (Majles) but with the Supreme Defence Council, the body that includes Rafsanjani, the President, and the Guards Commander among others. According to procedure the Council would 'submit a proposal to Ayatollah Khomeini for approval'. However, as the Guards Minister Rafiqdust has explained: 'the Ayatollah is against dealing with Saddam Hussein, so the line is already set. No one in the Council is against continuing the war'.[74]

Iran's inflexibility stems ultimately from the nature of its leadership, which, having defined the stakes in apocalyptic terms which brook no compromise, envisage no retreat, and allow no discussion of the issue, has made the issue of the war a continuing referendum on the regime, the revolution, and the Islamic republic.

4

Iraqi Politics and War Strategies

In fighting the war with Iran, Saddam Hussein has been obliged to pay careful attention to two different 'fronts'. The first is, of course, the war front, where the Iraqi forces have been committed to achieve certain objectives of their own, and to thwart those of the Iranian armed forces. The second has been the home front. Here the crucial consideration has been the maintenance of sufficient control to guarantee the absolute disposal of the country's resources as Saddam Hussein thinks fit, and, ultimately, to guarantee his own survival as supreme ruler. Understandably, the two are interconnected, since the future of Saddam Hussein is at stake in both areas. It has consequently been his determination to co-ordinate the military and political efforts involved. The utility of war and the disposition of force required to prosecute that war form parts of the same perception and definition of political advantage, and conform therefore to the same conscious and unconscious logic. It will be instructive to examine the ways in which this has affected Iraq's war strategies during the past seven years.

In a later chapter, a more detailed examination will be made of the effects of the war itself – the mobilization, sacrifice and damage involved in so prolonged an effort – on the polity presided over by Saddam Hussein, and therefore on his ability to control it. In this chapter, however, some assessment will be made of the ways in which the structure of that polity and its underlying, as well as public, rationale have affected the conduct of military operations and the goals towards which those operations are directed. In this respect, two major themes permeate the Iraqi conduct of hostilities, originating in the dual nature of political power in Iraq, referred to in chapter 2. The first, which flows from the traditional, deeply entrenched and autocratic view of power and of the imperatives of the ruler, characterized the first phase of the war. The second, corresponding to the duties arising from the claim to be ruling in the name of a collectivity like the modern nation-state, has surfaced with increasing frequency in the second and longer phase of the war, during which Iraq has been forced on the defensive. In both phases both themes have been visible. However, a shift in relative emphasis can be seen to have occurred, in part perhaps because the very nature of the enemy and his conduct of operations dictated that this should happen.

War as a demonstration of strength

The war initiated by Iraq's invasion of Iran in September 1980 was very largely a demonstrative war, conducted by the Iraqi political leadership under the limitations imposed by such a stylized form of warfare. The intention was to impress the Iranian leaders with the quality and resolve of Iraq's military strength in order to face them with the choice of escalation or concession. By the rules and assumptions underlying this form of warfare, there seem to have been few doubts among the Iraqi leaders that Iran's leadership would soon concede to Iraq's demands rather than attempt to mobilize for a war which Saddam Hussein believed them to be singularly ill-equipped to fight. The initial Iraqi onslaught, therefore, consisted of a land attack across the Iranian border at four points, and a poorly executed pre-emptive air strike against the Iranian air force. Iranian economic and civilian installations beyond the immediate battle zone were ignored, as was the considerable strength of the Iranian navy. Nor did there seem to be any concerted attempt by the Iraqis to bring the bulk of the Iranian armed forces to battle in order to defeat them decisively. Indeed, the tendency of Iraqi units to come to an abrupt halt when they encountered stiff Iranian resistance seems to have been due less to incompetence than to an uncertainty about what exactly their attitude should be to the opposing forces. Equally, the confusion of many Iraqi units when they came to significant targets within Iran, such as Ahwaz, Dezful and even Khorramshahr initially, seems to belie the notion that they had been given any very clear operational objectives.[1]

Instead, it seems that Saddam Hussein had briefed his commanders to mount an impressive show of force in Iran, demonstrating the capacity of the Iraqi armed forces to occupy territory, and to do so while remaining relatively intact and suffering minimal casualties. This seems to be quite likely in a war which was largely regarded in Baghdad not as a fight to the death with Iran, but simply as a means of compelling the Iranian leadership to give official recognition to Iraqi might. The initial Iranian riposte of using its air force to attack a range of vital economic and energy installations throughout Iraq may have made the Iraqi leadership somewhat uneasy about the Iranian leaders' capacity to understand the nature of the demonstration. It was noticeable that soon afterwards Saddam Hussein accepted the UN call for a ceasefire (Resolution 479 of 28 September 1980) and, when Iran rejected it, offered one of his own.[2]

At the same time, he ordered his forces to capture Khorramshahr (the old Muhammarrah), a site of considerable symbolic significance and – insofar as its fall might further impress the Iranian leadership – of strategic significance as well. Again, Saddam Hussein may have been dismayed by the cost in terms of lives and economic damage which Iraq was paying for this 'demonstration war'. Equally, the reports of isolated but ominous cases of dissent within the Iraqi armed forces concerning the legitimacy of war against Iran cannot have been reassuring.[3] Nevertheless, the Iraqi leadership seemed convinced that it was only a matter of time before the Iranian leaders responded as they were meant to do. As the then Minister of Foreign Affairs, Sa'dun Hammadi, stated: 'The *status quo* will be imposed on Iran and if they will not listen to the logic of understanding, they will listen to the logic of force'.[4]

In order to underline the 'logic of force', Iraqi forces proceeded with the capture of Khorramshahr (reducing it largely to rubble in the process) and laid siege to Abadan. At the same time, the Iraqi political leaders broadcast Iraq's 'historic and nationalist claims to Arabistan [Khuzestan]' and its oil, threatened to lend active encouragement to Iran's ethnic minorities with a view to dismembering the state, and urged the Iranian leadership to come to terms in the near future, otherwise the occupation of territory in the course of the war might create 'certain rights which did not exist before the war began'.[5] These appeared to be more in the nature of threats concerning what the Iranians might expect in the future if they did not give way to the current Iraqi demands, than any real set of war aims. The latter seem much more realistically encapsulated in the sentiments voiced by General Adnan Khayrallah when he stated that he believed that the Iraqi army's activities had dealt a 'strong and crushing blow to the Persian enemy, weakening his entity and denting his arrogance', and, further, that Iraq had 'almost reached all [its] objectives: the myth of Persian hegemony has ended, and Tehran's role of policeman has collapsed for ever'.[6] All that was required was that the leaders in Tehran should themselves publicly acknowledge the truth which Saddam Hussein claimed the prowess of the Iraqi armed forces had demonstrated: 'Iraq is rising, and Iran is collapsing'.[7]

In short, the war was to be a brief operation which would decisively convince the Iranian leaders that in the long-running competition between the rulers of the two countries, the Iraqi leadership now had the upper hand. 'Iraq has achieved military victory, and the Iranian army has been defeated in battle', consequently Iran's leaders should abide by the logic of autocratic competition and 'recognize [Iraq's] legitimate rights'.[8] Sensitive to the fact that many military commentators in the West had been remarking on the strangely parsimonious use of the Iraqi air force, Saddam Hussein felt obliged to spell out one of the implications of this form of warfare: 'We will not use our air force. We will keep it. Two years hence our air force will still be in a position to pound Bani Sadr and his collaborators'.[9] The virtual disappearance of the still substantial Iraqi air force from the battlefield, and indeed its dispersal out of range of Iranian attack, may well have been due to the sound military reason that, having failed to destroy the Iranian air force on the ground, the Iraqis found that their equipment was no match for the Iranians in the air. Nevertheless, three kinds of political considerations also appear to have come into play. Firstly, this war, as Saddam Hussein pointed out, was to be merely a brief episode in a long struggle, and consequently resources needed to be husbanded for future demonstration and conflict. Secondly, the simple fact of rapid Iraqi advance in strength into Iranian territory and the determination shown by the Iraqi leadership were supposed to be sufficiently impressive. In this calculation the persistent and co-ordinated use of the Iraqi air force seemed irrelevant. Thirdly, if the use of the air force was deemed irrelevant to the purpose of the war, it would be politically dangerous for Saddam Hussein to risk its decimation at the hands of the Iranians.

The problem, as Saddam Hussein was coming to realize, was that the Iranian leadership seemed neither impressed by the Iraqi show of force, nor inclined to see the war in the stylized terms predicated by the Iraqis. Political strife within Iran had once been thought of as an advantage to the Iraqi war effort, since, by the Iraqi reading of politics, this simply transformed Iran from a strong to a feeble autocracy, less able to resist the demands of Iraq's ruler.[10] As a consequence, war was a feasible, even a desirable option, since it could achieve the required outcome in a brief thrust. However, after a few months of warfare, which conspicuously failed to produce the necessary response from the Iranian leadership, the Iraqi leaders protested that the Iranian position was confused and incoherent. The divisions in Iranian politics seemed to prevent the formulation of a consistent, and as the Iraqis would see it, 'reasonable' response to the Iraqi use of force.[11] Saddam Hussein's preference for 'the war to last a week, provided we gain all our rights', was obliged to give way to the defiant claim that 'We have taken a protracted war into consideration . . . We will continue to fight until the enemy says: Yes, we have agreed to your rights'. However, it was clear from this same speech to the National Assembly that he was beginning to doubt whether war had in fact been the best way of proceeding in his relations with the Iranian leaders.[12] The long pause which then ensued in the fighting during 1981 was claimed by Saddam Hussein to be a consequence of his desire to give 'the Persian enemy' the opportunity to learn 'new lessons because he has refused to return to the path of peace'. However, it seems to have been due more to the fact that Saddam Hussein was uncertain what further 'lessons' the Iraqi armed forces could actually impart.[13]

At one of the most critical points of his career (in June 1982, soon after the Iranian forces had compelled the Iraqi army to withdraw from most of the territories held since 1980), he complained that the Iranian leadership had perversely refused to abide by the anticipated rules of war: 'Despite its military defeat in 1980, the Tehran regime insisted on its aggressive stands and expansionist trends'.[14] This juncture was critical, precisely because it marked a forced reappraisal by the Iraqi leadership of the nature of the war, its utility, the goals achievable through the continued use of force, and the strategies which might be used to achieve them. In doing so, it caused a not altogether disadvantageous shift from the 'war of demonstration' to the 'war of survival'. As such, the war became less of a demonstration of the personal prowess of Saddam Hussein, amplified through the armed forces at his disposal. Instead, it became an attempt to defend the Iraqi state, with which he had taken considerable care to identify himself, against the unmistakable ideological, political and military hostility of the 'Persian enemy'. From being a conflict in which the armed forces of the Iraqi state were the predominant instruments by which Iraq's ruler sought to impress his neighbours in the traditional competition for regional influence and domestic legitimacy, the war could be presented and understood as a collective endeavour, shaping an Iraqi identity where none had existed before.[15]

The war of survival

In many respects this was a more convincing rationale for the Iraqi war effort than any which had previously existed. However, the change caused a crisis for Saddam Hussein, precisely because it indicated that his earlier strategic calculations about the utility of war had been entirely mistaken. Not unnaturally, he attempted to present the earlier phase of the war as being identical to the situation in which the Iraqis found themselves in 1982. He claimed that the Iraqi attack on Iranian territory in 1980 had been motivated by the desire to pre-empt an imminent and massive Iranian assault on Iraqi territory, and to gain 'strategic depth', thus allowing the Iraqis to defend their own territory better.[16] Indeed, within the space of a few years, Saddam Hussein was to argue that the war had been a defensive one all along, since it had been initiated by Iran's 'aggression' of 4 September 1980 – the date on which the Iraqi Government now claims the war began. In doing so, he undoubtedly had in mind the prospect of the United Nations setting up a commission to establish responsibility for the war. However, more important was the need to convince a domestic audience of the fact that their predicament was not the result of a miscalculation by the political leadership, but rather the unavoidable outcome of Iran's aggressive intentions. As Saddam Hussein suggested in a speech to the 2nd Army Corps, this was an easier task for the Iraqi Government after 1982 than it had been prior to that date:[17]

> When we returned to the international border, we no longer had any difficulties. Our responsibility became simpler and less complicated. Dialogue with the Iraqis became simple; it was no longer complicated. When we told Iraqis that we were on Iranian territory . . . in defence of Diyala, Amara and Basra [towns in Iraq], some citizens – even some military personnel, except those who were well-informed – found it difficult to realize the connection between our presence in front of the target and protecting the vital target [i.e., Iraq].

Nevertheless, the considerably reduced Iraqi peace conditions of 1982 – in effect, indicating a willingness to return to the *status quo ante bellum* – implied recognition that the nature of the war had changed. In this there was an implicit admission that the war aims of 1980, once regarded as crucial to the maintenance and extension of Saddam Hussein's authority, had also perforce to be abandoned.[18]

Once Saddam Hussein had taken the necessary measures to ensure that this palpable reverse did not adversely affect his own power, the reduced inner core of the regime had to devise a defensive war strategy. This would be aimed in the first place at preventing an Iranian breakthrough, and subsequently at attempting to weaken the Iranian leadership's resolve to pursue the war. In this effort, one can sense a curious mixture or balance between the language and rationale of a nation-state at war, and the desire of the autocrat to address his fellow ruler directly. The belief seemed to persist that the latter's grasp of the rules of personalized warfare would lead him, as Saddam Hussein put it, 'to issue a *fatwa* ending the war, once he decides its continuation is harmful'.[19] The personalization of the conflict was, of course, not simply perpetuated by enduring Iraqi perceptions of the proper focus of political activity, nor by Saddam Hussein's attempt to form a bridge between this style of politics and those required by the languages of nationalism and mass politics through the 'cult of personality'. In a moral universe where the Iranian regime could demand the overthrow of Saddam Hussein himself as their major condition for ending the war, and where they could describe the launching of a surface-to-surface missile against Baghdad as 'a slap in the face for Saddam Hussein', it was not surprising that the Iraqi leadership should continue to see the war in part as a struggle between individual rulers.[20] Saddam Hussein's reported vow that he would lead Iraq in its war with Iran for ten more years rather than step down to meet one of Iran's main conditions for ending the war, meant that the Iraqi leadership had now to attend to the strategies which would make such a pledge sustainable.[21]

The decision to construct a line of defences along the Iraqi border which would be impregnable to Iranian assault appears to have been made some time before it was publicly acknowledged that Iraq's earlier war aims were redundant. Indeed, the fact that considerable preparations had already been made may well have contributed towards the orderly retreat of units of the Iraqi regular armed forces in the summer of 1982, as well as to their ability to resist subsequent Iranian attempts to pursue this apparent advantage. The price seems to have been the loss through death, but more particularly through capture, of large numbers of the poorly trained Iraqi People's Army. These unfortunates were then somewhat unfairly castigated by Saddam Hussein for having been 'a burden to the regular army because of the enemy's ability to appear in their rear'.[22] Nevertheless, the thoroughness of Iraq's defensive prepar-

ations, and the success with which the Iraqi forces were able to throw
back the Iranian offensive during 1982, seem to have put new heart into
the leadership and even encouraged them to believe that the war might be
brought to an end by this means. Iraqi soldiers were now exhorted by
Saddam Hussein not to think only of defending Iraq but also of ending
the war: 'should the enemy be destroyed to the same degree as in previous
attacks, the Iraqi leadership would consider the battle over from a military
viewpoint'.[23] Some months later, following the successful defence of
Basra, Sa'dun Hammadi echoed this by stating that the failure of recent
Iranian offensives could be considered an end to the war since it would
cause morale to deteriorate in Iran, and enhance the desire of its leaders
to end the war. Skirmishes might continue, but the war was as good as
over.[24]

Unfortunately for Iraq, these calculations were based on a continuing
erroneous assessment of the impact of apparent military failure on the
Iranian leadership. Consequently, for the next five years, the Iraqi war
effort was almost entirely preoccupied with thwarting repeated Iranian
land offensives. This was the *sine qua non* of the regime's political survival.
To this end an impressive array of skilfully designed and lavishly
equipped land fortifications was constructed, indicating the priority given
by the regime to this crucial defence effort.[25] It was hoped by Saddam
Hussein that the cost in human lives for the Iranians would not only
prevent a breakthrough but would also become so high that it would
jeopardize the relations of Iran's rulers with the Iranian people and create
the conditions under which 'it will be possible to freeze the war at a
certain point and allow it to take the form of small activities, or come to an
end'.[26]

In order to achieve both these results, the Iraqi armed forces were
permitted, or commanded, to use chemical weapons. This followed a
fairly explicit warning in 1983 from the Iraqi high command that Iraq was
now armed with 'modern weapons [which] will be used for the first time
in war', and which had 'not been used in previous attacks for
humanitarian and ethical reasons'. Hoping to demoralize the Iranian
troops poised to attack, the high command went on to declare that 'if you
execute the orders of Khomeini's regime . . . your death will be certain
because this time we will use a weapon that will destroy any moving
creature on the fronts'.[27] It is unclear whether chemical weapons were in
fact used that year. However, there was strong evidence to support
Iranian claims that they were used against the Iranian offensives in 1984,
1985, and 1986. So strong, indeed, was the evidence by 1986 that the
President of the UN Security Council roundly condemned the continued
use of such weapons by Iraq, following a UN report which for the first
time unequivocally apportioned blame to Iraq for having used them.[28]

The Iraqi leadership was eager to endorse the various international
calls for a cessation of hostilities and to present itself as the 'reasonable

party' in the conflict, with the explicit aim of 'bringing international pressure on Iran in order to limit its ability to continue the war'.[29] However, as far as chemical weapons were concerned, it was clearly not willing to cultivate international opinion to the extent that it put at risk its own strategies of self-defence and of inflicting massive casualties on the Iranian forces. Nevertheless, even the great human cost of these offensives did not have the effect the Iraqi leaders had hoped. As some of them were later to admit, 'we just cannot understand Khomeini's thought processes', and 'what is eluding us is how to persuade the Iranians that to export the revolution, to dictate the government of Iraq, is not negotiable, not achievable'.[30] At one stage, Saddam Hussein apparently pinned his hopes on the Iranian army: exhorting it to conserve its strength in order to play the political role which was its due, he seems to have seen it as a repository 'of logic and sound views', 'as a force whose organization is based on a rational order, allowing it to function both in war and peace . . . when both logic and common sense have forsaken the political leaders of Iran'.[31]

Interestingly, in groping for some thread of 'logic' by which he could understand the enemy, Saddam Hussein appeared to come close to an understanding of the nature and resilience of the regime in Iran, as well as of the daunting determination of its war effort.[32]

> The rulers of Iran cannot go on with the war without the earnest backing, in word and deed, of their supporters. Therefore, the need to influence the relationship between the rulers of Iran and their supporters, by creating divergence between them on the question of war and peace, is of paramount importance.

No doubt his own experiences, as the war became one of survival, of having to mobilize large numbers of Iraqis into a not wholly coerced war effort, had given him some idea of the power of voluntary collective endeavour. Nevertheless, there seemed to be genuine perplexity about how to address this key relationship. To be fair, it must be admitted that attempts to 'break' both civilian morale and the links which bind the population to their rulers in war, have never been particularly successful. However, the strategies employed by Iraq to bring the cost of the war home to the leaders and people of Iran seem to have veered between seeking consistently to break that vital link, and seeking to impress Iran's leadership with Iraq's capacity to cause potential, as well as actual, damage to their interests. The latter corresponds to the old idea of the 'game of war', whereas the former seems to be an expression of that form of warfare peculiar to the modern state and the mass society on which it is founded. Oscillation between the two may well have impaired Iraq's effectiveness in this regard. However, it can be seen as a genuine expression of the Iraqi leadership's political perspectives and of their growing uncertainty about the nature of the political phenomenon they were facing in the Islamic Republic of Iran.

The war of attrition

It was in these conditions that the idea arose of using Iraq's air force to inflict damage not simply on Iran's military resources but also on its economic infrastructure. Inevitably, targeting the latter meant targeting civilian areas. Frequently these were targets in any case – for reasons of revenge, deterrence or demonstration. The rationale behind this new strategy was twofold. First, there was the belief that it was politically imperative for the Iraqi armed forces to be seen to be active, since it clearly went against the regime's self-image to be thought of as forced on the defensive by Iranian military initiative.[33] Secondly, and more importantly, there was the belief that Iraq now had the right 'to select special means and methods to make Iran's rulers understand that the price of aggression is very high'.[34] Thus, the Iraqi armed forces would demonstrate, by holding the line, that any Iranian military effort on the front was doomed to fail. Meanwhile, the air force would demonstrate its capacity to damage Iran's economic infrastructure, to restrict its oil exports, and thus its foreign currency earnings, and to shake the faith of the Iranian population in their rulers' claim to be able to protect them from the ravages of war. By this means, it was hoped, 'the message would get back to the clerics in Tehran' and they would decide to end the war, since the choice before them would now be between 'peace or overall destructive war'.[35]

The particular problems facing the Iraqis lay in the execution of this strategy, and in the consistency with which it was pursued. The more general problem lay in the impact, or lack of impact, which it had on the determination of the Iranian regime to pursue the war. As the hiring of five Super-Etendards from France in the autumn of 1983 demonstrated, Iraq had not been well equipped to conduct the war of maritime denial in the waters around Kharg Island that it had declared prematurely in 1982.[36] During 1984, the bombardment of Iranian civilian targets had the severe drawback of bringing Iranian reprisals against Baghdad and Basra. This led to mutual agreement to desist from such a form of warfare, which, however, was broken and patched up in 1985, 1986 and 1987. Iraq was indeed discovering that Iran could also bring home to its enemies the fact that 'if they want comprehensive war, let them have comprehensive war'.[37] Consequently, although it was reported that the Iraqi air raids on Tehran during 1985 were creating a certain amount of civilian protest against the continuation of the war, it was politically dangerous for the Iraqi leadership to pursue such a strategy since the Iranian missile reprisals against Baghdad were equally causing rifts in Iraqi morale.

Nevertheless, at times of stress, the Iraqi air force would return to the bombardment of Iranian cities. This was most evident during the Iranian land offensives east of Basra in early 1987. During January and February, the Iraqi air force attacked a number of Iranian cities, making it clear that it was targeting not simply Iranian economic resources but also important population centres. This strategy was publicly justified by the Iraqi leadership as an appropriate response to the prolonged and indiscriminate Iranian artillery bombardment of Basra that accompanied their military operations along the front.[38] However, there appear to have been two other motives at work here as well. In the first place, some of the cities selected for attack seem to have been chosen because of their symbolic value to the Iranian clerical leadership. Thus, Qom, Isfahan and, of course, Tehran, were subjected to repeated air raids. In damaging these centres of religious and national significance, it was perhaps hoped by the Iraqi leadership that the cost of continuing the war could be brought home in a direct and painful way to the Iranian leaders. The damage was not great, but it was intended to be a warning of future devastation. This threat was apparently believed to have a more immediate effect on the Iranian leaders' political resolve than the slower and more uncertain effects of the erosion of Iran's economic base.[39]

Secondly, as Taha Ramadhan, Commander of the Popular Army, indicated in an interview at the time, Iraq's threat of massive escalation and of initiating 'a new style of war' intended to inflict many casualties, appears to have been part of an attempt to convince the Iranians that their leadership 'does not care for its people'.[40] Saddam Hussein was simultaneously seeking to persuade them to question Khomeini's claimed divine sanction for his rule and for the war effort when the latter had been so conspicuously unsuccessful. The Iranian inability to penetrate the Iraqi defences, he stated, 'was the means by which God wants his judgment to be clear'.[41] This was a return to the endeavour to undermine the Iranian Government's hold on the loyalties of the people by trying to persuade them that their leaders' determination to continue the war was serving neither their material nor their moral interests. Encouraging them to question the legitimacy of their rulers had led to Iraqi cultivation of, and provision of facilities to, one of the principal Iranian opposition organizations, the Mojahedin-e Khalq. It was significant, therefore, that when the Iraqi Government called a provisional halt to the 'war of the cities', in mid-February 1987, it did so ostensibly at the request of Mas'ud Rajavi, leader of the Mojahedin-e Khalq.[42] Such a gesture was designed, presumably, to demonstrate to the Iranian people that Rajavi's organization had a greater claim on their loyalty than had the government in Tehran, precisely because it was the Mojahedin, not the government, which had interceded on their behalf with the Iraqi Government. In fact, Iraq's bombing campaign against Iran's cities was suspended because the Iraqi leadership now felt confident that it had decisively defeated the

Iranian land offensives. With a reduction in the danger on the front, there was a less pressing immediate need to bring home to the Iranian leadership the direct costs of the war. In these circumstances, the price which Iraqis were themselves having to pay, in the form of the periodic explosions of Iranian surface-to-surface missiles in Baghdad, was less acceptable.

More successful, in terms of the measurable economic damage inflicted on Iran, was Iraq's mounting level of attacks on Iran's oil installations and on international shipping involved in the purchase of Iranian oil. When Iran threatened to close the Strait of Hormuz in retaliation for restrictions on its own capacity to export oil, this cannot have been unwelcome to the Iraqi leadership. The international intervention which would undoubtedly have followed such a move by Tehran was something which would have considerably supplemented Iraq's dwindling leverage on the Iranian regime. The latter, however, appears to have been equally well aware of the consequences of such a move and refrained from attempting to make the straits impassable – despite threats, harassment of some shipping and the installation of surface-to-surface missiles in the vicinity.

Once Saddam Hussein had been assured that Iraq had the capacity to inflict severe damage on Iran's economy, he seems to have believed that such a demonstration would in fact force the Iranian leadership to sue for peace. After the first major raid on Kharg Island in August 1985, he threatened that 'worse is yet to come'. He went on to explain that Iraq had not attacked Kharg earlier because he believed that the Iranian regime might yet move in the direction of peace. However, having 'found that the Iranian regime does not care for its property or wealth or even blood', he had decided to give them a taste of the 'comprehensive war' they seemed to desire.[43] Eighteen months later, he was to discover to his consternation that the Iranian leadership remained as insouciant as ever. This followed a prolonged period in which the intensity and accuracy of Iraqi air raids against Iran's economic infrastructure and oil-exporting facilities had noticeably improved. Kharg Island, although still functioning, was doing so at a reduced level and had become a danger zone for the large foreign tankers which had called in there until 1985. This had forced the Iranians to transport oil themselves from Kharg to Sirri Island in the lower Gulf by a convoy of ships. The Iraqi air force managed to do considerable damage to this shuttle service and, in August 1986, launched a devastating air raid against Sirri Island. This, in turn, obliged the Iranians to make use of the facilities at Larak Island by the Strait of Hormuz, in the belief that it would be out of range of the Iraqi air force. However, a raid in November 1986 by Iraqi planes using inflight refuelling disillusioned them on this score.[44]

Simultaneously, the Iraqi air force concentrated for the first time in a systematic way not simply on Iran's oil-exporting facilities, but also on other economic targets. During 1986, it attacked industrial plants, power generation facilities, communications centres, and hydro-electric schemes with a growing degree of accuracy.[45] As its commander, Lieut.-General Hamid Sha'ban, proudly if prematurely proclaimed:

> 1985 was the year of the eagles, and 1986 will be the year of the eagles and of decisiveness in implementing subsequent plans according to which no hostile target will be safe.

Nevertheless, despite the increasing destructiveness of these air strategies, they seemed as ineffective as previous strategies in forcing a decision. The crucial area of the Iranian regime's resolve to continue the war on the terms it had outlined from the outset appeared to have been unaffected both by Iraqi resistance on the battle front and by the Iraqi intention of carrying the war home to the Iranian population.

For Saddam Hussein, there were considerable frustrations to be borne. The land war, with its massed armies locked in mortal, if immobile, combat, seemed to be governed by the political logic stemming from its portrayal as a conflict of ideologies, of races, of nations – in short, of two distinct and opposed collectivities, destined to use war as a means of asserting collective superiority.[47] There were certain obligations flowing from such a state-based interpretation of war, which Saddam Hussein clearly found irksome. The chief of these seems to have been the question of territory. On the one hand, he recognized the value which the inculcation of a reverence for national territory had in the organization of a defence effort. On the other hand, territoriality clearly did not form a vital component in his own conception of the extension of his personal power. He appeared to be trying to persuade those he had rallied in the name of the defence of 'every inch of the homeland' that this was not so important if the ultimate aim of impressing the opposing leadership could be achieved:[48]

> We can accept any partial loss in return for a greater gain; any marginal loss in return for achieving the final objective; and any tactical loss whenever necessary in return for achieving the strategic objective.

As he discovered to his cost in 1986, after the loss of the Fao peninsula to determined Iranian assault, playing the game of nations and states in war did seem to involve obligations which could not be safely ignored – but the pursuit of which involved considerable risk. The initial response to the loss of Fao was to throw large numbers of Iraqi forces into the attempt to recapture it. The scale of the effort and the nature of the forces involved bespoke a compulsion out of all proportion to the value of the territory lost. The cost in terms of human lives which the Iranians were clearly able to exact caused Saddam Hussein to call off this assault, since the political gain of recovery of territory could not be offset against the political loss entailed by high casualties.[49] Instead, in one of his more disastrous strategic directives of the war, he ordered his forces to enter Iranian territory for the first time since 1982 and seize the area around the town of Mehran on the central sector of the front. This was lauded as a 'bold new strategy' and as 'a daring expression of the Iraqi leadership's political decision . . . to force the Iranian leaders to yield, preparing the way for peace'.[50]

In fact, as the constant references to Fao made plain, the Iraqi leadership clearly hoped to compensate for that territorial loss – and the loss of authority that accompanied it – by seizing, at considerably less cost in terms of Iraqi lives, an area of Iran which could be seen by the Iraqi home front as being in some senses equivalent to the lost Fao peninsula. Predictably, the capture of the redundant salient at Mehran was a military liability, and within two months the Iranians had driven the Iraqi forces back to the border. This was a military reverse which shook Saddam Hussein's political authority. However, it is difficult to say whether it damaged that authority more than if he had not made the attempt to acquire the Iranian territory in the first place.[51]

By contrast with the war on land, the war in the air seems for much of the time to have conformed more closely to Saddam Hussein's idea of demonstrative warfare between rulers. The air force had always been an area of his particular interest, partly because it had been a conspicuous actor in Iraqi political history and in the overthrow of governments; partly, perhaps, because its elite nature and technological sophistication accorded with his ideas about the proper function of the armed forces as instruments of personal power designed to overawe, if not destroy, his enemies.[52] This view of the function of the air force in the war largely determined the strategies for its utilization (although it was increasingly, if possibly reluctantly, used in battlefield support), and may be said to explain both the parsimony and the inconsistency of much of its activities up to 1986. It was then that a more systematic strategy was apparently adopted. It has been suggested that this was principally due to the blow to Saddam Hussein's authority caused by the misconceived 'Mehran strategy' of the summer.[53] It is just as likely, however, that the change was due to Saddam Hussein's reluctant realization that it was no use deploying the air force simply as an instrument of autocratic power, if the opposing regime refused to abide by the rules which made the conventional expression of that power effective.

During Iran's offensives in 1987, therefore, the Iraqi air force was not only sent on numerous missions into the interior of Iran, but was also used with greater frequency, and risk, in attacks on Iranian ground forces. Evidently, this task took a heavy toll of Iraq's warplanes. Iraqi officials were to admit that nearly fifty planes had been lost (roughly 10 per cent of the whole air force) during the Iranian offensives of late 1986 and early 1987.[54] These losses tended to suggest that the air force had been incorporated fully into Iraq's defensive strategy – a fact later confirmed by the commander of the air force himself.[55] Faced with the immediate danger of an Iranian breakthrough, Saddam Hussein had decided that this last preserve of the autocratic conception of warfare would have to be thrown into the fray in a way similar to the deployment of the massed armies of the Iraqi state. The decimation of the air force because of its activity over the battlefield was a price worth paying if the Iranian onslaught could be checked. At the same time, Saddam Hussein left the air force in no doubt as to those responsible for the heavy losses it had sustained. In a ceremony to award medals to pilots for bravery during the Iranian offensives, he acknowledged that anti-aircraft activity had been more intense than before and that it had taken a heavy toll of their comrades. This was due, he stated, to 'the Zionists and the Americans who supplied the Iranians with these weapons in order to inflict harm on Iraq and on the Iraqi armed forces'.[56]

One cannot know what effect such explanations had on the pilots. Certainly, the revelations concerning the shipments of American arms – particularly anti-aircraft missiles – to Iran received a good deal of publicity in Iraq. There has been speculation that the bitterness and resentment towards the United States which these revelations caused, played some part in the motives of the Iraqi pilot who was to fire two Exocet missiles at the American frigate, USS Stark, less than a month later. This incident was described by the Iraqi Government as 'unintentional'. Since no evidence has emerged to gainsay this, any other explanation must remain in the realm of speculation. Nevertheless, the incident underlined both the increasing scope and scale of Iraqi air force activity in the waters of the Gulf. It also heightened international concern over the dangers of such activity, or, more usually, of the Iranian response to such activity, for shipping using the waterway.

Precisely because of this connection, Iraqi air strikes against Iranian ships, or against ships carrying Iranian oil, seemed to be geared increasingly to two objectives. The first was the unchanging goal of forcing the Iranian Government to negotiate an end to the war by crippling its economy. The second was the aim of ensuring the continued anxiety of the international community, especially of the major powers, at the threat which the war represented to their own interests in the region. The hope in the latter case was that these powers would add their weight to that of Iraq in forcing the Iranian leadership to accept an immediate negotiated end to the war. These sentiments were especially in evidence after the passage of UN Security Council Resolution 598 in July 1987, and the subsequent inability of the UN to act with the urgency demanded by Iraq to enforce Iran's compliance with the resolution.[57]

With the resumption of Iraq's air attacks on maritime targets in the Gulf at the end of August 1987, these aspects of the air force's deployment were made explicit. At the same time, it was considered important by the Iraqi Government to assert that it was a strategy dictated by Iraq's military strength and capabilities, not by a desire to drag foreign powers – in particular the United States – into a war which Iraq was itself unable to end.[58] On the contrary, Saddam Hussein stated that 'In fact, the Iraqi people can defeat them [the Iranians] at any time, whether they like it or not'. However, he went on, if the Iranian leaders wanted a pretext to 'preserve their dignity, . . . if they want to say "We were not defeated in the face of Iraq, but in the face of the whole world", . . . then we will say that is fine'.[59] Unfortunately for the Iraqi leadership, the Iranian Government did not seem eager to seek this, or any other pretext, to end the war. Despite Iraq's air superiority and its continued attacks both on Iran's economic infrastructure and on its oil exports, Iran demonstrated that it could respond in kind: in the waters of the Gulf, mines and gunboats served its purpose in retaliating for Iraqi attacks on its own shipping; in Baghdad and Basra, the Iraqi people and government were only too well aware of Iran's capacity to do considerable damage, with surface-to-surface missiles and with long-range artillery, respectively.[60] Neither response seemed to suggest an Iranian willingness to be overawed by the deployment of Iraq's military might, let alone to acknowledge an Iraqi victory.

In these circumstances, Saddam Hussein has been compelled to redefine the victory he once hoped to win:[61]

> Iraq is now fighting only to prevent Iran from occupying Iraq. Technically speaking, the war may also end by one side achieving a military victory and occupying the land of the other. However, only the first alternative is realistic – one foiling the aim of the other. When one side fails to achieve its goals through war, it means defeat.

On these terms, Iraq has already been defeated, although few Iraqis would be audacious enough to point this out. Indeed, much of Saddam Hussein's effort has been directed at convincing the Iraqi people that 'Victory for us is to defend ourselves until the other side gives up'.[62] The major military task since 1982 has been to persuade the other side to give up its war aims. Even if this should succeed, the troubling question for Saddam Hussein must remain whether this will be regarded as sufficient to justify the sacrifices made during the years of war. The answer will depend in large measure on the effects which the war has had on the political fabric constructed by Saddam Hussein out of the disparate elements of Iraqi society in order to sustain his own authority.

5

Iran: War and Society

The war which the Islamic republic had imprudently provoked it has fought with sustained and implacable determination, conscious of a sense of moral rectitude: fierce, unforgiving, and tenacious, very much like the society itself. However, the war has not been the same in the seven years under study; it began for Iran as a defence of national territory (1980–82); it was transformed into a species of border war in the following two years, as Iran sought to defeat Iraq while the conflict remained confined to its western territory; and finally in 1984–7, it became a more total war, extending to the cities and the Gulf. Indeed, by 1987, 'the war', in the words of a Western journalist, was 'a central, inescapable fact of life in Iran'.[1] Its claim on the state's resources and capabilities had correspondingly grown. In this last period, some sort of equilibrium was finally reached between the stakes attributed to the conflict and the investment of resources in its prosecution.

One of the characteristics of revolutions in modern times has been their liberation of repressed social and political energies and their enlargement of state power. As J.F.C. Fuller put it:[2]

> The most striking aspect of the revolutionary state was the creation of a much stronger state bureaucracy which was able to mobilise resources for governmental use.

By increasing the state's 'extractive' power, revolutions expand state power and the capacity to wage war. In war, these newly energized states also find that their systems are being tested. As an historian of comparative revolutions and wars put it:[3]

> Armies in battle in major wars provide clear, definable and comparable measures, both qualitative and quantitative, of the effectiveness of a social system.

If Iran's revolution increased state power, mobilizing and tapping the energies of uncounted millions, the war came as a threat to it, not simply or even primarily as a question of territory but rather as a challenge to its very system. The war came to be defined in these terms rather quickly, albeit in Islamic terminology, but it was not until late 1984, after four years of war, that the leadership in Tehran decided that war 'on the cheap' would be impossible, and that the Islamic republic would have to throw on to the scales a great deal more, if it was to win what had become a test of two rival systems. The regime committed itself so totally to the war partly because it had very little else to offer, and also because the war was in some senses tailor-made for it. Certainly the war had become its 'most enduring legacy'.[4] Indeed, as time went by and costs increased, retreat or compromise became more difficult, commitments hardened, and the war came to represent all that the Islamic republic stood for. In August 1986, President Ali Khamenei could say: 'Ending the war victoriously is the key to solving all our difficulties'.[5] That the war impeded the tackling of other problems admitted of no doubt, but the 'mobilization regime' also found the war convenient and, some would argue, essential to its maintenance of power. By the end of 1986, the war and the revolution had merged in the consciousness of the Iranian people, and certainly in its mythology: the two were intimately connected not only in time and causation, but also in their ends. The war had helped the revolution: 'War and revolution have become intertwined in Iran and in so doing have helped to sustain the ayatollahs' regime'.[6] More interesting perhaps was the question whether a peace, especially a compromise peace registering a defeat of Iran's war aims, would also sustain the regime, or whether it would be judged harshly for its failure.

If the war has strengthened the regime, it has created problems for Iranian society. Appearances notwithstanding, in the prosecution of the war the government has been sensitive both to its utility and to its costs. The political management of the war at home has been keenly attuned to this, but the regime has been unable to resolve the central dilemma that the war represents for it, namely, that, however useful it may be politically, there is no practicable way short of victory to extricate itself from the conflict. Its fortunes are thus tied to the war, but outcomes of war are inherently unpredictable, and such a link is risky at best.

The war initially served the Islamic republic and especially its clerical adherents. While not unifying the country overnight (for, as we have seen, competition for the control and direction of the revolution continued between Bani Sadr and the Islamic Republican Party), the Iraqi invasion galvanized the nation, and gave the flagging revolution a second wind. It also gave it a 'focus', and increased its 'zealotry'.[7] It strengthened the militant wing of the clergy in the virtual civil war that took place in its immediate wake and became a major factor in the consolidation of power by the Islamic government.[8] By justifying repression of the opposition that could now be labelled 'traitors', and stilling the otherwise divisive debate that threatened the revolution at home, and by concentrating minds on foreign enemies, the war proved a convenient tool.

But the clerics were not its passive beneficiaries. The Islamic Republican Party used the war to entrench themselves in the seat of power and in what came to be known as the 'third revolution' to 'restructure' and thoroughly desecularize the country.[9] They did this in numerous ways: by eliminating their rivals, by gaining full control of the principal institution of violence (the Pasdar), by monopolizing the right to define the content of the revolution and giving it a clerical cast, by 'Islamicizing' the vocabulary of 'political discourse' relating to the war[10] and by using the war itself to smother or replace Persian culture with an Islamic one.[11]

The definition of the stakes at the start of the war served notice that the Islamic revolution was unable to prosecute a limited war; it launched a crusade. Khomeini and his disciples were not concerned about criticism. Their constituency was defined and their commitment beyond question:[12]

> . . . it was the people who established this government and this republic, not all the people, only the barefoot masses. The burden has been on the bazaaris, the middle class, and the oppressed . . . your government is the government of the deprived and it should work for the deprived masses.

And this constituency understood its responsibility. When Khomeini said that the war was an 'Islamic duty', he implied that it was not an option but a necessity. When he restated the proposition in 1986 in terms identical to those in 1980, that it must be won 'therefore continue your efforts, for killing or being killed will lead to your salvation',[13] he gave evidence of consistency and immovability.

Even though the decision to take the war to Iraq in mid-1982 had occasioned a debate in the Majles[14] (and stirred doubts in the military about its logistical feasibility), in practice the war did not become a controversial domestic issue until late 1984.[15] At first it was clearly a defensive war and later, after the Pasdar were given control of it in 1982, it became a canvas, as it were, for the revolution's creativity. But as long as it was limited to the frontier and involved mainly volunteers rather than conscripts, it was, in some respects, a distant affair. In any case the regime was not politically passive. It was especially careful to meet the needs of its supporters and to ensure to the extent possible that they were insulated from the hardships of the conflict. Economic inducements supplement the injunctions to follow Islamic duty in the war. The Pasdar and the Martyrs' Foundation, together with the revolutionary committees, oversee the distribution of goods made scarce by the war. (For further discussion, see the section on the war and the economy, below.) In one of his rare interventions in a specifically domestic policy issue, Khomeini, in the autumn of 1984, came out in favour of economic policy that allowed the politically important bazaar to retain control of trade, without excessive government interference.[16]

In addition, the regime allows a degree of opposition, the most striking instance being that of the Islamic Liberation Movement of Mehdi Bazargan, a kind of 'loyal' opposition which is tolerated though not always gracefully or unequivocally. In this particular case, even the issue of the war has been forcefully addressed (see below). In general, however, Khomeini has tended to rule the subject out of bounds, arguing that the 'whole world' is against Iran and that this critical juncture is not the time for frankness or criticism of the government or for seeking to replace a Prime Minister.[17] The regime has been skilful in trying to defuse potential tensions by introducing a period of fictional 'liberalization' in December 1982 after the bloody internal war with the Mojahedin, complete with a 14–point decree from Khomeini himself, or, when necessary, as in mid-June 1985, when opposition to the war was becoming widespread and more conspicuous, by organizing its supporters to form a huge rally in support of its war policy. At times, it has been relatively frank about the existence of differences between 'two relatively powerful factions' on the economic and social policies to be pursued by the Islamic republic, characterizing this, as Rafsanjani did, as normal and comparable to those between two political parties in a Western system of government.[18]

If the regime is not monolithic on domestic policy and admits it, its differences on the war are less conspicuous. There has been fairly general agreement on the war and on Khomeini's characterization of it (although it is altogether another question whether a different leader would have equated the war with Islam and ensured its consequent length and costs). The war has had its uses. It has served to keep the nation 'awake' in Khomeini's words. Rafsanjani has talked of this too: 'we have been able to use the war to awaken the people and to fight the problems that threaten the revolution'.[19] In keeping mobilized the revolution's most ardent supporters – the Guards, the Basij, and the domestic toughs known as the Hezbollah – it has enabled the regime to govern unconstrained by any qualms about democracy or debate, for in exceptional circumstances such as pertain these have to be sacrificed.

The state of war followed hard on the heels of the unrest of the revolution, allowing no time for 'normalcy'. This too has had its benefits. For example, the government that exists today still does so parallel to a host of revolutionary organizations which absorb resources and wield semi-autonomous power. The continuous state of emergency, the image of a beleaguered garrison state which is fed by the government's rhetoric about external conspiracies (for example, Musavi's 'We are surrounded by a great ocean of satanic forces') excuses a failure of performance in the economic sphere, and acts as an 'alibi'.[20] But the Islamic regime is not too concerned about this. In the first place there are compensations for a people steeled by war and by adversity – vigilance and resilience, for example. Musavi, making a virtue of necessity, has observed that such hardships are not just tolerable but also welcome: 'freedom and independence will be gained through the very difficulties'. Later he went further saying that 'the pressure from the imposed war has in all honesty made Iran and its people a better nation'.[21] Musavi gives voice to the belief (apparently widespread in contemporary Iran) that surmounting adversity will improve the moral fibre of society, and that 'resistance' is an article of faith[22]:

> We consider resistance for holy goals a victory and feel it a victory. It is very sweet for us to enter a war which is the embodiment of resistance, struggle and uprising against infidelity.
>
> We wish to declare that that which will be victorious in the world is the will of the faithful and pious humans not instruments of technology.

In the second place, the Islamic republic is not judged by its economic performance (see Chapter 7). However, it has made a point of emphasizing its interest in self-reliance and self-sufficiency, and the war and the arms embargo have given rise to various domestic projects which strengthen this. Nevertheless, the critical consideration is that the political culture is not in any fundamental sense materialist or geared to the production of goods and services. It evokes rather a set of values, a social system, a way of doing things anchored in the past and in the subconscious of the society. The system articulates discontent, exemplifies certain values, and provides an identity for its supporters. It is far weaker in providing answers to problems and so far has not been judged on this criterion. The war further postpones coming to grips with divisive issues by avoiding rather than resolving problems, for it habituates the populace to sacrifice or simply doing without. Even allowing for basic universal needs, one should not underestimate the liberating and at the same time enervating aspects of the war, which have released some people from an unbecoming materialism and allowed them to participate in a collective enterprise selflessly and in a light-hearted way that might under normal circumstances (outside of war and revolution) have been unthinkable. Scarcity simplifies life but it also fortifies the spirit, bringing it back to the essentials of family, tribe, clan and neighbourhood, and serving as a reminder of the values that the revolution is supposed to represent.[23]

Giving expression to these types of values and retaining a hold on the affections of the populace has not been easy, even if it has been helped by the war. It has been successfully achieved not only because of the suggestibility of the audience but also because of the considerable political skills of the clerics. As one might expect of a populist regime, it has for the most part been humble, open and truthful in regard to the war. One visitor wrote that the Iranians were less sensitive than the Iraqis about reporting casualties for they seem 'to reckon that it will most easily retain the popular support for the war by involving people in the fight'.[24] The regime does this most notably in the Friday sermon, an institution that serves as a rallying point, a place of worship, an act of social solidarity, and a political forum. The frankness of discourse, the range of international issues covered, the skilful use of local language and idiom, not to mention the potent and evocative symbolism of Shi'i Islam, all testify to the effective political use of this forum by the clerical regime, as a means of informing the people of current thinking as well as of mobilizing support for current policy. At times, it appears to the outsider that the officials are cynical in their manipulation of their audience's commitment and gullibility, but, even so, the discourse is honest and takes its audience seriously.

The war, it is sometimes said, has been the cause of political immobilism in the country, blocking or postponing the resolution of a host of issues concerning the revolution's domestic direction.[25] The reality is more complicated, for, far from creating immobilism the war diverts attention away from it. It displaces a potentially divisive issue (the direction of domestic change) by providing an external focus, on which there is much more consensus. In a sense, the war is not so much the cause of immobilism but rather a substitute for domestic politics. It may in effect block certain decisions but in doing so it postpones divisions within the ranks of the true believers. It thus acts as a unifying element, even at the price of a continued neglect of the internal front.[26] At the same time, it has both revived revolutionary energies and redirected them. A Western diplomat in Tehran is quoted as follows: 'Revolutionary inertia is down and it has been replaced by war fever'.[27] After the clash between Iranian pilgrims and Saudi security forces at Mecca in July 1987 which resulted in heavy loss of life, another Western diplomat based in Tehran was quoted as saying: 'They have to do something from time to time, apart from the war, to keep people alert on the revolution, to keep things alive'.[28]

This is not to imply that the Iranian leadership can discount any normal tendency on the part of the public to become bored or exhausted by the trials and tribulations of the war and turn upon its leaders. Indeed, so long as the prosecution of the war has been an asset, the leadership has had no problem in framing its maximalist goals. The difficulty has been to conceive of the sort of peace terms that might be feasible in a situation when the continuation of the war threatens the Islamic leadership's continued hold on power. Particularly vexatious would be a combination on the one hand of war-weariness and inflexibility among the regime's principal domestic supporters, and on the other inadequate military means either to win the war or to obtain adequate face-saving terms.

The current leaders are sufficiently politically astute to be aware that what has so far been an asset for them might at best turn into a political liability. Hashemi Rafsanjani gave a clear indication of this in an interview in mid-1987 when he referred to the general agreement in the leadership on the need to continue the war 'provided that Iran's internal administration could function normally'. He made it clear that his anxiety stemmed from any strategy that necessitated greater sacrifices from the

Mosta'zafin (the Oppressed) who had contributed most to the war effort, and who might well find any further belt-tightening onerous and objectionable.

At the same time that Rafsanjani alluded to the possibility that all-out war might provoke political discontent, he showed himself conscious of the problems of limited or incremental advances. This attrition strategy 'could be dangerous as our enemies can use the time against us, as seen in the Gulf crisis'. He concluded that while Iran had the capability (including logistically) to quadruple the rate of its mobilization in comparison to the previous year, 'it is a political choice and there are differences in making it'.[29] He returned to the political implications of devising a war strategy that would be both effective and politically feasible:[30]

> . . . if we want a quick end to the war we must mobilize the country's entire resources in order to co-ordinate a long and widespread offensive. Another solution is to continue this ordinary situation the way it is. Perhaps there is a third way between the two which would mean lessening the facilities for the public and giving more to the war.

Despite its many adverse consequences, the war has enabled the Islamic authorities to strengthen their political control of the country. Through the skilful use of the conflict they have manipulated themselves into a monopoly position as defenders of the revolution, while mobilizing the nation into support for a war of uncertain duration. To do this, however, they have had to increase the reach of the government, to enhance its 'extractive' capacity, and it is to this that we now turn.

Fighting a long war with an emphasis on manpower, faith and commitment required more than a new 'Islamic' man to volunteer for the crusade, it necessitated wholesale changes in a society that had not had, at least in modern times, any experience of warfare. Some of these changes, like the growth of a series of smaller industries to service the war effort, cannot be discussed here. But the broader impact of the war requires some attention if only because of its likely persistence, and the fact that its re-transformation will pose major political and social problems as well.

The Pasdar illustrate this perfectly. Growing from some 30,000 in 1980, by 1986 they had become a force of over 200,000 with internal and external security missions, with their own Commander, Minister, and Ministry, with plans to expand into specialized areas such as special forces, as well as into an air and naval arm. Expanded numerically and in mission, virtually an independent empire, (the Guards' budget in part is not accountable to the Majles), and with their special perks and benefits, the Guards Corps have become a formidable interest group. They would certainly resist the withdrawal of their privileges or their contraction to their previous internal security mission.

The Pasdar remain important to the government in a variety of ways, not least militarily where they combine Islamic dedication and skills acquired in combat with a degree of political reliability. They are thus the eyes and ears as well as the spear tip of the Islamic system. It was the Pasdar who announced the arrest of the Tudeh party leadership in 1983, thus testifying to the growth in their responsibilities.[31] The Guards have also 'trained' (or more likely supervised) the volunteer Basij who are the virtually untrained component of the national 'army of 20 million' which the regime early boasted of deploying. In reality, the Basiji are used to bring Iran's superior manpower to bear on the front, and to do so at a low cost, since they are the forces most motivated by Islam and least compensated by the Islamic government. So far some three million Basijis have been 'trained', of whom one-third have seen action at the front.[32] At any one time there are some 50,000 at the front, swelling to twice that number or more during offensives. The leadership has talked of using the Basij, its mobilized and faithful constituency, in construction jobs after the war. The government in wartime has vastly expanded the (in Musavi's phrase) 'creative, popular, and revolutionary forces' on whom it depends; the challenge will be in contracting them or in otherwise using them when the need for them at the front diminishes.

As the war continued and expanded, the demands made on the country and government correspondingly grew and signs of the institutionalization of the war became apparent in national life. A state that already demanded conformity in most areas of life (and that some understandably had already called 'totalitarian')[33] expanded its reach still further after 1984. (By the end of 1983 the government admitted the execution of over 5,000; a UN report put the figure at 7,000 by 1985.)[34] The war began to account for over 30 per cent of total government expenditures and to dictate or constrain all aspects of economic life. The war itself expanded beyond the western parts of the country and inhabitants of cities inland came to experience what their compatriots, who had fled the war zones earlier, huddling in the urban agglomerations like Tehran, had witnessed. The psychological impact of the Iraqi air raids and threats to stop international airlinks with Iran in the spring of 1985, together with attacks on shipping in the Gulf, convinced the government of the necessity of gearing up for a more total war.

In October, provisions were drawn up for sending government employees to the battlefront, up to 10 per cent of them on full pay. In December 1985, a decision was made to ensure that all future construction in the cities included space and provision for air-raid shelters.[35] The government orchestrated the dispatch of Basij volunteers to the front in 'Caravans of Karbala' (harking back to Imam Hussein's martyrdom at the historic battle) , and employed every device ranging from emotional and religious stimulation to financial inducement to increase the number of volunteers, while encouraging others to contribute financially to the war effort.[36] Kammal Kharrazi, the official in charge of

War Information, announced in October 1985 a decision to rely more heavily on Iran's manpower advantage by increasing the numbers at the front, and, for the first time, to use women in war-related tasks, behind the lines.[37] In the spring of 1986 plans were announced to give some 1.6 million civil servants on-the-job military training with some duty at army camps and refresher courses, and by the early summer emphasis had shifted (in the Guards' spokesman's phrase) to full mobilization of 'all the forces and resources of the country for the war.[38]

The decision to invest more in the war stemmed from both military and economic considerations: militarily the success at Fao in February had given the lie to the argument that a stalemate was inevitable,[39] while the Iraqi attacks on oil exports and the decline in oil prices made the prosecution of the war more difficult. Both considerations – that military victory was possible, and that it was economically necessary soon – combined to dictate a strategy for a rapid solution to the war. Hence the decision to broaden the mobilization base and transform the war into a 'real people's war' (in Reza'i's phrase).[40] This entailed in the first instance a new emphasis in mid-1986 on the involvement of all 'classes' and also all regions in the war effort. Mobilization was decentralized to 90 provincial councils, responsible for meeting recruitment quotas, which would be co-ordinated by the Supreme Council of War Support,[41] a body only slightly different from the Supreme Defence Council formed at the beginning of the war and charged with all the key issues relating to it (i.e. a form of super-Cabinet). The Guards Corps was given exceptional powers to call upon manpower from all sectors for the war effort, as needed, and all ministries were to assign personnel as requested.

The decision taken in November 1987 to move to a strategy of continuous offensives implying smaller-scale but rapid, repeated attacks, lies somewhere between a strategy of attrition and one of reliance on a grand breakthrough; in this sense, perhaps it may be considered a compromise. But two important components are the need for much broader recruitment and mobilization, and a greater contribution to the war effort by those classes not actively supporters of the war, or indeed of the regime. The catch phrases after November 1987 became 'personal jihad' and 'financial jihad', referring to the new policy in which, in Rafsanjani's phrase, 'we wish to enlist the greater financial support of the nation'. Those unable to serve at the front in combat were 'encouraged' (or required, more accurately) to substitute financial for personal jihad, and contribute through cash donations: 'at least pay the salaries of one fighter at the front for the three or four months when he goes to the front.'[42] The response to this appeal, principally to the well-off classes, was apparently disappointing.[43]

The decision to appeal for more contributions from the better-off coincided with an attempt to offset the decline in the number of volunteers for the war effort. Conscription began to supplement the dwindling stream of volunteers eager for martyrdom. In July 1987 the Head of National Conscription (Colonel Ramju) announced the extension of the period, for those unable to serve at the front, from 24 to 30 months. At the same time it became apparent that even the Pasdaran, which had hitherto been purely volunteer, was having problems of recruitment; it started taking conscripts.[44] The conscription of government employees and university students and their rotation to the front seemed to disquiet some of the regime's ideologues. Asked whether the dispatch of these latter groups to the front was compulsory, the IRGC spokesman (Afshar) replied that national service was a duty for everyone and that those conscripted must do this service. At the same time he insisted that: 'the power that has broken the back of the enemy and of global arrogance today is the volunteer and self-sacrificing spirit of the combatants'.[45]

The extension of conscript duty to 30 months and the beginning of the compulsory conscription of students indicated the problems faced by the government in meeting the manpower requirements of the new strategy.[46] The new approach announced in November may have been the product of political compromise, but it appeared rather similar to that articulated for some time by Morteza Reza'i which he linked with the move to self-sufficiency in arms production, and the formation of divisions of women for duties behind the lines. He said that the acceleration of the build-up and training of large reserve forces was to enable the authorities to mount repeated operations. He denied that what was taking place was 'mass mobilization . . . we are merely engaged in the formation of reserves in our country' but he also implied that such a mobilization would be a logical next step.[47]

The approach seemed to fit in with Reza'i's description in May 1986 of the sort of war that he believed should be waged.[48]

> So far in the imposed war only two per cent of the country's popular forces and twelve per cent of its economic forces have been utilized.
>
> . . . The war today should be completely transformed into a people's war, in accordance with a scheme in which all industrial schools will begin to manufacture military hardware and ammunition.
>
> It is sufficient for us to bring into the battlefield four times more infantry forces with light weapons than the Iraqis [to win] . . . We are on the threshold of a full-scale people's war and this is the only path.

The widening reach of government, the increase in its 'extractive' power as a result of the revolution and then the needs of the war, and the continuation of a 'state of permanent crisis', have thus virtually institutionalized the war in society. The Islamic republic's core constituency has been continuously mobilized since the revolution, and has been most involved in the war, and, at least in the popular base (i.e. excluding the Guards Corps), has suffered the most. The society has become militarized in the sense that all issues revolve around the war, are judged in relation to the war, and depend upon the war. The prolonged war, which now demands resources from deep within the country, has changed the face of society as well as its politics.

The war has increasingly affected all aspects of society. Only one other example is given here for illustrative purposes, namely that of the physicians. The war has increased the demand for medical services (see Chapter 7) and made it as it were a 'strategic' profession. Doctors are required to offer their services in the war and in outlying areas, according to government regulations. Yet these, of necessity, cannot be too strict if they are to have their desired effect and not lead to a further flight of medical expertise. In mid-1986, partly as a result of the desire to throw more resources into the struggle with Iraq, the government moved to assume direct control over the medical profession, by demanding control over the national association and talking of compulsory service at the front. When this was resisted as an unnecessary infringement on their professional independence, the doctors were accused of counter-revolutionary activity. Four hundred and fifty of them were arrested and many were tortured.[49]

The war and culture

However much the waging of war reflects aspects of the society waging it, it would be strange indeed if the situation were not reciprocal, that is, if the society itself were to emerge unscathed or untouched from such an experience. In Iran war has reinforced the sense of siege, embattlement and external conspiracy which is so central to Shi'i/Persian culture. The belief that deprivation is ennobling and adversity a test, has been added to the traditions of quietism and fatalism, which have themselves been replaced by militant messianism under Khomeini. The ambiguity or ambivalence remains; the shifts from utter self-confidence to moods of fatalism and acquiescence are notable in Khomeini's utterances on the war itself. For example, on Revolution Day 1985 he could argue that 'the war is the country's most important issue' and a month later observe that winning the war was not important – doing one's duty was the critical consideration. Still later in the year, he was to say that the war 'is something that will be sorted out'.[50]

The war has reinforced a sense of solidarity and a shared experience of historical dimensions, reduced differences among classes or regions, and infused a collective spirit. War in Iran (as in Beirut) brings out the good as well as the bad in man. On the home front the willingness to contribute jewellery or gold voluntarily and genuinely is matched by a willingness to do without, to accept rationing and shortages as simply a fact of life. War has increased demands on the citizen but has also helped in putting his life into perspective, stripping it of obsession with material comforts and 'false idols' and bringing it back to the essentials of the spirit – faith, family and kinsmen.

If strife and hardship have engendered intimacy, they have also reinforced the already prevalent sense of loss and disinheritance in Shi'i Iran. The nation's life in the war has been a daily enactment of Shi'i themes of sacrifice, dispossession, and mourning. The cult of martyrdom and martyrology is evident; Iran is a country 'where the dead rule'.[51] This is most evident in a subtle change in language; there are no longer any dead in Iran, only 'martyrs'. The government is aware of how to manipulate these deep and unresolved feelings and anxieties. It plays on the themes of guilt, suffering, and loss but it also makes a spectacle of them; the war has become a species of street theatre, a way of reinforcing the collective spirit, *and* a diversion for the urban population deprived of traditional outlets.[52]

The opposition to the war

The exertions and demands, the undoubted technical and military achievements, and above all the quality of commitment the war has called forth, have reinforced a sense of destiny and uniqueness in the country at large. This makes the government impervious to normal standards of judgement and ordinary criteria. The government of God is accountable only to God, not to the people, and this makes it peculiarly resistant to criticisms having an earthly flavour. As Robert Fisk observed, one either supports the war and what goes with it or one does not; if one does, the elements – faith, martyrdom, spiritual mission etc. – follow inexorably; if one does not, the war remains incomprehensible.[53]

Inevitably, the war has had its critics within Iran but these have been either marginal figures, or hidden, unseen, critics within the ranks of the regime. For reasons that we shall try to clarify, the leadership has enjoyed a quite surprising degree of support in what looks from a distance to be a wasteful, inglorious and futile quest. The immediate result of this has been the regime's capacity to wage war unhindered by domestic dissension, but the longer-term consequence is that, while the regime has not been reined in today, it has been left free to wager on an outcome which remains uncertain, at best, and which could cost it its moral authority.

The leadership has ensured that the war has not been publicly debated. Its monopolization of legitimacy has been one obvious asset. Khomeini's definition of the stakes as 'Islam versus blasphemy' also did little to encourage debate. The Islamicization of the political vocabulary, too, has helped to keep the debate to a minimum, as has Khomeini's own position, which has hardly been designed to foster inquiry and doubt among his colleagues. If political control as well as an adamantly stark and comprehensible position have strengthened the inhibitions on debate or questioning, so have Khomeini's policies. The revolution (he has said) was by and for the 'oppressed' class, and it is this class that supports the war, and this class that has given most in its cause. Consequently, the other classes, where dissenters are likely to be found, have no right to a say and will simply be ignored in any case as politically irrelevant.

There is furthermore a strong and general belief, transcending class, that Iraq is responsible for the war, and that for Iran it has been a 'defensive' war. Its continuation is now seen as necessary to ensure that Saddam Hussein is punished and does not survive to do the same thing again later, i.e. the war now is to ensure a 'true' peace, which must mean the removal of the 'roots' of aggression. Even among the classes opposed to the Islamic republic, hostility toward Saddam Hussein's Iraq is greater than their contempt for their own government.[54] (The Islamic authorities have tactically used nationalist symbols and imagery.) There is, in addition, the 'bandwagon' effect of the offensives; however limited the progress, however tenuous the 'victory', each gain can be depicted as another step forward justifying one more final effort to achieve a decisive result. The 'light at the end of the tunnel' motivates its supporters for one more supreme effort, attracts the sceptics and stills the voice of dissent. If victory, however incremental, is possible, how can critics argue for a compromise that would be injurious to the faith and sacrifice of the martyrs who have gone before? For their part, those who doubt that a victory is possible cannot be sure; conservative advice is not welcome in the flush of offensives that gain Iraqi territory. In truth, the situation works to the revolution's *short-term* political advantage either way; advances generate support for more effort, setbacks militate against compromises that devalue the memory of the martyrs who have gone before.

The opponents of the war have another problem, for they are often seen as opponents, in the first instance, of the Islamic republic, using the war as a stick with which to beat Khomeini. As the war has become one, and perhaps the only, achievement of the revolution, it has also become a gauge or yardstick for assessing support for the Islamic republic. As war and revolution have merged, one cannot pass judgement on one without assessing the other. And in this many of the Iranian critics of the regime *outside* the country are doubly handicapped: by their absence which suggests at best a lukewarm attitude towards the revolution, and by the fact that some of them, in particular the Mojahedin, are identified with, and funded by, the enemy, Iraq. Finally, by a curious alchemy present in crises like the Blitz or the war in Beirut, the bonds tying the people together in a common experience are such as to exclude others from passing judgement on them. Fear, danger and shortages breed anguish, exhilaration and in time nostalgia, and forbid too objective an analysis of the predicament.

The opposition abroad has been split on the issue. The monarchists seem to believe that the war is, or can become, a nationalist issue involving the future loyalty of the army, and have been unwilling to criticize the conduct of the war very seriously. Former Premier Shahpour Bakhtiar, somewhat tainted by his consultations with Iraq prior to the war, remains critical but on the sidelines. Mas'ud Rajavi, the leader of the Mojahedin, in April 1984 fell out with former President Bani Sadr on the issue of ties with Baghdad and now lives in Iraq. The radical Mojahedin based in Iraq, with access to arms and training and within reach of Iranian territory, have stepped up armed attacks on the Islamic republic's forces. These attacks remain irritants rather than a serious military problem. They could become more important in the event that Iran fails to achieve its war aims and political instability results. Bani Sadr and his former aides occasionally surface with the view that the Islamic regime needs the war to survive and to keep the army occupied on the frontier. In addition to all the problems that must be encountered in mobilizing opposition to the war (which most people identify with the revolution), the 'opposition' stance is no more unified on the war than on other issues.

The most significant opposition has come from within Iran itself. Privately, there have clearly been differences of view about the continuation of the war. Whether this extends to the core leadership itself cannot be judged. What is clear is that the regular military have at various times expressed doubts about the wisdom of continuing a war that is unwinnable militarily; unwinnable, not only because of Iraq's defences and access to complete weapons systems, but also because of Iran's logistical deficiencies, and above all because of the political involvement of the clerics and their protégés in the war operations. But these reservations are not opposition to the war as such. Khomeini has occasionally felt the need to respond to these unseen critics, presumably because they are potentially influential. Indeed, even in the wake of the victory at Fao, Khomeini adopted a very defensive tone in regard to the costs involved, pointing out to these critics:[35]

> The Holy Commander of the Faithful too was sorry about what would happen to the youth, but did he sit at home and say: We are sorry? Did he not go to war and participate in fighting as well as feeling sorry for those who had been martyred? And now should we just sit by and keep saying: What should we do, what can I do, and those things that they say . . .? . . . The big powers felt that Islam could never have such powers . . . Now they have understood this power is the power of Islam not the power of nationalism, it is the might of Islam which, in their minds, is placing the world in danger. They are now drawing up plots against the fundamentals of Islam. And should we just sit by and say we are responsible for the guardianship of Islam?

A Muslim who wants to eliminate Islam is worse than an infidel . . . Do you mean to say that God does not agree with defence? Today, we are talking about defence; it is not a question of going to war. No one wishes to wage war; it never was the case anyway. We are reiterating the same statement made by the Islamic republic at the very beginning concerning the war. Not a single word of it has changed. What we say is that as long as this Aflaqi party is in power we shall continue this war.

For in order to defend Islam, this tumour must be removed . . . otherwise this country will never experience peace; neither our country nor Iraq, nor all the Gulf states.

The most public criticism of the leadership's conduct of the war occurred in 1985 from the 'in-house' opposition, the Islamic Liberation Movement of Mehdi Bazargan. This came at a time when Iran's offensive at Howeiza (like its predecessor at Majnoon a year earlier) had proved particularly costly, and had given rise to Iraq's air bombardment of Iranian cities, including Tehran. Bazargan and some of his colleagues who came out in criticism were careful to express it in Islamic terms. On 4 February 1985, twenty-six personalities associated with the Islamic republic criticized the policies of the leadership in a manifesto that was circulated, referring to the human and material losses incurred in the war without explicit criticism of it. On 18 March, Bazargan and sixty supporters cabled the UN Secretary General about the war, labelling it unIslamic and illegal since mid-1982 (when Iran recovered its territory). There were signs of some clerical dissatisfaction as well. Ayatollah Hassan Qomi, in the first authoritative criticism of the war, on 5 March described it as 'religiously unlawful'. This was said to have been echoed by Ayatollahs Golpayegani and Morteza Haeri. It was also said that Ayatollahs Meshkini, Azeri Qomi, and Tabatabai, as well as the Prosecutor-General Sane'i, at various times voiced criticism of the continuation of the war.[56] Khomeini acknowledged these voices on 18 and 24 April and again on 6 May, arguing that such talk demoralized the military and could only be heard now that the going was tough. While Bazargan asked for negotiations with Iraq, Khomeini dismissed all such talk as defeatist; he was able to dismiss this criticism as mischievous and hostile to the Islamic republic. He was assisted in this, first, by the Mojahedin's parallel criticism of the war, which tarred Bazargan with the same brush as those 'collaborators', and also by Iraq's inexplicable decision in mid-June to discontinue the bombings which had been largely responsible for the upsurge in anti-war sentiment.[57]

Although Bazargan had 'gone public' on the issue and the ice had been broken, little momentum was achieved, partly because the focus of the war shifted again away from Tehran. Bazargan was disqualified from running for the Presidency later in the year, and his supporters were subject to occasional threats and abuse. Bazargan exemplifies the 'modernist' Muslim who is sufficiently pragmatic to realize that the stakes in the war cannot be so immense as to justify the suffering inflicted on both sides, and is aware of the disproportion between Iran's declared war aims – the deposition of Saddam Hussein and the Ba'th – and the costs expended. In January 1987 Bazargan surfaced with more direct criticism, on the war aims, on the conduct of the war (for example, the indiscriminate use of missiles against hapless Iraqi civilians), on the duplicity and mendacity regarding Iranian casualties suffered in recent offensives, and on the utility, and even necessity, of the war for the regime in maintaining itself in power.[58] (On all these points, the opposition would agree, but most of all on the last.)[59] But Bazargan's is a voice crying in the wilderness, tainted in the eyes of some by his collaboration with the clerics, and in the eyes of others by his call for half-measures.

Any movement toward peace risks raising all the unresolved and contentious issues, such as the future direction of the society, the successor to Khomeini, the nature of relations with the outside world (Islamic and non-Islamic), etc. etc. For Iran, which has not experienced a period of 'normalcy' devoid of crises or crusades in the past decade, and whose population has grown in the past ten years by some 14.5 million in a population which is more than 50 per cent under 15 years of age, the moment of truth is still to come. It will come when it has to try to harness all this youthful energy and dedication to productive peace-time enterprise.[60]

Meanwhile, the war remains stalemated on the battlefield: Iran's incremental gains have yet to translate themselves into a political collapse of Iraq or a military breakthrough at the front. At home, the society has habituated itself to the conflict. In 1984 costs caught up with the military, who took a long respite while refurnishing their stocks and resolving their differences on strategy. In 1985 Iraq's bombing of cities touched off anger against the Islamic regime, perhaps channelling discontent from other issues, and the clerics reacted by moving to a 'defensive jihad' of limited attacks. In 1986 the economic 'bite' of the war increased and dictated an acceleration of hostilities. In 1987 victory proved elusive, so Iran increased its reserves planning for a longer war, while hoping for political collapse in Iraq. The society has adapted to the war, but can it adapt to a peace? The clerics in Iran know that this depends on the nature of the peace; failure to achieve the oft-reiterated war aims will create problems in the government of the country. The cumulative costs of the war may then find expression, and may find their articulation in a person other than a cleric, or even in opposition to the clerics. In this sense the war is a two-edged sword, helping the regime up to a point but always threatening, in the event of failure, to rebound against those who have wielded it so long and so remorselessly.

6

The Impact of War on Iraqi Politics

In trying to assess the impact of the war on Iraqi politics, one is attempting to pursue inquiries in two major areas: firstly, the ways in which the war's effects and the effort necessary to prosecute it have touched, or perhaps transformed, the perceptions and activities of the rulers of the Iraqi state; secondly, the ways in which the perceptions and activities of their subjects have been similarly affected by the war and by the collective experience to which they are perforce committed as inhabitants of a country at war. In this connection, it seems important to ask what effects the war has had upon the moral and structural definition of the purported collectivity engaged upon it – namely, the Iraqi state. The regime would argue that the war has been responsible for forging a new Iraqi national community out of the ethnically diverse population bounded by the state's given territorial frontiers. The very persistence with which this argument is advanced, and the extent to which it has entered not only the official mythology of the state, but also the rationale for its continued domination by one man, Saddam Hussein, must make one question whether a new sense of collective Iraqi identity and purpose has indeed been generated by the war effort.

In some respects, it appears that the war has tended to atomize Iraqi society, throwing its members back on the security of primordial loyalties and collective identities in the face of catastrophe. Not the least eloquent testimony to this hypothesis has been the behaviour of Saddam Hussein himself and his dwindling band of intimate and trusted supporters. Similarly, a plausible explanation of the failure of the Shi'a of Iraq to make common cause with their Iranian co-religionists does not seem to lie in the success of the government propagation of the myth of Iraqi nationalism. Rather, it can be found in the previous absence of any widespread sense of specifically Shi'i identity in a community riven by the more urgent divisions of tribal, clan, urban and rural identities – nominally dominated by a remote and exclusive religious hierarchy. Under the pressure of war, these more fundamental values seem to have reasserted themselves, to the benefit of a regime intent on preventing the formation of any collective identity over which it has no control. Indeed, the example of the Kurds and the reassertion of Kurdish claims on the

Iraqi state, as well as the increasing level of Kurdish guerrilla activity, would seem to support the hypothesis that war's dangers and its opportunities have reinforced particularistic and traditional loyalties, at the expense of any loyalty to the Iraqi state *per se*.

The qualification that must be made in this respect concerns those individuals whom the regime has brought into the structure of state power as supportive dependants of the regime itself. Their adherence to the current definition of the Iraqi state has been given considerable legitimacy by the unrelenting hostility of the 'Persian enemy' and by the consequent impression of natural, and even virtuous, collective endeavour in the name of the 'Iraqi people'. Their interests, however, correspond more closely to their corporate, ethnic, or economic identities – in many cases significantly intertwined and reinforcing – which they believe have been assured by the particular nature of the state erected by Saddam Hussein in Iraq. They comprise a substantial number of people. However, it is too early to say whether they constitute a cohesive or coherent group with demands of its own, independent of its members' relationship with the structure of power from which they have derived such substantial benefits. Indeed, it seems possible that this will never be the case, since it has been one of the features of Saddam Hussein's regime, in peace as much as in war, that the position of Saddam Hussein, and the small group of 'insiders' clustered around the President, should not be restrained, let alone threatened, by any collective interest whatsoever. This has been the governing principle of Saddam Hussein's relations with the Ba'th, the armed forces, the economic entrepreneurs, and even, as was demonstrated in 1983, with members of his own clan. Precisely to avoid becoming beholden to any one of these groupings, despite the demands he must make of them during the war, Saddam Hussein has sought to play one off against the other. He has picked out particular individuals among them for special favour or disgrace, and has emphasized thereby their degree of dependence on himself alone and on his own authority. Destructive as this may be of any notion of community within Iraqi political society, it has greatly facilitated the construction of a thorough-going autocracy, focused on Saddam Hussein. Ironically, despite the fact that such a form of government is precarious at the best of times, the war, at least since 1982, appears to have facilitated Saddam Hussein's ambition of extending the circle of his personal authority into all sectors of Iraqi life.

argue that the war with Iran engendered the form
ddam Hussein has created in Iraq, however helpful
ation for war and the perceived nature of the enemy

have been for the reinforcement of both the moral and structural aspects of his rule. On the contrary, it seems more probable – as argued in Chapter 2 above – that the war owes its very origins to the nature of an autocracy establishing itself in a modern state. This endeavour led to the autocrat's consequent impulse to justify his authority with reference to some of the obligations introduced by the notion of statehood. These impulses were in evidence long before the war broke out and owed more to Saddam Hussein's own perception of the possibilities offered to him by Iraqi politics, following the ten years during which he had played a nominally subordinate role to his uncle, President Ahmad Hassan al-Bakr. His opportunity came in 1979, although it is clear that this was no sudden move but rather the calculated result of a long apprenticeship for absolute power.[1] Two particular features of that power were rapidly to become apparent, deriving from its very essence and from the vision of politics animating it.

These features can be characterized as those of 'mass-based autocracy': that is, the absolute rule of a single individual who yet attempts, for a variety of reasons, to address his subjects in the idiom, but necessarily without the mechanisms, of popular democracy. In many senses, this form of political dispensation is common to a number of states in the Third World. The latter have inherited not only their geographical boundaries, but also many of their institutional structures, as well as many of their ideologies, from the European states which had occupied their territories and in many cases created them. Nevertheless, these state structures are operating in societies where the dominant traditions, and indeed patterns of behaviour affecting the promotion of a political identity and the allocation of political authority, can diverge quite markedly from the European state tradition. Consequently, there has been a process of adaptation, whereby the administrative framework and sometimes the official myth-making of the rulers have been based on an inherited but alien idea of a state founded on a mass society. At the same time, the more exclusive imperatives which govern the perception, acquisition and maintenance of political power are rooted in an authentic but essentially clannish tradition, wholly at odds with the principles of mass participation publicly endorsed by the regime.

Saddam Hussein conforms well to this general type of autocrat. He endeavours to justify the power he holds through clan-based conspiracy with reference to a larger, all-embracing collective identity, encompassing all his subjects and giving him an exclusive right to speak in their name. Real power remains in his hands, and in the hands of the small group of associates whom he has picked as his lieutenants. These men he trusts for reasons of common personal or family experience, or because they are creatures entirely of his own making, without any significant power bases of their own. This, the core of the regime, and the men on whom he would rely to execute his orders in the future, had already been selected and put in place before Saddam Hussein thrust himself forward to become President of Iraq in 1979. However, in that year, as he prepared to become a more public figure of authority, he clearly found it necessary to pay greater attention to the public which he would soon dominate. To this end, he projected himself as a harbinger of significant political change, in the sense that the Iraqi people would now be encouraged to join *en masse* the hitherto exclusive and secretive Ba'th party which has ruled Iraq since 1968. Equally, general elections were promised for the first Iraqi National Assembly to meet since the overthrow of the monarchy in 1958.[2]

In fact, as the bloody series of events accompanying Saddam Hussein's assumption of the Presidency indicated, and as an examination of his subsequent organization of power bears out, neither the 'opening up' of the Ba'th nor the establishment of an Iraqi National Assembly signified any meaningful increase in the power of Iraqis to determine their own future. This lay, as ever, in the hands of the President and the Revolutionary Command Council (RCC). Nevertheless, both moves could be seen as part of Saddam Hussein's determination to be beholden neither to the Ba'th as a party, nor to the RCC itself: the party would no longer be an exclusive and formidable constituency, well entrenched in the structure of the Iraqi state and capable of fomenting independent criticism of the Head of State; and the RCC would provide less fertile ground for the hatching of conspiracies against its Chairman (the Head of State), in the knowledge that he enjoyed demonstrable public support in the nationally 'representative' form of the National Assembly. For precisely these reasons, therefore, Saddam Hussein was eager to project an image of himself as the 'people's champion' and 'leader of the nation'. It helped to distance him from his erstwhile peers, and convinced them that he alone might be able to maintain the myth of an Iraqi political community which was so necessary for the security of their own positions. It also opened up possibilities for him to create, through patronage or otherwise, his own constituency within Iraq, beyond the narrow circles of power.

A short but successful war against Iran was to be a spectacular means by which these processes would be advanced. In structural terms it was intended to strengthen the hold of Saddam Hussein's autocracy and the mechanisms by which it was enforced; in moral terms, it was to define the collective identity of Iraq and attach it indissolubly to the person of Saddam Hussein. 'Saddam's Qadisiyya' was to be the ordeal through which the ethnically diverse Iraqis would pass, forging in the process a united sense of Iraqi community and allowing for the development of a strong political system.[3] Just as the establishment of a National Assembly and other gestures towards a mass society were to be important on a largely symbolic level, so too with the war. The latter was intended to be brief, relatively painless in terms of casualties, largely cost-free for the bulk of the population, and producing, in the expected concessions of the Iranian Government, enormous political benefits for Saddam Hussein. One should not, therefore, underestimate the degree to which the Iraqi leadership believed that war, as envisaged in 1980, would be highly beneficial to the development of the 'mass autocracy' Saddam Hussein was creating in Iraq.

The war has in fact evolved in a way quite other than that hoped for and desired by Saddam Hussein. Nevertheless it is remarkable that the political system upholding his leadership has been able to cope so readily, both conceptually and organizationally, with the effects of a prolonged and defensive war. As we have seen, this can largely be explained by the dual nature of that political system. On the one hand, there is a small core of 'insiders', relatively homogeneous – even if that homogeneity has been somewhat ruthlessly created – and clustered around the figure of Saddam Hussein. These men, and the particular constituencies they in turn cultivate, are the repositories of a traditional and exclusive dispensation of power, from which they derive considerable benefit. On the other hand, there is the mass of 'outsiders', who are expected to play a strictly subordinate role to the self-designated rulers. However, they are addressed by them and regimented by them in the name of a national ideal and a national struggle. The purpose of this is to create out of the mass of Iraqis a malleable resource for the rulers in their competition with each other or with other rulers. Through the techniques of physical elimination and role-playing on a public stage, Saddam Hussein has sought to turn the political loyalties of this very heterogeneous mass towards himself, or at least away from any more authentic local leadership.

The effect of war on the first grouping, the core of insiders, has been to underline their common plight. Having reduced their numbers to sufficiently manageable and trustworthy proportions, Saddam Hussein could rely upon them to endorse his view of the way Iraq should be governed, as well as of the function of war in its future governance. The National Defence Council is composed of a select few from the already restricted circle of the Revolutionary Command Council, with the addition of a number of others, frequently related to Saddam Hussein, and thus appointed by him to positions of particular sensitivity.[4] It was almost certainly in this forum that the decision to go to war was taken, and it is here that the decisions are made on how best to cope with the effects of the war. It is unclear how collegial such a forum can be, but these men have more access to, and influence over, Saddam Hussein than any other group. Also, precisely because they are trusted for other reasons, they probably can speak to him with a greater degree of frankness, although they will have a very good idea of the suitability, and indeed safety, of the topics they raise with him.

Others, who believed themselves to be safe within the inner circle, have discovered to their cost that being outspoken on the subject of Saddam Hussein's own position can cost them their careers and even their lives. The latter appears to have been the fate of the late Minister of Health, Riyadh Ibrahim Hussein, executed in October 1982. He had reportedly suggested that Saddam Hussein might indeed relinquish the Presidency in order to comply with Iran's major condition for ending the war.[5] Na'im Haddad, even though it is uncertain whether he has suffered so extreme a fate, has seen his fortunes wane, possibly for similar reasons, until in 1986 he was officially dropped from the RCC.[6] The two years in which these rifts within the regime became apparent – 1982 and 1986 – were years in which the military and strategic judgment of Saddam Hussein had been demonstrated by Iranian military successes to have been wholly mis-guided. As a consequence, his authority as the paramount leader he had projected himself to be came into question, or at least he sensed that this might be the case. Just as in 1979, when he sensed a similar crystallizing of opposition to his leadership within the senior levels of the RCC, government and party, he acted ruthlessly to destroy it. He thus simultaneously narrowed the circle of those whom he could trust politically, and went to considerable lengths to emphasize his own personal authority and indispensability.

In 1982, the Iranian forces succeeded in driving Iraqi troops back to the international frontier, and demonstrated the Iranian regime's determination to pursue the objective of overthrowing Saddam Hussein. It was clear therefore that the original strategic conception of using war as a means of reinforcing the Iraqi regime through Iranian concessions had failed. Initially, Saddam Hussein sought to dissociate himself from the consequences of this for the Iraqi position. This led to the extraordinary meeting of the RCC, the National and Regional Commands of the Ba'th and the Military Command in his absence. The meeting resulted in the issuing of the Iraqi offer of a ceasefire, couched in language which appeared to be persuading the Iraqi people that the war had not been in vain and preparing them for the acceptance of the ending of the conflict on terms clearly disadvantageous for Iraq.[7] Khomeini's uncompromising rejection of this offer, together with his insistence that there should be a radical transformation of Iraq's political system, paradoxically allowed Saddam Hussein to reassert his authority. The explicit nature of the Iranian war aims now illustrated vividly for Saddam Hussein's colleagues that they were as much targets of Iranian enmity as was their leader. The singling out of Saddam Hussein by the Iranians as their chief target could not disguise the fact that in an autocracy of this nature it was not simply the autocrat whose future was in jeopardy, but also the future of all those who depended upon him and had been associated with him in his rise to power.[8]

Naturally, this was a point which Saddam Hussein took considerable pains to drive home. The fate of the unfortunate Minister of Health, who took the Iranian demands at their face value, was used by Saddam Hussein to underline the fact that all along the Iranian intention had been to topple the regime in Iraq 'not because a certain person was in that regime – we shall not allow any foreigner to discuss this or that person – but because this regime is nationalist and independent'. Consequently, any suggestion that he himself should step down was tantamount to treachery, and, as Saddam Hussein threateningly pointed out, the penalty for this was death, regardless of the individual's rank or privilege position.[9] In a successful bid to tighten and strengthen his own power base, making the senior echelons of party and state doubly dependent upon him and inextricably linked to his own fate, Saddam Hussein engaged in a general purge of the RCC, the top leadership of the Ba'th and of the government Ministers. At the same time, he appointed six special advisers to the Presidency (each with the rank of minister), underlining the degree to which political decisions would now be conducted from the Presidential Palace, with admission open only to those selected few whom the President himself trusted.[10]

This was achieved against the background of the 9th Ba'th Party Regional Congress which witnessed Saddam Hussein's formal appropriation of the Ba'th and its ideology to serve his own ends. The process whereby his influence had become paramount within the party had, of course, been in train since 1964. There were, however, a number of long-standing members of the party who either objected to Saddam Hussein's growing autocracy or who held fast to a dogmatic interpretation of the proper mission of the Ba'th and its members. In neither case could Saddam Hussein tolerate these obstacles to his own absolute exercise of power. He had succeeded in disposing of a number of personal opponents in the 1970s; at the 1982 Congress he succeeded in establishing that thenceforward 'on every matter, big or small, [he would be] cited as the authority'. As Ofra Bengio points out:[11]

> The more precarious Husayn's standing in the party became, the more he was inclined to enforce his line of thinking and to assert this authority. This . . . was reflected in the 'formula' which the report devised as his epithet, viz. the 'imperative leader' . . ., or the leader who represents historical and national 'necessity'. Forming a dialectical relation between Husayn and the party, the report warned members that 'disregarding this necessity or deviating from its strategic line' amounted to causing intentional and direct harm to the aspirations of the party and the people and their basic interests.

This 'strategic line' had been aptly expressed by Saddam Hussein several months previously when he stated in an interview that 'In changing conditions it is impermissible to adopt absolute stances'.[12]

The implications of these developments for members of the party, as for state officials, were made brutally plain by Saddam Hussein in an address to mayors from a number of Iraqi provinces in June 1987.[13]

As for what you said, namely that the people now argue with you and take my speeches and statements as evidence in their arguments, I would like to say that I mean it to be this way. In fact, I had intended it to be this way since the early days of the July 1968 revolution.

The first stage, he stated, had been to establish uniformity with his own views within the party. The second stage was

to get the help of the people against you . . . I wanted the people to make use of my words and my conduct so that nobody would come to tell them the opposite, or act in a contradictory manner, claiming that is the line adopted by the party . . . In this way we are activating the people's control and its role in society.

Using the language of democracy, Saddam Hussein was in fact impressing upon these officials the power of his own dictation. The party could have no existence independent of its leader, and its cadres should bear in mind the fact that he had the power, as head of the Iraqi state, to ensure total conformity with his wishes, since this was also, he suggested, the will of the people.

The war had not caused Saddam Hussein to move to this position of explicit personal domination, but it has provided him with both the incentive and the opportunity to do so. In the face of the explicit Iranian threat of 1982, two reactions appear to have taken place among those whom Saddam Hussein has most reason to fear, namely, among the members of the inner circle of the regime. There were those who saw this as an opportunity for giving vent to their already existing opposition to Saddam Hussein in the hope that his power might be curbed; however, there were also those who believed that more could be gained, at a number of levels, by manifesting their loyalty to Saddam Hussein, acquiescing in effect in the entrenchment of his autocratic power system. It was the latter who triumphed in the summer of 1982 and who have subsequently constituted the core of the regime. Indeed, the tenacity of the Iranian war effort during the years since 1982, and the unchanging, uncompromising and explicit nature of their war aims have, if anything, tended to cement relations among this group. The Iranians have given them a very real reason for the siege mentality they had already adopted in their conduct of politics, and have made the prospect of the removal of Saddam Hussein correspondingly alarming.

This is not to say that Saddam Hussein has not sensed himself to be under threat and in need of boosts to his authority within Iraq and among his own immediate following. In some ways, such a sense may be a necessary corollary of the construction of such an autocratic regime. However, it is uncertain whether Saddam Hussein constantly sees his environment in as threatening a manner as he is reported to have described it to a group of Egyptian reporters.[14] Nevertheless, there have clearly been times, such as 1982, when reversals in the war have caused rumblings whose significance has not been lost on the man who, after all, has claimed supreme leadership and supreme strategic insight in directing his country's war effort. The same sequence of events appears to have taken place in 1986, when it became clear that Saddam Hussein's attempt to compensate for the loss of the Fao penisula by authorizing the ill-considered capture of Mehran had ended in disaster.

Although this did not lead to purges and dismissals on the scale witnessed in 1982, it did lead to a noticeable tightening of Saddam Hussein's personal control within the RCC and the Ba'th, in part by the placing of yet more relatives and protégés in senior positions.[15] Equally, he felt it incumbent upon himself to summon an extraordinary Congress of the Ba'th Regional Command for the first time since 1982, at which he was re-elected Secretary General and his appointees were confirmed. He used this opportunity to deliver a speech in which he seemed to lay disproportionate emphasis on the portrayal of the war with Iran as part of a massive conspiracy against Iraq. In this way, it is to be supposed, he was seeking to absolve himself not only from the general charge of being responsible for initiating the war, but also from the particular charge of mishandling the way it had been conducted. Although the Ba'th hardly constituted a tribunal before which Saddam Hussein would have to exculpate himself, it is possible that he had another, narrower audience in mind which he wanted to impress with the inevitable show of solidarity he was able to elicit from the Ba'thist Congress.[16]

In organizing political power and in ensuring political control, it is noticeable that Saddam Hussein has been careful to place kinsmen within the power structure. This was true no less in the crisis besetting Iraqi politics in peacetime than it has been in the sharpened crisis of war. Although this ultimate circle of 'insiders' has been instrumental in maintaining Saddam Hussein in power, individual members of the circle have occasionally constituted something of an embarrassment, if not a danger. The reason for this has been a natural inclination on their part to overreach their authority and to see their close relationship to the President as constituting a licence to challenge him in certain particulars. At the same time, their intimate blood connection with Saddam Hussein makes them more aware than any outsider of the limitations and obligations he must accept if he is, in fact, to use their services to his own advantage.[17] In some respects, the nature of Saddam Hussein's relationship with his relatives is more like a bargain between equals than any of his other political relationships in Iraq. This traditionally based nexus of trust and blood loyalty lies at the heart of the regime and has in many senses been untouched by the war. Indeed, one could ascribe much of the resilience of Iraq's political system during the war to the original conspiratorial and exclusive nature of the regime. Based as this is on considerations which do not admit of any qualitative distinction between the efforts needed to sustain power in peace or in war, it is perhaps hardly surprising that it has been relatively immune to the kinds of pressures which might have built up under a more open or pluralistic form of government.

This is the heart of the structure of the Iraqi political leadership and constitutes the ultimate support of Saddam Hussein's autocracy. The war has not seriously affected its procedures nor the assumptions on which it is based. The war has, however, required that Saddam Hussein pay attention to the mass of Iraqis he claims to rule, and whom he hopes to mobilize. Even in this sphere, it is questionable whether the war has caused a qualitative rather than a quantitative change in the methods employed to affect the behaviour of the Iraqi population through the techniques of mass mobilization and surveillance, as well as the propaganda and myth-making that accompany them. The organization of the population through military and para-military bodies is not substantially different from the kinds of activity indulged in by the regime since it came to power in 1968. The Vanguards, intended to give military training and political indoctrination to children between the ages of nine and fourteen, already numbered 260,000 by 1978. Before the outbreak of war plans had been laid to expand this to 1 million children by 1980, thereby encompassing roughly three quarters of the relevant age group. A similar pattern existed for the Youth Brigades, formations which took in those aged fifteen to eighteen, preparatory to their conscription into the army. It was under the Ba'th that conscription itself was applied more rigorously, especially from 1970 onwards, leading to a standing army of about 250,000 on the eve of the war. This had been supplemented by the Ba'th Party's own militia, the Popular Army, founded in 1970, but greatly expanded after 1975 when military training was made compulsory for all party members between the ages of 18 and 45. By early 1980, it was claimed that nearly 250,000 men had received military training under its auspices.[18]

Naturally, mobilization for war, and especially for the large-scale defence effort required of Iraq since 1981/82, has meant that even larger numbers of men have been drafted into the armed forces and para-military organizations. By 1987, it was estimated that over 1.3 million men were serving in both the regular and auxiliary armed forces, although not all of the 500,000 or so Popular Army members would be serving at the same time. Nevertheless, even if not serving at the front, it was clear that the regime was organizing them to perform other crucial services in the rear, such as maintaining surveillance on and fund-raising among the people of their neighbourhoods.[19] Those actually mobilized in 1987 did not include their less fortunate predecessors who by that stage in the war were either dead, wounded or captured. It is estimated that these numbered, respectively, 80,000, 170,000, and 70,000.[20] These grim statistics point to the major qualitative difference between this form of regimentation in peacetime and in war. In war, the members of these units are, of course, expected to fight and, if necessary, to die in pursuit of the goal to which the leadership has committed them. It is, therefore, incumbent upon the leadership to convince those whom it expects to do its bidding that they are fighting and dying in their own collective interest.

In this respect, the myth of Iraqi nationhood and values, as well as the identification of the person of Saddam Hussein himself with that 'nation', has undergone an intensification rather than a radical change under the pressure of war. In the late 1970s family names denoting the place of origin of each Iraqi had been abolished, largely to avoid drawing attention to the fact that a disproportionate number of senior state and party officials came from the same clans and villages, or in general from the Sunni Arab northwest of the country.[21] Real power rested upon precisely such a narrow and exclusive clique. However, it would have been self-defeating to have made this apparent while this small group of people attempted to mobilize the population at large, and to justify their own tenure of power in the name of an all-embracing collectivity. Equally, when Saddam Hussein finally became President he was determined to project himself as an embodiment of unity, consensus and stable national politics.[22] This was rapidly developed, even before the war with Iran, into a personality cult of impressive dimensions. At the same time, it had been noticeable that the Ba'th, especially while it came increasingly under the influence and direction of Saddam Hussein, had been encouraging Iraqis to think of themselves as the inheritors of a distinctive national and cultural tradition, antedating the Arab–Islamic conquests. Many of the pan-Arabists in the Ba'th looked askance at this apparent erosion of the idea of Arab nationalism. However, for those who sought to wield power within the given territorial limits of the Iraqi state, it would be of considerable utility if the ethnically diverse inhabitants of that state could be persuaded that they shared a common identity. Even more useful would be the belief that this common identity imposed upon them an obligation to obey the individual who claimed to embody all the qualities of the national community.[23]

These efforts were a necessary adjunct of the Ba'th regime's attempts to displace other loyalties felt by Iraqis to alternative collectivities, be they those projected by the Iraqi Communist Party, by the non-Ba'thi Arab Nationalists, by the Kurdish Nationalists or by the advocates of an Islamic political community among the Shi'a. In Saddam Hussein's case, it was necessary that he ensure that there should be no alternative leadership to his own, whether this was among these various communities or indeed within the community with which he most closely identified. In peacetime, this was crucially important for political survival. It remains of vital importance in war, with the added consideration that the Iraqis are not simply being asked to rally in a vague way behind their sole leader but also to sacrifice themselves if necessary in defence of the values and the collectivity which that leader claims to represent. Even before the war had broken out, this was a message which Saddam Hussein was insistent on communicating to his subjects.[24]

In the early stages of the war, Saddam Hussein had evidently been perturbed by the fact that he had as yet been relatively unsuccessful in communicating his own sense of urgency to the people whom he expected to do the fighting for him. However, after the reverses of 1982, when it was clear that the Iraqi armed forces were fighting to prevent an Iranian invasion of their country, he was reassured that the very explicit nature of the Iranian threat was making his task correspondingly easier: 'The clearer the Iranian intentions become to the Iraqi forces, the more willing they become to offer sacrifices and to perform better'.[25] The changing nature of the war, although critical for Saddam Hussein's future, seemed to be allowing him greater opportunities to convince the Iraqis that 'in Iraq the people are one party, the party of great Iraqis defending the country and its sons' and that 'Al-Qadisiyya is not a Ba'th Party demonstration but is a battle in defence of Iraqi territory and dignity, in defence of its . . . past, present and future'. Indeed, so eager was he to persuade the population that they were not governed by a secret coterie, whether family or party based, that he made specific reference to the punishment he had meted out 'among my relatives, including my nephews, brothers and my son, who sometimes behaved badly' by failing to perform the military service demanded of them. In addition, he proclaimed that 'every Iraqi who took up arms and fought in defence of the homeland was an organized Ba'thist whose record was similar to that of the brave Ba'thist who continued struggling at the time of the secret work.'[26]

These efforts at myth-making and propaganda were supplemented by such moves as opening up the Ba'th party to general membership, transforming it into an instrument of mass mobilization in the service of the leader rather than a secretive vanguard which might call the leader to account for his actions. Indeed, under the pressure of war, Saddam Hussein clearly required efficient agencies and corresponding beliefs which would allow him not only to instil in the Iraqi people a sense of collective purpose, but also to define that purpose, unchallenged from below. In expecting the Iraqis to identify themselves with a specifically Iraqi community – 'to be Iraqis in heart, soul, conscience and action' – Saddam Hussein seemed aware that the creation of a sense of collective identity which would be effective politically, also implied a sense of participation among its members in determining their collective future: 'It is time for Iraqis to rule themselves by themselves in the true sense of the word'.[27] He had made a purely symbolic gesture in this direction through the creation of the National Assembly in 1980, its maintenance throughout the war, and the staging of general elections of a highly controlled kind for a new assembly in 1984.[28]

As ruler, Saddam Hussein stated that he was fulfilling his part of the bargain:[29]

> If God wants this war to continue for more than seven years, we must perform our national duty as dictated by our conscience and our responsibility . . . The official who does not safeguard his people's honour against a foreign occupation, should be pursued by the people. This also applies to us.

In his opinion the verdict of the people was evident in the way they had behaved during the war years. Claiming to see in the successful Iraqi defence effort 'a people's referendum' which more than substituted for his lack otherwise of an explicit popular mandate, Saddam Hussein seemed optimistic that war itself would create the necessary sense of community in Iraq:[30]

> It seems that the law of life stipulates that sacrificing blood is inevitable for an extraordinary construction. This is the history of nations and peoples and this is the history of Iraq and the Arab nation.

However, it was not his intention that this should lead to a definition of the nation's interest that was separate from his own. In fact, with the increasingly audible Iranian demand that Saddam Hussein himself should be sacrificed in order to bring the war to an end, it was vital that he should permit no separation between himself and the national community, and no distinction therefore between his own survival and that of the community. It was imperative that Iraqis should be convinced that in fighting to defend their country, they were also fighting to defend their leader.

As a result, the war has led to an even greater projection of Saddam Hussein as national leader in many guises, corresponding not only to the ethnic diversity of Iraq but also to his conception of the role of the 'populist autocrat'. This has become a marked feature of life in Iraq during the war years, with Saddam Hussein's image inescapable for the average Iraqi, in the cities, in the countryside, and above all in the mass media. The cult of personality has reached extravagant proportions, whether in the 'oceanic assemblies' of the people, demonstrating support for the leader in the streets of Baghdad, or in the reported oath of allegiance delivered to Saddam Hussein, amidst great publicity, by the members of the National Assembly, signed in their own blood.[31]

This exercise in self-projection is aimed not simply at the 'people' in a general sense, but also at Saddam Hussein's potential rivals among his colleagues and family. It is to persuade them that he has become an unparalleled focus of national loyalties, and indispensable, therefore, as a disguise for the clannish and restricted range of interests being protected and advanced by the current structure of power in Iraq. Sycophantic party officials may go to such lengths as to claim that by wearing the military uniform affected by Saddam Hussein, adorned by a badge of his face, it helps them 'to identify with the people'.[32] As far as the effect on non-official Iraqis is concerned, it is extraordinarily difficult to measure with any degree of accuracy the relative effects of their perceptions of government and of the Iranian enemy in motivating their war effort. Not only does this touch on the often enigmatic 'moral' side of politics, it is also something about which no research is tolerated in Iraq. Indeed, this very lack of tolerance, and the sensitivity or insecurity displayed by the regime in its relationship to its subjects, is a kind of testimony to its suspicion that the campaign to create a sense of Iraqi national identity has only a marginal hold on the imaginations of the general public when they assess their own political situation. Saddam Hussein intimated as much in June 1987, when he stated that 'the full mobilization of brains, resources and conscience to develop Iraq' had not happened to the extent that he had once expected.[33] Equally, the stridency of the 'personality cult' of Saddam Hussein may perhaps testify to the doubts he entertains regarding his ability to substitute his own desires and interests for those which might be allowed to emerge from a community which enjoyed freedom of debate, choice and association. While power is organized on the basis, and for the ultimate benefit, of the restricted circle of 'insiders' sustaining the autocracy of Saddam Hussein, this relationship between ruler and people is unlikely to change.

The crisis represented by the war has merely intensified the sense of beleaguered solidarity within the regime. However, by facing the bulk of the Iraqi population with an external crisis of similar proportions, the war has at least made them aware of the fragile predicament they share with their rulers. For the first time, perhaps, this idea of a common plight has made many Iraqis more susceptible to Saddam Hussein's exhortation that 'the most important thing about this battle is that it is the battle of the citizen's faith in his homeland, kinsfolk, aims, people and cause. You have a just cause. You are defending Iraq'.[34] It is unlikely that the basic social values have changed. However, whereas once the average Iraqi was faced with the problem of how best to survive and to preserve the interests of the most important social unit in his life – his kinsfolk – from the uncontrollable catastrophe of government, he has been confronted for the past seven or more years with the more immediate task of how to preserve those same interests from the equally relentless catastrophe of the Iranian armed forces. This, of course, is carried out in the full, or at least growing, knowledge of the treatment he can expect from his own government, should he be seen to fail in this newly imposed 'national' responsibility. Whether he is in fact fighting to defend his country or his family, the effect is much the same. Indeed, despite the rhetoric, there is a sense in which the regime might be considerably safer from recrimination in the long run if the latter were the case.

Consequently, it is doubtful whether the war has in fact lessened the sense of alienation that exists between subject and ruler in Iraq. Although this may in the long term work to the detriment of the security of any given Iraqi regime, in the short term it has been much exploited by Saddam Hussein and could be seen to constitute a crucial 'defensive perimeter' around the core of his regime. At the same time, the very visible peril of the war, and the nature of the Iranian enemy, has allowed him to tighten his control within that perimeter, as well as to extend his influence beyond it. In this respect, the war has allowed Saddam Hussein to impose a greater degree of conformity than heretofore. Structurally, there has been a proliferation of security organizations and of vehicles for the mobilization of society at large. Morally, the myths abound of a common Iraqi identity, as well as of his own role in defining and safeguarding that identity. Whether such conformity implies more than temporary and prudential obedience on the part of Saddam Hussein's subjects while the external danger of Iranian invasion persists, remains to be seen. However, a brief examination of the effects of the war on two very different communities – the Shi'i Arabs of southern Iraq, and the Sunni Kurds of the north – would suggest some of the strengths and weaknesses of the political system erected by Saddam Hussein, under the pressure of war.

The Shi'a

In October 1985, the ebullient Iraqi Minister of Culture and Information, Latif Nussayyif al-Jasim, declared in an interview with *Al-Hawadith*, that Iran's attempt to incite revolt among Iraq's Shi'i population had come to naught and that 'the Iraqi people has demonstrated its loyalty and its allegiance to the nation by defeating Khomeini's strategy to divide national ranks'.[35] Whether this was in fact the reason for the failure of the Shi'i majority in Iraq to make common cause with their Iranian co-religionists against the Sunni-dominated government, remains a moot point. Nevertheless, it was noticeable that despite the Iraqi Government's fears on this score and the rumours which spread at the start of the war concerning Shi'i disaffection within the Iraqi armed forces, there has been no very marked challenge during the years of war from this quarter. This has been the case despite the fact that specifically Shi'a-based political organizations have proliferated among Iraqi exiles in Iran. They have received the aid and encouragement of the Iranian Government to devote themselves to the twin goals of the overthrow of Saddam Hussein and the establishment of an Islamic republic in Iraq.[36]

The apparently rather limited effect of the war on the Shi'a community can be explained with reference to a number of factors, all of which, when taken together, can be seen to be more persuasive than the argument that some sense of loyalty to an imagined Iraqi nation has suddenly seized hold of their collective imagination. In the first place, although it is true that nearly 60 per cent of the population are Shi'i by faith, it is by no means true that this same 60 per cent constitute a distinct community, self-conscious and aware of a political identity defined by their faith. On the contrary, much of the rurally-based Shi'a population, which constituted the majority until a generation ago, were only nominally Shi'i: their political identities and loyalties were circumscribed and delineated by kinship relations and by the mutual obligations of tribal custom. Contact with the government was limited or mediated through tribal leaders, and it seems highly improbable that they saw themselves primarily as either Iraqis or Shi'a – rather as members of a particular tribal lineage.[37]

Equally, with migration into the towns and with the development of capitalist relations in agriculture and in industry, much of this community, while retaining links with their kinsfolk, began to see their situation not in sectarian terms, but in terms of their relations to their employers – who tended also to be Shi'a. As a result, they provided fertile ground for recruitment both by the Iraqi Communist Party and by the Ba'th. For many of the established urban Shi'a, there was equally an attraction towards these apparently 'modern' ideologies, as well as towards the educational, economic and administrative opportunities provided by the modern state. In both cases, it led to a marked lack of respect for the Shi'i *ulama* who were obliged to rely upon the diminishing traditional classes for their immediate following.[38]

As a result, there had never developed a strong political leadership which could unite the Shi'a into a self-conscious political community. The position of the *ulama* was indeed equivocal: while few may have regarded the government as legitimate, many advocated abstention from the political realm and an inward-looking concentration on spiritual matters. To this end, and following the pattern of Shi'a communities elsewhere, a strict division developed between those who were qualified to make authoritative pronouncements and those who were obliged to accept them, with an equally scrupulously observed hierarchy among the former. It was only the very rare and exceptional *alim*, such as Muhammad Baqr al-Sadr, who was able to bridge these formidable obstacles, and speak to a wider audience about his ideas for a more just society, to be governed by Islamic legists such as himself.[39]

Inevitably, these activities and the response they aroused within sections of the Shi'a community, alarmed a government jealous of its own exclusive authority. This led to severe restrictions on any perceived political activity connected with the authoritative leaders of the Shi'a, culminating in 1980 in the execution of Baqr al-Sadr himself. This was accompanied by the proscription of Al-Da'wa, a somewhat shadowy political organization based on Shi'i grievances. In addition the government expelled thousands of Shi'a of even the most tenuous Iranian connection and imposed government control over all Shi'i revenues, effectively transforming all Shi'i officials into government dependants.

These powers added to the already considerable and moderately successful government attempt to transform the Shi'i ulama of Iraq into a body as acquiescent to government demands as the Sunni ulama had traditionally been.[40] The exception has been the most notable and venerated of the Shi'i clerics of Iraq, Ayatollah Kho'i, who has persistently refused to submit to the government's demand that he make pronouncement sanctioning the Iraqi war effort and condemning the Iranian regime. He has paid for this by being placed under virtual house arrest. His silence seems to be due not so much to a feeling of sympathy for Ayatollah Khomeini's regime, the theological justification for which he is reported to view with unease, but rather to a disengagement from, and probably disdain for, the secular world of state power represented by the Baghdad regime.

As a result of this internal disarray, when war with Iran broke out, the Shi'i 'community' as such was in no position to offer resistance to the government's orders that its 'members' fight the Iranians. Conceptually and organizationally, Iraq's Shi'i inhabitants were unprepared either to make common cause with the Iranian Shi'a or to seize upon the fact of war as an opportunity for concerted action against the Iraqi government. The latter, however, was supremely well equipped to prevent the emergence of any such consciousness or organization. Saddam Hussein may have let slip at times of stress the cloak of Iraqi nationalism which he was seeking to fabricate, thus revealing a world view bounded by primordial and possibly sectarian loyalties.[41] However, this did not seriously hamper his pursuit of the traditional policies of material inducements and intimidation when dealing with the Shi'a. Indeed, as in his dealings with all communities, including his own, such a perception could be said to have helped him considerably.

The years of war have therefore witnessed a sustained effort by Saddam Hussein to placate the Shi'a symbolically and materially, while at the same time acting ruthlessly at the first sign of any challenge to his regime emanating from their ranks. On the symbolic level, he has ensured that the composition of the National Assembly should be about 40 per cent Shi'a and that its Speaker, both in 1980 and in 1984, should be a prominent Shi'a; he has lavished praise on the traditional heroes of Shi'i history, invoking them as Iraqi national heroes, and even going so far as to claim direct descent from the most prominent of them, the Caliph Ali, son-in-law of the Prophet; Shi'i festivals have been declared public holidays, to be observed by the government for the first time in Iraqi history. At the same time a number of other symbolic gestures of respect have been made to Islamic sensibilities.[42] On the material level, Saddam Hussein has greatly increased the amount of government money available to the Shi'i cities of Najaf and Karbala, both for impressive new municipal projects aimed at raising the standard of living of the inhabitants, and for the embellishment and restoration of the Shi'i shrines for which these cities are famous.[43]

Meanwhile, his security services have made it extremely difficult for any Shi'a-based political activity to take place. Even before the war, students at Shi'i theological colleges were exempted from military service. Publicly this measure was declared to be a token of respect for their calling. In fact, it was to prevent this most conscious stratum of the Shi'a from spreading sedition within the armed forces. Their place has been taken by more complaisant Shi'i ulama, subsidized by the government, who have been sent to army units at the front in order to convince any wavering souls that they have nothing in common with 'the Persians who call themselves Muslims but are Magians' facing them in the trenches opposite.[44] When, during 1982 and 1983, Al-Da'wa claimed responsibility for a number of bomb explosions in Iraq, and an umbrella organization for several Shi'i organizations (the Supreme Council for the Islamic Revolution in Iraq) was formed in Tehran, the regime took savage reprisals. Nearly one hundred members of the al-Hakim family, relatives of Hojjat al-Eslam Sayyid Mohammad Baqir al-Hakim, the chairman of SCIRI, were arrested by the Iraqi authorities. Six of them were executed in May 1983, with the warning that further executions would follow if Sayyid Mohammad and SCIRI did not cease their activities. In March 1985, the Iraqi authorities appear to have made good their promise by executing a further ten members of the al-Hakim hostages.[45] Although the details of the case are not yet known, the murder of Mehdi al-Hakim, the brother of Sayyid Mohammad, in Khartoum in January 1988, bears all the hallmarks of this highly clannish vendetta.

The war has had the effect of identifying any organized Shi'i political activity with the Iranian regime and its goals, making it simultaneously dependent on the vicissitudes of Iranian politics and on the favour of the Iranian Government. It has also made the organizational centres of such activity necessarily remote both physically and emotionally from the community it claims to represent. Indeed, the circumstances of the war are hardly likely to be conducive either to the emergence of a self-conscious Shi'i identity among the mass of Iraqi Shi'a, or to the creation of opportunities for organisations such as SCIRI to encourage the development of such political consciousness. As a result, Al-Da'wa and others which come under the umbrella of SCIRI have had to resort to unsystematic and short-lived campaigns of assassination and bombing within Iraq, to little obvious effect save that of increasing government repression.[46]

The prime target of such assassination attempts, Saddam Hussein, has hitherto escaped uninjured. Many of the reported attempts on his life have not necessarily been made by Al-Da'wa, or indeed by any self-conscious organization, poised to implement its own political programme.

Rather, they appear to be symptoms of the trend towards tyrannicide which regimes such as that of Saddam Hussein inspire. The dominant perception in this regard is that the death of the man who occupies so central a position within the political system will, in itself, cause violent and dramatic changes within that system, as well as being a fitting punishment for his tyranny. In Iraq, this is not an inappropriate perception of the instrumental and expressive uses of murder as an agent of political change. However thoroughgoing the autocracy, the weak link in the whole system is the individual survival of the autocrat himself. Given the means by which Saddam Hussein has ensured his own absolute power, there are many in Iraq who will have specific, highly personal reasons for wishing to plan his death, as well as those who regard his death as the principal means of realizing their own political programmes. Al-Da'wa's claimed attack on Saddam Hussein's motorcade as it neared Mosul in April 1987 showed a combination of these motives. Not only does he represent everything they oppose in politics; the timing of the attack – on the seventh anniversary of the execution of Ayatollah Baqr al-Sadr – clearly intended it to be a matter of personal retribution.[47]

The Iraqi authorities' reaction to this assassination attempt was reportedly to have sent the air force to attack the bases of Al-Da'wa in Kurdistan. This points to the direction in which the parties of SCIRI have been obliged to develop. In their dependence on Iran's military might, they have had to follow the protection of its armies, while at the same time attempting to assert their claim to be an authentic and independent alternative government for the people of Iraq. This led to increased association with the Iranian campaigns in Kurdistan, since it was only in this area that significant stretches of Iraqi territory were free from Iraqi control. In 1983, the capture of Haj Umran allowed them to establish an 'Iraqi government on Iraqi soil'. However, this was somewhat premature in conception and in execution: it evoked no audible echo of sympathy within Iraq; it also tended to antagonize other Iraqi opposition factions which had sought refuge in Kurdistan, but which had scant sympathy for SCIRI's vision of Islamic government. SCIRI has had some success in recruiting adherents from the many thousands of Iraqi Shi'i exiles living in Iran, as well as among some of the Iraqi prisoners of war. From these recruits, it has formed a nucleus of about 2,000 fighters which may not make them a very serious challenge to the Iraqi Government, but does lend them credibility in the opposition union formed in late 1986 (see below).[48]

Since it came to power, the Iraqi regime has been determined to ensure that no alternative sense of collective identity should emerge among the Shi'a of Iraq. In this respect, it was probably as much concerned by the strength of the Iraqi Communist Party as by the sectarian and communal calls of the ulama. The result has been that it has been engaged, since the mid-1970s, in a campaign to eliminate such alternatives, necessitating close attention to the material and symbolic wants of the Shi'a. These have been granted, as long as they do not touch on the central question of the distribution and organization of power. On this, Saddam Hussein has been adamant in insisting that religious considerations should play no part in determining the political programme of his regime.[49] More fundamental is the insistence that only he and the selected group around him should wield political power.

The Shi'a, like all other communities in Iraq, had been subject to this perception of power and its consequences for some years before the war. As a result, when war came, it found them without the conceptual or organizational apparatus to exploit these circumstances for sectarian ends. Instead, the regime has seized the opportunity to extend its control throughout the community by conscripting its members and subjecting them to an intense psychological bombardment. This emphasizes at the same time their separation from the Iranian enemy and the prudential considerations they must bear in mind if they and their families wish to survive the war.

The Iraqi leaders believe that the elaboration of the myth of a specifically Iraqi identity may help them in the former respect. Saddam Hussein has also taken pains to emphasize the qualitative difference between Arabic-speaking Muslims and others: the Arabs have a unique relationship with Islam which gives them a better understanding of its obligations; the Iranians are simply the latest manifestation of 'the enmity of the Shu'ubists against the Arabs, seeking to exploit religion to cause the Arabs to abandon their radiant role of leadership'. Returning to a theme he has made much use of, he has urged the Iraqi people not to be deceived by the Iranian Government's Islamic aspect, since this is simply a cover for Iranian nationalism – a force, it is alleged, deeply inimical to their own interests as Arabs and as Muslims.[50] As far as prudential considerations were concerned, the very visible presence of the government's security forces, and the degree of surveillance and supervision involved in regimenting people into the war effort, meant that few could escape the attentions of the authorities if they remained in their community.

For those members of the community for whom these pressures have been too great, desertion rather than political militancy was the principal option. In times of crisis, individual survival rather than collective action has become the priority. The numbers involved, now reportedly hiding in the southern marshes of Iraq, are said to be substantial and to constitute something of a security problem.[51] However, the fragmented nature of these groups, their physical isolation, their beleaguered attempts to survive and the very visible nature of their activities make them a reassuringly familiar phenomenon with which the regime finds it fairly straightforward to deal.

The periodic explosion of car bombs in the capital and the occasional attack on figures of authority in the provinces, as well as the reports of banditry and kidnapping around Nasiriyyah in the southern marshes, have caused concern to the authorities in Baghdad, but as a security problem rather than a direct political threat. Open defiance of this kind has evoked a harsh response from the government and has even led to the fall of those who had hitherto seemed part of the inner circle of power, such as Sa'dun Shakir, the Minister of the Interior until August 1987. Nevertheless, isolated acts of resistance such as these are less threatening politically than the much more insidious threat of communal disaffection. In dealing with the Shi'a, the energies of the Iraqi Government have been devoted as much to this endeavour as to the enforcement of the government's particular directives. The failure of the Iraqi Shi'a collectively to identify with the Iranian Shi'i enemy has certainly helped to encourage the government to believe that its strategies have had some success. However, it is no proof that they feel any collective loyalty towards the government which is commanding them to fight that enemy. The open hostility of the latter and the parochial loyalties among the Shi'a themselves would seem to exclude any surge of collective loyalty in either direction. More prudently, as individuals concerned with family identity and advantage, they wait to see which power has the capacity to do most harm to their interests and which needs placating most immediately.

The Kurds

The very different effect of the war upon the Kurds vividly demonstrates the differences between them and the Shi'a in their original organization and relationship to the state. However, it would be difficult to argue that the war has transformed either. Rather, what has occurred has been the opportunity provided by the Iraqi armed forces' distraction in the war for the Kurds to reassert, by force of arms, a traditional bargaining posture vis-à-vis the central government in Baghdad. All the Kurdish guerrilla organizations had, by the end of 1986, come to an agreement with each other and with a number of other Iraqi opposition groups, that the government of Saddam Hussein should be overthrown. However, this merely marked the end of a period during which some at least of the Kurdish groups entertained the illusion that they could negotiate with Saddam Hussein over the devolution of a significant degree of political power. As Mas'ud Barzani (at present the leader of the Kurdish Democratic Party) stated in 1985: 'We will live with the Arab people [in the state of Iraq], but not with a dictatorial regime'.[52]

The Kurdish community in Iraq is not homogeneous, divided as it is among two major linguistic groups and among the very different social and economic interests of those who inhabit the cities, the lowlands and the highlands of Kurdistan. Equally, it is a community fragmented by village, clan and tribal loyalties which in many respects have constituted a significant obstacle for those Kurdish nationalists who have sought to instil in their fellow Kurds a sense of collective identity. This fragmentation has been reflected in the Kurds' many political organiz- ations and in their differing relations with the central government, giving that government considerable latitude in the cultivation of acquiescence, if not loyalty, among its Kurdish subjects. However, it is also true that the cultural tradition of the Kurds, the history of their relations with successive governments and the very inaccessibility of much of their territory to close government control have given to each of their political organizations a military capability. Either to protect one's community against the impositions of central government, or to win greater concessions on non-interference from the latter, force has been seen as a legitimate and highly practical way of achieving one's aim.[53]

Within this scheme of things, the regional enemies of the Iraqi Government become useful allies, regardless of the lack of any other points of common interest. Equally, the apparent distraction or weaken- ing of the government in Baghdad, causing it to relax its military control of Kurdistan, is seen as an opportunity to reassert the Kurdish demands which the Iraqi military presence is designed to suppress. Consequently, following the Iranian revolution in 1979 and the subsequent deterioration of relations with Iraq, both the main Kurdish parties – the Kurdish Democratic Party and the Patriotic Union of Kurdistan – saw a chance for the revival of their fortunes. The KDP was considerably more successful in cultivating the new regime in Tehran, partly by offering its services in Tehran's campaign to eradicate the Iranian Kurdish autonom- ous movement. The PUK, whose origin was due partly to communal and ideological differences among the Kurds, and partly to a bitter feud between its leader, Jalal Talabani, and the Barzanis who head the KDP, could not bring itself to collaborate with Tehran in this respect. When war broke out between Iraq and Iran in 1980, the situation in Kurdistan was sufficiently confused to allow the Iraqi Government to feel fairly relaxed about its position there. Indeed, this confusion lasted for the first two years of the war, prompting Saddam Hussein to boast that the Kurdish organizations would never be able to achieve anything since they were hopelessly divided against each other and subservient to foreign powers. As a result, he claimed, the government was reducing its military presence in the region and putting Kurdish units of the People's Army in charge of Kurdistan's security.[54]

Nevertheless, this was only a short respite for the Baghdad Govern- ment. Subsequent years witnessed an attempt first to negotiate with the Kurdish groupings and, when these negotiations broke down, the resumption of full-scale military operations in Kurdistan. In some respects, it was the Iranian 1983 offensive into Kurdistan which set this process in motion. The arrival of Iranian forces in strength, and the apparent strategic importance of Kurdistan, gave the Kurdish guerrilla organizations greater value, and thus greater bargaining power, with both Baghdad and Tehran. The latter provided arms to the KDP and carried out attacks on the PUK allies of its own Kurdish dissidents.[55] The Baghdad Government therefore sought to come to terms with the PUK. However, it demonstrated a characteristic ruthlessness in its dealings with the KDP by rounding up about 8,000 members of the Barzani clan and despatching them to an unknown place of confinement. The fact that they have not been heard of again has caused many to believe that they have been killed, in part as a warning to the KDP and in part as a way of depriving the latter of a number of potential guerrilla fighters.[56]

As with the Shi'i community, Saddam Hussein pursued his policies of bribery and intimidation with the Kurds: the former encompassed symbolic and material gestures of generosity, stopping short, however, of any political concession; the latter involved calculated displays of government brutality as well as substantial, although only moderately successful, military campaigns. Saddam Hussein was clearly concerned by the number of Kurdish deserters from the armed forces. In the Kurdish context these constitute a double threat: not only do they significantly weaken the Iraqi armed forces' capacity to resist Iranian offensives in the area, they also have an alternative political and military organization to join, in the shape of the Kurdish guerrilla movements. Nor does the twin strategy of amnesty and reprisal seem to have had any very long-term effect.[57]

For the PUK, which was negotiating with Baghdad during 1983 and 1984, it was clear that even the pressure of war and their own threat to resume guerrilla operations would not wring substantive concessions from Saddam Hussein. The latter firmly resisted PUK demands that a fixed percentage of oil revenues should go to Kurdish development projects, that the Kurdish militia under government control should be disbanded, that the area of Kurdistan should be extended, or that there should be any meaningful political autonomy. Political power is clearly indivisible for Saddam Hussein and this has been the rock on which any negotiation with the Kurds has foundered.[58] As a result, the PUK was to join the KDP in armed operations against Iraqi government targets in 1985.

Subsequently, the aim of both main Kurdish guerrilla groups has been to sustain a campaign of harassment against Iraqi forces, sometimes in conjunction with Iranian forces. Equally important has been the intention displayed by both the KDP and the PUK to create areas in which they can be free of Iraqi government interference, thereby establishing a form of *de facto* autonomy. When these areas and the activities of the Kurdish groups have approached strategically vital resources such as the highway and pipeline to Turkey, the Iraqi Government has displayed considerable ruthlessness and tenacity in thwarting the aims of the Kurds.[59] At other times, it has been content to launch limited assaults against entrenched Kurdish positions, or to permit the Turkish armed forces to make incursions with the same end in view. This both serves to gain an operational advantage over the Kurds and has been used to demonstrate that the nature of Kurdish demands is such that the conflict is not simply between them and the government in Baghdad but involves other equally relentless forces in the region.[60]

This is, indeed, a problem for the Kurds and has given them some difficulties in the definition of their political aims. Calls for self-determination, rather than simply for provincial autonomy within an Iraqi state, arouse the suspicions and hostility not only of the government in Baghdad, but also of the governments in Ankara and in Tehran. Nevertheless, as the PUK seemed to recognize in 1987, the call for an independent Kurdistan is the more inspiring rallying cry.[61] An attempt to reconcile the various ideas on the desirability and practicality of independence, while not alienating their Iranian hosts, was evident in September 1987, when all the Kurdish parties united in a front which called for a future separate Kurdish state, 'confederated with a future democratic Iraq'.[62]

The *sine qua non* of such a future is recognized to be the removal of Saddam Hussein. However, in this respect as well, the Kurds suffer under the disability of the fact that they find it difficult to evoke any echo of sympathy for their cause in other parts of Iraq. Militarily, they can pose a threat to Iraqi government interests in the north. Politically, however, they tend to be excluded from consideration by those who are closer to the central structures of the Iraqi state and who may, therefore, be able to affect its future. Towards the end of 1987, it was noticeable that the leaders of both major Kurdish guerrilla organizations attempted to remedy this, by urging 'all patriotic Iraqis' to overthrow the regime. Mas'ud Barzani stated that 'the responsibility for the liberation of the Iraqi nation ... falls on the shoulders of every patriotic Iraqi'. Jalal Talabani, meanwhile, addressing himself directly to the Iraqi officer corps, warned them against believing Saddam Hussein's slogan that they were defending the country. On the contrary, he stated, they were merely defending the regime and 'defence of Saddam's regime is treachery against the aspirations of the Iraqi nation and treason against the country'.[63] In trying to secure their future, the Kurds have been obliged to appeal to the same idea of collective Iraqi identity as Saddam Hussein has been invoking. However, precisely because that idea is not firmly rooted as a rationale for political action, the Kurds are regarded as outsiders, with their own particular communal concerns, and are, therefore, likely to be an object of mistrust for other inhabitants of Iraq.

The Kurds, however, believe that by gaining territory they can achieve a number of aims: they can gain time and freedom from government control; they can establish themselves in a strong bargaining position vis-à-vis the government; they may, by their success, contribute towards the weakening and eventual overthrow of that government. These are in many respects the traditional goals of all Kurdish political movements. The war has given them the opportunity to pursue them with greater vigour than before, but it has not caused them to see themselves or their relationship to Baghdad, or the modalities of that relationship, in a radically different light. Much the same can be said of the government of Saddam Hussein. War with Iran may have placed constraints on the available resources with which to confront the perennial problem of the Kurds. However, it has not changed his perspective on that problem, nor his belief about the intolerable nature of the Kurdish groups' aspirations to political power. Equally, it has left unaltered Saddam Hussein's views on the utility of the means by which central government has sought to address the problem. Force, bribery, intimidation, the exploitation of inter-Kurdish rivalries, and the appeal to a range of self-interested motives will continue to be the major instruments in the hands of the government. These seem likely to remain more effective ways for the government to enlist the support of Kurds against their fellow Kurds and against the latter's Iranian allies, than any of Saddam Hussein's attempts to inculcate a sense of specifically Iraqi national identity among the inhabitants of Kurdistan.[64]

The Economy

It would be foolhardy to attempt to analyse with any degree of accuracy the effects of the war on the economic structure of Iraq. The release of detailed figures giving a breakdown of the economy has never been a marked characteristic of the Iraqi Government and, understandably, war has imposed an additional embargo on such statistics. It is perhaps more important to gain an understanding of the way in which the war has touched two particular areas of the economy, thereby affecting both the resources available to the regime and consequently its attempt to control its domestic and regional environment. These two areas are, first, the income at the disposal of the government which allows it to pursue its objectives in the war as well as inside Iraq. Secondly, there is the socio-economic balance within the country, through which economic realities are transformed into political facts. In both areas Saddam Hussein has sought to maintain an absolute control, commensurate with his view of the exclusivity and indivisibility of political power. He has been aided in this endeavour by the most salient feature of the pre-war economy, which has in no sense been eroded by the war itself: the overwhelming role of the state. The vast increase in oil revenues, due to the price rises of the 1970s, have meant, as Hanna Batatu points out, that the state has acquired a vital measure of financial autonomy and that consequently 'the relationship of individuals or groups to property has receded in importance and control of the apparatus of government has become the determinant of social action more conclusively than before'.[65] It is through this agency and the imperatives of government control that the economic effects of the war have been felt in Iraq.

In the first area, that of the revenues available to the government, it is of course self-evident that war is a costly business not only in human, but also in financial, terms. This has particular implications, however, for Saddam Hussein and for his tenure of power. Fundamental to the idea of a mass-based autocracy is the notion that absolute power can be justified not only by the manipulation of symbolic values through myth, but also by the material improvement of the lot of the people. This could be said to be an endeavour to purchase legitimacy *ex post facto* by attending to material wants, as a substitute for granting any meaningful share in power. Lavish expenditure on the servants of the state was supplemented by equally lavish expenditure on development projects. These were targeted either at particular communities whose loyalty was suspect, such as the Kurds and the Shi'a, or at the generality of Iraqis. The hope was that such a visible improvement in their standard of living would ensure their acquiescence to the regime responsible for that improvement.[66]

Development and its benefits were seen to be a fundamental part of the regime's attempt to legitimize itself and thus to reinforce the foundations of its power. The ability to 'deliver the revolution' was an element in Saddam Hussein's justification for his claim to power, as it had been for the Ba'th as a whole since 1968. Indeed, the identification of this feature as the regime's principal achievement has been constant in his efforts to project the idea of a common Iraqi identity defined and protected by his own leadership. In addition, he has sought to justify the degree of obedience which he demanded, with reference to his unique ability to protect the welfare of Iraqis from the envy of others who feared the success of the regime in creating prosperity and economic justice where none had existed before. This was to be an oft-repeated theme after 1982, as Saddam Hussein sought to explain to his subjects what exactly was at stake in the war, and why they were beginning to suffer a certain amount of economic hardship.[67]

The fact that until that date Saddam Hussein's regime had successfully insulated the Iraqi people from the economic effects of the war, at enormous economic cost, testifies to the importance attached by the Iraqi leadership to this aspect of its relationship with its subjects. After nine months of war, the Minister of Industry and Minerals could boast that the government had signed $2.7 billion worth of contracts for industrial projects and that it was going ahead with its planned development regardless.[68] Visitors to Baghdad noted the continued feverish pace of construction in the capital, the plentiful supply of consumer goods, the absence of a blackout and the curious lack of the impression of a city at war in a country where the investment budget for 1981 had increased by 28 per cent. The total value of contracts signed in that year for development projects, capital equipment, and consumer goods alone totalled $24.3 billion.[69] These expenditures were going ahead despite the fact that Iraq was estimated to be spending between $500 million and $1 billion per month on the prosecution of the war itself. In addition, during the first few days of the war Iraqi oil exports had been more than halved through Iranian military action, leading to a fall in revenues from oil exports from $26.1 billion in 1980 to $10.4 billion in 1981.[70]

It was only towards the end of 1982 and the beginning of 1983 that Saddam Hussein was finally forced to concede that 'we need to adjust our economic conditions in the light of the circumstances of the war', as he warned the country of austerity to come.[71] Syria's closure of Iraq's major oil pipeline in April 1982, the running down of Iraq's foreign-exchange reserves, which had stood at an estimated $35 billion in 1980, the increasing cost of the line of fortifications along the border with Iran, as well as the need to replace much of the equipment lost during the war, and the possible reluctance of some of Iraq's regional allies to continue subsidizing it on the scale to which it had become accustomed – all of these inescapable constraints on the revenue available to the regime obliged it to recognize that the costs of the war could no longer be borne by the state Exchequer alone.

Initially, the government had attempted to disguise the distortions of the labour market caused by increased conscription by importing foreign labour on a massive scale. In 1983 it was estimated that nearly 35 out of every 100 in the Iraqi workforce were serving in the armed forces and that these had been replaced by a claimed 2 million foreign workers.[72] The cost of the remittances which they sent out of the country was, however, becoming apparent. Measures were taken to restrict this flow of capital, enforced occasionally with considerable harshness in order to deter evasion.[73] For Iraqi nationals, currency transfers were forbidden, as was foreign travel, except for government officials; the Dinar was devalued; imports of consumer goods were drastically reduced. In addition, the government instituted a campaign to encourage the donation of substantial sums of private wealth to the war effort. The alleged voluntary nature of these contributions was used by the regime as an illustration of the solidarity of the people behind its leadership, although it seems that there was little voluntary about it.[74]

With inflation running at an estimated 28 per cent, these measures brought home to the population the economic cost of the war. Nevertheless, the regime was clearly determined that, despite economic constraints, certain sensitive communities should not be dramatically affected, hence the grants to Kurdish and Shi'a areas. It also involved those families who had lost a relative in the fighting. The latter now received a number of direct economic benefits, ranging from cash grants to gifts of land and loans to finance house building, as well as easier access to higher education.[75] Despite the rallying calls for greater sacrifice in the name of the Iraqi nation and its leadership, it was apparent that Saddam Hussein did not have great faith in the capacity of the spirit of collective endeavour to overcome the real hardships of the war.[76] Attempting to soften the blow through economic largesse still seemed to be the appropriate strategy.

This was made manifest as the revenues of the government increased after 1983: substantial loans were negotiated from Western Europe, Japan and the United States; contributions were forthcoming from Saudi Arabia and Kuwait, in the form of financial aid and oil 'loans'; the expansion of the existing pipeline through Turkey and the construction of a new one through Saudi Arabia brought the prospect of a large increase in oil exports. The financial resources thus acquired were put not only towards the military effort, but once again towards the improvement of living conditions by increasing imports, continuing the subsidization of basic items and stepping up investment in the local production of consumer goods.[77] The burden of debt thus acquired was considerable, but as a massive debtor in an apparently precarious military position, the Iraqi Government found that it was in a relatively strong bargaining position vis-à-vis its creditors. At the same time, it was evident that the regime viewed the internal and external efforts to survive as inseparable, and consequently equally deserving of the scale of expenditure that would ensure such survival – even if this meant that economic resources were put to rather exotic uses at times.[78]

Although Saddam Hussein could publicly declare that 'frugality will lead to final victory', this was not a policy which he himself could afford to pursue.[79] An estimate of the overall cost of the war up to 1985, including military expenditure, lost oil revenues, and losses in Gross National Product, but excluding the war damage, puts it at $175.7 billion.[80] Whatever the accuracy of this figure, there can be little doubt that the economic cost has been on a truly massive scale. Yet, largely because the cost has been borne by the past and future production of a resource – oil – which is detached in some important ways from the social relations of production, it has not been transmitted into the fabric of society itself, as would be the case in a highly industrialized society. This has given the regime, in the short term at least, the latitude to attend to the wants of a mass society accustomed to being pensioners of the state, while at the same time financing the equally crucial military effort. These are short-term calculations based on the immediate requirements of political survival on both fronts, bolstered by the belief that Iraq's proven oil reserves will offset – in the long term – its present indebtedness.

At the same time, the war has provided Saddam Hussein with the opportunity, sometimes disguised as necessity, of attending to the social relations of production in agriculture and in industry. The marked increase in the encouragement of the private sector in both these areas testifies to his belief not only in the economic utility of such a development, but also in its political utility. The latter feature had been perceived by Saddam Hussein as an important contribution to his rise to absolute power. The cultivation and patronage of private entrepreneurs were undertaken secure in the knowledge that the regime possessed the predominant economic resources of the state through its control of oil revenues. However, the promise of greater economic liberalization appealed to an important constituency within Iraq and within the Ba'th, since in many respects the success of private entrepreneurs was due to close family and other connections with members of the party and state hierarchy. By encouraging this sector, therefore, Saddam Hussein was simultaneously encouraging the emergence of a group whose economic interests would be closely bound up with the survival of his own highly personalized rule, and outflanking the more doctrinaire socialists of the Ba'th to whom he did not intend to be beholden. It was to be a means of transforming the Ba'th into an organization wholly subordinated to his will, and of cementing the loyalty of the 'insiders' whom he was expected to reward.[81]

This process had begun long before the outbreak of war. However, the war, coinciding with and in some senses contributing to the entrenchment of Saddam Hussein's autocracy, has hastened its development. In agriculture, the number of collective farms has been reduced by more than a third since 1980 and the number of agricultural co-operatives has undergone a similarly dramatic reduction. In 1983, following the reinforcement of Saddam Hussein's power at the 9th Ba'th Congress in 1982, Law 35 was promulgated, giving government blessing to the privatization of agriculture.[82] At the same time, the final report of the Congress was published (the delay of some six months has been taken to indicate Saddam Hussein's need to overcome considerable resistance to his personal takeover of the Ba'th). It not only contained a scathing attack on the record of the public sector and on the socialist measures which had brought it into existence, but also explicitly urged the expansion of the private sector. This was to be justified not only in terms of greater economic efficiency, but also with reference to the demands which the war effort was making on the economy. The marked rise in output of some domestically produced food items, especially those which are capital-intensive, appears to have vindicated the government's claim that by encouraging this form of enterprise both consumer and producer would benefit.[83] Certainly, the regime itself seems to have benefited. The assured supply of foodstuffs to the markets of the capital has been an important part of its effort to convince the Iraqi people that their leaders can cope with the effects of the war. Equally, the economic interests of the producers appear to have been guaranteed by the regime, helping to create a significant constituency of support.

This led to the deregulation of prices in 1987, whereby the state maintained subsidies on basic items but the entrepreneurs who were responsible for marketing a wide variety of products were able to make a substantial profit. This accorded with Saddam Hussein's directive that 'an active and prosperous private sector' should be created as a supplement and encouragement to the state sector. In his exhortation that 'all officials have to pay as much attention to economic affairs as to political ideology', he was suggesting that such considerations were likely to be more effective both in sustaining the Iraqi war effort and in maintaining support for the regime.[84]

It remains true that the majority of those who have gained most spectacularly from these liberalizing policies are those who have managed to make the most of the opportunities offered by their close relationship by blood or background with members of the regime. Nevertheless, there are many others who have also gained thereby, becoming in some senses beneficiaries but also dependants of the state. The advantages of this system for Saddam Hussein are twofold. First, economic interests can cut across and overcome communal or sectarian interests. This was indeed the procedure used by the *ancien régime* under the monarchy, to end the rebelliousness of the Shi'i tribal sheikhs and integrate them into the dominant economic structure of Iraq. Similarly, the expulsion of many nominally Iranian Shi'a in 1980 and the confiscation of their property made the subsequent beneficiaries of government land sales in some respects accomplices in the regime's action, regardless of sectarian identification. At the same time, it has been noticeable that a number of the leaders of the Shi'a community have been engaged in real estate and capital investment, profiting from the regime's intention to grant them a measure of economic power as a substitute for political power. Meanwhile, Saddam Hussein can represent this process as evidence of 'service to the homeland' at a time of supreme national crisis.[85]

The second advantage is that Saddam Hussein is helping to create a class of state dependants, who cannot hope to challenge the economic power of the state, and who see their interests best served by placating it and those who control it. Isam al-Khafaji cites a revealing instance in July 1983 when Saddam Hussein summoned a group of Iraqi contractors and persuaded them to increase their 'voluntary' contributions to the war effort, by reminding them that the state had made their fortunes and it was now their turn to help the state. At a similar meeting, convened for the same purpose, he threatened his audience with 'the anger of the masses'.[86] This is the authentic voice of the man who has constructed a 'mass-based autocracy': the apparent direct communion which he enjoys with his mass constituency is used not only to placate the latter, but also to intimidate those who are in reality closer to the inside circle of decision-making and power. The war can thus be used as a pretext both for advancing the economic interests of the people needed to sustain the structure of the state, and for ensuring that they remain subservient to Saddam Hussein's will. If they show any signs of independent, let alone opposition, activity, he will not hesitate to point out that 'the enemies are not only in Khomeini's trenches but are also those [in Iraq] who tamper with the people's resources'.[87] As in the case of the six Iraqi businessmen executed on charges of corruption in August 1986, examples can, if necessary, be made, and punishments appropriate to wartime enemies of the state meted out.[88]

In a regime of this nature, where the dominant political impulse is that of the autocrat seeking absolute control of his environment, economic resources and the economic interests of particular sectors of society are assessed only insofar as they aid his objectives. War cannot be allowed to interfere with this. In Iraq, the effort by Saddam Hussein to ensure that the financial burden of the war should neither weaken nor significantly alter the structure on which his power is based has been a constant preoccupation. Indeed without it, the war effort itself would be meaningless. The long-term indebtedness of the Iraqi state and the possible future political implications of the promotion of a class of capitalist entrepreneurs with strong links to the hierarchies of that state are consequences both of the war and of Saddam Hussein's efforts to mediate its effects. They may eventually prove fatal to him and his style of government, but there can be little doubt that in the short term these two features have been instrumental in enabling him to survive 'the war on two fronts'.

The armed forces

The use of force to achieve or retain political power has been a constant theme of Iraqi politics. Consequently, it has been of prime concern to all Iraqi leaders that they should pay close attention to the loyalties and ambitions of the officer corps of the armed forces. For the leaders of the Ba'th who emerged after the short-lived experience of Ba'thist rule in 1963 this lesson was driven home with particular sharpness, since failure to do so had cost the party its hold on power. In 1968, it was their turn to use the armed forces as the vehicle for their return to power. This was made possible not only through the exploitation of their military sympathizers, but also by the fact that a number of the leading Ba'thists were themselves officers in the army. The most prominent of these, Ahmad Hassan al-Bakr, was to become President of Iraq and Chairman of the RCC until he was replaced in 1979 by Saddam Hussein. The latter, however, clearly perceived the danger to his own position as a non-military figure from those in the leadership who could back up their claims to power with the following they had accrued within the armed forces. The history of the early years of Ba'thist rule is largely that of the attempt by Saddam Hussein – and others – to ensure the expulsion, and in some cases liquidation, of these military Ba'thists. By the early 1970s, this had largely been achieved, leaving only al-Bakr, Saddam Hussein's uncle, in a position of considerable, although not absolute, power.[89]

It was under the auspices of al-Bakr and Saddam Hussein, therefore, that a massive programme of military expansion was initiated, facilitated first by Soviet aid and then by the growing oil revenues at the disposal of the government. Two features of this expansion were noteworthy. First, the regime was clearly endeavouring to construct a military organization commensurate with its own ambitions internally and in the region. To this end, the professional and technical capabilities of the armed forces were enhanced in order to equip them to perform the most pressing military task of subduing Kurdish guerrilla activity, as well as to pose as a fitting expression of Iraqi state power in the region.[90] Secondly, the regime was equally determined that such an orientation should not lead to the formation of a collective corporate identity independent of its own control. Consequently, parallel with the expansion of the armed forces came the expansion of the means by which the state leadership could continue to exert close surveillance over the officer corps. This was to be achieved through direct patronage and the appointment of kinsmen to key positions in the military hierarchy. It was supplemented by the activities of the Ba'th party Military Bureau, responsible for vetting officer cadets, for implanting Ba'thist political guidance officers in military units, and for making recommendations on questions of promotion and transfer based on the perceived political loyalties of the officers in question. For the Ba'thist faithful, whom Saddam Hussein was still obliged to cultivate, this could be justified by the proclaimed intention of creating 'the Ideological Army' with an explicit dual purpose: to be a militant instrument of the Ba'th party, fulfilling the party's objectives, and to be an active and modern fighting force, capable of rapid and effective deployment.[91]

When Saddam Hussein assumed absolute power in 1979, promoting himself to Field Marshal in the process, he could feel reassured that he had at his command a politically reliable and militarily effective instrument. As a deterrent to any ambitious officers whose political affiliations had somehow escaped the net of surveillance and who might be tempted to challenge his primacy, special units had long been in existence whose main function was to guard against such an eventuality. These included not only the Republican Guard, the Special Forces and the armoured brigades of the Baghdad Garrison, but also the militia of the Popular Army. Under the command of a close associate of Saddam Hussein, Taha Yasin Ramadhan, this formation had undergone a steady expansion since the mid-1970s and represented as much an obstacle to

Saddam Hussein's enemies within the Ba'th as to any attempted military takeover.[92]

It took the first few months of the war to impress upon the political leadership that political control and military efficiency might not necessarily be compatible, and indeed that the requirements of the former might seriously impair the latter. Nevertheless, as far as Saddam Hussein was concerned, military success without the political subordination of the military organization itself was meaningless, if not positively dangerous. The attempt to accommodate these two fundamental requirements has been a constant theme of the regime's efforts to manage both the situation on the battlefront and the domestic political dimensions of the conflict. At times, the strain which has resulted between Saddam Hussein and individual military commanders has been noticeable. However, equally noteworthy has been the relative success with which Saddam Hussein has managed this crucial constituency. In many respects the fact of war, as well as the nature of the war itself during the past seven years, has allowed this to happen.

Perhaps the most dangerous time for Saddam Hussein was in the period 1980–82. It was then that the disabling effects of close political supervision of the armed forces' operations became most noticeable and that the political premise on which the invasion of Iran had been based was shown to be false. Saddam Hussein appeared to allude to these problems himself, both at the time and later, when assessing the relative weaknesses and strengths of the Iraqi armed forces before and after the forced withdrawal from Iranian territory in 1982.[93] While some military commanders may have grown restive at the constraints under which they were forced to operate, and may have questioned the purpose of the war itself, the political leadership, possibly as a way of disguising the political failure of the enterprise, seemed inclined to blame the professional incompetence of some of the senior commanders. Inappropriate military doctrine and the failings of individual officers, it was implied, had contributed to the inability of the armed forces to achieve the war aims determined by the political leaders. Following the success of the Iranian forces in 1982, this crisis appears to have come to a head (as did the crisis of political leadership itself within the Ba'th). From it, Saddam Hussein emerged strengthened, having succeeded in eliminating those who questioned his leadership both within the Ba'th and within the armed forces.[94]

He had been able to achieve this, in part because of his ruthless political skills, but also because the nature of the war itself allowed him to make common cause with his military commanders in a way which no amount of Ba'thist indoctrination had been able to achieve. The war had unmistakably become one for the defence both of Iraq and of the political system from which the largely Sunni officer corps had derived considerable benefits. Based on this community of interest, a form of tacit contract appears to have emerged between Saddam Hussein and the senior officers. Professional competence was now to be rewarded and the high command was to be drawn into a process of apparently collegial decision-making with the political leadership. They were to be jointly engaged on the relatively uncontroversial task of defeating the initiatives of the external enemy. To this end, increasing financial and technical resources were devoted to the armed forces, presenting them with a professional challenge. Facing up to this challenge and mastering it underlined the specialized function of the armed forces, and demanded their energies and attention. At the same time, it coincided with the supreme political desideratum of Saddam Hussein: the solidarity and efficiency of the armed forces in defeating the Iranian military onslaught and the political objectives which lay behind it.[95]

With the success of the armed forces in blunting the Iranian offensives during the following years, this system paid considerable dividends. Saddam Hussein's personal links with the armed forces were reinforced, strengthening his position vis-à-vis other groups within the country. While the overall strategy which was responsible for the massive casualties inflicted on the Iranian forces was attributed to Saddam Hussein's military genius, it was noticeable that individual officers were increasingly praised for the efficiency and determination with which they executed this strategy.[96] In explicit recognition of the identity between the defence of Iraq and the defence of the regime, Saddam Hussein despatched units of his Republican Guard to key sectors of the front, stating that 'special guards who do not fight in defence of Iraq in Sulaymaniyya, Basra and the Misan borders, cannot defend the regime in the Presidential Palace'.[97] Furthermore, he publicly acknowledged the debt which the state and the Ba'thist revolution owed to the army when he praised its continuity as an institution and its contribution to the economic, political and social development of the country.[98]

The emphasis placed on the professional identity of the armed forces and on their dedication to the goals appropriate to them as a military organization, did not imply any lessening of the degree of political control Saddam Hussein expected to exert. 'Political guidance' officers were still very much in evidence to supervise loyalty, although their role in military operations was reportedly reduced. Saddam Hussein's personal favouritism and his determination to cement personal loyalties through blood ties were equally obvious. The judgments passed on officers according to criteria of professional competence also allowed him considerable latitude in the dismissal or transfer of officers who might have felt resentful at the conditions under which they were expected to carry out their duties. Nor would such resentment find much echo among their peers when the latter could clearly perceive the nature of the external threat, and saw in the failure of colleagues an opportunity for their own advancement. In addition, the reports of disagreements in the collegial atmosphere of the

National Defence Council were not evidence of political dissent so much as substitutes for it. These were arguments about the most efficient means to achieve a common political end.[99]

As might be expected, cracks in this system have become evident in the face of military reverses. This was the case in 1986, when the Iranian capture of Fao and the misjudged Iraqi attempt to 'compensate' for this loss by the occupation of Mehran placed considerable strain on the relationship between Saddam Hussein and some of his military commanders. The public nature of these setbacks meant that they could not be disguised. Consequently, both the 'military genius' of the political leadership and the military efficiency of the army commanders were thrown into question, leading to mutual recriminations and a sense of future unease. Reportedly, the frustration of the Iraqi forces' attempts to recapture Fao led to a confrontation between Saddam Hussein and one of his senior army commanders, Major-General Mahir Abd al-Rashid. The latter comes from the same village as Saddam Hussein and is related to him by marriage. He had been placed in overall command of the three columns attempting to dislodge the Iranians from their positions on the Fao peninsula but his failure to do so, according to one account, caused Saddam Hussein to recall him to Baghdad with the intention of disgracing him. This intention was thwarted, however, when the officers under Abd al-Rashid's command threatened in effect to go on strike unless he was confirmed in his position. Thereupon, Saddam Hussein backed down and Abd al-Rashid returned to his men. It has not been possible to confirm this account, but there is reason to suppose that Saddam Hussein may have felt threatened by the position which Abd al-Rashid was establishing for himself.

Precisely because he came from the 'insiders' of the regime, Abd al-Rashid had, in previous years, evidently felt that he had the licence to comment extensively on the military situation to the foreign as well as the domestic media. His military success in preventing an Iranian breakthrough after their offensive in the Majnoon islands and his later recapture of these islands had made him something of a national hero.[100] Perhaps even more disturbing for Saddam Hussein were the implications of his outspoken comments to a delegation from the Kuwaiti National Assembly when the Iraqi forces under his command were halted on the Fao peninsula. He stated then that the Iraqis had suffered 'huge casualties', that he was simply waiting 'until the Iraqi leadership allowed him to begin the liberation [of Fao]', and that 'the Kuwaitis, like the Iraqis, had the right to wonder why the final onslaught was delayed'. The fact that he also more or less admitted to using chemical weapons and that the Kuwaitis proceeded to lavish praise on him, rather than on the political leadership he was apparently indicting, cannot have endeared him to Saddam Hussein.[101]

The latter's determination to avoid adding to the 'huge casualties' mentioned by Abd al-Rashid, had been long in evidence. It had, indeed, been part of his perspective on the political utility and the costs of war from the very beginning of hostilities. Nor was he in any mood to change his perspective at this juncture in the war.[102] Yet it was clear that in this instance, the professional judgment of a military officer seemed to require that some such change should be made. This was not a price which Saddam Hussein was willing to pay in order to achieve a military success. Instead, he sought to deflect attention by ordering his army commanders to capture Mehran – a move heralded by the general responsible for its capture as 'a daring expression of the Iraqi leadership's political decision'.[103] When it fell a few months later to the Iranian forces there could be little doubt where the responsibility lay.

This precipitated a crisis in Iraq, to which Saddam Hussein responded by a further tightening of his control within the political structure.[104] As far as his position vis-à-vis the commanders of the armed forces was concerned, it was reported that it had led to a collective decision on their part to curtail his military powers and to forbid him from intervening militarily in the war.[105] Although logical from their point of view, this would seem improbable, at least in the dramatic form in which it was reported. Instead, what appears to have happened is a restatement of the terms of the 'contract' between Saddam Hussein and his military commanders. The latter had demanded and won greater freedom of independent decision-making at the front, without having to refer to Baghdad. They had also been reassured about continued unimpeded access to all the resources in terms of money and matériel which would make their agreed task possible.[106] For his part, Saddam Hussein retained the apparatus of political surveillance and patronage throughout the armed forces which ensured that such independence of action at the front would not lead to any dangerous thoughts about the dispensation of power in Baghdad. At the same time, it was noticeable that he reinforced his personal following at the 'collegial' meetings between himself and the armed forces commanders by bringing in on a regular basis his dependant, Latif Nussayyif al-Jasim, the Minister of Culture and Information, as well as, and more pertinently, Ali Hasan al-Majid, his kinsman, the Director General of Security.[107]

The effect of the war on the armed forces has, therefore, been to orient them towards a professional task, technically defined. It is a professional task, however, carried out within the setting of the Iraqi political system of which they constitute an important element. It has been Saddam Hussein's endeavour to ensure that he should remain the dominant element in that system, and consequently he has sought to mediate the demands which their wartime professional requirements make of him, while retaining overall control. This has so far been achieved by the methods outlined above. However, there is always a danger that, irrespective of serious political differences, of which there is at present scant evidence, given the nature of the war, the very professionalism of the armed forces may breed a sense of collective, corporate identity and interest. There is clearly some potential here for severe conflict with the political leadership should perceptions on the utility of the war, or on the best means of conducting it, change. Whilst this was certainly far from being his intention, Major-General Hamid Ahmad al-Ward's article in praise of Saddam Hussein, published in *Al-Thawra*, could be interpreted as containing a hint of future menace:[108]

> It is no exaggeration to say that President Saddam Hussein would not have made a fateful decision, such as the one to counter the aggression, had he not taken into account all of the probabilities and reached the perfect conviction that victory would be realized.

Problems are likely to arise if the outcome is in fact considerably less glorious than the anticipated victory.

Conclusion

Seven years of war have tended to demonstrate how well equipped the Iraqi regime has been both ideologically and organizationally to cope with the immediate effects of the state of siege imposed by the war. The perceptions of power, and the means used to ensure its exclusivity, developed in the period preceding the outbreak of war, have in many senses been reinforced by the unmistakable threat posed by Iran. Indeed, in the short term, Saddam Hussein has benefited both from the critical nature of that threat and by its externalization. The former has helped him to assert his authority among his colleagues, the 'insiders' of the regime itself. Realization of their shared collective plight in the face of Iran's stated war aims has led to a tightening of the circle, as well as a certain suspension of their critical faculties in assessing the powers Saddam Hussein claims to need in order to manage the effects of war. In the wider sphere of Iraqi society, the externalization of the threat appears to have had considerable impact. Hitherto government itself was seen by many as a somewhat arbitrary misfortune. Now, however, the Iranian armies, and the political impulse behind them, tend to be seen as a greater one. This may not have changed attitudes towards the government, but it has certainly placed them for the first time within a scale of relative values. Indeed, despite the fact that the war has required real and painful sacrifices, it has also provided many with considerable material opportunities: the officer corps of the army, the entrepreneurial and landed 'classes', whatever their ethnic or sectarian affiliation, and state officials have all discovered that war has given them substantial possibilities to advance their interests, albeit within a framework dictated by the regime.

The crucial question is whether the experience of war has caused any lasting transformations in attitudes to political power or to the personal authority of Saddam Hussein himself. This seems to be a much more dubious contention. In many respects, the very fact that the phenomenon of war has been incorporated with such facility into the fabric of Iraqi politics is testimony to the resilience of the moral and structural universe which underlies those politics. For Saddam Hussein and those around him, war has necessitated pragmatic bargains in order to allow a more effective use of Iraq's human and other resources in the war effort. However, these have been struck on Saddam Hussein's own terms: the question of the dispensation of political power has been specifically excluded. For society at large, and a society as fragmented as that of Iraq, government remains an organ to be placated and feared, despite the exhortations to common effort in repelling the greater threat on the borders. Indeed, in the absence of institutionally guaranteed participation, not simply in the war effort but in the process of government itself, it is difficult to see how this could be otherwise.

The regime has succeeded in mobilizing and arming a large proportion of the Iraqi people as a means of organizing their survival and thus determining their fate as regards the Iranian enemy. This, as Saddam Hussein has not tired of saying, is the 'referendum' by which he himself has been confirmed in power. It has been a deliberate intention of the mechanisms by which this takes place, and of the myths with which it is surrounded, that it should in no way encourage the kinds of sentiments or aspirations which would lead the Iraqis to believe that they have a right to determine their fate as regards their own government. Nevertheless, the question arises as to whether this process in itself, however well controlled, might give rise to such sentiments. Saddam Hussein himself has been proud to state that one of the beneficial effects of mobilization for war has been that[109]

In Iraq, leaders are being built every day ... We had ten efficient political leaders at the beginning of the war; we now have dozens of efficient leaders. We had ten military leaders at the beginning of the war; we now have dozens of better trained and more capable leaders.

Whilst this may be of benefit to the Iraqi war effort, the development of the consciousness of such capability and of the political rights which accompany it, can constitute a challenge both to the regime and to Saddam Hussein.

In some areas, the promotion of a collective consciousness both of power and of the conditions necessary for the efficient exercise of that power, appears already to be occurring. The Kurds, prepared to a certain extent perceptually and organizationally for the exploitation of such opportunities vis-à-vis the Baghdad Government, have clearly been stimulated in this direction by the fact of war. Although important, they remain, however, a province, in more than one sense, of Iraqi politics.

More interesting, but by its very nature considerably less easy to discover, is the degree to which such developments have been taking place within the Iraqi armed forces. It is here that a sense of corporate identity among an increasingly professional officer corps may overlap, or reinforce, other socially given identities to the extent that the 'amateurs' in government are seen to thwart their collective interests on a number of levels. This may constitute a threat of particular sharpness to Saddam Hussein and his own clan.[110]

For the rest of Iraqi society, however, the effects of war, and the management of those effects by the regime, appear to have led to its further atomization, as individuals concentrate on the tasks of surviving both government and Iranian attention. In the short term, this has made the society more malleable in the hands of the regime, although it seems also to have produced the relatively frequent, but significantly isolated, attempts on Saddam Hussein's life. Personal extinction is, after all, the basic flaw in the autocratic system of power. In the longer term, this very fragmentation, and the anomie it engenders, may contribute to the underlying instability of Iraqi politics. In the absence of any institutions given legitimacy and permanence by popular participation, there are few ways of transforming the current apparent collective solidarity in the face of the Iranian threat, into long-term collective acceptance of the Iraqi regime and the political system on which it is based.

This is precisely the dilemma of autocracy. In a 'mass-based autocracy' which is engaged in war, the dilemma is particularly acute. War appears to have frozen political attitudes and relations in the modes of exclusivity and mistrust which gave birth to autocracy. At the same time, the relentless appeal to the projected interests of an imagined community which is taken to justify so absolute a hold on power, brings with it the obligation to be seen to serve those interests. This is the mechanism which was to a large extent responsible for the war's initiation, and it seems probable that it will remain in operation at the war's termination. Saddam Hussein may then discover that the very determination with which he has pursued the aim of freeing himself from dependence on any sector of society makes him personally vulnerable. As in the case of previous rulers of Iraq, he may find himself accused of having placed in jeopardy, or of having betrayed, the supposed collective interests by reference to which he had himself once justified his claim to absolute power.

7

Iran: The War and the Economy

Introduction

As with other parts of the society, Iran's revolutionary leaders rejected the economy they inherited. Broadly their goals (rather than their programme) consisted of reversing what they saw to be in existence. Sometimes dressed up as 'Islamic economics', these aims had an intellectual trendiness identified with the 'small is beautiful' and 'dependencia' schools combined with an emphasis on *tiers-mondisme* or Third World solidarity. To replace large industrial projects they emphasized self-sufficiency in agriculture; to escape from the inevitable dependency arising from trade with industrialized countries, they promoted trade with the Third World. They also sought to reduce if not to eliminate the importation of useless consumer goods, and, as we have seen, to reduce military expenditures by creating a citizen or people's army. Oil, the principal motor for economic growth, was to be de-emphasized, production reduced, and reliance on it for foreign exchange sharply cut.

The war with its own needs soon overtook the revolution, first acting as a constraint on the achievement of its aims and subsequently simply displacing them. Speaking at the end of 1987 the Prime Minister chose to emphasize this:[1]

> It can safely be claimed that one can see the seal of war on all the state apparatus. Allocation of some 41 per cent of expenditure in the general budget and over 52 per cent of the total current allocations for the government to military and security affairs is another proof of the value and importance which the government attaches to the issue of the war as the most important problem of the country.

The war has had its own dictates, necessitating increased reliance on oil exports for foreign exchange to finance the purchase of arms and supplies, and high military expenditures to maintain large numbers of men under arms and to continue hostilities. In response, the authorities have improvized by:

i) seeking to keep oil exports flowing at a sufficiently high volume to finance essential imports (arms, food, pharmaceuticals);

ii) substituting men for arms and light for heavy or sophisticated weapons;

iii) diversifying sources of arms and types of weapons systems to increase their flexibility;

iv) increasing indigenous weapons production capabilities to substitute for imports and reduce foreign-exchange outflow.

The demands of the war have not been totally at odds with those of the Islamic republic. The mood of crisis and self-sacrifice, the emphasis on the collectivity over the individual, the urgent requirement for unity that represses dissent, the all-purpose excuse that the war has priority and is responsible for any government shortcomings – none of these elements have been foreign to the thinking of the authorities or, one suspects, completely unwelcome.

Without money or access to financing Iran could scarcely have sustained the war for more than seven years. In this respect, at least, the conflict is not typical of the situation in most developing countries. But if funds are a necessary, they are not a sufficient, condition for explaining the length of the war. For this one must examine the adversaries' political structures and alliances. The impact of the revolution on the Iranian economy has been profound, but its effect on the spirit was still more important. The economy ground to a virtual standstill in 1978–9 in the prelude to, and the aftermath of, the upheaval. The war which followed did so before there was any sign of a recovery or indeed of any coherent national economic planning or programme. Many commentators surveying the scene of 2.5 million unemployed, 30 per cent inflation and an industrial turnover at some 40 per cent of the pre-revolutionary period believed (like Eric Rouleau) that, without a major improvement, the authorities faced serious political discontent.[2] But this underestimated the moral transformation launched by the revolution and assessed it by 'normal' criteria. In addition to becoming accustomed to diminished material expectations, the people engaged in the revolution judged the government by different standards; the regime's legitimacy gave it greater leeway and consequently greater resilience to deal with scarcity and adversity. Indeed, it was part of the regime's ideology and continuing refrain that it represented a spiritual revolution that did not set out to improve the material well-being of the people but to see to their spiritual and moral needs. The authorities were thus managing a less demanding nation and could call upon the vast reserves of goodwill, support and sense of solidarity that existed between the people and the revolutionary leadership to surmount or at least tolerate what might, in another political context, have been impossible.

The Iranian Government was relatively secure and confident of its capacity to call upon the nation for sacrifice, but it was not oblivious to the need to placate its revolutionary constituency. It treated the war as an 'opportunity', a chance to extol the virtues of sacrifice and self-reliance. At the same time, it did not neglect its core constituency, and tailored its economic policies to meet their needs while squeezing those it did not consider true revolutionaries, believers or 'oppressed'. Nor did its rhetoric interfere with its willingness to exercise pragmatic restraint and compromise (for instance, in OPEC) when its interests so dictated. And it showed considerable ingenuity in devising means to maintain the flow of oil, repair installations, defend terminals and find markets.

Although oil accounts for some 80 per cent of government revenues and 90 per cent of foreign-exchange earnings, without which no modern war of such duration would have been possible, the oil factor has also been a complication. In theory, it has been the country's Achilles heel, open to attack on its vulnerable infrastructure. In practice, this failed to materialize on a significant scale in the early period of the war. Nevertheless, because of price fluctuations and the related uncertainty about export volumes, planning has been difficult. Oil prices tripled in 1979–80, providing the Islamic republic with a windfall that enabled it to earn adequate revenues while reducing production. Hashemi Rafsanjani could observe in late 1982 that with an average production of 1 million barrels/day since the beginning of the war, Iran was able to manage very well because of the tripling of prices.[3] But the fluctuations were not only in one direction. From 1984, because of more accurate and aggressive bombing by Iraq, Iran's oil exports were reduced. From 1985 weakened demand for Gulf oil slashed the price from around $30 to $10 a barrel, stabilizing somewhat throughout 1987 at $18/barrel. Combined with the slide in the value of the dollar (in which oil prices are denominated) and the specific difficulties Iran had in maintaining the level of its exports, anticipating annual oil revenues became a hazardous enterprise. In each

Table 7.1   Chart of revenue fluctuations ($ bn)

	Military expenditures[a]	Oil revenues
1980–81	4.2	approx. 12
1981–82	4.4	approx. 12
1982–83	15.5	23
1983–84	17.37	18
1984–85	20.16	12.5
1985–86	14.891	12.0
1986–87	15.89	6–8

[a] Military expenditure figures are approximate at best.
  Adapted from International Institute for Strategic Studies, *Military Balance* (annual/ 1980/81–1986/7); *Middle East Economic Digest* 1980–87; *Middle East Economic Survey* and published Iranian sources.

year since the record $23 billion in 1982–3, Iran's actual revenues have failed to come close to those projected. See Table 7.1 above.

Oil prices have fluctuated and production and export volumes have varied. Exports were 700,000 b/d in November 1980; by Spring 1982 they were 1.5 million b/d, and in the following year they averaged 2.3 million b/d. Thereafter fluctuations in the market and Iraq's extension of the war made anticipation of oil revenues much more difficult. It should be emphasized that this has occurred precisely at the time when the needs for financing the war have increased, for the demands of the war have not been the same from year to year. Indeed, one could usefully divide the war into two principal phases, 1980–84 and 1984–87.

In the first period it remained a species of frontier war, Iran's oil exports were relatively unscathed by Iraq's attacks, and the Islamic republic was able to rely on stocks of weapons systems inherited from the Shah. For Iran this was a manpower-intensive phase of the war. As a consequence, the war made claims on only 15–20 per cent of the government's revenues, and there was talk of investment in development continuing alongside the war effort.[4]

The second period, witnessing an intensification and geographical expansion of the conflict to the Gulf's waters and Iran's inland cities, was also the period when access to new sources of arms supplies became necessary owing to the attrition of existing stocks. It also became more difficult, because of the arms embargo that the United States in particular sought (with considerable success) to impose on Iran. In this phase, the Iranian authorities admitted that the war was costing more than a third of the national budget and argued that it was responsible for inflation and shortages and that it must assume absolute priority.[5] The war came to be equated with 'our life' and, as a clearcut military victory continued to be elusive, while the economic costs of the war increased, the Iranian leaders in 1986 sought to find a means of using their advantages in numbers and individual motivation to bring the war to a victorious conclusion. They were unambiguous in attributing the new sense of urgency to economic pressures. Hence the reliance (after February 1986) on a 'final offensive' to end the war can be traced to the economic conditions arising from it.[6]

The war has imposed uneven demands on the Islamic republic in its first seven years. In the first period both guns and butter appeared possible as revenues soared to $23 billion in 1982–3. The consistent revenue decline thereafter has posed political choices for the authorities. In 1983–4 they chose not to alienate their constituency in the bazaar, and opted for deficit financing rather than the restriction of 'non-essential' imports. After 1984 they clamped down on imports but ensured that their loyal supporters had access to goods and supplies and were insulated from the costs of the war. Although it has resorted to counter-trade the Islamic republic has avoided borrowing. While it has the advantage of a broad political base and a mobilized and 'aware' population inured to sacrifice and deprivation, it has been handicapped in the prosecution of the war by an inability to gain access to compatible and complete weapons systems from other governments (as opposed to the rather more expensive and haphazard arms market). Nor does Iran have any rich or generous allies, a fact which compounds the problems of financing the war, and which serves to stress the quite different conditions of the two adversaries: Iran, self-reliant, innovative and committed, contrasted with Iraq a 'dependent tool', awash with money, pampered by allies, but unable to defeat its united enemy.

The economics of war

Wars can be short or long, sustained or sporadic, limited or total, but without funds they would not be possible on a significant scale for very long. Economic factors may strengthen or weaken the war effort, affect the cost calculations of the belligerents, and make them more amenable to outside pressure, or to domestic pressures arising from the war. If the stakes in the war are limited and the adversaries are in some sort of communication, the conflict can be wound down, made the subject of negotiations, or the issue conceded by one side. In the present conflict, none of these conditions obtained as long as Khomeini saw the stakes in the war in absolute terms, motivated the people accordingly, and had the national means to prosecute the war. The economic dimension is of interest here insofar as it can demonstrate the relationship between oil income and the ability to finance the war, sketch the relationship between economic resources and the conduct of the war, examine in general terms the cost of the war and discuss the political management of an economy at war.

For convenience, we shall start by breaking down the direct costs of the war into three categories; those directly affecting its prosecution, those arising from war damage, and the particular set of costs relating to the oil industry, including the production and export of oil, repairs, and defence.

– Direct costs include: increased military expenditures, arms purchases, etc.; expansion of the armed forces; the need for more doctors, imported pharmaceuticals, etc.

– Damage: to agriculture, industries, installations, ports, etc.; relocation of refugees; manpower losses (deaths, invalids); martyr subsidies, etc.

– Oil industry: Abadan refinery; repair and defence of other terminals, e.g. Kharg, Ghanaveh; costs of shuttle, hiring, convoying and storage; discounting and subsidizing oil exports to cover risk premiums.

Using different classifications, the Iranian Government has claimed that the war had cost it in cumulative damage, up to September 1985, $309 billion, of which $160 billion was in the oil sector.[ ] More recently, the Minister of Economy, Irfani, put the figure at $150 billion.[8] In 1985, Hashemi Rafsanjani, reflecting the tendency to attribute all the country's difficulties to the war, said:[9]

> If we had spent the budget allocation of four and a half years of the imposed war, that is 4,000–5,000 billion rials ($43.4–54.3 billion), on industry, today we would be one of the most powerful industrial countries in the world.

Such talk demonstrates a surprising amnesia about the expressed intent of the Islamic authorities to de-industralize Iran, but it does capture the sense of the astronomic costs of the war.

The actual costs of waging the war are sensitive to starting assumptions and vary with the sources used. Hence these figures can only be suggestive. The costs can be broken down into manpower costs, replacement of arms and operating costs. Without counting volunteers in the Basij, we know that the military, both regulars and revolutionary guards, have tripled from some 204,000 in 1980 to 705,000.[10] Arms imports are more difficult to cost accurately. Sources in Washington put total arms imports in the period 1979–86 at $9 billion, with $5.2 billion in 1979–83, and $3.8 billion in 1984–6.[11] These figures would appear to be conservative. Purchases on the open market are notoriously expensive and of uneven quality, and the attempts by Iran to circumvent the US arms embargo have entailed a willingness to pay considerably more than the market price for the items desired. Rafsanjani implied in late 1986 that Iran was spending in one year $1.5 billion on arms purchases. We may take this figure as the average (or more likely minimum) annual cost of purchases. Another source, for example, put defence spending at $3 billion in foreign exchange *plus* 1 billion rials.[12]

Bearing in mind Iran's reliance on manpower over technology, we must suppose that the true costs of the war are likely to be in operating costs and above all in that of volunteer manpower, which we cannot begin to cost here. Estimates as to operating costs are indicative. In mid-1984 an informed Western source calculated that the war cost $250 million a month *in foreign exchange alone*. By the following year, the same source quoted *total* costs at $300 million a month and $500 million for offensives.[13] Iranian sources have noted that the defence budget more than tripled between 1979–80 and 1984–5. However, in the draft budget for 1985–6, the direct allocation to the war was half that of 'war-related' expenses, including relocation of war refugees, subsidies to martyrs' families, etc., totalling $12.8 billion for the year.[14] In the following year, while actual revenues shrank by 50 per cent (against anticipated revenues), the defence budget was increased by 12.5 per cent or some $300 million to $4.53 billion, and additional or supplemental allocations of $500 million were later made to the revolutionary guards and the military. In the 1987–8 budget approved by the Majles, the *foreign exchange* allocation for the war was increased to $2.8 billion from the $2 billion requested, and the total defence budget was *increased* by $3.6 billion *more* than that requested by the government. Yet Rafsanjani was claiming in May that Iran fought 'cheaply', spending less than $3 billion.[15]

Estimating military expenditure is normally difficult enough; in wartime it becomes more so. It is clear that Iran's expenses have fluctuated. To take the figures in Table 7.1 as suggestive rather than definitive, one could note that from an early figure of $4.2 billion (in 1980–81) they tripled to $15.5 and then to $17.3 billion in 1982–3 and 1983–4, and then rose again to some $20 billion in 1984–5, declining to $15 billion in 1985–6, and possibly to some $16 billion in both 1986–7 and 1987–8.[16] The variation can be accounted for by the wearing down of stock and the cost of replacement, fluctuations in the tempo of the war, and the growth in the numbers of war casualties and refugees.

What seems clear is that the war is costing more at a time when foreign-exchange receipts are fluctuating, no longer growing, and indeed are generally less dependable, *and* when the other costs of the war, infrastructure damage and plant and equipment attrition, are also increasing. In March 1986–March 1987 (Iranian year 1365) 'the government had the smallest amount of foreign exchange income in the past twelve years. However, it allocated more foreign exchange and rials to the war in comparison to previous years.'[17]

The situation is by no means hopeless. One bright spot is the fact that the current account deficit is thought to be running at less than $1 billion a year. Iran now owes only some $5.6 billion in trade credits.[18] Against this it is believed to have $5–6 billion in foreign reserves. (Contrast the situation of Iraq with rich allies and with a foreign debt of $64 billion.)

A second area of relative strength and resilience is in the build-up of a domestic arms industry. This serves three functions: to affirm the belief in self-reliance; to substitute for expensive imports; and to insulate Iran's war effort from any international embargo that might be imposed on arms sales. Iran's strategy in the war, as we have seen, has always emphasized the decisive role of ground forces and individual commitment over technology. The soldiers of the Islamic republic are thus equipped with light arms, and conveniently these can be produced mostly at home.

Officials compete in extolling the virtues and productivity of the indigenous arms industry. A Deputy Minister for Industries was established within the Ministry of the Islamic Republic Guards Corps (IRGC or Pasdaran) in 1983, responsible for the work of 13 industrial groups charged with research related to arms production. This includes work on retro-fitting, reconditioning and repair of existing equipment as well as the production of munitions, shells, light arms, work on anti-tank missiles, air defence (SAM) and surface-to-surface missiles (e.g. the *Oghab*, an adapted *Scud* SSM missile), and continuing research on the future production of submarines, aircraft, and drones (remotely piloted

vehicles) used for reconnaissance and intelligence.[19] The Guards
Minister Rafiqdust claims that Iran can now produce 70–80 percent of its
own ammunition; and the Guards Corps Commander, Reza'i, also claims
that it is self-sufficient in bullets and mortar shells, and produces RPG-7s
and other anti-tank missiles and will soon manufacture SAMs and
SSMs.[20]

The current Defence Minister has reported that Iran can now produce
47 types of ammunition (as against 7 in 1979) thus saving a considerable
amount of foreign exchange. The Guards Commander has put a figure to
this saving which he says amounted to $1.5 billion in 1986–7 and should
increase in 1987–8 as production quintuples. Prime Minister Musavi in
presenting his budget for 1988–9 (1367) to the Majles dwelt at length on
the import substitution made possible by domestic arms production,
without giving any precise figure for it.[21]

One of the costs of the war has been in the agricultural sector. The
initial fighting was in one of the richer agricultural provinces, which
suffered badly. Iran claimed damages amounting to $22 billion in the
agriculture sector in the first two years of the war; this was increased to
$41 billion for the period September 1980–March 1983. By 1983 food
subsidies amounted to $1.6 billion and food items were among the biggest
imports after war matériel.[22] This could lnot be attributed wholly to the
war, for political and ideological differences within the leadership
prevented efficient development of the sector. Nevertheless, the war was
responsible for the virtual cessation of activity in the rich province of
Khuzestan and for a large-scale exodus which required the housing of
refugees away from the war zone.[23] (The figure of one and a half million
refugees from the war is commonly accepted.) By the end of 1984, the
government claimed to have spent some $2.2 billion in reconstruction *in
the war zone*.[24]

The war has become a great drain on manpower to feed a seemingly
endless supply of conscripts and volunteers for combat.[25] The Basij in
particular, the 'volunteer' para-military element in the armed forces,
recruited from the rural areas, seems to have been responsible for the
development of a manpower problem in agriculture. An Iranian
economist has observed that:[26]

> Males in the 15–24 age group in rural areas, who assume many important
> agricultural tasks, number 1.5 million, if only half of the numbers estimated
> (conservatively) to have died or been maimed in the war are of rural origin,
> there has been a loss of nearly 10 per cent of the rural labour force in this age
> group.

Since the decision in late 1987 to increase the number of reserves-in-
being and to accelerate conscription, the number of youth fleeing the
country to evade the draft, already large, has increased.

Another expense directly related to the war is the cost of meeting the increased demand for medical care. Iran experienced a serious loss of doctors abroad as a result of the revolution, but the resultant shortage would not have been so critical if there had not been a surge in demand for medical services because of the war. In December 1983 one estimate gave the figure of 600,000 dead and injured and reported that Iran was looking for doctors abroad to add to the 200 Indian doctors it had recruited, and seeking to attract back those who had left.[27] According to one estimate, half of Iran's doctors had fled the country, and of the remaining 15,000 half live in Tehran. Legislation was accordingly passed requiring them to spend one month per year in 'deprived' areas.[28] Imports of pharmaceuticals and their use in the war zones were given priority. A not unexpected result was the tendency for this to lead to their hoarding.

The political management of the war economy

The Islamic republic had made a cult of its intention to elevate principles and self-sacrifice into watchwords and to remain indifferent to the 'normal' considerations that were supposed to constrain choice, and of its determination to pursue its goals oblivious to the hostility of the rest of the world. In the conduct of the war, the regime has shown skill in continuing to motivate its supporters by such appeals, while deftly ensuring that they are in fact insulated from severe shortages, thus protecting its own political base.

As we saw in Chapter 5, Khomeini has made it clear that the Islamic republic is not to be judged on its economic performance. Any criticisms along these lines demonstrate a fundamental failure to comprehend the aims of the revolution:[29]

> If the motive behind the revolution had been to establish a lower cost of living . . . to enjoy welfare . . . if that is what the motive was, then those who want to complain may go on complaining . . . Needless to say, the people's masses have no complaint. Those who do complain are the ones who have been deprived of their meetings.
>
> What you wanted was Islam, what you wanted was an Islamic Republic, what you wanted was neither West nor East. All these objectives have been achieved.

At other times he has disparagingly referred to the idea that revolutions are concerned with such mundane issues as the 'price of watermelons'.

Following Khomeini's lead, Prime Minister Musavi, who is in charge of running the economy, has sought to depict the war as indistinguishable from the building of an Islamic society, rather than in competition with it.[30] The defence of Islam starts with the defence of the Islamic republic; to safeguard Islam, Iran must win the war. However, as the costs of the war have increased, the tone has become less confident. Increasingly Khomeini argues that criticism of the government's economic performance should be stopped.[31] By 1985 the tone had become more shrill. On the seventh anniversary of the revolution, Khomeini appealed for support:[32]

> If there are certain shortages as a result of the war imposed on us by the superpowers, today Islam is confronting the entire world of blasphemy. If there is the slightest hesitation on this vital issue we will deliver such a blow that it will not be remedied very easily. The enthusiasm and fervour for defending the Islamic homeland and Islam should be kept alive in all hearts.

Eighteen months later, he repeated the plea:[33]

> You are in a state of revolution ... the government has been successful ... The government has been beset with difficulties ... We are in a state of war! We are under a blockade ...

The Prime Minister in turn has emphasized the therapeutic and character-building values of adversity, saying that although Iran 'naturally' has problems because of the war, 'it believed that freedom and independence will be gained through the very difficulties'.[34] More realistically, he alluded to the resilience of the populace:

> If the Islamic spirit did not prevail ... and the economic trends were not towards domestic production of resources, we would no doubt be in dire economic circumstances.[35]

The costs of the war have become increasingly evident in the daily life of the nation. The government already has a programme for subsidizing basic goods at stable prices.[36] However, power cuts since 1985 and petrol rationing since autumn 1986, together with food rationing, have become commonplace. In 1987 the gap long evident between official exchange rates or quoted prices and those of the black market became particularly striking. Hoarding, profiteering and inflation increased. So too did complaints about the material inequalities prevailing in the Islamic Republic. In June Khomeini agreed that the government ought to fix the price of certain staple items by law, over the objection of some of the conservative clergy in the Council of Guardians. The media carried bitter commentaries on the 'economic terrorism' and 'profiteering' prevalent.[37] It may have been due to this new mood of class rancour directed particularly at the better-off and the bazaar, that the decision was made in November to ask (or rather require) increased contributions from them for the war effort.

It would be mistaken to underestimate the unifying impact of the initial Iraqi invasion, or the real sense of achievement felt by the Iranian people in the course of the war, not least because of the ingenuity required to offset the technologically more advanced equipment that its foe was receiving; or to forget the comparable sense of solidarity and exhilaration unleashed by war in the European experience. In the military area alone, there is little doubt that resourcefulness and tinkering have allowed Iran to use its own means and thereby to save on precious foreign exchange. But this motivation could not endure over seven years without skilful leadership. A constant refrain here was the theme of external conspiracy and domestic pride: 'Despite all their [i.e. foreigners'] predictions and conspiracies', said the Prime Minister in 1986, 'our system became stronger daily'.[38]

Without the dedicated commitment of the populace, Iran's war effort would have been quickly nullified. In the conduct of military operations – making a virtue of necessity – the regime relied on numbers and zeal to offset Iraq's superior access to technology and resources. The Basij, the so-called 'army of 20 million', numbered several hundred thousand at any one time. Whether press-ganged, brainwashed or simply manipulated, they went to war as volunteers, generally not only uncomplaining but positively enthusiastic. When the conflict turned into a war of attrition Iran depended on its people's greater tolerance for belt-tightening and self-denial. In the functioning of the economy in general – as in agriculture – it relied on the participation of the people to keep things going. A Tehran radio commentary caught this spirit: 'The economic self-sufficiency of the country cannot be attained without the all-out crusade of the entire masses'.[39]

The government's approach to problems was precisely to use the commitment of the already mobilized population to make up for shortfalls in other areas. The 'Reconstruction Crusade' organization became a form of alternative to the military draft, for deployment primarily to the rural areas. (Indeed, in October 1986 the government acknowledged it as such by exempting its members from military service.) During the war, the 'Foundation for the Oppressed' (*Bonyad-e Mosta'zafin*) was superseded by the new 'Martyrs Foundation' (*Bonyad-e Shahidan*). Both drew their 'membership' essentially from the same pool of committed believers in the revolution, who volunteered for military service. And it was this same stratum – usually serving in the Basij – that paid most heavily in human life during the conflict.

The government was by no means oblivious to this, and it funnelled large amounts of funds for the war effort into the Bonyad-e Shahidan precisely to ensure that the commitment to the regime and the war should not turn sour as a result of casualties. The families of war martyrs received a grant of 2 million rials (roughly $30,000), while those crippled (*shahidan-e zendeh*) were given priority in acquiring scarce goods, government jobs and university places.[40] Five thousand residential units were built for the military and martyrs' families in April 1986; interest-free loans for servicemen 'to meet their essential needs' were announced in August 1986; and long-service volunteers were to be any government jobs as of January 1987.

Since 1979 the government sector has expanded considerably, the bureaucracy virtually doubling to some 2 million as the leadership maintained a set of parallel institutions. The demands of the war and the languishing private sector have done little to change this. If the charge on the public exchequer has been correspondingly heavy, it has provided the government with a large constituency whose fortunes are subject to manipulation. Food rationing, price controls, petrol rationing, all are under the control of the revolutionary guards and committees. They can and have controlled these and other essentials selectively in ways that benefit themselves and the 'true' supporters of the revolution. And this has been the clear intention. One report perhaps went too far in this vein when it observed that support for the war was maintained by the judicious mixture of threat and incentive, making the avoidance of military service impossible, on the one hand, and the practice of volunteering profitable, on the other. While pointing to the 'widespread discontent' arising as a result of the war, the author concluded that the families of martyrs are 'virtually a privileged class' with bonuses and fringe benefits.[41]

The government has made it clear that the revolution was made by and for the disinherited. Because the revolution also depends on the more hard-headed 'bazaar' for investment and for managing and distributing imports, it has sought to placate this group by pursuing economic policies which otherwise make little sense for revolutionary Iran.[42] Unable to find a way to end the war on its own terms, the government has sought to insulate its more impressionable – less commerce-minded – core constituency from the costs of a war for which it has no solution.

Oil, the economy and the war

Access to foreign exchange to fund the arms that fuel the war has been important to both sides, and oil accounts for at least 90 per cent of the adversaries' foreign exchange. The oil sector of the enemy's economy has thus been a logical target in the hostilities. Yet, with the exception of the initial exchanges in the first months of the war, and Iran's success in blocking Iraq's access to the Gulf for its oil exports, and some attacks on offshore sites, Iran's oil installations did not come under *sustained* attack in the first years of the war. It shifted exports to terminals further south, out of reach of Iraq's artillery or aircraft. In seeking to increase production to meet increasing foreign-exchange needs[43] the Islamic leadership had to discard their strongly held belief that Iran should reduce its dependence on oil.[44] But apart from forcing Iran to expand its OPEC quota to fund the conflict, the war made few demands on the country's oil industry until 1984. In February of that year, Iraq declared a 'total exclusion zone' around Kharg island, Iran's principal export terminal, and threatened tankers with its newly-acquired Super-Etendard aircraft carrying the Exocet air-to-surface missile.

To reduce Iran's capacity to continue the war, Iraq sought to stop or diminish Iran's oil exports by inhibiting tankers from loading at its terminals and by damaging these installations. It was able to impose a war premium on a 7-day voyage to Kharg of 2–3 per cent of the hull's value. To maintain its exports Iran was forced to absorb this additional cost, and resorted to discounting its oil at the price of $21 as against an official $29/barrel.[45] After Iraqi attacks on Bandar Khomeini and Kharg, shipping was inhibited, and Iran's exports declined to roughly 1.4 million b/d. By the end of 1984, the threat from Iraq combined with market and price uncertainties had reduced this to 1 million b/d. However, the threat soon receded as businessmen and crews in a world with a surplus of tankers found the risk worthwhile. Iran ingeniously deployed decoys to misguide or spoof the Exocet. By early 1985 it was discounting oil at $25 as against the official $28/barrel price (a $2 discount was to cover risk premiums).[46]

To offset the Iraqi threat, Iran started up a tanker shuttle to ferry oil from Kharg to Sirri and Lavan islands in the lower Gulf, thought to be out of range of Iraqi aircraft. But this could account for only some 300,000 b/d, and the remainder from Kharg became the object of sustained aerial attack from mid-August 1985. By the end of the year, Iraq claimed 77 sorties against Kharg alone (rising to 120 in a full year), and despite the surplus capacity of this facility and countermeasures, Iran's oil exports were significantly affected. Its average export level was lowered to 1 million as against a preferred level of 1.6 million b/d. Iraq's rather more effective attacks brought uncertainty into the export picture. As a result of this and market uncertainties, only 60 per cent of expected oil income was realized in 1985.[47]

Iran's reaction, in addition to improving the defence of these installations, was threefold:

i) It retaliated by increasing what had been an intermittent surveillance of shipping for war matériel that might be destined for Iraq, to a full-scale programme of intercepting, boarding and searching suspected vessels irrespective of flag or provenance.

ii) It announced what was to become a standard refrain intended as a warning to the Gulf states and the oil consumers to restrain Iraq, namely, that if Iran's oil exports were interrupted, everyone else's would be as well. Rafsanjani, emerging from a Supreme Defence Council meeting, observed:[48]

> If the Persian Gulf were to become unsafe for us, the natural reaction would be to stop Iraq's making indirect use by making it unsafe for others.

iii) It announced plans to diversify its oil export terminals and specifically to use Ghanaveh and terminals south of Bushire.[49] There were also suggestions that it might build a pipeline with a 500,000 b/d capacity to deliver crude to Lavan island, but it was recognized that this would be expensive and would take at least one year to construct.[50]

Iran soon faced additional difficulties. Oil prices plummeted from $28 to $14/b in the period January–March 1986. At the same time, Iraq continued its attacks on Kharg and Ghanaveh, reducing Iran's exports to 800,000 b/d and complicating the problems of the Islamic leadership in planning the economic management of the war. Iran also found itself confronted in the spring of 1986 with what looked suspiciously like a Saudi-led 'oil conspiracy', in which the other producers increased their exports in a soft market, but did this in the name of economic policy rather than as part of an effort to weaken Iran's oil exports and hence its war effort. The results were in any case the same, for prices were driven down further – at one point to $9 a barrel. Iran's reaction is discussed in chapter 9 on relations with the Gulf states. Here it suffices to note that the issue was resolved amicably at the August 1986 OPEC meeting, when Tehran was able to convince Riyadh that continuation of this policy could only be seen as a sign of active belligerence. Underlining this was the report by *Petroleum Intelligence Weekly* in July that Iran had suffered one of the (two) largest drops in OPEC revenues in the period January–June 1986, when it had seen its revenues drop to $16 million a day in June as against $32.5 million in January.[51]

Iraq maintained the pressure by attacking the Kharg–Sirri shuttle tankers (5 out of 11 tankers were reported hit in mid-1986); by stepping up attacks on tankers near Iran (over 100 ships were hit in 1986, double that of the previous year); and – by aerial refuelling – attacking Sirri itself, very effectively in August.[52] It surprised Iran even more in November by attacking Larak, 250 kilometres east of Sirri, and repeated this in 1987. So effective was this campaign that Iran's leaders now sought to end the war quickly by adopting a final push rather than a strategy of attrition. Iran's oil exports were squeezed to 1.1 million b/d, while to maintain even this level of exports it was obliged to pay for chartered tankers ($60 million for the shuttle) and for oil storage at various places without storage tanks. The shuttle tankers were thought to cost $20,000, and the storage tankers $10,000 a day. In addition to the cost of the shuttle tankers destroyed, there were increased insurance premiums (rates on ships and cargoes having tripled) to be paid. In all, the tanker war cost Iran millions of dollars in expenses and in exports forgone. But as one reporter noted, this would affect the war effort decisively only if Iran's exports could be reduced to 750,000 b/d at $12/b for a *sustained* period.[53]

This evidently was Iraq's strategy. Saddam Hussein remarked:[54]

> The economic field remains a basic one in the existing conflict. The Iranian regime spends all of its revenues upon its war machine. Any increase in Iran's revenues over Iraq's means in practice ... increasing the ability [of Iran] to prolong the war and to threaten the security and stability of the region.

The Iranians did not see it that way: 'Our enemy in running its war machine depends more on its oil revenues', observed Rafsanjani, alluding to Iran's policy of self-reliance, diversification of oil terminals and popular support.[55] Be that as it may, there was little question that Iraq's air attacks were proving effective. Throughout 1986, but particularly after May, repeated attacks on the refineries in Tehran, Isfahan, and Tabriz caused significant damage, forcing Iran to triple the rate of its imports of refined products for domestic consumption (to some 300,000 b/d) and finally to impose petrol rationing in October.[56] In the same month, its exports were down to 6–700,000 b/d, but the average export level over the year still reached 1.3 million b/d, generating some $6–8 billion in revenue.[57]

By the turn of the year, Iraq's air attacks had diminished and the price of oil had risen to $18/b. Early in 1987, Iraq reverted to counter-city attacks, perhaps because of suspicions that Iran had improved its air defences. In any event, Iran (showing what *The Economist* called 'nimble-footedness') had survived a difficult year. The Prime Minister, in presenting the budget for the following one, termed it a 'restrictive' one.

Despite much talk of building overland pipelines for the export of oil (and routes through Turkey, the USSR and southern Iran to Chah Bahar in the Gulf of Oman have been discussed), no action has been taken. Perhaps this is due to the prohibitive expense of such undertakings, or to the Iranian leadership's expectations of a rapid victory. In any event by the end of 1987 Iran remained dependent on security in the waters of the Gulf for the export of its oil, while Iraq's exports were now all overland. Thus it was now Iran that was the more vulnerable of the two to the threat of an interruption in its oil exports, an exact reversal of the situation in 1983. At the same time as being more vulnerable to an oil cut-off, Iran also had become the weaker of the two in its capacity to export, i.e. Iraq was now producing and regularly exporting more oil than Iran.

Iran's oil income has varied markedly during the war (see Table 7.1). Iraqi air attacks were only one part of the story: an unstable market, currency fluctuations and changes in national oil policy[58] also contributed to the uncertainty. Iran has kept the war going without resort to borrowing from friends or international institutions. It has done so by counteracting the Iraqi air threat, by taking military countermeasures, by using its natural advantage of a long coastline, by pressing Iraq's paymasters to counsel restraint, and by using its political advantage of being able to motivate its troops even in a period of belt-tightening. At the same time, it has ensured that the most ardent supporters of the revolution and the war are well cared-for.

Conclusion

Iran has shown considerable ingenuity in meeting the challenge of war. It has reduced non-essential imports and managed to keep its oil flowing despite periodic air attacks. It has diversified the sources of its arms supplies, bought on the open market and from apparent enemies, and increased its ability to manufacture its own requirements and save foreign exchange. It has capitalized on the support of the masses for the war, while squeezing the well-to-do and coddling the bazaar, on which it still depends. The war has to all intents and purposes become the sole criterion for judging the Islamic republic.

Iran has been able to export adequate amounts of oil to fund the war in the harsh economic and military conditions of the past three years, and there is no reason to expect this to change in the future. The conflict, in truth, is fuelled more by passion on the Iranian side. Throughout the war there has been little if any investment in basic infrastructure; agricultural production is stagnant, and the invaluable inherited military stock (that was so much criticized) is now virtually exhausted. Peace, when it comes, will not bring with it much of a dividend. For it will have to start with a ceasefire and only time will bring about the confidence necessary between two neighbours, in order to reduce military expenditures. The fact that none of the economic problems have fundamentally changed the regime's determination to continue the war 'until victory', testifies to the sagacity of Adam Smith's remark to the effect that 'there is a good deal of ruin in a nation'.

8

Iraq and the Region

Saddam Hussein's vision of the utility of war which led to the invasion of Iran in September 1980 also contained a regional dimension. The demonstrative use of force was intended to impress the rulers of Iraq's neighbouring states as much as the rulers of Iran, and the humiliation of the latter was expected to reap considerable benefits for Iraq, and thus for its ruler, in the wider domains of Gulf and Arab politics. For the Gulf rulers, it would show that Iraq could indeed be relied upon to protect them from the disturbing consequences of the Iranian revolution; for states elsewhere in the Arab world, an Iraqi victory of this magnitude would serve to justify its claim to act as inspiration and leader of the Arab community of states. Even those who recoiled from this prospect might be intimidated by the strength of will and the martial prowess at the disposal of Saddam Hussein.

Saddam Hussein had long been preparing the ground to this end. The opportunity presented by Egypt's signature of the Camp David accords with Israel and the subsequent peace treaty, was rapidly exploited by Saddam Hussein through the organization of the Baghdad Summits of November 1978 and March 1979 respectively. It was then that an Arab consensus emerged, sponsored by Iraq. The latter showed itself to be a much needed moderator between the elements which were later to form the 'Steadfastness Front' and the more cautious Arab states.[1] Largely because of the peculiarly unsettling dynamics of intra-Ba'th politics, Saddam Hussein could not, and would not, maintain as close relations with the former as with the latter. As a result, despite the 1978 'Charter of Joint National Action' signed with Syria, a coolness soon appeared in their relations. This intensified, following alleged Syrian involvement in the plot which Saddam Hussein claimed to have uncovered soon after assuming the Presidency.[2]

However, he had been assiduous in cultivating other Arab states. This included not only Jordan – a useful ally against Syria – but more especially the Arab states of the Gulf. It was here that he believed Iraq could have a special role to play, particularly in view of the concern caused by developments in Iran. Iraq was, therefore, projected as the protector of the *status quo* in the Gulf, reassuring the troubled rulers of Arabia that it had the capacity to prevent their regimes from succumbing either to internal subversion or external aggression.[3] This leading role, not simply in the Gulf but in the Arab world as a whole, was increasingly portrayed by Iraq's leaders as an integral part of its destiny and formed, therefore, a binding obligation on the state and its rulers. The instruments which would allow them, and indeed which required them, to carry out this obligation were the armed forces of the state:[4]

> Iraq is building an army not to defend just its own borders, but to serve as the shield and sword of the Arab nation against its enemies.

As relations with Iran deteriorated, so the intensity of Saddam Hussein's claims to have both the right and the means to oppose 'Iran's aggressive designs in the region' increased: war had once been threatened and, he suggested, it was perhaps incumbent upon him to make good that threat.[5] Although it is hard to prove, it seems probable that some, at least, of the Gulf states were informed of Iraq's intention to invade Iran and that their rulers approved the scheme, believing, as did Saddam Hussein, that this would be a short salutary campaign. The Iranian menace would have been averted. Even if the price of this was to be the self-aggrandizement of Iraq and its ruler, this was nevertheless preferable to a belligerent and ill-intentioned Iran.[6]

The war, when it came, soon proved to be different from that which Saddam Hussein had expected. So too, apparently, were the attitudes of the Arab states on whose behalf he claimed to have committed Iraq's armed forces. By November 1980 Saddam Hussein had discovered that the Arab states he had hoped to lead fell into three categories: the firm allies who gave complete support to Iraq's efforts; the supporters who could be more forthcoming in their assistance; and the renegades who had betrayed their Arab identity by siding with Iran.[7] Disappointingly for Iraq, only Jordan came into the first category; the Gulf states gave support but not of the wholehearted and uncritical nature expected by Saddam Hussein; Syria, Libya, the People's Democratic Republic of Yemen and – initially – Algeria fell into the category which made a point of declaring their support for Iran.

Thereafter, Iraq's pan-Arab and regional endeavours were geared not so much towards preparing the way for the pan-Arab impact of a victory which had in any case eluded it, but rather towards mobilizing the resources of the Arab world in order to use them in sustaining the Iraqi war effort. Saddam Hussein has, therefore, devoted considerable energy to the task of persuading his regional neighbours that they share a community of interest with Iraq in its attempts to thwart the aims of the Iranian armed forces and to bring the war to an end. On one level, this has meant the identification of Iraq's cause with the larger pan-Arab cause, thus creating obligations for those who claim to subscribe to the latter.[8] On another level, it has taken the form of a direct appeal to the self-interest of certain Arab rulers, threatening them with the probable consequences of an Iraqi military collapse, and simultaneously promising them the financial or political gifts which Iraq still has at its disposal.[9]

Given the perception of what was at stake in a war with revolutionary Iran, as well as of the opportunities offered by a closer association with Iraq, these appeals have had a significant effect on the assistance given to Iraq by a number of Arab states. Financial aid, logistical support and the supply of military equipment and advisers have been forthcoming. They have had a marked effect on Iraq's capacity to bear the burden of a war of attrition. In addition, Iraq has witnessed a gratifying tendency over the years – most evident at the Arab Summit in Amman in November 1987 – for the Arab states to subscribe to Saddam Hussein's argument that the Iranian threat 'is as serious – if not more so in the long run – as the threats which the Arab League dealt with on various levels' at different times in the past.[10] Thus, far from being a 'little local difficulty' faced by Iraq and its Arab neighbours in the Gulf, the conflict with Iran has been agreed to be of vital importance to the future of that elusive, but emotively powerful, entity, the Arab nation. It has been Saddam Hussein's primary task in the region to ensure that, whatever the vicissitudes of the conflict, this interpretation of the war, and the consequent level of support flowing to Iraq, should be maintained.

This is important, and perhaps crucial, for Saddam Hussein in two ways. Firstly, the logistical and financial help of a number of Arab states has been of inestimable worth in sustaining the Iraqi war effort. Secondly, and equally significantly, the fact of Arab solidarity has been a visible reminder to Iraqis that they are fighting in a struggle legitimated by their common identity as Arabs. Despite the fact that the regime has been assiduous in cultivating the idea that Iraqis share a common, specifically Iraqi, identity, it is clear that there are doubts about whether such a notion has, in fact, captured the collective imagination of the country's inhabitants. In these circumstances, and in view of the pan-Arab propaganda to which Iraqis have been subjected since the troubled beginnings of the state, Saddam Hussein has found it useful and possibly necessary to convince his soldiers that they are fighting for a truly Arab cause. The ambiguity of this endeavour was apparent in a speech intended to boost morale which Saddam Hussein delivered to troops defending Basra in December 1987, as they awaited an Iranian assault:[11]

> The martyrs' blood was not shed in defence of great Iraq only – although it deserves this – but it is the ransom that has preserved Arab land and dignity from the Atlantic Ocean to the Arabian Gulf.

The endorsement of such sentiments by the other Arab states is seen, therefore, as a vital element in support of the domestic legitimacy of the regime, just as their material aid has been crucial in maintaining the war effort against Iran.

In addition to Iraq's cultivation of its fellow Arab states, it has also established increasingly close relations with Turkey. These links have been of great utility to Iraq's war effort and have established a common interest of both governments in two spheres: firstly, the economic and, for Iraq, strategic interests constituted by the oil pipeline from its northern oilfields to Turkey's Mediterranean coast; and secondly, the political and military interests represented by the desire of both governments to curb Kurdish guerrilla activity along their common border. After the cutting of the pipeline to Banias in Syria in 1982, and before the construction of the pipelines across Saudi Arabia, the pipeline through Turkey represented Iraq's sole facility for the export of oil in bulk. Its security was therefore vital to the Iraqi war effort, as was the plan to increase its capacity. In both these areas, Turkey co-operated closely.[12]

This raised the question of the vulnerability of the pipeline and of the parallel highway to the activities of Kurdish guerrillas. Before the war, Turkey and Iraq had already signed an agreement in 1978 under which troops from either country had the right to pursue Kurdish guerrillas up to fifteen kilometres inside the other's territory, as long as prior notification was given. In May 1983, following Iran's first major offensive into Iraqi Kurdistan and the KDP's subsequent extension of the territory under its control, Turkish forces made their first incursion into Iraq since the agreement. They attacked Kurdish encampments and reportedly sent Turkish troops thirty kilometres into Iraqi territory, with the approval of the Baghdad Government. In fact, so successful was this operation, that Tariq Aziz went to Ankara to explore ways in which security co-operation in this area could be strengthened.[13] The visit resulted in a further accord between the two states in 1984, facilitating cross-border operations, the results of which were seen in October that year when Turkish forces staged a second major attack on Kurdish rebel bases. These have been followed by Turkish air force attacks on Kurdish bases in both 1986 and 1987.[14]

It is apparent, therefore, that the war has compelled Iraq to pay close attention to an important area of common strategic interest with Turkey. Successive governments in Baghdad, of which the present one was no exception, have tended to mistrust Turkey – because of its historical associations, because of the suspicion that it covets the north-western, oil-rich provinces of Iraq and because it is a member of NATO. However, the demands of war have allowed Saddam Hussein to justify the utility of the controversial 1978 agreement. Even before the war, he had perceived that the two states had much in common. During the war, he can point to the vital part which Turkish security co-operation has played in the protection of Iraqi interests, thereby explicitly arguing that the requirements of the latter should constitute a prime obligation. Important as this trend has become in Iraq's dealings with Turkey, it is, however, in the arena of Arab politics that the competition between the imperatives of state interest and wider moral or ideological considerations has taken on most significance for the politics and policies of Iraq itself.

Iraq, Jordan, Egypt and Syria

Iraq's war-time relations with Jordan, Egypt and Syria have vividly illustrated these themes. All three of these countries have materially affected Iraq's capacity to wage war – Jordan and Egypt positively, and Syria negatively. Of equal importance for Saddam Hussein has been the symbolic, pan-Arab resonance of the relationships Iraq has established with these states. Their attitudes towards the war against Iran have had a direct impact on his thesis that 'Iraq's policies are based on Iraqi national interests and on the Arab nation's pan-Arab interests'.[15] The vehemence with which he has attempted to maintain an identity between the two testifies to the practical and ideological importance attached to this endeavour. It has also necessitated a redefinition of the 'Arab national interest'.

Prior to the war with Iran, this was almost exclusively defined with reference to the conflict with Israel. Arab governments were judged by sections of their own population and by their fellow Arab rulers on the basis of their proven degree of commitment to the struggle to establish an Arab state in Palestine. This was the test of their devotion to pan-Arabism and any backsliding was denounced as a betrayal of the Arab nation. Treachery of this order justified their overthrow in the eyes of those who saw themselves as more virtuous and rigorous trustees of the Arab cause. The Ba'th party, first as a revolutionary movement and then as the Iraqi Government itself, justified its activities in precisely these terms. The governments of Jordan, Egypt and Syria – the 'front-line' states – were regarded as having a special role to play in selflessly devoting their resources to the prosecution of the fight against Zionism. Any tendency to compromise, or to plead other, more locally based priorities, was portrayed in Baghdad as sufficient grounds for questioning their right to rule and for seeking to hasten their downfall. The Iraqi regime, by setting itself up as the guardian of the Arab nation's conscience and of its security, sought to create for itself a dominant position in the Arab world and an unassailable stance of Arab rectitude within Iraq itself. This was most evident at the Baghdad Summit of 1979, when Egypt was expelled from the Arab League for having broken ranks and flouted the prevailing consensus by signing a peace treaty with Israel. The denunciation of the Egyptian Government suggested that one of its primary sins had been to have acted out of self-interest, disregarding the greater Arab good.[16]

In 1980, when Saddam Hussein decided that his own and, by association, Iraq's security required that Iraq should go to war with Iran, it was imperative that he should maintain that this was in some respects a selfless act, whereby Iraq was defending not simply its own interests but those of the Arab nation. Claiming that Iran had forced Iraq to go to war, Saddam Hussein stated that Iraq would[17]

> deal with this accursed foreigner and, on behalf of the Arab nation, do honour to the name of Arabism in this battle . . . the Iraqis are bearing the honour and mission of the Arab nation.

Expanding upon this theme, he went on to link Iraq's plight with the perennial Israeli threat:

> The Zionist entity had its own aims in this war and inspired the Iranians to launch it. This explains their persistent evil-doing against Iraq and the Arab nation.

Addressing the Iraqi people at the outset of the war, he justified the attack on Iran by stating that 'this glorious hour for the Iraqi Army is preparing it to liberate Palestine: victories against Iran are paving the road to Jerusalem'.[18] Sensitive, no doubt, at the time to the accusation that the Iraqi troops were facing in the wrong direction for this particular task, Saddam Hussein explained how it was that, by fighting Iran, Iraq was really taking on Israel. Not only was the Iranian Government ritually denounced as 'Zionist', but, it was claimed, only through their military efforts against Iran could the Iraqi armed forces go on 'to liberate Palestine'. Indeed, Saddam Hussein used the Israeli attack on the Iraqi nuclear reactor in 1981 to illustrate his thesis that Iraq's advanced technology and the military prowess it had shown on the battlefield had sufficiently disturbed Israel for Iraq to become a military target.[19] At the same time, he acknowledged that 'the war has restricted – or, rather limited – utilizing the Iraqi capabilities, which could not thus be used on another front'.[20] It was all the more important, therefore, for him to maintain that the front on which his own forces were in fact fighting was as crucial for the future of the Arab nation as the front facing Israel.

In this respect, the government of Jordan has been the most consistent in subscribing to the thesis that Iraq was fighting 'not only for its own territory but for the fate of the entire Arab nation'.[21] This has been backed up by practical aid in a number of ways: crucial trans-shipment rights through the port of Aqaba for war matériel and other goods destined for Iraq; the grant of facilities for the dispersal of Iraqi aircraft to Jordanian airfields at the outset of the war; the secondment to Iraq of Jordanian military advisers and possibly also of a number of Jordanian volunteers, although the impact of the latter on the war effort must be considered minimal.[22]

In return, Jordan has derived considerable benefits. Firstly, even though Saddam Hussein may not have been able to deliver the quick victory over the Iranian revolutionary regime once promised, he has managed to lead a successful Iraqi defence effort which appears to have blocked Iran's regional ambitions. Secondly, there has been a certain financial reward for Jordan, although as Iraq's economic situation deteriorated, this has considerably diminished. Lastly, and perhaps most importantly, Jordan has profited politically from a situation in which Iraq now looks on its relations with Jordan as being, in Taha Ramadhan's words, 'a model of what relations should be between two fraternal countries to serve the two countries' mutual interests and the Arab nation's objectives'.[23] This situation has allowed Jordan to repay the debt which Iraq's pre-war assistance had been building up and which might have proved irksome in the future.

It has also given Jordan a considerably freer hand than hitherto in its delicate negotiations with the Palestinians. In a marked departure from previous intransigent statements on the issue, Saddam Hussein could declare in 1982 that[24]

> We will not oppose any solution that is acceptable to the Palestinians . . . The Palestinians could well accept some form of relationship with Jordan of their own free will . . . such a relationship between two Arab regimes facing up to the future is natural. We are not against it.

This interview is interesting for a number of reasons. Firstly, it seemed to depart from the previous Ba'thist claim that its General Secretary, as the repository of knowledge concerning the true interests of the Arab nation, would know better than the Palestinian leadership what course they should be pursuing. Secondly, it seemed to reflect an increasing tendency on the part of Saddam Hussein to acknowledge that the states of the Arab world did indeed have their own legitimate interests, which imposed certain obligations on their rulers. In 1980, he had portrayed the division of the Arab nation as an unnatural act, brought about by the conspiracies of 'imperialism, Zionism and powers interested in dividing the Arab nation into twenty-two parts'.[25] By September 1982, he was advocating that the Arabs should accept this state of affairs: 'The Arab reality is that the Arabs are now twenty-two states and we have to behave accordingly'.[26] In the meantime, he had profited by the crises of that summer to reinforce his own control over the Ba'th party, eliminating the last of those who might have wanted to hold him accountable to its ideological tenets. In their place, he had established himself as the supreme guide of the party, whose pronouncements and directives would of themselves constitute its ideology.

These moves allowed Saddam Hussein to act upon the principles he had enunciated by embarking on an increasingly necessary rapprochement with Egypt, regardless of the latter's continued adherence to the treaty with Israel. As early as 1981, and under the guise of pan-Arab solidarity, Egypt began to supply Iraq with quantities of war matériel. This has subsequently grown into a substantial flow, with an estimated value of $1 billion in 1982, rising to $2 billion by 1985.[27] The ability of Iraq to draw on the industrial capacity of Egypt's military establishment, as well as on the services of Egyptian military advisers, has evidently been of great utility to the war effort. In view of Saddam Hussein's pre-war denunciation of Egypt's 'betrayal' of the Arab cause, and indeed the implicit challenge he had thrown down to Egypt's pre-eminence in the Arab world, it is clear that the exigencies of war have led to a re-appraisal of Egypt's role. Urging all Arab governments to resume normal ties with Egypt, without insisting on the latter's renunciation of the Camp David accords, Saddam Hussein was able to justify his own change of position in a highly characteristic way by stating simply that 'Husni Mubarak is not Anwar Sadat'.[28] The enthusiasm with which the Egyptian press and Egyptian officials publicly subscribed to Saddam Hussein's pan-Arab definition of the conflict with Iran was clearly welcomed by the Iraqi regime. It not only brought benefits, in terms of Egyptian support, but also reinforced the message through which that regime was seeking to mobilize support throughout the Arab world.[29]

As in the case of Jordan, Egypt, in turn, gained substantial political and economic benefits from its support of the Iraqi war effort. Although Egypt was in no sense threatened militarily by Iran, the prospect of the military victory of the self-proclaimed Islamic republic could only be a disturbing one for its rulers. They are, after all, highly aware of the capacity of political discontent within Egypt itself to take on the form of an explicitly Islamic challenge to the authorities. By supporting Iraq in the name of pan-Arab solidarity, the Egyptian Government was also able to serve Egypt's national interests, harmed to some extent by the isolation of the country following the treaty with Israel. Nor was the economic benefit of the arms trade and other commercial agreements negligible. The austerity measures introduced by Iraq had severely reduced the substantial flow of remittances sent back to Egypt by the million or so Egyptians working in Iraq. To a large extent this could be offset by the increasing official links between the two countries.[30]

These had begun when the Egyptian Minister of State for Foreign Affairs, Butros Butros Ghali, had met the present Iraqi Minister of Foreign Affairs, Tariq Aziz, in France in 1982. In February 1983, when Iraq was facing an Iranian offensive in the south, Butros Ghali and the special adviser to President Mubarak, Osama al-Baz, visited Baghdad in a show of support.[31] In an even more dramatic demonstration of pan-Arab solidarity, President Mubarak himself, together with King Hussein of Jordan, flew into Baghdad in March 1985 to express their support for Iraq at a time when the Iranian forces were launching one of their more vigorous offensives of the war.[32] Despite the fact that the Iraqi Government still felt that the time was not ripe for restoring diplomatic relations with Egypt, contacts between the two governments increased, as did practical co-operation measures, especially in the production of armaments. This was praised by Taha Ramadhan as an example of much needed pan-Arab co-operation, and as part of the 'overall plan for developing the Arab nation's capability to confront its enemies'.[33] On the anniversary of the Ba'thist revolution, Saddam Hussein reinforced this message, declaring:[34]

> Arab solidarity cannot be strong and effective without Egypt . . . Egypt is part of the Arab nation . . . [we must] not let an important Arab power like Egypt fail to participate with the group.

This ambition was achieved at the Arab Summit in Amman in 1987. Although the heads of state assembled there did not take the decision to re-admit Egypt to the Arab League, they did accede to the Iraqi request that relations with Egypt should be reconsidered. This led to the re-establishment of diplomatic relations with Cairo by the majority of Arab states, with Iraq itself in the forefront, thereby officially ending the isolation imposed on Egypt at the Baghdad Summit of 1979.[35] In many respects the Amman Summit represented a considerable triumph for Saddam Hussein's determination to persuade the Arab world that Iraq was fulfilling a major Arab duty by acting as a steadfast bulwark against Iranian aggression. The consensus achieved on the condemnation of Iran, on the support for Iraq's position regarding a negotiated end to the war, and on the expression of solidarity with Iraq, gave important symbolic recognition to its claim to be acting in the true interests of the Arab nation. As Taha Ramadhan suggested at the time, it was this crucial pan-Arab legitimation of the Iraqi war effort, rather than any specific material aid, which the Iraqi Government desired above all else.[36]

The summit was also noteworthy in having brought about a public meeting, even if not exactly a reconciliation, between Saddam Hussein and President Hafez al-Assad of Syria.[37] Ironically, the antagonism which has existed between the two leaders has been a function of the fact that their regimes are remarkably similar, both in their structures and in their attitudes towards the Ba'thist ideals which they claim as legitimizing their rule. In both countries, an autocratic President rules the state through a mixture of coercion and largesse, dispensed through a network of 'insiders', many of whom are part of his extended family or provincial community. This is sustained by an uncompromising hold on the armed forces. Both rulers have successfully ensured that the Ba'th party and its ideology should not constitute an independent force in politics, but should be subordinate to the needs of maintaining power in states where the inhabitants have little sense of collective identity. Both are insecure, knowing full well that the reality of their power is very different from the image each wishes to propagate. Furthermore, each is aware of the vulnerability of his own position not only to internal conspiracy, but above all to the ability of the other to expose the fiction by which he justifies his hold on power, through the accusation that he has betrayed the causes of Arabism, of Socialism and of Freedom on which the Ba'thist creed is founded.

For these very reasons, at periods when they sense themselves to be most vulnerable domestically, their antagonism has been at its height. In 1979, when Saddam Hussein made his move and became President of Iraq, he claimed to have uncovered a plot to overthrow him. He used this as a pretext for an extensive purge of the upper echelons of the regime, in effect disposing of those figures in the Ba'th who might have stood in the way of the extension of his own personal power by making him adhere to a set of goals dictated by the party, rather than by himself. It was alleged at the time that these individuals were advocating immediate union with Syria and consequently that Syria had a hand in the conspiracy. Whether they received, or needed, encouragement from Syria is unclear. However, it was clear that Saddam Hussein resented any attempt to curb his own interpretation of the matters needing urgent attention in Iraq and regarded any interference from Damascus as illegitimate. A noticeable coolness between the two regimes set in, where only shortly before there had been vows of undying brotherhood. After some months, the war of words began, as each accused the other of an identical set of crimes, the most prominent and significant of which was 'the betrayal of the Arab nation'.[38]

When the real war broke out between Iraq and Iran, the antagonism existing between the two Ba'thist regimes was such that Assad in Syria could only see Saddam Hussein's plight as his possible gain – and particularly after it had become clear that there was no hope of a quick, decisive military victory. Syria had no hesitation in condemning Iraq for having started the war and went on to accuse Saddam Hussein of having done so as part of a greater betrayal of the Arab nation: he was alleged to be collaborating with the United States and Israel, since he was attacking a fiercely anti-Zionist Islamic state and depriving the Arab states of the 'strategic depth' needed in the confrontation with Israel.[39]

Syria's exploitation of the situation was not confined to denunciation alone. Damascus became the base, in the early years of the war, for a wide variety of Iraqi opposition groups, pledged to the overthrow of Saddam Hussein. Syria became a conduit for the transfer of considerable amounts of Soviet and Eastern bloc weaponry to Iran. And in April 1982, at a time when Iraq was particularly hard-pressed on the war front, Syria closed the Banias pipeline carrying Iraqi oil to the Mediterranean, thereby halving Iraq's already diminished oil exports.[40]

Insofar as it could, Iraq reciprocated. The charge that Saddam Hussein had acted out of overweening ambition, placing in jeopardy the balance of power in the Middle East, clearly touched a raw nerve and drew forth a vituperative response. The very vulnerability of the Iraqi regime to this charge during 1980–81 redoubled the ferocity and volume of its refutation of a thesis which, if widely accepted, might indeed have weakened the pan-Arab support on which Saddam Hussein would have to rely for his survival.[41] As Iraq's plight worsened and the violence and determination of the Iranian counter-attack became apparent, so Syria's position began to seem rather anomalous to a number of Arab states. When this was combined with the rift which developed in 1982–3 between President Assad and the chairman of the Palestine Liberation Organization, Yasser Arafat, it was used by the Iraqi Government to support its thesis that it was the Syrian regime which was 'betraying the Arab nation': in the east it was allied with Khomeini's Iran; in the West it was serving Zionism by helping to divide and weaken the PLO.[42] Saddam Hussein was to use these themes time and again during the years that followed. Not only did they serve to discredit Syria in the eyes of the Gulf states – on whose falling oil revenues both Iraq and Syria were increasingly dependent; they also underlined Saddam Hussein's determination to demonstrate to his own people and to the Arab world the fact that, as he put it, 'Iraq is being attacked by the same poisonous daggers in the east as those which attack the Lebanese and the Palestinians and which threaten the Arab Gulf states.'[43]

By 1985, in fact, Iraq could feel confident that its own interpretation of the war was gaining ground. Syria appeared to be increasingly isolated. Iraq tried to make the most of this by calling for the adoption of majority voting, rather than unanimity, as the means of arriving at Arab League decisions. This was particularly evident at the Casablanca Summit in August 1985. In the absence of Syria and Libya, which were boycotting the meeting, a communiqué was issued, strongly condemning Iran and supporting Iraq.[44] A similar alignment was apparent at the Arab League Council meeting of March 1986, summoned to discuss the recent Iranian occupation of the Fao peninsula. Against severe reservations on the part of Syria and Libya, the Council condemned the Iranian occupation of Iraqi territory and expressed the 'member states' all-out solidarity with Iraq in its legitimate defence of national sovereignty, security and territorial integrity'.[45] Syria's claim that the Iraqi regime had 'ignited the Iran–Iraq war to remove Iraq from the equation of struggle against the Zionist enemy' and that the war should be seen 'within the framework of US–Zionist plans for the region, by removing both Iraq and Iran from confrontation with Israel', looked increasingly implausible, since it was clearly Iran's determination to continue the war until victory that kept the conflict going.[46]

Furthermore, the Iraqi Government was obviously delighted by the revelations of 1986 and 1987, concerning the role of Israel in the transfer of American arms to Iran. Adnan Khayrallah called a press conference at the end of December 1986 to explain, as he put it, 'the dimensions of arms co-operation between the two Zionist entities in Tehran and Tel-Aviv, on the one hand, and the role of world imperialism on the other'.[47] It was expanded upon by Saddam Hussein in his Army Day speech of January 1987, in which he stated that the links between Iran and Israel only confirmed what he had been saying all along about the true nature of the Iranian regime.[48] This had been a constant theme of the Iraqi Government's message to its own people and to the Arab world. The war was portrayed as the result of a Zionist conspiracy which had inspired the Iranian regime to force Iraq into war, pinning down the forces of the Arabs at a time when they should have been united in confronting Israel.[49] The Iranian refusal to end the war was taken as further evidence of this malign conspiracy. Indeed, the Iraqi Government used the pretext of the Israeli invasion of Lebanon in 1982 to put before Iran its markedly reduced conditions for an end to hostilities.[50] Equally, the charge of Israeli complicity had been used to discredit the claimed Islamic aspects of Khomeini's mission. In this respect, it was the Iraqi contention that the sectarian message of the Iranian revolution was serving the Israeli aim of destroying Arab unity, since it sought to persuade the Arabs to identify themselves as members of various religious sects, rather than as Arabs.[51]

Iraq also made a move to exploit the rift between Arafat and Assad, by inviting the PLO in 1987 to set up its headquarters in Baghdad. Appropriation of this talisman of pan-Arab commitment was important symbolically for Saddam Hussein, since it allowed him to underline Syria's lukewarm, if not overtly hostile, attitude towards the 'sole legitimate representative of the Palestinian people'. Much was made at the time of the fact that this demonstrated Iraq's steadfast commitment to the cause of Arab Palestine – sentiments which were warmly endorsed by Arafat who had his own reasons for wishing to discredit the Syrian Government.[52]

Iraq had long before provided a refuge for another emblem of Arab nationalism, in the shape of Michel Aflaq, founder of the Ba'th party and currently Secretary General of the Ba'th Party National Command (a powerless body which in theory represents the apex of the Ba'th's pan-Arab organization). Having fled from Syria in the 1960s, when he discovered that the Damascus regime, although calling itself Ba'thist, had no intention of acknowledging his authority or following his suggestions, Aflaq had no reason to feel kindly towards the Assad government Although it seems improbable that he can regard with equanimity what the Ba'th has become at the hands of Saddam Hussein, he has found shelter in Baghdad and has become a pensioner of the government. In that capacity, he has been expected to play the role of public legitimator of Saddam Hussein's rule. This inevitably means giving vent periodically to a virulent denunciation of the Assad regime in Syria. Such a role has been regarded as useful by the Baghdad Government, as was made clear when Aflaq made a speech on the fortieth anniversary of the founding of the Ba'th party, in April 1987, much of which was devoted to a fierce denunciation of the Syrian regime, accusing it of being unpopular, corrupt, dictatorial, anti-Arab and 'hiding under the slogans of the Ba'th'. From this perspective, 'its alliance with Iran and its attempt to liquidate the Palestinian cause betray its true nature'.[53]

In these circumstances, the Iraqi Government could be fairly relaxed about attempts to mediate a reconciliation with Syria. King Hussein of Jordan was particularly energetic in this field. He claimed that the Gulf war could not have continued so long had all the Arab states adopted a single stance on the side of Iraq, since Iran took heart from Arab disunity.[54] He also had his own reasons, connected with his concern over the Palestinian question, for not wishing to see Jordan a target of Syrian enmity. Nevertheless, he appeared to receive encouragement from Saddam Hussein in late 1985 and early 1986 to bring about a reconciliation. In terms of inter-Arab politics, Saddam Hussein had much to gain from such a move. It would require no concessions from Iraq. On the contrary, reconciliation was more likely to be at the expense of Syria's relationship with Iran, suggesting that Syria had been in the wrong for the past six years, and Iraq in the right. By coming to some form of public agreement with Iraq, Syria could be portrayed as 'rejoining Arab ranks'.[55] Assad also had his own reasons at this stage for encouraging the idea of a grand reconciliation. He was to use the prospect of rapprochement with Iraq as a means of forcing greater economic and political concessions out of the Iranian Government which had become rather neglectful of its only significant Arab ally. Once this became clear in Iraq, Saddam Hussein claimed to see it as characteristic of a regime he regarded as beyond the pale and therefore no worse than he had expected.[56]

This setback did not discourage King Hussein, since there seemed to be grounds for believing that Syria was not getting as much out of the alliance with Iran as it had hoped. Assad was also becoming sensitive to the cost which Syria's support for Iran was inflicting on the state, given the sense of beleaguered solidarity with Iraq which had increasingly marked the policies of the major Gulf states. It was on this basis that a meeting was arranged between Assad and Saddam Hussein in Jordan in late April 1987. Despite the optimistic account which appeared in the Kuwaiti press, the encounter between the two uncompromising autocrats did not seem to have been a great success.[57] Syria was soon to reaffirm its support for the 'Islamic revolution of Iran', and Iraq was to repeat its denunciation of Assad's 'treachery' and urge his overthrow and the destruction of his regime.[58]

King Hussein persisted in his efforts, which were presumably not helped by Iraq's shooting down of a Syrian warplane that had strayed into Iraqi airspace in July 1987.[59] However, the King linked the reconciliation to the convening of the Arab Summit conference at Amman in November 1987. Here, at least, his efforts were rewarded with a kind of success. Although it was scarcely a penitent Assad who came to Amman, there was an unmistakable impression that the summit itself was a personal triumph for Saddam Hussein. He had received the imprimatur of an Arab consensus on his long maintained argument that the struggle with Iran, far from being a distraction from the Arab nation's major concern with Palestine, was in fact fundamental to the future identity and survival of the nation. Iraq's war effort was therefore sanctified by its dedication to a greater goal, in the achievement of which, Saddam Hussein suggested, the Iraqi armed forces had acquitted themselves considerably better than those Arab armies which had fought Israel.[60]

There are a number of unsubstantiated reports about the nature of the meeting between Assad and Saddam Hussein in Amman. Memories of insults exchanged, conspiracies hatched and the very transparency of each regime to the other cannot have made it a particularly soothing encounter. Nevertheless, something was achieved, even if it was only the letting off of steam. The Iraqi leadership claimed to see a change in Syria's position on the war and were encouraged by its endorsement of the summit resolution supporting Iraq.[61] The fact that, once back in Damascus, Assad reassured Iran of Syria's support did not seem to bring the tentative moves towards an Iraqi–Syrian dialogue to an end. Low-level visits aimed at improving economic relations followed, although Iraq claimed not to be interested in reopening the oil pipeline to Banias. At this stage, it was clearly felt that such a move would give too great a hostage to fortune. In addition, Iraq did not want to be distracted from the expansion of the pipeline across Saudi Arabia.[62] While the re-establishment of diplomatic relations did not take place immediately, it was nevertheless noticeable that both Syria and Iraq considerably reduced the hostile, indeed vituperative, tone of their media when commenting on each other's affairs.

Iraq and the Gulf States

The importance of the Amman Summit did not only lie in the sphere of Iraqi–Syrian or Iraqi–Egyptian relations. It also underlined, in a way highly advantageous to Iraq, the identity of its fate with that of Saudi Arabia and Kuwait in 'the face of Iranian threats and aggression'.[63] Throughout the war, but especially since 1982, it has been crucial for the war effort that Saddam Hussein should be able to draw on the financial and oil resources of these two Gulf states in particular. The insistence with which he has maintained that Iraq is fighting on behalf of the Arab nation has been directed as much at the Arab states of the Gulf as at the rest of the Arab world. It has been a means of reminding them that they have a moral obligation to sustain and subsidize the defence of Iraq and, by implication, of Saddam Hussein's regime. In fact, the vulnerability of these Gulf states is such that they have, in general, needed little reminder that the military collapse of Iraq would be a catastrophe for them. Even so, Saddam Hussein has found it incumbent upon himself to stress the fact that an Iranian military victory would mean not only the devastation of Iraq, but also of the Arab states of the Gulf:[64]

> All Gulf countries are aware of Iran's ambitions in targeting them ... They know that had it not been for Iraq, they would have been taken as prisoners to the lands of the Persians ... I think they know that, and if they do not, then that is an even graver problem.[64]

This was said at a time when Saddam Hussein was evidently disappointed at the level of financial assistance which Iraq was receiving from the Gulf states. He felt that it was commensurate neither with the gravity of Iraq's military and economic plight, nor with the interests of the Gulf states which Iraq was serving by engaging the armed forces of Iran.[65] Iraq's fear was that the very scale of the Iranian threat would intimidate the Gulf states into reducing and possibly ending their financial aid, in the hope of working out some form of compromise settlement with Iran over the corpse of Saddam Hussein. It was for this reason that Saddam Hussein was somewhat mistrustful of the sporadic attempts by the Gulf states to mediate an end to the war. While Iraq publicly welcomed any efforts by third parties to persuade Iran to abandon its war aims, this was tempered by Saddam Hussein's determination that it should not be achieved at the expense of his own interests.[66] Nor was the Iraqi Government particularly reassured by the prospect of mediation by its fellow Arab states. As Tariq Aziz said:[67]

> Iraq does not expect mediation from its brothers. From them, Iraq expects solidarity that stems from their commitments in accordance with the Arab League Charter and the collective defence pact.

In the case of the Gulf states, there was evidently concern that, since they lacked the leverage considered by Saddam Hussein as necessary in order to force the Iranian regime into negotiating an end to the war, mediation of this nature would simply allow Iran to persuade them to reduce the level of their support for Iraq. This was particularly true of the increased contacts between Iran and the Gulf states during 1985. The Iranian 'peace offensive' of that year, seeking to draw the Gulf states away from their position of support for Iraq, was vehemently denounced by Saddam Hussein. He warned them that Iran's professions of friendship were a sham and that they should be aware of the fact that behind the reassurances lay an unmistakable threat of internal subversion and external aggression. As he reminded them once again, 'had it not been for Iraq's steadfastness, black and greedy Khomeinism would have stormed through all the region's countries'.[68]

Nevertheless, for the most part Saddam Hussein could be satisfied that the attitude of Iran itself, with its 'friendly warnings' and overt threats to Iraq's Gulf supporters, would ensure that they would continue to see Iraq as the main bulwark against Iran.[69] An attempt to assassinate the Emir of

Kuwait and a series of bomb explosions in the city of Kuwait were claimed by groups which seemed to draw their inspiration from Iran. This formed a curious backdrop to Iranian professions of goodwill, as Saddam Hussein pointed out.[70] Taken together with the inability of the Saudi intermediaries to find much common ground with the Iranian position on the war, it simply served to confirm for the Gulf states that they had little alternative but to continue their financial support for Iraq's war effort.[71]

In fact, despite Saddam Hussein's occasional grumbles, the aid given to Iraq by the Gulf states has been substantial and could be said to have been a decisive factor in enabling the regime to withstand the rigours of an extended war. Although the size of the financial loans cannot be known definitively, estimates of the sums involved range from $35 billion to $50 billion since the beginning of the war, and its seems certain that very little of this is a loan in the strict commercial sense, but rather an outright gift.[72] Kuwait and Saudi Arabia have supplemented this financial help with the opening up of their ports for the shipment of goods bound for Iraq, as well as with the sale of oil on Iraq's behalf. In addition, Iraq has constructed a major oil pipeline through Saudi Arabia which, together with the pipeline through Turkey and other measures, enabled it to export an estimated 2.7 million barrels of oil per day by late 1987.[73]

Iraq's growing dependence on the Arab Gulf states has therefore been an important outcome of the war, even though it may have dented Saddam Hussein's earlier pretensions to play a dominant political and security role in the region. His original attitude of hurt disappointment when the Gulf states established the Gulf Co-operation Council in 1981, specifically excluding Iraq, has necessarily been forced to give way to an acceptance of the organization. Tariq Aziz commented in 1984 that the policy of seeking regional domination by one country or leader was outdated and that there was now a need for co-operation. This was a far cry from the boast made in *Al-Thawra* in 1979 that Iraq opposed any form of military alliance or regional bloc, since it alone had the capacity to ensure the security of the Gulf.[74] Nevertheless, the importance of ensuring the uninterrupted flow of Gulf financial aid has overtaken all other considerations, at least for the present. Efforts by Iraq to draw the Gulf states more closely into its war operations have been constrained not only by the limited assistance they can give in this sphere, but also by the knowledge that this should not be allowed to jeopardize their most important contribution – their financial resources.[75]

It is in this respect, of course, that the Iraqi strategy of extending its military operations to the waters of the Gulf, by targeting Iran's oil exports, has inevitably had a direct impact on the interests of the Gulf states. The occasional attack by Iraqi warplanes, in the early months of this strategy's implementation, on ships belonging to or doing business with their Gulf allies may have been something of an embarrassment. However, it could equally be seen as a demonstration of Iraqi resolve in pursuing the only strategy which the leadership believed would cause Iran to reconsider its war aims. It was, and has remained, imperative for Saddam Hussein to reject any limitations on his conduct of the war, regardless of the nature of the aid he has received or the anxieties and cautions of those from whom he expects aid to be freely given. For the Gulf states, it was perturbing enough that Iran should regard them with undisguised hostility because of their financial support for Iraq. Once Iraq began in earnest to bomb Iran's oil installations and to attack the tankers loading Iranian oil, it was unavoidable that Iran should reciprocate by attacking shipping trading with Iraq's allies in the Gulf. Undoubtedly, the destructive consequence of this, as well as the anxiety it caused many of the Arab Gulf states, led to the search in 1985 for some common ground with Iran. The failure to find such common ground and the lack of leverage over Iraqi war strategies resulted, it would appear, in their agreement with Iraq's thesis that only by crippling the Iranian economy could the Tehran Government be compelled to modify its war aims and negotiate an end to hostilities.[76]

However, such acquiescence also meant that the Gulf states would have to accept the consequences, spelt out by the Iranian Minister of Foreign Affairs in early 1986:[77]

> We wish to live in peace and co-operation with our neighbours. But we cannot allow some countries to sell oil on behalf of our enemy and calmly transport the oil in the Persian Gulf.

It has been Iraq's task subsequently to steel the resolve of those Gulf states which are most obviously at risk and to ensure the failure, in Tariq Aziz's words, of the 'attempt to use the Iranian paper tiger to peddle schemes of hegemony in the Gulf'.[78] This has meant continually stressing the fact that Iran's attacks on Gulf states' interests – especially on those of Kuwait and Saudi Arabia – are not simply the result of any particular war strategy pursued by Iraq, but stem from a deeper Iranian hostility, based ultimately on the desire to subject the whole Arab littoral to Iranian control.[79] After the occupation of the Fao peninsula, and the alarm it caused in the Gulf, it was therefore important for Iraq to draw the appropriate lesson for the benefit of its neighbours. This it succeeded in doing during a visit of the GCC Ministers of Information to Baghdad, where they were reported as having jointly condemned Iran's attack on Iraqi territory as 'aggression which seeks to threaten the Arabian Gulf and control its waters'.[80]

For Iraq, therefore, the intensification of Iranian threats against and attacks on the shipping of Kuwait, Saudi Arabia and other Gulf states has been by no means an unwelcome consequence of its own strategies in the waters of the Gulf. Quite apart from the increased international involvement in 1987 which resulted from Kuwait's fears for the security of its shipping, there was the unmistakable impression that, by the middle

of the year, Iran regarded Kuwait and Saudi Arabia as little better than
co-belligerents. This was an impression which Iraq did much to foster.
The riots and demonstrations inspired by Iran during the Haj in Mecca
at the end of July were used by Saddam Hussein as examples of the kind
of threat which Iran represented:[81]

> Muslims, Arabs and the entire world . . . [now] have legitimate justification for
> launching a war against Khomeini, because he distorts Islam and threatens the
> Arabs and their security, sanctity and property.

Furthermore, the declarations of the Arab League now grouped
Kuwait and Saudi Arabia with Iraq as the beleaguered victims of Iranian
aggression, encouraging Saddam Hussein to underline the selfless nature
of Iraq's war effort, as its forces dedicated themselves to the task of
defending all three states:[82]

> Iraq's policy always considers Iraqi national security to be an indivisible part of
> pan-Arab security . . . Arab Gulf states are currently being exposed to certain
> circumstances and threats. In the light of this fact, Iraq considers its national
> security an integral part of the security of the brothers in Saudi Arabia and
> Kuwait. What threatens or harms them also threatens and harms Iraq.

At the beginning of September 1987, after the launching of an Iranian
surface-to-surface missile against a target in Kuwait, Iraq went so far as
to link its own strategy of attacks on Iranian economic targets directly with
the fate of Kuwait, calling its own efforts 'a day of revenge to underscore
the bonds of blood, religion, history and destiny between Iraq and Kuwait
and as a salute from Iraq'.[83]

Kuwait might well have preferred to have foregone such 'salutes', but
the nature of the war and the logic of its own situation meant that its
government had scarcely any choice in the matter. Much the same logic
could be said to apply to Saudi Arabia. Because of the crucial role they
have played in sustaining Iraq's war effort, these two states are the ones
which Iraq has been at most pains to cultivate. The vacillations and
anxieties expressed periodically by the small states in the lower Gulf, and
their occasional attempts to placate a wrathful Iran, have been of little
importance to Iraq. However, they have provided Saddam Hussein with
some good opportunities to talk reproachfully about the proper duties of
Arab brothers, as if to remind others, with greater resources at their
disposal, that they must not forsake Iraq.

In managing relations with the Arab states in the region, Saddam
Hussein has succeeded in drawing upon their resources for Iraq's benefit,
whilst at the same time sustaining the impression that such aid has been
given in the spirit of pan-Arab co-operation. This has been as useful for
the rulers of the states concerned, as for Saddam Hussein himself. It has
helped to reinforce the image, believed fundamental to the legitimacy of
all the governments involved, that they are serving the greater cause of the

Arab nation. At the same time, the help which they have given has enabled Iraq to withstand seven years of war without succumbing either to military or economic collapse. In averting such a catastrophe, they have also served their own particular interests. It is not only in Iraq that this ambiguity has been apparent, between dedication to a lofty ideal beyond the state and the requirements of maintaining the power of individual regimes within the given boundaries of the state. More than any of them, Saddam Hussein, during the war, has been forced to come to terms with the twin obligations of government in this regard, as he made plain in his speech to the Amman Summit of 1987:[84]

> We must take into account our actual state of affairs. We are a number of countries, each with its own concerns, problems and circumstances, which are usually similar, but sometimes different.

He acknowledged that this demanded a new basis for relations between Arab states, in which the sovereignty of each state must finally be recognized:

> We should first eliminate a problem from which the Arabs have suffered – namely, the bane of interference in the affairs of others, based on claims and illusions about populations, geographical areas or other factors that tempt some to impose trusteeship on others and interfere in their affairs. Without eliminating this problem, the Arab condition will never be rectified.

The reassurance which the assembled Arab rulers could draw from witnessing an Iraqi Ba'thist President making such an improbable declaration, would have depended upon their degree of trust in his sincerity. However, the fact that he could voice such sentiments, in so public a forum, is testimony to his confidence in having bent not only a domestic, but also a regional, environment to his will. The success he has had in handling the latter in many senses reflects his domination of the former. In both cases, the war has created a pressing need on the part of many of those involved to support 'Saddam's Qadisiyya', whatever reservations they may have about Saddam Hussein himself, precisely because the prospect of defeat in that battle is even more alarming.

9

Iran and the Region

Relations with the Gulf states

The Iran–Iraq war has thrown into sharper relief the paramount issue facing the Arab states of the Gulf: how to deal with the Iranian revolution. For Iran too, quite apart from the war, relations with these neighbouring Muslim states have been an important consideration since the inception of the Islamic republic. These states are its closest neighbours, and the most susceptible to its power and influence. (However, ambitious revolutionary Iran has not conceived a breakthrough in influence in Turkey, Pakistan, the USSR or Afghanistan, comparable to that which its leaders had already envisaged in the Gulf in 1980.)

The Gulf states were bound to become a prime target, by virtue of their proximity and size. Geography and demography made them susceptible to Iran's power whether exercised by traditional means or through the large Iranian and Shi'i communities sprinkled on the Arab littoral of the Gulf. However, they became even more so as a result both of Iran's claims to the leadership of the Islamic world and of the war, in which they became, in most cases unwittingly, virtual participants.

As both an Islamic state and revolution, Iran has claimed a unique position in the contemporary Islamic world, as vanguard, model and leader. Because at the same time it is the only existing Shi'i state (and the Shi'a are themselves a minority of only 20 per cent in the Muslim world, and sizeable largely in the non-Arab world) these claims have been to the Islamic *ummah* – the entire community of believers – a much broader constituency than that available had sectarian considerations been paramount. The need to escape any 'Shi'i ghetto' and to affirm the universal applicability of its mission on a much broader stage has been an essential element in Iran's propagation of its message. It has thus emphasized its role as an Islamic state rather than as a state motivated by patriotism, nationalism, or sectarian motives. From the outset of the war the Iranian leaders have depicted the conflict as one between 'Islam and blasphemy' and, despite its increasingly national dimensions in 1987, have repeated this. President Khamenei put it this way:[1]

If expressions of nationalism are intended to create barriers between Muslims, cause separations among them and threaten their fraternity, then this is 100 per cent forbidden. *There are no Arabs and non-Arabs in Islam.* (Emphasis added.)

Inevitably Iran's claims to such a role and the exclusive right to judge the Islamic credentials of its neighbours, would have created strains with its neighbours in the Gulf. So too would its alleged right to appeal to Muslims over the heads of their governments and its practice of seeking to undermine their leaders politically for not being hostile enough towards Israel, or being too supine and dependent on the 'Great Satan', i.e. the United States. These pretensions were already causing concern in the Gulf states throughout 1979–80. The Saudi Government as the 'Keeper of the Holy Places' had always emphasized its religious credentials as an integral aspect of its dynasty's legitimacy, and felt particularly threatened. In addition, there was a question of *amour propre*, for the Arab states were less disposed to see Iranians as Islamic Iran chose, i.e. as co-religionists, but equally as Persians and traditional rivals of the Arabs, with their own distinctive national claims on their neighbours, and as Shi'a, representing a minority, not to say deviant, form of Islam.

If the Iranians have Islamicized the war, appealing for neutrality at least from the Arab states, while continuing their attempts to expunge corruption, Iraq has sought to Arabize it and depict it as a concrete revolutionary threat to the Arab states of the Gulf, the Arab world as a whole, and to Arab Nationalism as a doctrine. Iran has threatened the Gulf states with the consequences of thwarting the Islamic tide, and has cultivated Syria's friendship. The latter is crucial less for any concrete benefit it provides than for the entrée it gives Iran to the broader Islamic world, and for the support it gives to its argument that, indeed, the conflict is not about Persian versus Arab.

The outbreak of the war put the Gulf states in a dilemma, confronting them with the need for decisions they would have preferred to postpone. For these states there is no optimum policy to deal with the war, which at times threatens some of them in a daily way, directly, and the outcome of which would affect them all. Their situation is not identical. To take but one dimension, their Shi'a populations vary; from some 60 per cent of the population in Bahrain, 30 per cent in Kuwait, 15 per cent in Saudi Arabia, 5 per cent in the United Arab Emirates to virtually none in Oman. Geographic location also affects involvement in the war. Kuwait is most directly implicated because of its adjacence to Iraq, and consequent pressures from both belligerents; but Bahrain and Saudi Arabia in the northern Gulf are also more involved, while the more southerly states of the UAE, Qatar and Oman are less so.

They all need to be sensitive in varying degrees to the threat of subversion in their countries stirred up by Iran, and particularly amongst the Shi'a communities. At the same time, while none of them wishes to take sides in the conflict, because it may turn out to be the losing side, each is aware of the consequences of an Iranian victory for the region's security. On the other hand, they are also reluctant to tilt too far towards Iraq, for they neither trust Baghdad nor wish to have a vindictive and defeated Iran as a neighbour. Similar considerations inhibit their reliance on the United States for assurance of their security. This could be a political liability for them domestically, and in any case none of them is content to rely on the durability of the US commitment, and most have doubts about the sagacity of any US government. The upshot of all these contradictory considerations is policies that appear inconsistent or worse. There is a strong tendency to balance relations with both adversaries, to avoid 'provocation' of Iran, to keep channels open (because isolating a regional great power is impossible), to defuse crises by conciliation or even appeasement.[2]

The war has escalated and widened into the Gulf's waters since 1983–4, and particularly since 1985 when Iraqi attacks against Iranian oil terminals elicited Iranian attacks on the shipping of the Gulf states suspected of complicity in Iraq's war effort. Attacks on third party shipping, attacks on the facilities of the Gulf states, and even an Iranian ground offensive near Kuwait, all threaten to drag the Gulf states into the war. Pressures have built up especially in 1987 threatening their precarious, and (one must add) in some cases largely fictitious, neutrality. At times in the past seven years the fact of the war has been rather distant, almost a theoretical concern; this is no longer the case. The risks associated with its continuation now probably overwhelm the earlier estimate that the war, at a low level, served some useful purpose in keeping the combatants preoccupied.

Iran's attitude toward the Gulf states has also reflected ambivalence. Notwithstanding the Islamic-moral claims on them, contemporary Iran has exhibited aspects of great power arrogance combined with the traditional Persian contempt for the Arab states. Khomeini's references to Saudi Arabia as the 'Kingdom of Hejaz', and Ayatollah Montazeri's frequent contemptuous comments about the 'Wahhabi' are thus mixed with more conventional comments about Iran's rights as a regional great power. Iran has tended to mix reassurances about guaranteeing the security of the Gulf with dire predictions about the dangers of thwarting its will and the dark fate awaiting these reactionary regimes.

Iran has had some success in Islamicizing the conflict, and reducing any automatic polarization of the region into Persian versus Arab. In this it has been helped by the differences among the Arab Gulf states, some of whom have traditionally been close to it (e.g. Dubai), and others distant from Saudi Arabia (e.g. Oman), as well as by its ties with Syria (which we discuss below). Its attempts to reassure the Arab states of the Gulf and to seek their detachment from what in practical terms has been a near-universal tilt towards Iraq, has been constrained by its own insistence on continuing a dualistic policy. On the one hand, it has waged conventional war against Iraq and sought to keep its neighbours out of it while, on the other hand, it has not relinquished its claim to interfere in their affairs or to destabilize them at the earliest possible opportunity. The net result, seen most vividly in the case of Kuwait, is a dual-track policy of intimidating Kuwait with bomb attacks and sabotage by various front organizations, while insisting that it be genuinely neutral in regard to a war whose outcome may directly threaten it.

A paradoxical situation is thus created which is not easily sustained. Iran wants a 'neutrality' from the Gulf states that allows it to win the war: the Gulf states, in turn, want to buttress Iraq for their own security, but also to keep out of the war. In the case of Kuwait, a vicious circle is at work whereby Iran's attempts to detach Kuwait from Iraq through intimidation only increase Kuwait's suspicions about the loyalty of its Shi'a population, stimulating their repressive treatment which further inflames Iran. Similarly the more pressure Iran brings to bear on the Gulf states to force them away from Iraq, and the more intimidation it practises, the more these states are convinced of the need for at least clandestine support for Iraq. Yet if Iran is to forgo this pressure, how is it to convince them of the need for genuine neutrality? Clearly the needs of the war have come to require their neutralization, yet it would seem that the only terms under which this can be achieved – the effective and credible assurance that Iran poses no threat to them – entail the renunciation of any claims on them. In brief, to detach these states from Iraq and to win the war, Iran would have to convince them that its dispute concerns only Iraq, its neighbour, and renounce any messianic Islamic mission – a price too high for the Islamic republic to contemplate.

Iran has sought to depict its war aims as reasonable, the punishment of the aggressor being the prerequisite for any restoration of a true peace. Khomeini put it characteristically:[3]

> For in order to defend Islam, this tumour must be removed; . . . otherwise this country will never experience peace; neither our country nor Iraq, nor all the Gulf states. These Gulf states do not realize what Saddam would do to them if he won.

Iran has depicted the defeat of Saddam Hussein as the prerequisite for effective action against Israel: 'the road to Jerusalem goes through Baghdad'. In 1985 the Iranian Foreign Minister, Velayati, on the first official visit to Saudi Arabia since the revolution, told his counterpart that it was his country's view that the failure of past efforts against Israel had been due to their lack of 'Islamic essence'.[4]

As the war and Iranian politics have evolved so have Iran's attitudes and policies been modified. The war has been an education, obliging the authorities in Tehran to balance their ideological goals with their practical needs, to harmonize their principles and their priorities, to modify their rhetoric and their peremptory claims vis-à-vis their neighbours, to admit the need for, and even desirability of, co-existence and to relinquish any early expectation of a voluntary alliance. Our primary interest in this section is this evolution in Iran's perspective and policy toward the Gulf states. Part of the evolution is natural, following the passage of time and the tempering effects of responsibility and experience, but part of it is due to the war, which creates its own demands and priorities. As we have seen repeatedly in the seven years covered in this study, the period 1984/5 marked a turning point, when it was recognized that there would be no quick or easy victory, and policies were adjusted accordingly. In Iran's relations with the Gulf states, this dividing line is visible, even if not its exact date.

i) *The first phase 1980–4: revolutionary claims, warnings and demands*

The Islamic republic inherited a situation in the Gulf that was very advantageous, with good relations with all the littoral states and no significant outstanding differences. The Shah's Iran had made claims on its neighbours, particularly in its efforts to support a regional arrangement hostile to Communism and regarding some islands which he considered strategically important, but had otherwise made no effort to order the internal structure of the Gulf states. The 1975 Algiers agreement between Iran and Iraq regulating the overall relationship as well as adjusting respective border claims had been a triumph of pragmatism over ideology on both sides. Revolutionary Iran managed virtually overnight to destroy the *modus vivendi* laboriously achieved, by the nature of the claims it made on its neighbours. Even before the war, Iranian officials spoke of their mission to take true Islam to the 'masses' and of their right and duty to 'export the revolution'. Iran appeared to be intent on undermining the Gulf states, monarchical or republican, rejecting them as secular, oppressive and corrupt, and determined to bring its version of a radical universal Islam into the forefront of Middle East politics.[5] In this policy, it possessed formidable assets: traditional regimes controlling societies in transition, the frustrations and dislocations of change, and the diminished appeal of secular ideologies. In addition, it had the advantage of the powerful appeal of revolutionary Islam among all Muslims, the specific attraction for the 'oppressed', often Shi'a, communities sprinkled all over the Gulf states (with majorities in Iraq and Bahrain) and the natural constituency of overseas Iranians settled on the opposite littoral of the Gulf.[6] Iran could pose a threat of subversion to the Gulf states which was, and remains, virtually inescapable.

By virtue of its revolution, its claims of leadership, and its rejection of the concept of national territories or 'intervention' as principles that could inhibit Islamic duty, Islamic Iran was seen as the primary threat to their security. On the eve of the war, it had managed to push them into the lap of Iraq, which was now seen as a potential bulwark against an unpredictably volatile and powerful neighbour. There was thus little question that the Gulf states, and especially Saudi Arabia and Kuwait, were aware of the Iraqi plan to attack Iran, and did little to restrain Baghdad, possibly offering some assurances to encourage the attack. Iraq's dispersal of its air force into the territory of some of these states, and its deployment of helicopters on their territory for use as a staging post for an attack, almost saw the Gulf states directly involved in hostilities. In the event, this threat was defused but the Gulf states were to pursue a very tenuous form of neutrality.

· Any disappointment felt in Iran was swamped by the belief that these 'regimes' did not reflect their people and would in due course be swept away, and by a confidence in Iran's revolutionary élan to win the war and to deal with the Gulf states at its leisure. Iran disclaimed any intention of posing a threat to the Gulf states and adopted a tone of injured innocence, combining blandishments with intimidation. Besides providing a sanctuary for Iraqi dissidents and sponsoring an Iraqi government-in-exile, it also funded, trained and supported opposition parties and groupings in the Gulf states. It appears to have supported and trained terrorist groups such as the Islamic Jihad and the Iraqi Mojahedin and Al-Da'wa, as well as various groups whose nomenclature changes with their mission. In addition to propaganda, it used its network of Shi'i clerics and international groups of Muslims (such as the Organization of Friday Prayer Leaders) to urge the necessity for radical change. It refused to accept the distinction between religion and politics, arguing that worship was implicitly a political act, and that the annual pilgrimage, the haj, should be used to awaken Muslims. It allocated a division of revolutionary guards for support to liberation movements and a small detachment was soon sent to the Beka in Lebanon to testify to its concern for its co-religionists.

The threat posed by Iran stimulated the Gulf states into formal co-operation and the creation of the Gulf Co-operation Council in May 1981, which excluded both Iran and Iraq. The GCC came to emphasize security and defence after the revelations of Iranian support for an attempted coup in Bahrain in December 1981 that was thwarted in the nick of time. At a meeting in early 1982 the GCC, whilst increasing defence co-operation, declared that an attack on any one state would be considered an attack on all members of the GCC, and condemned Iran's attempts at regional destabilization.[7] Iranian comments varied from Tehran Radio's call for the overthrow of the 'corrupt' Saudi regime, to Rafsanjani's more resigned: 'We know that the Gulf states are helping Iraq with its war effort . . . but we forgive them'.[8] As the war appeared to be moving toward a swift Iranian victory in 1982, Iran renewed its demand that the Gulf states stop their support for Iraq. In May 1982 the GCC Ministers held emergency discussions.[9]

Iranian officials like Rafsanjani sought to allay fears about the consequences of an Iranian victory:[10]

> the Islamic republic of Iran is not adventurous. The IRI realizes that the oil is essential for the world's economy today and it does not want the oil cut . . . in this region we are in greater need of security than the Gulf sheikhs. The security which we will maintain will stop others who want to violate it.

Successful counterattacks after the recapture of Khorramshahr led to the expulsion of Iraqi forces from Iran. In taking the war into Iraq and insisting on the 'punishment' of Saddam Hussein, Iran appeared to be doing more than prosecute a war against Iraq. Such suspicions were fed by Khomeini's attitude which appeared to expect the Gulf states to fall into Iran's lap once Iraq had been dealt with:[11]

> If the war continues and if in the war Iran defeats Iraq, Iraq will be annexed to Iran; that is, the nation of Iraq, the oppressed people of Iraq, will free themselves from the talons of the tyrannical clique and will link themselves with the Iranian nation. They will set up their own government according to their wishes – an Islamic one. If Iran and Iraq can merge and be amalgamated, all the diminutive nations of the region will join them.

Khomeini, who habitually used the phrase 'palace dwellers' for the Gulf states' rulers, tended to talk ambiguously, sometimes implying a spontaneous unity, sometimes an enforced one. In any event, his stern and hectoring tone was not encouraging and the Gulf states in mid-1982 regarded with horror the imminent prospect of an Iranian-led Islamic juggernaut rolling south from Baghdad to Basra and into their principalities. Khomeini warned them about assistance to Iraq: 'they are creating trouble for their future; helping Saddam is treason against Islam'.[12]

Iranian statements reflecting the various strands within Tehran were not consistent, and seemed to mix assurances with threats in a most *un*reassuring way. Most of the Gulf states shared the vision articulated by Patrick Seale of a 'Shi'a commonwealth of Iran and Iraq under Khomeini',[13] with its implications for themselves and the wider balance of power in the region. It was not comforting. They dropped their inhibitions about political co-operation, and in the light of the palpable vulnerability of their societies to the effects of the war, moved away from their 'false neutrality' to more obvious alignment with Iraq.[14] GCC statements openly condemned Iran for continuing the war and destabilizing the region, while individual states disbursed interest-free aid to Iraq to the tune of some $20 billion by 1982. The threat perceived from the war was threefold: a) the impact of an Iranian victory and the direct consequences for the region; b) the impact of a continuing war, which might expand to include their territories or facilities; c) the contagious nature of radical Islam which might take root in their own countries, by appropriating the channels of protest and the symbols of legitimacy in opposing the established order.

By the second anniversary of the war, the lines had become drawn. The Gulf states had shown themselves uncharacteristically determined. A Saudi Radio commentary reflected this tone: 'There is no way to thwart those (Iranian) plans and foil them, except by supporting Iraq financially and militarily in order to destroy the Iranian war machine'.[15] Iran in turn could point, as Rafsanjani did in listing ten points, to transgressions by the Arab states in favour of Iraq. 'We have been very patient for the sake of Islam and the Muslim peoples. However, patience . . . has limits'.[16] Continued Arab financial support for Iraq compensated for its inability to export oil and generate foreign exchange for its war needs.

The issue of the haj pilgrimage continued to fester. Khomeini wanted it to constitute a political factor:[17]

> From its inception the political dimension of the Haj has never been anything less than its dimension as an act of worship . . . The harm suffered by these palace-appointed preachers is greater than that inflicted by America.

Saudi warnings that misbehaviour could see the end of the haj for Iranians led to Khomeini threatening 'an explosion within Islam . . . as a result of which there will no longer be a shaykh and any more American lackeys left'. The question, in some ways a side-issue to the central problem of the war, reflected the attitudes on either side: Khomeini betraying his contempt for the Gulf states in his language, the latter concerned that political agitation would be disguised as legitimate worship. Indeed, Khomeini never differentiated Iran's interests from those of Islam, thus making his claims difficult to disentangle.[18]

> The government of the Hijaz will wake up some day when the issue is over. It should start now to mend its ways. I warn the governments of the Gulf . . . to stop opposing Iran and assisting Saddam . . . An Islamic government is better for all the shaykhs of the region than the flimsy American power.

At the same time, while Iran's Foreign Minister sought to assure the Gulf states that they had no cause for worry and that Iran paid attention to the interests of its neighbours,[19] others in and out of government made contradictory statements. The Army Commander-in-Chief told a Western magazine:[20]

> Our strategy is designed to liberate not only the occupied territories but also Jerusalem and all Islamic countries where people feel the need to vanquish tyranny.

The discordance was not intentional and referred to two different levels of activity and aspiration, but it was nonetheless chilling for the Gulf states following Iran's war operations.

Seemingly impervious to casualties, losses and deficiencies in equipment, Iran threw its soldiers into offensive after offensive with little result, but with apparently undiminished determination. Iraq, emerging from a period of cautious restocking, now sought to escape from exclusive reliance on defence and to broaden the war by attacking Iran's oil exports. This threatened to involve the Gulf states directly, especially if Iran reacted in revenge by attacking its more vulnerable neighbours in the Gulf. Iran, in turn, was finding the inability to breach Iraq's defences or bring about a political collapse in Baghdad frustrating. The Gulf states' assistance was turning out to be more than a nuisance; it had become the critical economic and psychological factor in 1983. Yet it was not in Iran's interest to widen the war to the Gulf states or waters, however blatant the support of these states for Iraq. For Iran, victory would have to come on land, and other entanglements could only hinder this.

Iran repeatedly sought to affirm its support for the unhindered flow of oil, with the proviso that it could only accept this as long as its own oil was flowing; attacks incapacitating its ability to export, it was implied, risked the closure of the straits for all states.[21] Playing on its interest in limiting rather than extending the war, its spokesmen emphasized the compatibility of interests with the Gulf states. As Rafsanjani put it:[22]

> The nations in our neighbouring countries should know that the Islamic Republic first and foremost desires security in the Persian Gulf; we have proved this ... We call on you not to become partners in this war. We can guarantee your security.

The Gulf states' response to the widening war and the possibility of an Iranian air threat was to improve the co-ordination of their air defences within the GCC, and individually to request improved short-range air-defence missiles (*Stingers*) from the United States.[23] Emergency meetings of Arab ministers and the Arab League Council meeting in Tunis focused on Iran's attacks on Arab tankers (usually in retaliation for Iraqi attacks) rather than on Iraq's actions. Similarly the US-led naval patrol tended to see Iran as the culprit for not ending the war, rather than Iraq for extending it. In any case, there was a deep resentment in Iran at this type of double standard, which depicted Iran as unreasonable or irrational, condemned its pursuance of the war as stubborn, and acted in panic at its successes, but had been mute when Iranian territory had earlier been invested and destroyed by the Iraqis. Iranian newspapers did not always follow the moderate line of some spokesmen. *Kayhan* asked why Iran had to put up with the 'hostile' attitude of Kuwait and Saudi Arabia when it had the means to overfly them? *Jomhuri-ye Eslami* warned:[24]

> The more the Arab reactionaries display their sensitivity to the expansion of Islam, the more they will reveal their main weakness to Muslim nations.

A major turning point in relations was the shooting down by Saudi aircraft over Saudi waters of an ageing Iranian F-4 fighter on 5 June 1984. The Iranian reaction was illustrative of a change in attitude and policy that had been becoming evident but which was crystallized by this event. It was neither threatening nor contemptuous; it sought to reassure the Saudis about its aims and to argue for a more even-handed policy. The protest note referred to 'the IRI's repeated efforts aimed at the creation of stability and the elimination of tension from the Persian Gulf region'. It warned that Iran would respond severely to any further attacks on its aircraft, but went on to explain that they 'are assigned only the task of creating stability in and eliminating tension from the region' and concluded: 'We use this opportunity to renew our highest regards.'[25]

The tone was as conciliatory as possible, reflecting a change in the war situation. As the defeat of Iraq receded into the future and confidence that the Gulf states would soon fall into its lap declined, Iran sought to adjust its policies by moving initially to a war of attrition and later in 1985 to emphasis on more limited offensives (ending up again in 1986 with a return to large-scale offensives). Part of this rethinking entailed a recognition that Iran's own acts and declarations had had the effect of virtually isolating it in the war, and giving Iraq a free ride as the less odious of the two combatants. Failure to distinguish between aspiration and policy, and state and 'revolution', and between the 'export of the revolution' as a model and as an active policy, had alienated many of Iran's neighbours. In retrospect rather needlessly, Iran, in the first flush of revolutionary confidence and hubris, had imposed constraints on its own war effort by pushing the Gulf states into the opposite camp. It had demanded of them total reform, the ending of ties with the United States and the installation of Islamic governments. Now, with the war in its fourth year, and with shortages in equipment looming, Iraq's *de facto* allies needed to be decoupled from Baghdad by soft words rather than threats. Threats appeared only to harden their determination to resist; further-more, Iran had a diminishing capability to carry them out. It had also become clear that, in the event of an attack on the Gulf states, Iran would become entangled with the United States, an eventuality that did not hold true if the war was limited to Iraq.

The theme of reassurance, and the aspect of sweet reasonableness, began to make its unaccustomed appearance. The Iranian President made no threats but simply asked whether those states supplying Iraq with money ought not to use their influence to stop it from escalating the war into the Gulf.[26] *Jomhuri-ye Eslami* asked whether it might not be helpful for the region's stability if the Gulf states relied a little more on themselves for their security.[27] The Deputy Foreign Minister observed that, despite their support for Iraq, there were signs that these states were beginning to understand Iran's policies.[28] The Speaker of the Majles emphasized that export of the revolution did not imply the use of the sword, but that 'We wish to provide the divine message to the deprived meek people of the world'.[29] President Khamenei echoed the theme that the export of the revolution did not imply the use of force.[30] Iranian commentaries took to an emphasis on the potential for co-operation with the Gulf states, though always with one proviso:[31]

> [Iran's policy] is stable, especially toward co-operation with the neighbouring GCC and within the framework of non-interference in internal policy. But it is not possible for the region to be secure while the Baghdad regime exists.

Iran thus sought to project a new image in the region. It denied any involvement in outbreaks of violence such as the assassination attempt on the Emir of Kuwait or explosions in Riyadh, and insisted on its desire for good-neighbourly relations. It accused Iraq of sponsoring these incidents to destabilize the region and to blackmail the Gulf states to arrest the normalization of relations with Iran.[3]

Tehran now sought to depict Saddam Hussein as at least as great a threat to the Gulf states as he was to Iran. This was particularly true, it was observed, of his policy of trying to entangle the Gulf states in the war. One commentator doubted that he could be a serious threat to Iran, but rather 'to the Gulf states, since he tries to draw them into the battlefield while they are powerless'.[33] In return for the punishment of Saddam Hussein, Iranian leaders now offered assurances to neighbouring countries that they would not subsequently attack them or try to destabilize them.[34] At the same time, Iran adhered to the position that it would retaliate for attacks on its own oil exports by attacks on others:[35]

> If the Persian Gulf were to become unsafe for us, the natural reaction would be to stop Iraq's indirect use by making it unsafe for others.

From the standpoint of its Gulf neighbours, Iran's more soothing tone and more restrained policies, particularly regarding the escalation of the war, soon began to contrast favourably with the policies of Iraq, their putative ally. In an increasing attempt to break out of the desperate stalemate on land, Iraq resorted to an extension of the war; by attacks on tankers in 1984, on Iran's cities in the spring of 1985, and on Kharg Island and other export terminals thereafter. In all these attempts, what was put at risk was not only Iraq's aircraft and Iran's terminals but also the security of the Gulf states.[36] At the same time, as it had for Iran, the prolongation of the war raised new considerations. A quick decisive victory had not been achieved and any sort of victory over Iran appeared increasingly remote. If revolutionary Iran was here to stay, a fact of life, there were practical reasons for learning to live with it and helping it to mellow. At the very least, the opening up of channels would give the Gulf states an additional option, and possibly somewhat more leverage than they possessed in a tight enforced alignment with Iraq, or in a position of institutional dependence on Saudi Arabia.

The breaking of the ice with the June 1984 F-4 incident led to informal soundings between Tehran and Riyadh (who already co-operated, if not always harmoniously, inside OPEC). The possibility was broached of a visit to the Saudi Kingdom by Rafsanjani, but it was considered premature; nonetheless the channel had been opened. By May 1985, the Saudi Foreign Minister had made a visit to Tehran in an atmosphere of 'frankness and clarity' and by the end of the year his Iranian counterpart had returned it. No concrete results were evident at the time but the visits indicated greater realism and pragmatism (in contrast to ideological militancy) on the part of Iran, and a more prudent posture in relation to the war on the part of Saudi Arabia. Tehran could reassure Riyadh that it had no territorial ambitions, and point to the 'bad feeling' created by aid to Iraq, and to its belief that the security of the region was best assured by the littoral states. Riyadh could argue for an end to the war and point to agreement on the Palestine and Afghanistan questions.[37]

The Gulf states too, taking Iran's reassurances into account, had reasons for opening up their channels to Tehran. This was particularly true of the United Arab Emirates, of which Dubai had always had especially close ties with Iran.[38] The different traditions and varied needs of the Gulf states made it inevitable that they would react flexibly if given an incentive by Tehran. The diplomacy of broad smiles launched by Tehran in 1985 fitted this description nicely and the exchange of official visits and delegations increased. The upshot was that by the time of the GCC summit in November 1985 in Muscat, while there was still talk of military co-operation measures (e.g. a GCC navy), there was now a distinct emphasis in the final communiqué on a more correct, neutral, even-handed approach to the conflict. Iran was quick to note the change and to encourage it. The Foreign Minister referred to the 'friendly gestures', *Jomhuri-ye Eslami* saw it as the 'beginning of the road', and a radio commentary noted that the 'change in the stance of some of the littoral Gulf states indicates an evolution to a more realistic attitude toward events in the region'.[39]

Iran's neighbours would have seen the commentary as applying at least as much to the evolution in Iran's perceptions and policies as to themselves. Iran saw the change as a recognition of its power. As Prime Minister Musavi put it: 'They have to recognize it (Iran) as the most determining factor in the region and the Islamic sphere'.[40] Of Iran's power and predominance in the region there had never been any question, particularly in relation to the Gulf states. The issues had been how that power would be used and Iran's universalist and regionalist ambitions. Now that Iran's demands had been modified to encompass the concerns of its neighbours, the continuation of a state of frozen animosity made no sense. On Iran's part too, the war required concentration of resources and energies that made it imperative to retrench and consolidate ambitions as well as commitments, at least in the short term.

ii) *1985–7: Tensions and adjustments*

If 1984–5 had been a turning point on many levels for Iran, reflecting a recognition that the war would not be won without considerable effort and some adaptation, and leading to a scaling down of demands vis-à-vis its neighbours and a softer, less confident, more tolerant disposition toward the smaller Gulf states, this did not mean that a sea-change in the relationship occurred overnight. Just as, in the prosecution of the war itself, Iran had been disappointed by the failure of the Shi'a in Iraq to rise up and shake off the 'corrupt' Ba'th regime, so in its relations with the Gulf states the Iranian religious leadership had been frustrated by the failure of its message to take firm root and lead to spontaneous imitation. It is difficult to pinpoint the date by which the allure of the Islamic Revolution as a model had worn off amongst the people in the Gulf states, but one can confidently say that this was indeed the case by the end of 1985.[41] Iran recognized this and denied any desire to force its model on its neighbours. But this did not imply any satisfaction with its neighbours' policies either. Under threats and provocations they had responded by siding with Iraq in almost every way short of a formal declaration of belligerency. They had intensified military ties among themselves in a grouping that looked from Tehran to be suspiciously like an anti-Iran axis, and had increased their military ties and contacts with the United States. As if these were not enough, substantive disputes remained in Iran's relations with the Gulf states relating to the conduct of the war. These had primarily to do with Kuwait and Saudi Arabia and the measures each took to assist Iraq, while trying to improve ties with Iran.

The question how far support for Iraq was compatible with good relations with Iran was to be raised in acute form in 1986. On the one hand, Iran's demands on the Gulf states had been scaled down. As Rafsanjani put it: 'If secular issues prevent you from co-operating with us, your neutrality would be acceptable to us. We expect no more from you'.[42] On the other, the war continued and the closer Iran came to victory, the more elusive it seemed to become, and the more infuriating Gulf support for Iraq appeared. Thus, Iran's needs and the dynamics of the war were such as to make a rapprochement difficult.

From Kuwait's perspective Iran remained a serious threat. It had been directly implicated in a series of bombings in Kuwait in December 1983. Kuwait tightened its alignment with Iraq and resisted Iran's threats. For Iran, oblivious to its own past policies, the primary issue was Kuwait's continued aid to Iraq. In addition to financial assistance, there was the direct help Kuwait was providing in the trans-shipment of arms and supplies from its major port overland to Iraq. This served to weaken the effect of Iran's naval control of the Gulf and encouraged Tehran to adopt a policy of intercepting and inspecting maritime traffic that it considered likely to be carrying war-related cargo destined for Iraq. This policy was initiated in 1984 and intensified in 1985–6. There were other signs of Kuwait's partiality for Iraq in the tenor of its public statements and allegations of Iranian responsibility for terrorism in the Emirate, in the continuing expulsion of large numbers of Iranian nationals, and in a general unwillingness to achieve a better balance in its relations with the two combatants. After Iran's successful offensive in February 1986 that saw the capture of Fao and the stationing of troops a few kilometres from Kuwait, the Iranians warned that any aid to Iraq, such as the leasing of Bubiyan island, would be considered an unfriendly act. The Fao operations, warned Rafsanjani, 'constitute a warning that is stronger than any others to the reactionary defenders of Iraq in the southern Persian Gulf'.[43]

Kuwait denied or rather 'regretted' allegations of helping Iraq and protested against Iran's harassment. Iran continued its criticism of Kuwait's 'double position' but made clear its readiness to 'ignore the past'. Alternatively, 'If they do not discontinue their support and indifference, they will be answerable in the future'.[44] Iran's threatening noises and newly established positions close to the frontier increased the pressures on the small emirate. In March, it organized demonstrations against Kuwait and Saudi Arabia. After sabotage in the country, the Emir of Kuwait dissolved the National Assembly, alluding to the external problems: 'We were not content with Kuwait's internal problems . . . but we have also entered into external battles which are not compulsory for us'.[45]

It was not possible for Iran to continue the war successfully without threatening the Gulf states, or to fall out with Kuwait without souring its relations with the other states. The GCC Ministerial Council reverted to its earlier role of criticizing Iran, calling on it to withdraw, and warning of the possibility that the conflict might expand. Iran in turn caustically remarked:[46]

> The GCC was formed while Iraqi forces were occupying part of our Islamic homeland . . . [but now that the tables are turned] they have suddenly decided to condemn what they call the occupation of an Arab country.

Resentment at the hypocrisy and effrontery of the GCC, never far from the surface in Iran, spilled over when the Council focused on what Iran saw as its *reactions* to Iraq, rather than the original Iraqi actions that had precipitated Iran's response. One Iranian commentary accurately observed that 'The theory of Gulf security is based on the creation of a counterforce that can face the Islamic revolution'. Another pointedly noted that it was the 'Persian Gulf Co-operation Council'. In the Iranian view, GCC actions as well as views had been far too biased: 'It has robbed itself of any credibility with regard to any impartial mediation'.[47]

As in the course of 1986 the land war intensified, so did the tanker war and Iraq's attacks on Iran's oil facilities. GCC ministerial statements tended to focus on 'regret' that Iran was not willing to be responsive to the good offices of various parties and to relinquish the use of force.[48] But from mid-summer the GCC's concern for the security of shipping was increased both by the tanker war and by Iran's intensified interception of shipping. In August, the Council 'noted with regret the escalation of Iranian threats directed at the security and sovereignty of some member states' and expressed 'its extreme concern' over Iran's interceptions.[49] Nothing was said about Iraq's attacks on Iran's oil facilities, and its attacks on tankers, about the GCC members' continued assistance to Iraq in the prosecution of the war, or indeed, about Iraq's actual initiation of the war. For all these reasons Iran considered such declarations by the GCC as invalid and lacking any authority or even moral force. This did not, of course, stop the Council from making them. The novelty of multilateral diplomacy and the sense of solidarity engendered by regular meetings, and defence co-operation, tended to give the GCC rather exalted airs, insisting that an attack on one would be regarded as an attack on all, and calling on Iran to negotiate, and for measures to protect 'third party' shipping.[50]

The Iranian position repeated time and again was to let bygones be bygones, to affirm its interest in the security and stability of the Gulf, to disclaim any ambitions in any of the littoral states, and to argue that if the region was to enjoy any peace in the future Iran's war with Iraq could be ended only with the removal of Saddam Hussein. In July 1986 Rafsanjani referred to 'our neighbouring countries with whom we have no wish to become involved' and to Iran's intention to limit not widen the war, reserving within this framework the right to consider states helping Iraq 'as partners in this crime'.[51] He put Iran's case more fully later:[50]

> Our past history shows that we have not been in favour of adventurism, given the excuses provided by the littoral states of the Persian Gulf on many occasions by their open aid to Iraq − they sell oil on Iraq's behalf, provide funds, make their roads and ports and perhaps even their airspace available to Iraq for military purposes − and knowing that it is easy to punish them. [Yet] We have no intention of expanding the war.

He went on to argue that it was palpably false to argue that Iraq was some sort of protector for the Gulf states, and that Iran was somehow prevented by the war from waging war against them. He observed that had Iran had such an intention, given its resources, the additional effort required for this would have been marginal.[52]

Another concrete point of contention was with Saudi Arabia. The success of Iranian troops at Fao coincided with the slide in the price of oil in world markets (from some $30 a barrel to under $10 at one point). Iran's position, based on its ideology, was that production should be curbed to increase prices. To bring some discipline into OPEC and to concentrate the minds of the producers on the need for some sort of quota system if overproduction was to be avoided, Saudi Arabia adopted a policy of *increasing* its own production. The result was a sharper fall in the price of oil. Whether or not this was intended as purely a question of oil policy, it was interpreted in Tehran as part of an Arab war effort to constrain Iran's capacity to continue the war by limiting its access to funds. What came to be known as the 'oil conspiracy' was continuously and spiritedly denounced by Iranian officials. Khomeini's designated successor, Montazeri, observed in March:

> They sell oil which belongs to the Muslims and the oppressed, God-given wealth at bargain prices. They pour it into the pockets of the superpowers at cheap prices in order to defeat revolutionary Iran.

Rafsanjani also referred to the 'conspiracies of Iran's enemies to reduce the price of oil', while President Khamenei warned that 'the price war is no less important to us than the military war'.[53]

By August, Iran's pressure – bilateral and within OPEC – was enough to reverse the Saudi position, and to establish *de facto* co-operation within OPEC. In October, as one illustration of this, Riyadh dismissed Sheikh Yamani, the experienced oil Minister, whom the Iranians considered unfriendly. The Saudis' *volte face* stemmed from various considerations, amongst which the need to maintain some semblance of neutrality in the war certainly figured. The Iranians remained in a position to damage the Saudis' standing both in the Gulf and within OPEC – especially in depicting Saudi oil policy as a sell-out of the Muslims' birthright. The Iranian case that Saudi oil policy was not neutral but actually very hostile to Iran was certainly persuasive, and equally so were the list of possibilities for Iranian subversion and intimidation (starting with the haj and extending to the Shi'a in the eastern province) and extending to attacks on shipping and oil facilities. Iran had frequently intimated that it could retaliate against the Gulf states for Iraq's increasingly long-range attacks on its oil exports, and had blamed them for extending assistance to Iraq in covering the air ranges involved.[54]

As the year came to an end, Iran's threatened 'final offensive' had not yet materialized, but the extension of the war to the southern Gulf and the intensification of the tanker war (attacks on ships in 1986 alone totalled 105 versus a total of 152 between May 1981 and December 1985) only increased the risk of a spread of the conflict to the Gulf states.[55] Both the Gulf states and international shippers were therefore becoming more concerned about the safety of shipping and looking for a means to ensure it. At the same time, Iraq continued to use its air force to widen the war, and to try to internationalize it to bring pressure to bear on Iran to end the conflict. Iran's interest, by contrast, remained what it had been for some time: to win the war on the ground, to cultivate the genuine neutrality of the Gulf states, and to leave the Gulf free for navigation, while ensuring that war-related goods did not reach Iraq.

Iran's attempts to reassure the Gulf states had not had much lasting success. Its advances on the ground at Fao tended to cancel out whatever goodwill was engendered by a softer diplomatic line. Furthermore, the need to mix non-specific threats about future 'punishment' or 'accounting' for current unfriendliness (especially vis-à-vis Kuwait) undermined protestations of peaceful intent. Iran's efforts to abort the holding of the Islamic Conference Organization's meeting in Kuwait in January 1987 (on the grounds that it was not a truly neutral venue or a safe one) illustrated the problem. Iran boycotted the meeting, and various shadowy groupings threatened terrorist acts in the Emirate.

In 1987 the odd situation in which Iran responded to Iraqi air attacks against its oil tankers and terminals by attacks on tankers serving Iraq's Gulf friends, came to a head. This triangular relationship reflected the fact that Iraq now exported its own oil overland, and found it in its interests to try and sever Iran's waterborne oil exports by air attack. In the absence of any equivalent Iraqi targets, Iran attacked the other Gulf states both to warn them of the costs of continued support for Iraq, and to give them an incentive to try and restrain Iraq's air attacks. Iraq, however, was not disposed to limit its attacks, and Iran's retaliation on the other states in the Gulf nicely served its purpose of trying to internationalize the war in order to get assistance in ending it. The increase in attacks on tankers in 1986 (when Iraqi attacks numbered twice those of Iran) had affected Kuwait, which Iran singled out for particular pressure with an increase in domestic bombings and terrorist incidents against it.

Kuwait sought to escape from this pressure by inviting the two superpowers to take its tanker fleet (or part of it) under their protection. After initial hesitation, the United States accepted, justifying the decision by reference to the need to guarantee freedom of shipping in the waterway. Other considerations, including preventing Soviet inroads into the region and reassuring the Gulf states about its reliability as an ally, were more dominant in the decision. While the US began by emphasizing Iran's military threat to shipping by giving prominence to its acquisition of a mobile SSM from China known as *Silkworm*, with a 50-mile range, there was little doubt that Iran's interest in keeping the Gulf open for shipping was second to none, for, of all the Gulf oil producers, it was the most dependent on the waterway for its exports (and imports). The US' desire to efface the memory of the Irangate arms scandal appeared to Iran to be a more likely explanation for its response. To Iran the US decision in July, following an Iraqi attack on a US ship, the *USS Stark*, in May and coinciding with a United Nations effort to end the war (Security Council resolution 598 of 20 July), seemed to be a sign that the United States was taking sides in the war. The US presence could only inhibit Iranian responses to Iraqi air attacks, while doing nothing about the prime cause – Iraq's air war against Iran.

If Kuwait's principal concern was to escape from the mounting pressure from the two belligerents, and to gain some reassurance from the superpowers in the event of an Iranian breakthrough on land, it found little relief.[56] Iran treated the decision as a hostile act designed to tilt the war in Iraq's favour. It also resented the invitation of outside powers into the region as a violation of regional norms, and a threat to its own regional standing, which was diluted and challenged by this presence. Its response was characteristically uncompromising; accepting the implicit challenge, it continued to retaliate for Iraqi attacks, while stepping up its own campaign of intimidation against Kuwait. Ayatollah Montazeri told a domestic audience:[57]

> The region's reactionaries want to drag the superpowers into the Persian Gulf to prevent Islam and Islamic Fundamentalism, as they put it, from spreading to other countries.

The Iranian Foreign Ministry sought to demonstrate that Kuwait's invitation was not popular with the other Gulf states, which saw a foreign presence as dangerous. Kuwait was invited to mend its ways:[58]

> Whenever Kuwait ceases supporting the initiator of the war we can have normal relations with it similar to our present tie with other regional countries such as the United Arab Emirates, Oman, Qatar, and Bahrain.

Iran sought to make its displeasure known in concrete ways. For the first time in six years it sought to use the annual haj, or pilgrimage to Mecca, to make a political point. The comments of Hojjat el-Eslam Khoini'a, a former supervisor of the haj and currently State Prosecutor General (and known as hard-liner), nicely capture the revolutionary approach:

> We hope, and we are very optimistic about this hope, that the day will come when governments will shake due to the haj. The governments which act treacherously ... Why is Saudi Arabia afraid of the Islamic Republic raising the issue of the Iran–Iraq war and putting it to a vote?

Khoini'a went on to argue that the people should decide, and that the haj should be used not merely as a 'march or demonstration' but as a 'referendum': 'let the people be asked whether the actions undertaken by the governments (Saudi Arabia, Kuwait) are good or not'.[59]

King Fahd of Saudi Arabia in turn condemned the use of religion by pretenders to undermine 'security in certain Arab and Islamic countries'.[60] In seeking to exert pressure on Saudi Arabia, to separate it from Kuwait, and to inhibit it from military co-operation with the United States (e.g. in widening the use of its air surveillance through AWACs and sharing the product with the US fleet), Iran was determined to exploit the Saudis' sensitivity about their role as Guardian of the Holy Places at the most important time – during the high season of the pilgrimage. The upshot of its attempt to organize demonstrations on 30 July, to which the Saudi security officials over-reacted, was the death of nearly 400 pilgrims, three quarters of them Iranian.

The attempt to apply pressure on Saudi Arabia backfired, creating a new (if temporary) polarization between Arab and Iranian. Iran was widely seen as having desecrated the Holy Places by its ill-judged demonstrations. Rather than unnerving the Saudis, Iran's action strengthened their determination to stand up to their neighbour. The *modus vivendi* that had been fashioned between the two states since 1984/5, and which had been extended in 1986 to an agreement in which Iran forwent attacks on Saudi tankers, while the Kingdom ceased its overproduction of oil which drove prices down, was now in disarray.[61]

Iran clearly overplayed its hand at Mecca. No doubt this was due to a real sense of frustration, of being cornered by the international community and not being given a fair chance. This feeling of embattlement quickly gave way to a willingness to take up the challenge; after all, the land war was in a seasonal lull, and the sense of purpose in the war needed revival. The arrival of several European fleets in the Gulf in the early autumn only reinforced the sense of conspiracy and whetted its appetite for confrontation. Perhaps this explains Iran's second false step, being caught red-handed in September in the mining of some shipping channels, which provided retroactive validation to the claim of its enemies that freedom of navigation was indeed the paramount stake in the Gulf.

Throughout the autumn of 1987 Iran continued to probe and test the strength and extent of the US commitment to the Gulf states, and the firmness of these states in their support for Kuwait. The latter expelled five (out of a total of seven) Iranian diplomats, accusing their country of missile attacks on Kuwaiti territory.[62] Iran massed a number of speedboats near the offshore Saudi oil field of Kaifi (whose production revenue goes to finance Iraq) but in the face of Saudi warnings and military responses passed the episode off as a training exercise.[63] More serious were the pressures brought to bear on Kuwait by missile attacks on shipping in its territorial waters (and thus not covered by the US convoy), and other shipping not under the US flag (there were only 12 thus covered). Iran also attacked an important offshore terminal, Sea Island, again in Kuwait's territorial waters.[64] In December it warned Kuwait strongly against allowing the deployment of a barge, to act as a floating base for US forces, in its offshore waters.[65]

These acts of coercion (or of defiance, as the Iranians saw them) were intended to put across Iran's central message, that the involvement of the superpowers in the region would not be to the benefit of any of the littoral states. Prime Minister Musavi emphasized this in the wake of the missile attacks and Iran's clashes with the US:[66]

> We have repeatedly advised these countries, as you know, that the arrival of large powers is not in their interest and now they are beginning to feel this.

In October Rafsanjani tried to put Iran's case more positively. He offered the Gulf states and the United States three 'options' in order to restore peace in the Gulf:

  i) to stop or hinder Iraq from attacking Iranian tankers in the Gulf;
 ii) to designate Iraq as the aggressor in the war;
iii) to cease all military and financial assistance to Iraq and assume a position of true neutrality.[67]

Iran's position in the tanker war was quite clear in that it sought neither an extension of the war nor the involvement of more powers. The Iranian leaders consistently differentiated between the land war, which they would not terminate without victory, and the conflict in the Gulf waters, which they would stop as soon as Iraq did the same.[68] Again and again they emphasized the limited nature of their claims on the Gulf states:[69]

> We do not want anything of you except that you stay neutral. Do not give (the enemy) oil, air space, pipelines, roads and ports so that the Iraqis can come to make the Persian Gulf insecure. Don't give them intelligence, and switch your propaganda to the side of neutrality. If you do so you will have a good neighbour to the north, who will be your friend and has the readiness to forgive you for your sins. But this Saddam's sins are such that he cannot be forgiven; he must be punished.

But the nature of Iran's conflict with Iraq, the demands of the war and the interests of the Gulf states in its outcome, preclude their true neutrality. Furthermore, there remains the question of Iran's true intentions post-war. Although there were reasons to believe Rafsanjani when he told a Western journalist[70] that Iran did not consider Kuwait as being as ripe for an Islamic revolution as Afghanistan or Lebanon, there were also cogent reasons to doubt that this attitude would survive an Iranian victory. Moreover, it was not clear to Kuwait, which had become the object of (presumably an Iranian) terrorist campaign (with over a dozen bombings in 1987), that even a position of true neutrality – if that were feasible – would be satisfactory to both belligerents, and devoid of comparable pressures.

The internationalization of the war, the precipitate deterioration of relations with Saudi Arabia, and the virtual state of war with Kuwait, all indicate that Iran lost control of events in 1987 and, indeed, had been trapped into a series of false moves in response to Iraqi pressures. For example, it said something about Iran's poor relations with these states that, while they had deflected pressures to invite US assistance in their defence in 1984, they were prepared to do so in the face of Iran's inevitable fury in 1987. It was none the less evident that, even whilst it welcomed the opportunity to confront the regional and outside powers in 1987, Iran's actual policies remained far more moderate than its rhetoric. The sense of aggrievement and resentment in Iran is at least as strong as any instinct of bellicosity. Both are discernible in a Tehran television commentary on the eve of the Arab League Summit at Amman in November 1987.[71]

> If this conference is Arab and sincere, it must view the aggressive colonialist war imposed on the Islamic revolution fairly and justly and not from a bigoted tribal perspective.

Besides a sense of pragmatism stemming from its war needs and the natural mellowing of a revolutionary state confronted by adversity, Iran has been much helped by the structure of Gulf politics, which are not conducive to polarization. The smaller Gulf states are not anxious to relinquish their independence by a close alignment with any power, or to bank on any one protagonist in the current or any future war. For them the aim is to maintain a balance, to keep channels of contact open, and to reduce tensions; if the price of this is a degree of appeasement, they are prepared to pay it. Thus they have proved unwilling to follow Saudi Arabia's initial inclination after July 1987 to sever diplomatic ties with Iran. Apart from 'condemnation' of Iran at the Arab League summit, the Gulf states have subsequently shown themselves even more keen on maintaining a dialogue with Tehran (as in the very moderate communiqué adopted at the eighth GCC Summit Conference in Riyadh in December 1987). While hinting at a willingness to invite outside powers into the region to assure its security, the prevailing tone of the meeting was a desire to keep channels to Iran open. The Saudi Foreign Minister admitted at a press conference that the dialogue with Iran 'had not stopped, it was continuing and would continue in the future'.[72]

Despite its attempts at improving its image in the Gulf states, Iran is still seen as the greater threat to their security. An extreme but not unrepresentative view of Iran was voiced by a Jordanian official:[73]

> If Iran wins here, all the Gulf states are finished . . . Iran will simply dispatch its chosen governor at the head of an army of 10,000 revolutionary guards to Kuwait, Saudi Arabia, Bahrain, and so on, and who will dare to fight them? It will be the Ottoman conquests all over again.

After seven years of war, despite considerable diplomatic effort, more circumspect rhetoric, and the advantage of being a proximate power that the smaller states need to cultivate for their own security, Iran's success in detaching the Gulf states from Iraq or altering their perceptions of threat, has been limited. In one way the Gulf states have become more confident, for the stalemate has shown that Iran is not the mighty military power that it had seemed when it kept its military arsenal in reserve. Co-operation in the GCC has also increased contacts and created confidence in at least a degree of local solidarity. Iran, for its part, can scarcely look on the Gulf states with benevolent magnanimity; circumstances may have necessitated the cultivation of these small states, but there can be little doubt that in some cases they have virtually been co-belligerents on Iraq's side.[74] Depending on the outcome of the war, and on Iran's domestic needs, there would be adequate time for a reckoning. At the very least, one can expect an Iran interested in either disbanding the GCC or expanding it to include itself. Islamic Iran may have only itself to blame for misjudging the appeal of Islam as a bridge over the Persian/Arab cultural chasm and specifically for the distrust between Iran and the Gulf states.

Iran's policy toward the Gulf states has evolved over the past seven years but there is little to show for it. While its tone has fluctuated between aggrievement and imperial contempt for the Gulf states, the reality is a mood of irritation and at times impotent fury. Unwilling to widen the war and involve the great powers because this would only further reduce its prospects of victory, Iran has also been unable to convince the Gulf states of the need for genuine neutrality.

Iran and Syria: a pragmatic arrangement

The war with Iraq has (in Iran's parlance) 'imposed' many things, and not least a degree of co-operation between Islamic Iran and secular Ba'thist Syria. The arrangement, which is sometimes referred to as 'strategic' by the participants, is born of a tactical convergence of interest against Saddam Hussein's Iraq, and little else. But to infer from the narrow foundation of the relationship any especial fragility would be mistaken; in the annals of Middle Eastern diplomacy, the friendship, already six years old, is a relatively long-lived one. This section will discuss the benefits to the two states of their co-operation, and address the issues which threaten to weaken, dilute or even reverse the partnership, from the perspective of Iran's policy in the Gulf war.

In the spring of 1982, as Iran began to push back the Iraqi forces and liberate areas occupied by the enemy, victory seemed within its grasp. To weaken Iraq's still considerable military capability further, Iran obtained agreement from Iraq's arch rival, Syria, to exert economic pressure on Iraq. On 8 April, Syria closed its borders, and two days later closed the trans-Syrian oil pipeline. Iraq, which had been exporting a volume of up to 3.4 million b/d before the war, had as a result of the conflict lost access to the Gulf for its foreign-exchange-generating exports, and had thus become more dependent on overland routes. The trans-Syria pipeline, with its capacity of 700,000 barrels, accounted for half these exports, the remainder coming from the similar outlet of approximately the same capacity through (Dortyol) Turkey. Deprived of the Syrian outlet, Iraq would find that the halving of its vital oil exports made a serious impact on its funding of the war. At the same time, enforced reliance on only one export terminal, and that through an area susceptible to Iranian or Kurdish sabotage, increased its sense of insecurity. The net result was to cut by a half an already greatly diminished flow of oil, at a loss of $17 million a day, in a country already some $20 billion in debt.[75]

Iran's concrete benefit from this move was a financially weaker enemy. This was, and remains, an important factor in a state like Iraq, which is keen to insulate its population from the war and more dependent than Iran on foreign exchange in the prosecution of the war. Iran's relationship with Syria has had other advantages, some concrete, some more abstract. An obviously pressing problem in the war – arms supplies – was one area in which Syria was helpful. Iran was able to buy arms from the Soviet bloc via Syria without having any direct relationship with the Eastern bloc. With Soviet approval arms were supplied to Iran from Syria, sometimes, it appears, from the USSR itself, at other times from Eastern Europe. This was particularly the case in the early stages of the war and in 1982, when shipments were 'extensive'. Express Soviet approval may not have been forthcoming by the time of the 'war of the cities' in 1985 when Soviet missiles found their way to Iran, but by then the pattern of co-operation had already been set.[76]

In addition, the massing of Syrian troops on Iraq's western borders threatened it with a war on two fronts and forced it to deploy troops away from the Iranian front to deal with such a contingency. Both in practical terms and from the psychological pressure exerted, Syria's action was of substantial benefit to Iran.

In the Iranians' minds there was no question about the basis for the relationship. Foreign Minister Velayati observed: 'Our relations with Syria are strategic and we view the political, economic, and cultural relations between the two countries as strategic'.[77] There is little reason to dispute this characterization of a relationship which has been correct and restrained rather than warm and enthusiastic, and which is supported by few cultural or popular bonds between the two nations. For Iran, the Syria connection appears to have been important from the miliary point of view. The presence of the Commander and Minister of the Revolutionary Guards, Morteza Reza'i and Mohsen Rafiqdust, in the delegations that shuttle to Damascus several times a year, and the fact that the Guards are primarily supplied with East bloc weaponry, is at least indicative of a military dimension to the relationship.

An important aspect of the arrangement also stems from Iran's sense of mission in the Islamic, and especially the Shi'i, world. Without the agreement or acquiescence of Syria, Iran would not have access to Lebanon, where a third of the total population of 3 million are comprised of Shi'a in precisely that condition of quintessential political and economic oppression which Khomeini believes must be fought and eliminated. Not only is Lebanon important because its proportion of Shi'a is relatively high (only in Iraq and Bahrain is it higher), traditionally underrepresented and disadvantaged politically, but it is in Lebanon that another charismatic Shi'i leader, Musa Sadr, started a similar, if peaceful, crusade on the part of the Shi'a, before Khomeini came to power.[78] Furthermore, Lebanon has the advantage of a weak government in disarray, unable to resist Iran's political incursions.

Iran's need to extend its constituency, to broaden the platform of its international actions, to transcend the limitations of being merely another national actor in a world of nation-states, should not be underestimated. As a revolution it claims a universalistic message; as an Islamic model it demands an especially attentive audience in the Islamic world. Its appeal would become atrophied if its message were to be limited to the narrow stage encompassed by Iran and Iranians. As Khomeini put it in 1980:[79]

> We should try hard to export our revolution to the world, and we should set aside the thought that we do not export the revolution, because Islam does not regard various countries differently and is the supporter of all the oppressed people of the world ... If we remain in an enclosed environment we shall definitely face defeat.

The Shi'i dimension is thus important and Iran has Syria to thank for facilitating its presence in Lebanon, which has both practical and symbolic dimensions. But it is not all. There is also the broader Persian/Arab question that needs to be sublimated, transcended or overcome, if Iran is to play a wider role consistent with its sense of mission. Iran's co-operation with Syria serves this function of broadening its constituency as well as de-polarizing the Gulf conflict, undermining any suggestion that the Iran–Iraq war is an extension of the historical Persian–Arab conflict. Despite the fact that Iran's Islamic revolution had, as it were, no Arab content, there was no doubt of its appeal (at least initially) in the Arab world.[80] Nevertheless, this was a far cry from understanding, let alone support, for Iran's position in the Gulf war. The Syrian connection was, in the words of one of its major supporters, 'effective in dispelling the misconception perpetrated by imperialism which attempts to depict the war as an Arab–Persian conflict and not a war against oppression'.[81]

Iran's desire to play a region-wide role has been helped by the relationship with Syria. As President Assad was to say in defence of the tie: 'The Iran of Khomeini is anti-Israel. Iran was the only country to send forces when Israel invaded Lebanon in 1982'.[82] Iran's dispatch of elements of a Revolutionary Guard brigade numbering perhaps 2,000 men was no less effective for being largely symbolic. Since 1982 a detachment[83] of the Guards force has remained in Lebanon at Baalbek in the Beka valley, with the agreement and under the sometimes watchful eye of the Syrian Government. These 'volunteers' are part of the branch of the Guards devoted to the 'export of the Revolution'. They are a tangible symbol of Iran's interest in the fate of the Shi'a and in the future of Lebanon. Together with Iran's diplomatic representation and clerical network, they provide training, funding, arms and support for the more militant Shi'i groupings such as the Hezbollah (or Islamic Amal). They appear also to have been involved with groups implicated in various terrorist activities such as Islamic Jihad. Even the more moderate, mainstream Shi'i group Amal, which refuses to have any ties with the radical and violence-prone Hezbollah, admits its connection with Iran; Nabih Berri, the Amal leader, compared the Lebanese Shi'i attitude to Khomeini to that between the population of a Catholic country and the Pope.[84]

Iran's interest has not been exclusively strategic or military; humanitarian interest is also evident in Lebanon. Iran has been active at the grass roots level, building a hospital, clinics, and schools and providing medical care and financial stipends for the families of martyrs and active members of the Hezbollah. In providing such community services in a country where the state is weak and the economy in disarray, Iran has, at the comparatively low cost of some $60–70 million a year, increased its level of influence in Lebanon.[85]

While historically Iran has always had a degree of contact with the Shi'a community in Lebanon, today that relationship is particularly important for the Islamic republic's foreign policy. From the outset of the war support for Iran was evident in the Shi'a community. However, as the war has continued Lebanon has become a place where Iran coyly admits to having only a certain amount of influence over some of its 'friends' where the issue of hostage-taking is concerned. The fact that the various abductions are represented as the products of spontaneous indigenous indignation at Western policies in the Gulf war, and are intended as a means of altering individual states' policies in this regard, is a convenient fiction in which all sides tacitly collude. Nor has Iran's strategy of indirect terrorism been unproductive; witness the long list of Western countries that have been prepared to do business on these terms.

The Iran–Syria connection, a veritable 'odd couple' even by the standards of the Middle East, has not been cemented by complete agreement on all issues but rather by substantial agreement on a very important one. The relationship is based on a negative – opposition to Saddam Hussein's Iraq – not on any positive agreement, let alone vision.[86] In other circumstances, the relationship between a clerically run Islamic state and a secular Ba'th state run by an 'Alawi minority that ruthlessly represses its religious opposition would be very different. As a Western diplomat observed: 'Without Iraq, Iran would be a potential enemy of Syria'.[87] However, given the fact of Iraq, Iran is a tactical ally of Syria. There is much to Tariq Aziz's comment that the only thing uniting Iran and Syria is 'a negative stand consisting of hatred of Iraq and their blackmail of the Gulf'.[88] Certainly the strongest part of the stream of their joint communiqués is usually the section that refers to 'the crazy war waged by the fascist regime of Iraq'.[89]

What Syria gains from this relationship concerns us less and may be summarized. Above all, a Syria alienated from Egypt, Iraq, Jordan, and the PLO and with no special ties with Algeria, is a country isolated. Iran, a militant rejectionist, has provided Syria with a strategic depth and a political base of which it would otherwise be deprived, in relations with both Israel and the Arab world. Again and again Syria has played the 'Iran card', thereby persuading the Gulf states that its special relationship with Tehran is a guarantee of their security and suggesting that it has managed to get Iran to accept the limitation of the war in the Gulf and the principle of non-annexation of any Iraqi (i.e. Arab) territory.[90] Syria has thus cashed in on the tie with Iran in the form of increased subventions from the Gulf states. In addition, to some extent the acceptance by the Islamic republic of the 'Alawite-run regime of Hafez al Assad is of assistance in the legitimation of that minority regime.

Doubtless of more practical value has been the economic dimension of the relationship, especially in an era of declining oil revenues and grants from the Gulf states, and deteriorating economic circumstances within Syria itself. The immediate payoff for Syria's closure of the Iraqi pipeline in April 1982 was of the order of $1 billion, of which $600 million was in grants. This stemmed from an agreement whereby Iran was to provide 1 million tons of oil per annum free, and supply some 5–7 million tons of crude oil at a discount of one-third posted prices. In essence, of this latter component, Syria paid for half in foreign exchange and half in Syrian goods.[91] A report two years after the agreement was signed cited the figure of 6.2 million tons of crude oil from Iran in 1983 (of which 1 million tons were free), the total representing 70 per cent of Syria's total refined product.[92]

By 1986 this arrangement had encountered difficulties stemming from Syria's inability to repay part of its oil debt amounting now to some $2 billion. Iran's increased need for income in that year because of Iraqi bombing and the slide in oil prices compounded the problem. Iran reportedly suspended oil shipments pending a new agreement.[93] This was quickly reached after reports of a possible Syrian–Iraqi rapprochement through the good offices of Jordan, and was for Iran to supply 2.5 million tons to cover a period of six months from October 1986 to March 1987.[94] A similar scenario unfolded in 1987 with rumours of a meeting between Assad and Saddam Hussein, difficulties in the Syrian repayment of its Iranian debt, and differences over Lebanon.[95]

Because of Syria's straitened economic situation there were grounds in 1986–7 for believing that it would be more susceptible to economic inducements from other Arab states to end its support of Iran.[96] In the event Iran renewed its economic relationship, extended repayment schedules and continued its supply of some 20,000 barrels/day of free oil.[97]

Syria has proved adept at exploiting the relationship with Iran to gain benefits from both sides. To the Gulf Arabs it presents itself as the bridge to Iran, a channel of communication and above all a restraining influence on Tehran.[98] Periodically, under pressure it gives demonstrative 'warnings' to Iran about the inviolability of the Arab homeland.[99] Yet even when seemingly isolated as at the Arab League Summit at Amman in November 1987, it manages to wriggle free, accepting the condemnation of Iran but in the same breath denying any change in its stance and assuring Tehran of its solidarity on the war.[100]

The respective aims of Iran and Syria in Lebanon may not be compatible either in theory or, for very much longer, in practice. Iran has supported the Hezbollah, who appear to be eager to set up an Islamic republic in Lebanon on Iranian lines. In the process they have succeeded in radicalizing the Syrian-preferred, moderate, pragmatic Amal (who seek only a more representative system within a reconstituted political order), and undermining Syria's claim to be the arbiter of Lebanon's politics. The Hezbollah, financed, trained and armed by Tehran, are effectively Iran's proxy in Lebanon. They have pushed the South Lebanese Shi'a into confrontation with Israel and the United Nations force UNIFIL and have clashed with Syrian forces sent to restore order in West Beirut.[101]

The Hezbollah's abductions of foreign citizens have at times embarrassed Syria and particularly in 1987 there were occasions when clashes with the Syrian security forces seemed likely to escalate. The abduction of US newspaperman Charles Glass in June was one such incident in which Iranians or Iranian agents appeared to have been involved. Syria reacted by restricting the activities of the Hezbollah.[102] The Iranian Government sought to depict the issue as a US-inspired conspiracy, intended to harm its relations with Syria; Rafsanjani referred to 'pressure' on Damascus to confront the Hezbollah, something which he insisted was a 'mistake we consider to be remote from Syria'.[103]

Despite differences over the sort of Lebanon desired, there are cogent reasons for both Iran and Syria to limit their actions in order to preserve their relationship. Without being a partnership, it remains a useful diplomatic asset for each, giving them an incentive to defuse incidents in order to prevent a full-blown crisis. Nevertheless, volatility is given to this aspect of their relations by the presence of free-lancers in Lebanon, who share ties with each state but are not always answerable to them.

To be sure, Iran has supported Syria too on a number of regional issues of particular interest to the Assad Government. Tehran was highly critical of the agreement of 17 May 1983 between Lebanon and Israel, expressed support for Syria when there were rumours of an impending Israeli attack in May 1986, and again in the autumn of that year when Syria was under international pressure over involvement in terrorist activities. Syria's support for Iran stems from its belief that the revolutionary state is an objective ally against Israel and imperialism. 'While opposing the Iraqi war against Iran . . . Syria is also opposed to fabricating an Arab–Iranian conflict that will draw the Arabs away from their real battle against the Israeli enemy'.[104] Iraq, for its part, sees its relationship with Syria as revolving around neither abstract ideological nor general strategic issues, nor even around strictly bilateral issues, but around its position in the war.[105]

Syria's value to Iran increases in proportion to the deterioration of Iran's relations with other Arab states. Thus in 1987 as hostilities began to expand into the Gulf with consequences for Iran's relations with many of the states of that region, Syrian leverage correspondingly grew. This leverage does not extend to influencing Iran's decision to carry on or stop the war. But Syria is important for Iran, not for strategic purposes (for Iraq now exports its oil by other routes) nor for any military utility, but for its political usefulness. For Iran Syria is a ticket to the Arab–Islamic world, a means of broadening its otherwise narrow constituency, and of giving the lie to the allegation that it is driven by Shi'i or exclusively Persian rather than Islamic interests. Iran is prepared to pay the price for this ticket in terms of gifts of oil, subsidized supplies and postponed payments, because of the importance of maintaining access to this broader community in order to keep the universal Islamic mission alive.

Syria in turn finds that contacts with Iran are most fruitful in its relations with the Arab world when Iran is most isolated. It is then that Damascus can play the role of the indispensable bridge, the moderator of Iran's actions, picking up cheques from both parties without having to make a choice. (It plays the same role with Western states too, implying that it has a channel to Tehran.) The most sensitive area of relations is in Lebanon, where ultimate interests do not coincide, and the Hezbollah periodically challenges Syria's authority or tests its credibility. Neither Iran nor Syria have an interest in allowing these incidents to imperil their ties, and they have worked out channels of communication that are activated during such crises. The fencing between their clients in Lebanon, and the support each gives its respective allies in these manoeuvres, constitutes a form of diplomatic signalling between the two limited allies. Neither holds a clear advantage, and neither is willing to pay the costs of putting differences to the test, or, indeed, paying the price that that would entail. The balance is not any less of a balance for being precarious.

Rumours of a rupture between Iran and Syria are always plausible, given both the unnatural and the limited basis of their relationship. The inherent treachery of Middle East politics where the reversal of alliances may hang on the size of a cheque, or the fate or even the whim of a particular leader, also makes for caution about predicting their longevity. That said, reports about the demise of the Iran–Syria tie have tended to be premature, as in 1984 when differences on Lebanon came to the fore.[106] Today these differences persist and are even more acute, yet neither country wishes to pursue them to a complete breach. Similarly, in the event of an Iranian victory, differences on the fate of Iraq will manifest themselves. The constantly divided Arab world has been helpless in dealing with either the Iran–Iraq war or the continuing problems with Israel. Changing alignments or a changed balance of incentives could lead to the defection of Syria from the relationship with Iran. There are many potential areas of dispute. The principal area of agreement – opposition to Saddam Hussein – may not be immutable either. But it has endured so far for over six years, and by the standards of the Middle East that can be considered an achievement.

Iran has certainly exploited and affected its regional environment in the course of the war. It has used Syria's rivalry with Iraq to some effect, thereby dividing the Arab world, and some would say diverting it from its principal mission against Israel. At the same time, while railing against the 'Zionists', it has pragmatically though covertly dealt with the Jewish state. This is particularly true in regard to the supply of spare parts for equipment of US origin. For our purposes, it is sufficient to note that this pragmatism regarding sources of arms supplies, commendable in military terms, has had a high cost in terms of Iran's credibility in the Arab/ Islamic world. In the Gulf Iran created rather than inherited a hostile environment. In the past three years, in trying to soften this situation, it has been faced with the difficulty of building trust while fighting a war. Without a military victory, or a major success in Lebanon, the efforts of the past seven years will have been of little avail. Not least because as the resonance of the revolution has faded, the accomplishments of the Islamic republic outside the war remain imperceptible, and in the war itself, negligible.

Conclusion

The Islamic republic of Iran, in the prosecution of its war with Iraq, sought to use its regional environment. In the process it influenced it considerably. It found an Arab world already divided on Camp David, and with Syria and Iraq in competition. It established a basis for converting Syria's rivalry with Iraq into a tactical arrangement, which gave it one important 'ally' in the Arab world and an opening to the Lebanon. The price of this for the Arab/Islamic world was an even greater schism among the Arabs/Islam. For Iran, it entailed payment; Iran's one regional ally has to be bought or rather hired. Even so, the relationship is a narrow one able to endure during the war but unlikely to survive it. The Lebanon remains important for Iran for symbolic and emotive reasons. Failure in the war would leave only Lebanon where Iran could claim a mission beyond its national self-interest, yet it is unlikely to find Syria accommodating.

In the Gulf, the Shah's Iran had left a working relationship of goodwill: even with Iraq passable relations had been established after 1975.

Revolutionary Iran was to squander this inheritance in the name of its regional and universal mission. Its neighbours were unwilling to take sides but were driven to do so by its plots and claims against them. By 1984–5, less confident of its ability to attain victory single-handed with the entire Gulf arrayed against it, the Islamic republic set about repairing the self-inflicted damage by pragmatically adjusting its rhetoric and goals. The change – if change it really was – was not easy for Iran's smaller neighbours to accept on trust. Iran's strident behaviour impelled them to seek security under the wing of Saudi Arabia and the Gulf Co-operation Council; the resulting arrangement was not easy to undo. Revolutionary Iran's threat to the Gulf states accomplished what nearly a decade of entreaties by the Shah had failed to achieve – the creation of a regional security arrangement. Unfortunately, the accomplishment was a negative one, as it had been possible to achieve only under the threat of Iranian guns and subversion, and on the basis of defence *against* Iran. Repairing the damage of the early years of the revolution has taken considerable time and effort and made little progress. Iran is thus faced with a regional environment that is at best suspicious and may rather more accurately be characterized as defensively antagonistic. The more Iran denies any claim to a special regional role, the more it risks becoming just another ordinary state.

10

Iraq and the Superpowers

As in all other spheres of activity, Saddam Hussein's prime consideration regarding the nature of Iraq's relations with outside powers has been the degree to which that relationship will facilitate his task of political survival and the consolidation of his regime. This has been no less the case during the war with Iran than it was in the years preceding it when he was working to establish his own undisputed claim to rule Iraq. In both cases, it has been important that he should ensure access to the resources of outside powers with a minimum of constraint on his own freedom of action or of contradiction with the purposes by which he has sought to justify his hold on power. It was vital, therefore, that during the war external aid should not be allowed to infringe the jealously guarded political autonomy of the regime. Whatever help he might elicit under the duress of war, mere military survival would be worthless if he placed in jeopardy his own political future by being seen seriously to compromise the dictates of Iraqi independence. As *Al-Jumhuriyya* expressed it, 'Iraq will refuse to permit its relations with a world power to become the relations of servant to master.'[1]

Prior to the war, the massive and rapid increase in oil revenues had allowed the Iraqi Government to steer an increasingly non-aligned course. During the 1970s and under Saddam Hussein's growing influence, this had meant weakening Iraq's hitherto almost exclusive reliance on the aid and support of the Soviet Union. In a relatively short space of time, between 1974 and 1979, the Soviet Union lost its position as Iraq's major trading partner to a number of Western states. Its monopoly in the supply of military equipment to the expanding Iraqi armed forces was eroded by Iraqi purchases of major weapons systems from France. Furthermore, significant differences emerged in Iraqi and Soviet perceptions of regional issues, from the Horn of Africa to Afghanistan.[2] Growing economic independence gave Saddam Hussein the ability to ensure the autonomy of the Iraqi political system under his own direction. From this position he could guarantee that his regime would be able to deliver to Iraqis the material fruits of the Ba'thist revolution, whilst at the same time championing Iraq's non-alignment and independence as the basis for an extension of its influence in the region.[3]

It was acknowledged that outside powers, and the two superpowers in particular, had resources in their gift which might be of great utility to the domestic and regional projects on which the Iraqi leadership was embarked. Such resources were primarily material, in the sense of military supplies, economic goods and technological co-operation. However, there was also a moral or ideological component, in the sense that association with one or the other of the superpowers – and by implication with the political and economic systems which they respectively represent – was taken to be an indication of the broader inclinations of the Iraqi regime, affecting in the process the claims on which it based its right to rule. This has little to do with the actual proclivities and priorities of Saddam Hussein, who has taken some trouble to free himself from having to become answerable to any defined, let alone externally oriented, ideology. However, it has much to do with the political myth on which his power is founded – that is, with the wider goals and principles which he claims to be serving.

Domestically, it was clear that alignment with the Soviet Union was proving as confining and potentially troublesome in this respect, as forced reliance on its relatively poor material resources. In the late 1960s and early 1970s the proclaimed solidarity between the Ba'th Socialist Party and the Communist Party of the Soviet Union might have been a useful asset in confronting the Ba'th's many internal enemies and rivals, not least the Communist Party of Iraq. However, for Saddam Hussein, who seemed determined to free himself from any ideological encumbrance, such affinity appeared dangerous on two counts. Firstly, it would oblige the Iraqi Government to pursue socialist policies, especially in agriculture and industry, which would deny it support in key areas of society, as well as being unlikely to produce the type of prosperity Saddam Hussein hoped to encourage. Secondly, and equally dangerously, it seemed likely to enhance the status of those in the Ba'th who adhered to a rigid interpretation of its ideological tenets and wished to make the political leadership answerable to them. A warning to this group and an indication of their future fate came in late 1978 and early 1979, when members of the Iraqi Communist Party and some of their alleged sympathizers in the Ba'th were arrested.[4] Members of the Iraqi Government stated at the time that they did not believe that these measures would affect Iraq's relations with the USSR. In terms of *Realpolitik* and inter-state relations, this was almost certainly true. However, it did signal Saddam Hussein's determination to shape the course of Iraq's domestic and foreign policy in a way which he thought best suited to his own definition of Iraqi state interests.

As Saddam Hussein stated at the time, if these could be promoted by restoring Iraqi relations with the United States, then Iraq would not hesitate to restore them. However, he added the proviso that it would have to be demonstrated that such a move would serve not only Iraqi national interests, but also the 'Arab nation's pan-Arab interests'.[5] Service to the latter was, after all, an important part of the legitimation of the Iraqi Government's claim to rule. Rapprochement with the states of Western Europe, with Japan and with the conservative and generally 'pro-Western' states of the Arab world, did not bring with it any of the still risky symbolic overtones of re-establishing relations with Israel's chief ally and superpower patron, the United States. Diplomatic relations with the United States had been broken off in the aftermath of the 1967 Arab–Israeli war by the Arif Government in Iraq. This government had been overthrown a year later by the Ba'th, a major part of whose indictment of the Arif regime had been its lack of dedication to the pan-Arab cause. It would, therefore, have been impossible for the new Ba'thist regime to have gone back on one of the few gestures made in this direction by its derided predecessor. Nor was there any pressing reason or inclination to do so. On the contrary, the maintenance of a posture of vehement hostility to the plots and conspiracies of 'world imperialism' served a number of useful purposes at the time.

In 1984, however, Iraq and the United States re-established formal diplomatic relations. This was merely the culmination of a number of years of increasingly cordial relations between the two states, coinciding with the years since the outbreak of the war with Iran. Ostensibly, therefore, despite the fact that the Iraqi media maintain their anti-imperialist rhetoric, the conditions of the war have brought a significant change in the nature of Iraq's relations with the superpowers. In fact, it would be truer to say that Iraq's plight in the war, especially after 1982, has brought about a re-appraisal by its regime of the relative utility of the assistance which both the Soviet Union and the United States can offer. In the autumn of 1980, soon after Iraq had invaded Iran, Tariq Aziz (at the time Saddam Hussein's special adviser for foreign affairs) visited the Soviet Union. The purpose of his visit seems to have been strictly utilitarian: he wanted to ensure that the Soviet Union would continue to supply Iraq with the military assistance it required, and would not take any action that might cheat it of its expected victory.[6] The nature of the war, however, soon demonstrated that such a victory would prove elusive. It became clear that the resources of Iraq itself were insufficient to allow its ruler to fulfil his ambitions, whether on the war front on in the related task of maintaining internal order.

Consequently, Saddam Hussein sought to solicit the resources – military, political and economic – of outside powers, particularly of the superpowers, to enable him to achieve his now reduced war aims. After 1982, these amounted to simple military survival and an internationally guaranteed return to the *status quo ante bellum*. He was to discover that the very precariousness of Iraq's military situation strengthened his own hand in his dealings with outside powers. This factor had worked to his advantage in consolidating his domestic political base and in rallying regional support throughout the Arab world. He could equally make a virtue of it in his relations with the superpowers, when he boasted that[7]

> this is the first time in contemporary history that a Third World country has been able to wage a successful defensive war – the longest conventional war since the Second World War – without being forced to place itself under the umbrella of a military alliance or the influence of a great power.

The superpowers and the Iraqi war effort

Soon after the Iraqi invasion of Iran in 1980, Saddam Hussein discovered to his chagrin that the Soviet Union clearly did not wish to be seen as an accessory to his own independent initiative. Tariq Aziz, on his visit to Moscow in the autumn of that year, discovered that the Soviet Government strongly disapproved of the invasion and that Soviet arms shipments to Iraq would thenceforth be curtailed. The reasons which Saddam Hussein had given for the previous Iraqi humiliation at the hands of Iran in 1975 – the Soviet failure to supply Iraq with the arms and ammunition it required to achieve its objectives in Kurdistan – seemed likely to be repeated.[8] Although this may not have caused great anxiety as long as a rapid termination to the conflict was expected, the situation became more serious when it was realized that Iraq was likely to be engaged in a protracted conflict.

The alarm this caused in Baghdad can be measured by the growing criticism of the Soviet attitude – in particular by the references to the Soviet failure to live up to the obligations stemming from the 1972 Treaty of Friendship and Co-operation, as interpreted by the Iraqi leadership.[9] It could also be seen in Iraq's overtures to the United States, on the pretext that a new administration in Washington could herald a new chapter in US–Iraqi relations. The moves which constituted this overture were not particularly significant in themselves, but in the context of the hitherto frozen US–Iraqi relationship and of the growing coolness in relations between Iraq and Soviet Union, they seemed to be a pointer to the future. It was no doubt gratifying for Saddam Hussein that the Soviet Union was quick to pick up the signal. Closer contacts were established and, reportedly, some Soviet war matériel began to arrive once again in Iraq.[10]

A substantial change, however, in the Soviet attitude towards the Iraqi war effort was only to emerge in 1982, when it became clear both that Iraq had lost the initiative and that its very survival was now at risk. The Soviet Union may have had few illusions by this stage about the nature of the Iraqi regime, and thus about the nature of Soviet–Iraqi relations, but it clearly did not consider an Iranian military victory to be in its own interests. Despite purchases of arms from other sources during the 1970s, the bulk of the Iraqi armed forces was still wholly dependent on Soviet military equipment. It was, therefore, imperative that the Soviet Union should ensure that Iraq had an overwhelming superiority in military hardware, if its ground forces were to survive the mass assaults of the highly motivated Iranian forces. Accordingly, Soviet military resupply of Iraq began in earnest. The agreements reached during the following years set generous terms for this major operation. In addition, they involved a scale of supply commensurate with Iraq's determination to construct an impenetrable defence network along much of its border with Iran. By 1987, therefore, the Soviet Union was in effect underwriting much of the Iraqi defence effort.[11]

The tone of Iraqi comment on the relationship has, therefore, become correspondingly warmer. At times of military crisis, the Iraqi leadership has clearly thought it necessary to underline to the Soviet Government the value of the regime's survival. This was perhaps the chief reason for the 'reinforcing' visits of Tariq Aziz and Saddam Hussein himself to Moscow in 1984 and 1985, respectively.[12] At the same time, it has been important for Saddam Hussein to stress that the military resupply operation was to be conducted on Iraq's own terms. This was explicit in the text of the report of the 9th Ba'th Party Congress which included not only a condemnation of the 'socialist model of development', but also a clause to the effect that the diversification of arms supplies was essential for the preservation of national independence.[13]

This has been the political reality behind the gestures and statements of mutual goodwill that have accompanied the growing number of visits between officials of the two countries during the war. The release of some two hundred Iraqi Communists from prison in late 1982 and the joint use of the rhetoric of anti-imperialism and of 'progressive' politics by spokesmen of the two governments have served the symbolic purposes of both regimes.[14] The opportunity afforded in April 1987 by the fifteenth anniversary of the signing of the Iraqi–Soviet Treaty of Friendship and Co-operation allowed for an elaboration of these purposes: the Soviet Government could give the impression of a steadfast ally, anxious to help its partner in its hour of need; Saddam Hussein could demonstrate to Iran and to his own people that he had successfullly retained the support of the Soviet Union, pointing out that it was in broad agreement with Iraq's major conditions for ending the conflict.[15] Underlying these professions of goodwill, however, was Saddam Hussein's rather more frank summing up of the Soviet–Iraqi relationship: 'Friendship and co-operation, yes. Satellization or the adoption of the Soviet Union's viewpoint, no'.[16]

Saddam Hussein had few inhibitions about using the prospect of a rapprochement with the United States as a means of ensuring that the proprieties of the Soviet–Iraqi relationship should be observed. If this

could be achieved by judicious hints on his part that 'it is in our interest
that the United States should be present in the region, when any other big
or superpower is present', so much the better.[17] However, it was not
simply with the idea of using leverage on the Soviet Union that a closer
relationship with the United States began to develop. The United States
had material resources of which Iraq was to stand ever more clearly in
need, if it was to survive the developing war of attrition against Iran. As
Saddam Hussein said, when referring to the prospect of a US–Iraqi
rapprochement in 1982:[18]

> No country can claim independence by shutting its doors to the world and at
> the same time keeping pace with world development and science.

This argument raised the question of the primacy of the requirements of
Iraq's national independence, both with reference to the Soviet Union
and to access to the Western, especially American, technology required in
its war effort. It was used increasingly by the Iraqi Government and
appears to have been a crucial part of its attempt to justify ever closer
relations with a superpower that continued to be identified as a linchpin of
the 'imperialist-Zionist conspiracies' which the Iraqi people were
constantly being urged to confront.

When the independence, indeed the existence, of Iraq as a state was
under threat, the Iraqi Government suggested, help from any source was
permissible. The United States lost little time in reciprocating. Official
contacts increased and by the end of 1982 Iraq had been removed from
the US Government's list of states 'supporting international terrorism',
thereby allowing further contacts and increased trade. This did not
include items of military equipment as such, but it did extend to Iraqi
purchases of American technology, as well as transport planes, vehicles
and helicopters, all of which were useful in the defence effort.[19] As far as
non-Soviet military supplies were concerned, Iraq's major object of
attention in the West was France, as it had been for several years before
the war. Because of Iraq's financial difficulties from 1982 onwards,
France also found itself underwriting the Iraqi defence effort. The size of
the debt which Iraq had incurred in purchasing French arms was such
that, quite apart from other considerations of French regional interest,
France had a strong commercial incentive to ensure that an Iraqi military
collapse should not occur. As a result, it became eager to provide Iraq
with the means of preventing it.[20]

At the same time, Iraq has been able to receive from the United States
intelligence information which should theoretically make its use of the
massive arsenal it has built up increasingly effective. Since the restoration
of US–Iraqi diplomatic relations in 1984, and possibly before, Iraq has
been able to acquire data on Iranian military activities. This came initially

from the AWACS supplied by the United States to Saudi Arabia. Subsequently, and more importantly, it has come from American satellites passing over the battlefronts.[21] The advantage of this system for the Iraqi leadership has been that, quite apart from the real military value of the information received, Saddam Hussein has been able to take the credit for his extraordinary prescience and military acumen whenever the Iraqi armed forces have responded successfully to a predicted Iranian attack. This occurred in the defeat of the Iranian offensives of 1985 across the Howeiz marshes. However, when the Iraqi forces failed to deal so effectively with an Iranian onslaught, as in early 1986 and 1987, the blame could be placed conveniently on the United States, which was accused of 'misleading' the Iraqis for its own nefarious ends.[22]

In withstanding the rigours of a war of attrition, the extraction of economic aid and credit has been an equally important part of the Iraqi war effort. By 1982 the Soviet Union had reportedly seen its trade with Iraq fall to less than one third that of Iraq's trade with the United States. It therefore attempted to remedy this by embarking on a number of joint projects with Iraq in the important fields of oil exploration and power generation.[23] The United States has meanwhile arranged considerable credits for the Iraqi purchase of American technology and agricultural products.[24] After the financial crisis of 1982–3, Iraq was obliged to reschedule the estimated $2 billion due on its foreign debts to non-Arab states, which was deferred until 1985. In that year, it paid the instalments due to its European creditors, but negotiated a further rescheduling of its debt to Japan. The latter, precisely because of the size of the debt, had little choice but to agree. When the Iraqi economy was further hit by the collapse of oil prices in 1986, this was an experience which most of its Western creditors were also obliged to go through.[25] Iraq was discovering some of the power which a spectacular debtor can exert in Western financial markets. Since it could also point out that its economic collapse might lead directly to a military collapse and to the disappearance of the regime which had incurred the debts, its case appeared to be doubly persuasive.

Saddam Hussein had found that he could use Iraq's apparent vulnerability to reinforce his own position. The apocalyptic vision with which he had threatened both his country and the region should the Iranians succeed in achieving their war aims, had rallied both domestic and regional forces to his side. It appeared to have an equally galvanizing effect on the external powers. Paradoxically, although Iraq had become more dependent than ever before on outside assistance, it was dependent on such a range of powers for so many resources and its plight seemed so desperate, that Saddam Hussein had won considerable independence of action. He could thus afford to play one set of anxious backers off against another, confident in the knowledge that they regarded his mere survival, rather than any particular policy he might pursue, as an asset in itself.

Materially, this has been of enormous worth in enhancing his capacity to deal with both the Iranian front and the domestic front. Domestically, it has also been of considerable value in reinforcing the impression which he has wished to create, portraying him as the guardian of Iraq's independence.

The superpowers and the ending of the war

The successful exploitation of the resources of outside powers has helped Iraq over the years to fend off numerous Iranian offensives and thus to thwart Iran's achievement of its war aims. However, Saddam Hussein and the Iraqi leadership have repeatedly voiced their resentment at the fact that these same powers – and the superpowers in particular – have shown little or no inclination to force Iran to cease these offensives and to sue for peace.[26] Iraq's inability to extract itself from the war, and the apparent unwillingness of the superpowers to help it do so, have been the cause of much concern. Saddam Hussein's Army Day speech of 1982 clearly showed what he expected of the superpowers. He stated that they should first condemn Iran for continuing the war and then impose an effective boycott on Iran to deny it the means of doing so. The fact that neither the Soviet Union nor the United States seemed willing at the time to take any active measures in this direction was portrayed by him, characteristically, as evidence of an international conspiracy aimed at forcing Iraq 'to give up its independent stand . . . and to curb its non-alignment'.[27] When the military situation become more critical later in the year, he returned to this theme with considerable vehemence, stating that he found it beyond belief that a war should be allowed to rage for two years in 'one of the most dangerous and vital regions of the world', without any serious attempt by the superpowers to stop it.[28]

Increasingly, therefore, Iraq's attitude towards the superpowers has been determined not simply by the material contributions they can make towards its defence effort, but also by the degree of resolve they have shown in persuading or compelling Iran to abandon its war aims and negotiate an end to the conflict. Apart from the immediate defence of its territory, Iraq's war strategy during most of the past seven years has been geared towards forcing the Iranian Government to call off its armies and agree to settle outstanding issues through negotiation. It has been for this reason that Iraq has made a point of accepting the eight United Nations Security Council resolutions which have called for an end to hostilities. In 1986, Tariq Aziz declared that Iraq had already convinced the world that it was imperative to concentrate on a comprehensive settlement of the conflict and that its diplomatic efforts were aimed at 'convincing the world that it must bring pressure on Iran to limit its ability to continue the war'.[29] In addition, since the forced Iraqi withdrawal from Iranian territory in 1982, and the consequently much reduced Iraqi conditions for an end to the conflict published in that year, Saddam Hussein has repeated the Iraqi terms at regular intervals. In essence, these terms imply a return to the *status quo ante bellum*, with the withdrawal of forces to 'internationally recognized boundaries' and the signing of a peace and non-aggression treaty.[30] There was perhaps little surprise in Baghdad that the Iranian leadership continued to reject these various proposals. However, there was evident exasperation at the apparent disinclination of the international community, and specifically the superpowers, to compel the Iranian leadership to change its mind.

Nor had Iraqi war strategy succeeded in provoking Iran to bring down on its own head the international retribution which Iraq increasingly saw as the most effective way of ending the war. The Iraqi attacks on shipping in the Gulf and on Iran's oil installations after 1982 were primarily intended to put direct pressure on Iran and to limit the economic resources at its disposal. However, there was always the hope that these moves might tempt the Iranian leaders to make good their threat to close the Strait of Hormuz should their oil-exporting capacity be seriously disrupted. The repeated assurances by the United States that it would, if necessary, use force to prevent Iran from doing so, held out the welcome prospect of international involvement in the conflict in a way that seemed likely to work in Iraq's favour.[31] Undoubtedly aware of these implications, the Iranian Government had shown little inclination to provoke such a direct intervention by the United States, despite the ferocity of the rhetoric of the Iranian leadership.

Nevertheless, it could not fail to respond in some measure to the mounting intensity and accuracy of the Iraqi attacks during 1985 and 1986. Iranian reprisals against shipping belonging to or doing business with the Arab states of the Gulf led to the requests by Kuwait to both the Soviet Union and the United States for some form of naval protection for its own oil exports. This resulted in 1987 in Kuwait's chartering of Soviet tankers and in the placing of half of the Kuwaiti tanker fleet under the American flag. As far as Iraq was concerned, this was an encouraging development, since it seemed to guarantee an engagement of the superpowers to an extent that they had hitherto shown themselves perversely able to resist. In the waters of the Gulf, the reinforcement of US naval strength was interpreted by Tariq Aziz as a direct result of Iraq's proven capacity to defeat the Iranian war effort on land. This had, he claimed, led to desperation on the part of the Iranian leadership, increasing the danger for all users of the Gulf and obliging outside powers to take the Iranian threat seriously for the first time.[32] However, it was important for Iraq to convince the superpowers that it was not enough simply to protect shipping. Rather, they should exert themselves to end the war itself, since it was the existence of conflict which was putting the ships in danger in the first place. The Iraqi fear was that the more effective American and other efforts were in preventing Iranian attacks on their own shipping, the less inclined they would be to tackle the central question of the ending of hostilities. It was this fundamental issue which was the principal concern of the Iraqi government.[33]

Consequently, Iraq was keen to encourage moves at the UN which seemed designed to address precisely this question. There was the oft-repeated hope in Iraq that its own acceptance and Iran's rejection of successive UN calls for an end to the war would eventually lead to decisive UN action to force Iran to comply – and, as Iraq made clear, such a display of resolve could only come about if the two superpowers decided that it was in their best interests to do so.[34] As a result, the Iraqi leadership flattered and cajoled both the Soviet Union and the United States to a marked extent during the first half of 1987. A spate of Soviet diplomatic visits to Iraq allowed Saddam Hussein to stress the identity of Soviet and Iraqi views on the need to end the war and to underline the co-operation between the two countries.[35]

Much the same applied to the United States, which was anxious in any case to repair the damage caused to its reputation in the Arab world by the continuing revelations of the 'Irangate' scandal.[36] When, in May 1987, an Iraqi warplane attacked the US frigate *USS Stark* in the Gulf, Saddam Hussein was quick to apologize. Apart from offering compensation, he used the opportunity to express the hope that this unintentional action would in no way affect the cordial state of US–Iraqi relations. At the same time, he used the incident to illustrate the urgent 'need for joint efforts to end the war and force the Iranian regime to agree to peace in accordance with the principles of international law and UN resolutions'.[37] President Reagan's conciliatory reply echoed these sentiments and stated that the United States would be working actively for a peaceful solution to the war, in co-operation with Iraq and others. This message received considerable publicity in the Iraqi media.[38]

It has been vital for Iraq not only that the war be taken seriously by the superpowers, but also that Iraqi interests be taken into consideration and treated as a priority. In this respect, there has been repeated evidence of Iraqi concern that both the superpowers might regard Iran as the greater strategic asset and tailor their policies accordingly. Despite the continuing and manifest differences between the Soviet Union and Iran over the latter's uncompromising stand on the war, the growing economic and diplomatic relationship between the two countries, especially after 1985, cannot have been reassuring for the Iraqi Government. Nor can the reports of the indirect supply of Soviet arms to Iran. It was not surprising, therefore, that Taha Ramadhan, on his return from a visit to the Soviet Union in July 1987 to solicit help, should vehemently deny such reports. Maintaining that the Soviet leaders were determined to work for a UN resolution that would take some action against 'the party that would not

respond to international resolutions and conventions', he stated unequivocally that 'They are on our side'.[39]

It was in order to impress upon the superpowers that the Iraqi side was
the one it was worth being on, that repeated reference was made to the
permanence and durability of Iraq, compared to the instability and
uncertain future of Iran. The message of Iraqi unity and of the existence
of a specifically Iraqi identity was undoubtedly aimed simultaneously at a
domestic audience of uncertain loyalties. Nevertheless, it was also clear
that Saddam Hussein intended that the superpowers should not
underrate Iraq, when he instructed them to remember that 'Iraq does not
exist only geographically, but also as a will . . . No power can force it to
retreat'.[40] As he was later to state, the war would not weaken this will and
the 'world powers' should know that 'This people, who possesses a
civilization five thousand years old, will not give in'. It was, therefore,
incumbent upon those powers to take 'strong, co-ordinated international
action . . . to contain this hostile barbarism which is becoming more
arrogant and hostile with appeasement'.[41]

The appeasement apparent in the covert American arms deals with
Iran was clearly disturbing. In public, the Iraqi leaders claimed to see in
these moves further proof of the US–Zionist conspiracy. Indeed, they
sought to make some political capital out of it, by using it as an illustration
of the righteousness of their own war effort. However, they also showed
that they were aware of the strategic implications, in which it could be
argued that American national interests were better served by cultivating
Iran. Nevertheless, they took some comfort from the fact that the nature
of American interests in the Arab world as a whole would soon cause
the United States to reassess such a policy. It was expected in Iraq,
therefore, that the US Government would take pains to repair the damage
done to American interests and that, since most of the Arab world was
aligned with Iraq, this would work in Iraq's favour.[42]

More disturbing, clearly, for the Iraqi Government was the attitude of
the Soviet Union following the passage of the UN Security Council
resolution 598 in July 1987. This resolution had been similar to many
previous ones, in that it called for a cease-fire, a withdrawal of forces to
international boundaries and a negotiated end to the conflict. However, it
also contained, for the first time, the suggestion that the UN might take
some form of action against the party which rejected its terms. In a well
organized display of unity, Saddam Hussein, after presiding over a joint
meeting of the Revolutionary Command Council and the Ba'th Regional
Command, summoned an extraordinary meeting of the National
Assembly. Here Iraq's acceptance of the terms of the resolution received
unanimous approval. The resolution itself was described as 'a new
political and diplomatic victory for Iraq and the embodiment of a wide-
scale world response which has helped crystallize a joint international
will'.[43]

It was clearly hoped that this will would now manifest itself by concrete steps being taken to force Iran to accept the resolution as well. Any attempt to delay its implementation or to seek to implement it piecemeal was regarded by the Iraqi Government as giving an unacceptable advantage to Iran, since it was feared that Iran would simply use the temporary respite to gather its forces for fresh offensives against Iraq. The Iraqi Government was therefore adamant that Iran should be judged swiftly on its attitude to the resolution as a whole and that UN sanctions should be applied against it in the case of equivocation or rejection.[44] This was the thrust of a series of letters addressed by the Iraqi Minister of Foreign Affairs, Tariq Aziz, to the UN Secretary General in the months following the passing of the resolution. In them, he expressed Iraq's concern at the 'delay in drawing clear conclusions as defined in the provisions of the resolution [which] will grant the recalcitrant Iranian Government permission to continue its war of aggression against Iraq'. He also expressed Iraq's displeasure at seeing attempts being made at the UN to dilute the comprehensive nature of resolution 598.[45]

The role of the Soviet Union in this lobbying was regarded as particularly worrying. The visit of Yuli Vorontsov (Soviet First Deputy Minister of Foreign Affairs) to Baghdad at the end of July was described as 'warm and friendly' by the Iraqi media since the discussion centred on 'the early implementation of the Security Council resolution'.[46] Once he had left, visiting Tehran before returning to Moscow, Iraqi exasperation did not take long to surface. The superpowers were reminded that the implementation of Security Council resolution 598 was a test of their credibility and that 'experience shows that once it loses its credibility, it is difficult for a big power to regain it'. Threatening not only permanent Iraqi and Arab disaffection, the Iraqi press went on to stress the illusory nature of any gains which the Soviet Union – for this was clearly the big power in question – might hope to make in cultivating Iran:[47]

> Those who believe they can adopt stands that will ensure they will not lose either belligerent in the war are mistaken. The Iranian regime cannot represent the Iranian peoples and their interests. It is a regime that has no future and lacks consistency and political stability.

As Iraqi frustration and suspicion of the Soviet Union's motives increased, so the Iraqi Government's criticism became more explicit. The Soviet media were taken to task for suggesting that the escalation of Iraqi attacks on Iranian economic targets was at the instigation of the United States.[48] Soon the Iraqi Government was expressing its dissatisfaction directly to the Soviet Union for hesitating to impose economic sanctions on Iran. Furthermore, Saddam Hussein explicitly rejected a Soviet proposal that Iraq should accept an immediate 'informal' cease-fire, while an enquiry began into the responsibility for starting the war. This was regarded in Baghdad as an unmistakable and unacceptable capitulation to the demands of the Iranian Government.[49]

As the Iraqi Minister of Information, Latif Nusayyif al-Jasim, put it, the strong, friendly relations between Iraq and the Soviet Union 'do not mean that we cannot criticize it, but such criticisms should not affect the essence of long-term friendship between the two countries'.[50] The maintenance of such a relationship is clearly crucial for the success of Iraq's defence effort and must, therefore, place restraints on any concrete expression of Iraqi dissatisfaction. Whatever the level of frustration in Iraq at the behaviour of the Soviet Union, this is not the time to lose the support of a superpower. Much the same could be said to apply, although on a rather different scale, to the Iraqi relationship with the United States.

Saddam Hussein has shown considerable skill in exploiting Iraq's predicament to gain the superpowers' support for its war effort, relatively unencumbered by conditions that might limit his freedom of action. Where he has been less successful has been in inducing those powers to extricate Iraq from that predicament on terms which he would find acceptable. This dilemma relates not simply to the perceptions and interests of the powers involved, but also to the nature of the enemy and thus of the war itself. Although Saddam Hussein can draw some satisfaction from the fact that both the United States and the Soviet Union wish to prevent an Iranian victory, he is clearly less reassured about their joint determination to allow Iraq to emerge from the conflict under conditions which Saddam Hussein could claim as a 'victory'. Yet he believes that such an outcome is necessary to ensure his own political survival. These conditions are at present defined by the 'Five Principles' enunciated by Saddam Hussein in his 'Open Letter to the Iranian People' of 2 August 1986:[51]

i) Ceasefire on land, sea and air, accompanied by complete withdrawal to internationally recognized boundaries.
ii) Complete exchange of prisoners.
iii) Signing of peace and non-agression treaty.
iv) Pledge of non-interference in each other's internal affairs – each country to respect the other's options.
v) Iraq and Iran should be positive elements in ensuring security and stability in the region and the Arab Gulf in particular.

As he has subsequently been at pains to point out, 'Iraq has the determination, the ability and the legitimacy that supports our stand to continue the struggle' until they are achieved.[52]

The unpleasant suspicion of superpower collusion and conspiracy in preventing their achievement is never far from Saddam Hussein's view of the conflict. It also plays a basic and necessary part in explaining to the Iraqi public why it is that the war continues, despite the claim that Iraq has 'defeated aggressive Khomeinism' and that it is now in a position to force Iran to accept peace.[53] In these circumstances, Saddam Hussein hopes that the superpowers will take note of the fact that[54]

> their game of prolonging the war might not lead to what they wish. It might even lead to certain surprises with a reverse impact not only on the tactical level, but also on the strategic level.

The propagation of the idea that the war is a form of conspiracy against Iraq has been used widely by the government, with reference both to regional alignments and to the role of the superpowers. It seems to be an attempt by the Iraqi leadership, and by Saddam Hussein in particular, to explain not only why the war is continuing, but also why it began. In this connection, it serves to disguise the fact that their original belief that war would be an instrument of regional dominance was so disastrous a miscalculation. At moments of domestic crisis, the temptation to fall back on the theory of conspiracy as a substitute for explanation and as a justification for equally conspiratorial action has been a marked feature of Iraqi politics under the Ba'th. It is, therefore, scarcely surprising that a similar perspective exists with regard to the international system. In this way deficiencies of leadership, of strategy and of execution are concealed not only from the public gaze, but also from the kind of scrutiny that might disrupt the cohesion of the inner circle of power.

Saddam Hussein has frequently had recourse to this level of conspiratorial explanation in his dealings with the superpowers. Nevertheless, in seeking to calculate how they will react, he seems to have been made aware of some of the fundamental rules of international politics. Although he was ostensibly referring to Iran, one might be tempted to see a trace of self-analysis in his assessment of the war, nearly seven years after the Iraqi forces crossed the border into Iran:[55]

> War can break out even without prior intentions, when the parties involved find no other means of relations but war to achieve their objectives. A war erupting as a result of its parties' own will need not simply be caused by miscalculation – that is, when the rulers commit an error in this direction – but also when the regional, internal and international situation can attract these rulers into committing such an error.

As Saddam Hussein himself has discovered, it may have been very tempting to start a war against a state which had no external superpower patron or ally, precisely because of the opportunity this seemed to provide him to achieve his war aims. However, when the latter were shown to be wholly inappropriate, the opposite applied. Thus, where once Iraq sought to gain unilateral advantage by a war conducted without the impediments of superpower restraints, so now Iran seems to be set on the same course. Defiant in its insistence that the war must end with the overthrow of Saddam Hussein, Iran seems intent on resisting superpower pressure to moderate its war aims or to end its war effort. Although the situation now works to Iraq's disadvantage, Saddam Hussein appears unable to escape from the logic of a situation which he himself helped to create.

11

Iran and the Superpowers

The demands of the war and the pressures that it has created in the light of the supreme importance attached to its victorious conclusion, have given Iran every incentive to modify its other policies in order to attain its primary goal. Foremost among these have been its policies towards the superpowers which it early identified as the cause of most of the problems of the 'oppressed'. The war has created new realities, needs, and priorities, and in response to them Iran's policies, and the attitudes undergirding them, have evolved considerably. One can see this as a collision of the Islamic republic's principles (ideology) with the realities of the war. The war is a 'baptism of fire' imposing demands and necessitating choices, and it entails the moderating of ideology to the needs of the state. The impingement of the external environment, which conditions the exercise of Iran's foreign relations, on its Islamic-revolutionary values and rhetoric is clearly obvious. In this sense, the war has served to accelerate a 'learning' and a mellowing process.

A new tactical flexibility or pragmatism has evolved in Iran's attitude towards the superpowers. This is a significant modification of its earlier images rather than a fundamental shift in viewpoint or a repudiation of earlier attitudes. The Islamic republic's principal interest has been to protect the revolution. To do this, since the war and the revolution are inextricably intertwined, the Islamic republic must not only survive the war but emerge from it victorious. Yet it has been evident from the outset that, even if the superpowers were not in a position to dictate outcomes in the region, they were and are, singly or jointly, in a position to make some outcomes less likely, to raise the price of certain policies, and to deny even the 'victor' the fruits of victory or to make them bitter. In addition, there has been some evidence for the proposition that, while the superpowers' rivalry has prevented their concerting their policies on the war, they have shared a preference to see it end in a stalemate rather than an Iranian victory.

While seeking the means to achieve victory, Iran has sought to do so without compromising its fundamental values. The war has precipitated a rethinking and re-evaluation of positions vis-à-vis the superpowers. This has included the need to consider whether the equation of Moscow and

Washington serves Iran's purpose, or to put it differently, whether Iran is not paying too high a price for its simultaneous antagonization of both superpowers. Iran has tried to exploit its own strategic importance and the superpowers' rivalry to increase its room for manoeuvre and to harmonize its ideology with its practical needs. It is now clear that Tehran initiated as well as accepted contacts with the United States in 1985, and has never been without an indirect channel to Washington. Relations with the USSR have varied, but the Islamic authorities have refused to drop their opposition to Soviet policy in Afghanistan, despite an obvious need for Soviet goodwill. In sum, Iran's war needs have not dictated policy, which still has to consider principles, ideology and image. Yet even if they had, it remains doubtful whether it is within Iran's capability to choose or decide issues unilaterally. Despite their competition, and also because of it, the superpowers have pursued their interests with some restraint, unwilling to relinquish control of their policies or their wider concerns to the demands of their bilateral interests with Tehran.[1]

The war has raised complex questions for the superpowers, relating to the primacy of the need to avoid crises, their bilateral interests with a strategic state, and the sort of regional order that they wish to encourage in the Gulf and the Middle East as a whole. They have each sought to benefit from Iran's needs and the exigencies of the war to improve their respective positions in Tehran. The United States, which had diplomatic ties with neither adversary in September 1980, has sought to use the war as a means of opening relations with Iran. US policy has been guided by two considerations, which have had to be balanced, leading often to a two-track or dual policy: the need, on the one hand, to cultivate Iran as the strategic linch-pin of the region and as a buffer to the Soviet Union, and, on the other, the sometimes competing necessity of preventing its 'export of the revolution' and the destabilization of the region.[2] In maintaining an equilibrium between the two necessities of cultivation and containment, the US has alternated between blandishments and stern warnings, between hints of rewards and threats of punishment. For the US, Iran remains the principal proximate geographic and political obstacle to Soviet penetration of the Gulf region, a potential ally and a force independently for good or ill as regards US interests in the entire Middle East and Islamic world.

The USSR started off in a better position, enjoying relations with both adversaries when the war broke out, and in a somewhat less strained position with Tehran. For the USSR, Iran represents a major interest as a neighbouring power that can create strategic problems as well as opportunities for it in the Gulf, the Indian Ocean, and in South and Southwest Asia and the Islamic world. Moscow has been anxious to ensure that it does not lose its advantage vis-à-vis Washington and that the war does not allow the US to improve its ties with the belligerents or its military position in the region. While the USSR has not been keen to take sides definitively with either of the adversaries, or to see an Iranian victory, it is equally concerned to ensure that a prolonged stalemate does not strengthen the American presence in the region, or the combatants' incentives to lean towards the US. At the same time, it has exploited the war to put across an image of restraint and reasonableness, both in the region (where it is combined with the value or 'relevance' of the Soviet connection) and vis-à-vis the US.

It is, however, Iran's reaction to the war and the evolution of its policies in the light of its needs that primarily concerns us here. Briefly one can summarize this as an attempt to balance the demands of the war and the importance it attaches to other values, such as independence and self-reliance. It has sought to maximize its own room for manouevre without becoming a client state, and without losing its identity or becoming 'dependent'. Its aim is to neutralize support for Iraq, to gain access to supplies for its war effort, and to achieve at least acquiescence in the possibility of an Iranian military victory. Its relations with the superpowers can be summarized in phases:

i) 1980–82. Rhetorical equation of the superpowers not matched by policy, which tilted towards Moscow while relations with the US were hostile.

ii) 1983–4. Relations with both superpowers bad; war seems stalemated, costs of antagonization appear high and limit manoeuvrability.

iii) 1984/5–7. Improvement of 'correct' relations with USSR, agreement to disagree; opening of channel with US, to increase options. A form of balance between the superpowers prevails, with no decisive impact on the war.

The Islamic republic was established by a clerical leadership that insisted on the proposition that all the ills of the world – inequality, an unjust international system, exploitation, oppression, the bullying of the weak by the strong – emanated from the 'arrogant' superpowers or their 'agents'.[3] In this view, the superpowers were in collusion and were equally guilty. Khomeini saw Iran's condition in particular as the result of a conspiracy between the Shah and the West, to make Iran culturally and politically dependent. If the US was seen as the main threat to the revolution, the 'Great Satan', it was primarily because of cultural contamination and only secondarily as a result of its military power. Iranians held the contradictory view of the US as at one and the same time impotent and omnipotent; the Islamic authorities feared US military power while also ridiculing it. Paradoxically, the Soviet Union was seen as a less immediate threat despite its proximity, because the Islamic leadership implicitly relied on *Realpolitik* and countervailing American power. Equally important, the revolution's leaders saw threats primarily in terms of their own position, not in terms of the nation-state; this led them to focus on counter-revolutionaries, and especially the US-trained officer corps in the military forces that they inherited from the Shah.

It was an article of faith of Islamic Iran that true independence entailed a rejection of foreign values, a repudiation of standard procedures that ratified the domination of the weak by the strong. It accepted that this might mean a period of scarcity, but saw it as a necessary phase in a purging of the culture from foreign influences. Self-reliance became synonymous with authenticity, a value that made some hardships tolerable and perhaps even necessary. The idea of compromise, trimming, adjustment to the demands of an unforgiving world, has been rejected time and again, even if in practice it has become increasingly operational in policy. In 1984, as the war ground to a stalemate, Khomeini put the case against adjustment thus:[4]

> Our revolution is a great one; it does not rely on any power, either East or West . . .
>
> Today, Iran is standing on its own feet. Therefore, it must put up with the difficulties and conspiracies.
>
> Certain individuals . . . may say, well let us come to terms with the superpowers. However, they must bear in mind that any compromise today would be tantamount to eternal annihilation; that would be the end of Islam for ever.
>
> . . . Resist for your victory is a victory over the two superpowers. To triumph over one power through the support and backing of the other superpower is not important. You must stand up to both superpowers.

Relations with the United States

In Iran's view the war launched by Saddam Hussein in September 1980 could only be explained by US complicity and encouragement. The crisis over the seizure of American hostages served, in this view, to encourage an attempt by the US and its regional 'agent' Saddam Hussein to strangle the young revolution. In support of this argument, Iranians point to the absurdity and inherent improbability of Saddam Hussein 'daring' to embark on such an adventure against a foe three times the size of Iraq, and to the low-key US reaction to the attack and its obvious interest in reversing the blow to its fortunes in the region represented by the revolution. Iranian statements since the outbreak of war emphasize the United States' complicity in the Iraqi attack, 'the US hand emerging from Saddam's sleeve', and less prominently the superpowers' equally objectionable policies on the war both bilaterally and in the United Nations.[5]

Phase (i).   In the first phase of the war, victory took second place to the needs of assuring the revolution's immediate security. As we have seen, the domestic power struggle, the 'third revolution', the consolidation of power by the clerical IRP, enjoyed priority over war strategy or the needs of the military. Indeed, distrust of the military led to their being set up as potential scapegoats rather than fitted out as saviours. The upshot was a low priority given to the needs of the military, and even more, an obstructionist attitude toward any policy that might envisage a reconstitution of the military relationship with the US. The clerics saw an arms relationship as the thin end of the wedge, or a new umbilical cord which would drag Iran down again into a position of dependency, and more important, give the military real clout domestically. In sabotaging the supply of arms (already paid for and held up because of the hostage dispute), which the US was willing to furnish under the Algiers accord of 1981, the IRP hamstrung the Iranian war effort. Ironically, it is the same people (e.g. Hashemi Rafsanjani) who have since 1986 blamed the US for a failure to return Iran's assets.

At the outset of the war, Iran had a large store of spare parts on which it could draw and which the Shah had accumulated for precisely such an eventuality. Nevertheless, the degree of reliance on American weapons should be noted, for it included all of the air force, much of the navy including reconnaissance aircraft, air defence, hundreds of helicopters, most electronic components including air to air, air to surface and surface to air missiles, as well as anti-tank missiles.[6] Because of rapid attrition of stocks in combat, and the difficulty of locating some matériel, Iran quickly found it had to look for new supplies, but had to do so with its hands tied because of its own policies. And supplies, when available, were costly.[7] Nevertheless, the requirements of the revolution prevailed and Iran was able to reorganize and counterattack without compromising its principles. If the priority was the revolution rather than the war, Iran was at first cushioned from having to make any real choice by the momentum of the revolution, the country's geographic depth and the enemy's ineptitude. By Summer 1982, it was poised to move into Iraq itself whither Iraqi forces had withdrawn after a succession of defeats. It looked as if Iran had achieved victory without outside assistance and despite external hostility.

US 'policy' towards Iran throughout this phase of the war had been one of barely concealed satisfaction at the Iraqi attack, combined with the hope that the hostages would be quickly released, the limited offer of the supply of arms which had been paid for, and consultations with the USSR at the United Nations.[8] Doubts as to Iran's ability to continue the war were mixed with awe at its willingness to accept casualties, but while neither adversary had much of a popular constituency in its favour within the US, after the trauma of the hostage crisis Iran was the more unpopular of the two. Kissinger's aphorism, 'too bad they can't both lose', reflected both official and popular feeling, but not policy. This was simply confined to making sure that the conflict did not spread, that allies in the Gulf were reassured by means of a multilateral naval presence, the deployment of early-warnings (AWACS) aircraft, and warnings about the need to ensure the flow of oil and the freedom of navigation.

As Iran's military position improved, the US found its interests more directly threatened. While an expansionist Iran threatened the stability of the Gulf, a policy of confronting Iran would risk pushing that country – 'the strategic centrepiece of the region' – towards the Soviet Union.[9] The problem of containing and cultivating revolutionary Iran posed itself in acute form and still remains the central dilemma of US policy in the region. The US response in this period was to become more involved, warning Iran that its neutrality should not be construed as 'indifference' to the outcome of the war, and making plain that its tolerance of Iran's actions in the Gulf was limited.[10] Defense Secretary Weinberger underlined US interest in an end to the war but not to *any* end: 'We want to see the war end in a way that doesn't destabilize the area . . . An Iranian victory is certainly not in our national interest'.[11] To give substance to these statements, the US authorized the sale of cargo planes to Iraq.[12] Reiterated US calls for an end to the war seemed to Iran to be due only to its battlefield successes; Washington had been mute during its travails in 1980–81.[13] Yet the US presented some semblance of evenhandedness, calling for negotiations, affirming its support for the territorial integrity of both belligerents, and reproaching Jordan for its decision to dispatch volunteers to Iraq, as a widening of the war.[14] At the same time, it maintained a naval presence and continued to exercise its forces (e.g. with Oman in the autumn of 1982) in order to be able to project power into the region quickly if called upon.

Phase (ii).   The second phase saw Iran take the war to Iraq, but remain unable to force a military decision. This was a period in which the Pasdar controlled military operations and with a combination of hubris and zeal sought to rewrite the principles governing warfare. Iran continued to reject both the idea and the need to seek any sort of relationship with the United States, confident of its ability to win the war on its own terms. At the same time, its alliance with Syria had given the Islamic republic access to Lebanon and to the largest constituency of that country, the dispossessed Shi'a. Its support for radical groupings such as Islamic Amal, Hezbollah, and the terrorist Islamic Jihad, served not so much as a diversion from the war as ancillary to it, testifying to Iran's regional constituency and demonstrating the continuing vitality and reach of the revolution. As a result of its insistence on the right to attack US interests anywhere,[15] it clashed with the United States on the issue of terrorism, which in turn influenced the tenor of relations in the Gulf war. At the same time, by the end of this period, the problems of arms resupply had become more acute as existing stocks were used up and replacements became harder to obtain as a result of the US policy of tightening up on its own leakages and arresting third-party supplies in what was known as 'Operation Staunch'.

The second phase in relations started predictably enough with US calls for negotiations to end the war.[16] US nervousness about the expansion of the war increased as Iraq took possession of French Exocets and Super-Etendards and threatened Kharg island. Tehran's position was that if its exports were threatened by Iraqi air attacks, it was in a position to make sure that no oil was exported through the Gulf by closing the Strait of Hormuz. Putting aside the question of its technical feasibility, this threat was clearly intended to exert pressure on the Gulf states and the US to act to restrain Iraq from such attacks.[17] The threat was a 'reasonable' one only if it was accepted that Iran had the right to deny Iraq the use of the Gulf for its oil exports, but that Baghdad did not have an equal right. The US position was that this was a threat to the freedom of navigation, and that it would not stand for 'blackmail' or allow the closure of the straits by anyone. US naval patrols were stepped up accordingly.[18]

The hardening of respective positions continued in 1984. As a result of its apparent involvement in the Beirut bombing of a US marine barracks, Iran was designated a terrorist state, thus further restricting its access to military technology from the US.[19] By 1984 US policy had shifted to one of preventing an Iranian victory in the war, implying a definite tilt towards Iraq.[20] Iraq now received access to US intelligence data gathered by the AWACS in Saudi Arabia. The official US position was that it was Iran that was refusing to end the war not Iraq, which had accepted UN Security Council resolution 540 of October 1983. Also it was argued that while Iraq confined its air attacks on Gulf shipping to a defined war zone, Iran attacked non-belligerents in international waters.[21] The tilt towards Iraq was also evident in the use of US good offices in the search for assurances concerning the security of a new pipeline to be built by Bechtel and intended to bypass the Gulf.

The other side of this policy was an increase in the rhetoric of confrontation with Iran. Warnings against a closure of the straits, backed up by an expanded naval presence of nineteen ships, including a carrier (*USS Midway*), were coupled with stepped-up planning against an oil emergency, and consultations with allies. The US position remained one that envisaged intervention as a last resort; it looked to multilateral co-operation with its allies rather than unilateral action, and stipulated that it would only act on a request from its regional friends. While the Gulf states were reassured by these moves and by US willingness to supply air-defence equipment (*Stinger* SAMs), they were in no hurry to alienate Iran by offering the United States bases.[22]

The US sought to ensure that the combatants were under no illusions as to the risks entailed in widening the war. This meant in the first instance deterring any Iranian attack on the Gulf states as a riposte for an Iraqi attack on Kharg island. Formally, as Assistant Secretary Murphy told Congress, the US position was one that wished to see neither side emerge as victor.[23] In practice, there was no question of an Iraqi victory and this formulation became shorthand for a desire to prevent an Iranian victory. While President Reagan called upon Iran to stop this 'terrible bloodletting',[24] the US had moved to tighten up on arms transfers to Iran. In the first instance, this meant stopping leaks of spare parts from the US itself and secondly raising the issue seriously with more complaisant allies such as the British.[25] Ambassador Richard Fairbanks was assigned to this job and seems to have made the embargo on Iran effective (Iraq continued to enjoy access to the armouries of other states, especially the USSR and France). Reflecting their desperation, reports of Iranian efforts to buy arms from US sources in 1985 were matched by the number of arrests and interceptions within the US.[26]

Phase (iii). By now the war was in its fifth and the revolution in its seventh year. The newly re-elected Reagan Administration, chastened by its experience in Beirut, was no longer so confident of a policy of unrelenting pressure, and was conscious of the need to find a *modus vivendi* with the 'strategic centrepiece' of the area. For their part, Iran's revolutionary leaders no longer felt as insecure as before, but neither did they feel as militant or as confident of their ability to win the war without new sources of arms supplies. The basis for a possible 'deal' could be glimpsed at this juncture.

The US continued its calls on Iran for a negotiated end to the war. It continued to admonish 'terrorist states' about the risks they ran, and to warn Iran explicitly of its responsibility and accountability for the lives of US citizens kidnapped by Islamic Jihad in Lebanon.[27] But the tone had changed. The US now put pressure on Iraq not to indulge in unlimited air attacks on Iran's economic infrastructure during the 'war of the cities'.[28] The State Department made efforts to appease Iran by criticizing Iraq's use of chemical weapons in the war in the United Nations. Iran, for its part, also made an effort. It opened up a dialogue with the Gulf states – including the dispatch of its Foreign Minister to Saudi Arabia for the first time – and sought to reassure them of its pacific intentions. In the form of Hashemi Rafsanjani, Iran played a helpful role in the resolution of the TWA hijacking in Beirut in June. Later that month Rafsanjani sent a signal to the US when he mentioned the possibility of eventually restoring 'normal' relations, under certain rather vague conditions.

US interest in Iran had not diminished with the reduction of its oil imports from the Gulf region. The need to contain the Gulf war and deter Iran from regional mischief-making could not substitute for a long-range policy of opening channels to an Iran that might moderate its aims over time. Indeed, the US-led arms squeeze had already accelerated this process of rethinking in Iran. The US covert strategic dialogue with Iran had never been completely severed. In 1982 a KGB defector, Vladimir Kuzichkin, stationed in Iran, had disclosed the scope of the Soviet Union's undercover network to Washington and London. This information had been passed on to Tehran and may have stimulated the widespread arrests of members of the Tudeh party and the expulsion of eighteen Soviet diplomats, for spying, in the spring of 1983. In addition, the US had supplied Iran with intelligence on Soviet military dispositions on the Iranian frontier.[29] As President Reagan was to put it subsequently, the US interest in opening a channel to Iran was a) to establish contacts with moderates in Tehran, b) to gain some leverage in Iran to prevent a completely open field for the Soviet Union in that country, and c) possibly to assist in the freeing of US citizens kidnapped and held as hostages by groups subject to Iran's influence.[30]

In 1985, Iran's situation in the war had deteriorated. The war seemed unwinnable without a new infusion of arms and unnegotiable because of Iran's own intransigence. The margin for manoeuvre was limited by the regime's insistence that the war was a defence of Islam. At the same time, the policy of hostility towards both superpowers had proved costly. The US embargo damaged Iran in virtually every category of arms, and substitution was simply not possible in the case of an entire air force.[31] If the costs of hostility to the US appeared to be tolerable in September 1980, five years later, with the political imperative of victory in the war and with seriously depleted stocks, the US connection no longer seemed as dangerous or political ties as unthinkable. Iran's interest in new contacts was evident: a) to gain access to weapons systems and spares, usually referred to as the 'return of Iran's assets' (i.e. weapons bought and paid for but impounded by the US during the hostage episode and the war); b) to increase its room for manoeuvre vis-à-vis the USSR; c) to gain some reduction in the flow of aid to Iraq; and d) to obtain recognition of the revolution as a historical fact.[32] None of this suggested a basic reformulation of Iran's aims. It still considered the US to be aiming at stalemate in the war, that is, a 'peace without justice' for which its 'neutrality' was a smokescreen. And it insisted that Gulf security was an issue that concerned Iran, as the dominant power, and not the US or other outside powers.[33]

The revelations of Iran-US contacts that came to light in late 1986 served to underscore both the basis for, and the problems and limitations involved in, even a limited dialogue. The primary problem was that, while Iran sought arms to win a war in which it was bogged down, the US sought ties primarily to release its hostages, but also to open up channels for future influence.[34] By making arms the currency of the dialogue, the US raised a host of questions about its intentions, its judgment, and its firmness when it came to dealing with 'terrorist' states. For our purposes, it is sufficient to note that the direct supply of US arms appears to have included some 2,000 TOW (anti-tank missiles) and some 235 HAWK (air defence, SAM) missiles (the Iranians deny receiving any HAWKs).[35] These weapons were valued at approximately $40 million and did not come from Iran's confiscated assets. They were delivered in three instalments in June, 1985, July 1986, and October 1986.

In addition, the US sanctioned, or at least had knowledge of, Israeli arms shipments to Iran including parts for tanks (M-60s) and aircraft, mainly F-4s and radar. The admission of the Israeli connection only served to focus interest on the continuing role of Israel in the supply of arms to Iran throughout the entire period of the Gulf war. Although some reports of the cumulative dollar value of this supply channel seem exaggerated, and many explanations appear self-serving in the heat of public inquiry, the important point for our analysis is that this channel had been tacitly endorsed (or quietly ignored), precisely as a means of maintaining some indirect links with Iran.[36] The US, while supplying Iraq with intelligence relevant to the conduct of the war since 1984, has also misled it about Israeli arms shipments to Iran.[37] At the same time, it appears that, as part of its bargaining with Iran, it may also have provided that country with intelligence useful for the prosecution of the war.[38]

The Iranians condemned the US supply of information to Iraq and claimed that Washington (and Moscow) wanted a stalemate in the war because they were fearful of the repercussions of an Iranian victory.[39] The arms actually delivered (which were, after all, limited in numbers and interrupted by their public disclosure) do not appear to have had a decisive impact on operations. However, they do seem to have inhibited the use of Iraqi airpower in late 1986, and may have accounted for the loss of some 45 aircraft in the engagements of January–February 1987. In addition, the increased activity of Iran's air force might be attributable to these supplies.[40]

More important than the improved air defence and anti-tank capability, and the increased operability of the remaining aircraft, was the political and psychological impact of the publicity surrounding the disclosure of US arms supplies to Iran. Iraq's allies felt the need to move to recognize the 'historical fact' of the Islamic revolution and to reinsure against the possibility of an Iranian victory. The 'revolution' was now publicly 'recognized', negotiated with, and accorded importance by its greatest adversary, a source of legitimacy as well as gratification for the Islamic republic. And the resumption of 'Operation Staunch' would now be difficult, given the dilution of US credibility on the issue.

To some extent, after the 'arms for hostages' scandal relations between Iran and the US appeared to have reverted to normal. Tehran continued to call upon the US to admit its errors, unfreeze Iran's assets, and curtail its relations with Israel, and to insist that Iran would not subordinate its foreign policy goals to its arms needs.[41] Khomeini rejected any idea of a rapprochement and this was seconded by his designated successor Montazeri and President Ali Khamenei.[42] And he still insisted that 'The superpowers beginning with the United States [were] . . . the prime cause of all world corruption'.[43] Yet, something important had been broached in the act of contact. Iran had survived the political revelations about the contacts and the even more embarrassing links with Israel which made nonsense of the proposition that Tehran wanted to liberate Baghdad as a first step towards Jerusalem. Rafsanjani continued to threaten to close the straits, to criticize the US retention of Iran's assets and to pose conditions for a renewal of formal relations, but he also referred with some regularity to the channels established and the eventual resumption of ties.[44]

The US, for its part, was more defensive, having achieved very little. It resumed 'Operation Staunch', starting with requests for China's restraint in arms supplies, it increased its warnings to Iran about not tolerating 'blackmail' in the Strait of Hormuz', it stepped up its naval presence in the region, and through Secretary Weinberger declared that an Iranian victory would not be in the US interest.[45] But there was now a submotif evident in US policy. The US authorized the sale of a non-strategic computer to Iran but denied the sale of cargo planes to Iraq.[46] While insisting that the US did not agree with Iran's continuation of the war, Secretary Shultz argued in December 1986 that there was 'no permanent conflict' with Iran, going further, a month later, to say (in reference to Afghanistan) that the US and Iran might indeed share some strategic concerns.[47]

It was one thing to see movement in Iran–US relations, another to see meaningful progress. For Iran the United States remained an adversary, a threat, the embodiment of materalism devoid of any faith or religion. As a superpower, it represented all that was unfair and unequal in the world. It was a continuing challenge perhaps to be dealt with tactically but otherwise to be spurned publicly, rejected, and (if possible) justly humiliated for the indignities of the past. Iran continued to see the US as, at one and the same time, all-powerful and impotent. Yet it also looked to it as a sort of yardstick, a test of its own credentials, a mirror of its own achievements. This meant that the impulse to confront and humiliate the US (a recurring word and image where the US is concerned) was sometimes matched by a tendency to convince or convert it. In either case the US continued to serve a useful role – as all-purpose bogey – in Iran's politics.

The Iranian leaders depicted the 'Irangate' scandal as a famous victory for the revolution. The revelations of the contacts with the US came on the eve of the anniversary of the seizure of the US embassy hostages. Rafsanjani pointed out that: 'The USA has accepted that Iran is standing invincibly on its own feet'. This theme was echoed by Khomeini, who said that the episode was 'an issue greater than all your victories' for the US, after making threats, had been forced to eat humble pie and its representatives had 'presented themselves meekly and humbly at the door of this nation and wish to establish relations. They wish to apologise for their mistake, whereas out nation rejects them'.[48]

Besides using the episode for domestic political purposes, there seems to have been a desire to at least test the possibility of some sort of continuing contact with the US, if only for tactical purposes, to increase the scope for international manoeuvre. The Iranians were therefore genuinely mystified by the next chapter in this unhappy relationship, when the United States in early 1987 started to play up the dangers posed to the freedom of navigation by Iran's acquisition of the *Silkworm* anti-ship missile, a modified form of the old *Styx* missile, from the Eastern bloc. It seemed to them that the US had moved rather abruptly from courting them to threatening them, and they attributed this to a combination of ignorance and conspiracy. Rafsanjani referred (with considerable justice) to the former thus:[49]

> The Americans . . . despite their satellites, spies, the CIA and the rest are so immensely uninformed about our region; uninformed about our internal affairs; how many half-baked analyses they tend to make.

The US decision to become directly involved in the Gulf stemmed from several overlapping and not wholly compatible considerations: a desire, as the war intensified, to reassure the Gulf states (especially Kuwait), to pre-empt any Soviet role in the Gulf, and to serve notice of concern about the safety of navigation. The immediate catalyst for US involvement was the request by Kuwait that the US reflag twelve of its tankers and assign them the appropriate naval protection. The US decision was influenced and speeded up by the threat of Soviet acceptance of a comparable offer. Ironically, it was only reinforced by the apparently accidental bombing of the frigate *USS Stark* (with attendant loss of life) by an Iraqi warplane, in May 1987. President Reagan justified the need for an expanded US naval presence in the Gulf thus:[50]

> The use of the vital sea lanes of the Persian Gulf will not be dictated by the Iranians. These lanes will not be allowed to come under the control of the Soviet Union. The Persian Gulf will remain open to navigation by the nations of the world.

Iran welcomed the recognition implicit in President Reagan's defence of his offer of arms to Iran earlier: 'Without Iran's co-operation, we cannot bring an end to the Persian Gulf war; without Iran's concurrence, there can be no enduring peace in the Middle East'.[51] Now it appeared that the US was trying to coerce it into 'an imposed peace', for a large US naval force permanently cruising in the Gulf's waters could not be a neutral act.

In the first place, it diluted Iran's naval supremacy while 'international-izing' the war, as Iraq had long sought to do. Secondly, however confused in substance,[52] it was a policy clearly aimed against Iran: it was framed and articulated as such, and in implementation would have that effect. For the US decision to protect the newly reflagged Kuwaiti vessels would serve to constrain or inhibit Iranian attacks against them while doing nothing about the principal cause of these retaliatory attacks, namely, Iraq's air attacks on Iranian installations and tankers. (Nor did it address the prime cause of the spread of the tanker war, the increase in Iraq's air attacks). Indeed, US policy-makers specifically denied any intention of attempting to restrain Iraq from these catalytic attacks, the cause of Iran's attacks on third parties.[53] It was precisely because of this *de facto* 'tilt' towards Iraq that some thoughtful Americans, like Senator Sam Nunn, questioned the policy.[54]

US policy was also extraordinarily bellicose, fixing first on the threat from the anti-ship missiles and the possibility of pre-emptive attacks on them, and then on the possibility of mining Iran's ports to force it to stop its attacks in the Gulf (Representative Les Aspin's pet project). The United States was also keen, after it succeeded in getting agreement in the UN Security Council on resolution 598 of 20 July 1987 calling for a ceasefire, to move to a tough second resolution imposing mandatory sanctions on the party refusing to accept its terms – namely, Iran. Apart from anything else, this flexing of muscles appeared to satisfy a basic political need in the US – to purge the administration after the Irangate episode by confronting the 'ragheads' in Tehran. (Iran appeared as necessary for the US psyche as the US for Iran.)

The deployment of some 30 vessels into the Gulf and the institution of a convoy system for the reflagged tankers (of course, a very small percentage of the tankers plying those waters), and the difficulties encountered by the threat of mines, the damage to the ship *USS Bridgeton*, the decision to increase the number of minesweepers and the parallel but formally unco-ordinated decision by five European states, France, the United Kingdom, Italy, Belgium, and Holland, with indirect assistance from West Germany and Japan, all this need not concern us here. What is relevant to our analysis is the fact that the unprecedented international concern and focus on the war in the United Nations and in the Gulf's waters, with the extraordinary and unprecedented participation of many European NATO states in an 'out of area' operation, ushered in a new phase. It seemed that the international community had suddenly discovered the war, but this did not mean that even this frenetic, belated activism would leave much impression on its conduct.

The US as the leader of this multinational convoy could scarcely be called its mastermind; activism rather than strategy seemed to be the order of the day. As the convoys continued and Iraqi air attacks invited Iranian responses, the US presence appeared more and more like support for Iraq. *The Economist* observed in early September: 'The Americans are now getting uncomfortably close to fighting Iraq's war for it'.[55] As the inevitable clashes with Iran occurred (see below) the questions for the US became clearer: did it want to become a party to the war and lose whatever moral authority it possessed as a neutral in trying to achieve a settlement through the UN? Could it afford to alienate Iran which still remained of critical strategic importance? Precisely what did the US military presence in the region seek to achieve in the context of the war?

In the new atmosphere of confrontation it was not difficult to get agreement in the US to embargo trade with Iran.[56] More elusive was the devising of a means of applying pressure and offering incentives to Iran in the service of a policy that preserved US interests in both Iran and the other Gulf states. The tensions in US interests were reflected in a policy that appeared ambivalent at best. In a single year it had shifted from appeasement to confrontation. Now it risked war with Iran for uncertain ends. The *Wall Street Journal* reminded its readers:[57]

> Ayatollah or no ayatollah, Iran is and will remain the most valuable sovereign land mass in the Persian Gulf. It is critically important that the US not make a future rapprochement with Iran all but impossible.

The aims outlined in public by President Reagan in May 1987 had by October merged imperceptibly into another, that of stopping the war, or at least an Iranian victory. One British newspaper believed that this was both desirable and feasible but undermined its own case by stipulating requirements that are inherently in short supply, if not beyond the scope of the US political system:[58]

> If the real American aim is to prevent Iran from winning the war, this should be stated. It is a respectable goal and it is also achievable, but only so long as American will and consistency remain strong.

There were signs by the end of the year that the United States had not wholly changed tack, and that Washington still sought contact with Tehran. Indicative of this was the implicit dialogue behind the release of Charles Glass (presumably with Tehran's consent as a gesture), and Rafsanjani's offer to help in other cases. Although the US rejected the offer, Rafsanjani pointedly observed that Iran did not consider itself weak and 'we do not fear having relations and negotiations with them'.[59] Subsequently it was revealed that the US had again sought a direct dialogue but had been rebuffed; Iran's condition remained the supply of arms contracted for but embargoed since November 1979.[60] It is to Iran's response to the new US policy that we now turn.

Tehran's first reaction to the new set of pressures that accompanied the internationalization of the war, was one of caution. Rafsanjani observed that the US presence in the Gulf was intended to 'reduce our pressure' on Iraq. He reiterated Iran's position that it would block the flow of oil in the waterway only if 'they bring the situation to the point that Iran cannot use the Persian Gulf'.[61] Later in the year he reverted to the theme that Iran's principal concern should be the land war, implying that the furore in the Gulf, where the US was acting as a bully, was a sideshow.[62]

> Meanwhile, we should get ready to give the main answer to America in the battlefields against the Iraqi Ba'thists who were the main reason for the American presence.

President Khamenei likened the US after Irangate to a 'wounded snake', and Iranian commentaries tended to see in the activity in the United Nations, and in the deterioration of relations with France and Britain, proof of an international conspiracy to confront Iran.[63] Yet the same Khamenei, aware of the dangers of toying with such a beast, was also careful to reiterate that unless there was a direct threat to Iran's oil exports: 'We have declared that we will not pre-empt or stoke any fire. We will not involve the USA in any war with ourselves'.[64] Prime Minister Musavi put Iran's view bluntly:[65]

> We believe that the way to end the existing crisis is for these forces to pull out. [They] . . . are here in order to set up bases, establish domination and help the Saddam regime; they are here to safeguard the illegitimate US interests in the region.

Once the US naval presence became an established fact, Iran sought to demonstrate that security in the Gulf had actually declined as a result. To do this without directly confronting the United States took considerable skill and luck, which Iran did not always succeed in mustering. It sought to play on US domestic political sensitivities and reluctance to see blood shed by drawing analogies with the experience in Lebanon in 1983 and by painting images of flag-draped coffins returning home to the United States. Rafsanjani put the matter characteristically: 'If even one single drop of blood is shed by the United States in the Persian Gulf, there will be rivers of blood throughout the world'.[66]

In practical terms Iran's actions were considerably more subdued. It did not reject the possibility of ending the tanker war and made a distinction between this, which could be settled (if Iraq stopped its air attacks), and the land war which was not negotiable.[67] It did not reject out of hand the Security Council's resolution on the war, despite its belief that the United Nations had forfeited its credibility by its failure to act at the beginning of hostilities. Instead, it proposed other conditions while clarifying the nature of its own objections, (primarily its insistence that the aggressor be identified before and not after a ceasefire). When the *Bridgeton* hit a mine in late July, it was careful not to claim responsibility for the act, alluding instead to 'invisible hands'.

No doubt because of the vast disparity in military power, Iran was careful to try not to confront the United States directly. After an Iranian naval vessel was caught by the US laying mines in September, its crew taken prisoner (and later returned), and the ship scuttled, the Iranian leaders said that a confrontation was a distinct possibility and even inevitable, and that 'we shall most certainly take revenge'. Later Rafsanjani gave what he called an 'explicit warning' to the US that Iran would soon be engaged on another front.[68] In the following month the opportunity to confront the United States presented itself when US helicopters sank three Iranian patrol boats, killing two of the crew and capturing four others. Iran vowed a 'crushing response'.[69] On 16 October an Iranian missile hit *Sea Island City* flying the US flag, inside Kuwait's territorial waters, blinding the captain, a US national. The US response was to destroy two Iranian offshore oil platforms (equipped with radar for surveillance) on 19 October. Three days later, rejecting the offer to 'call it quits', Iran hit the Kuwaiti deep-water Sea Island terminal.

This exchange of blows was notable because of Iran's care not to attack the US directly but to target its regional allies. In general, the most Iran did was to probe the extent and scope of the US commitment in order to find the weak links, the grey areas. Yet it did over-reach itself when it was caught red-handed in minelaying, thus unwittingly providing ammunition to those who argued that it was Iran that constituted a menace to the freedom of navigation. Evidently it found the impulse to defy the United States, whatever the consequences, irresistible, providing the revolution with the high drama that it so cherished, even at the risk of diverting from the principle issue – the land war. At the same time, the Iranian leaders were confident that the US presence could not last forever, that sooner or later the expense of the enterprise and the distraction of other issues (such as the Presidential election) would see a withdrawal of the US fleet.

If Iran was more moderate in deed than in rhetoric (particularly the rhetoric designed for home consumption), it was because the revolution continued to need constant cultivation. Iran used the brinkmanship for domestic political purposes. Indeed what originally, and correctly, had been seen as a diversion from the main event – the war with Iraq, which would be decided on land – came to be embraced and given priority. Perhaps this was due to Iran's penchant – repeatedly noted – for giving priority to revolutionary posture and form over the achievement of specific results; perhaps it was simply due to the fact that the seasonal lull in the land war allowed greater emphasis on, and exploitation of, the confrontation at sea. Perhaps this new confrontation was welcomed precisely because the land war was at an impasse, and Tehran hoped that the novelty would revive the people's flagging enthusiasm for the crusade. One suspects in any case that the change in focus, however accidental, was not unwelcome to Iran's leaders who sought to capitalize on it. Hashemi Rafsanjani sought to depict American involvement in the war as a new chapter in the heroic epic of the revolution:[70]

> If we had won the war last year, everyone would have said that a 50 million strong country was victorious over a 14 million strong country. But if we win this year, everyone will know that we are victorious over the United States.

As the clashes and near-misses continued throughout the year the benefits of refocusing attention on the 'international conspiracy' became evident. Rafsanjani (as usual) was frank about the heightening of the revolutionary spirit:[71]

So long as we were arrayed against Iraq and others like her our nation did not feel the need for sacrifice too much. Since the day the Americans came the people are bringing so much pressure – pressure that we must expand the war – mobilize forces and use all our capabilities for the war. [Thus] we managed to strengthen the backing for the war.

In early October Iran reported that half a million volunteers were prepared for 'martyrdom-seeking operations' to resist the United States in the Gulf. On 4 November (the anniversary of the seizure of the US embassy) popular anti-US demonstrations were of a size and vigour unmatched in the immediately preceding years.[72] As one journalist remarked:[73]

anti-Americanism has continued to be a useful tool for the Iranian regime. The US presence in the Gulf has helped revive diminishing popular support for the Gulf war.

The Iranian leadership saw their strategy of probing without confronting the United States as paying off, weakening the credibility of the US with its Gulf allies, exasperating its own military, and drawing it further and further away from a posture of aloof impartiality to one of messy partisanship. Rafsanjani compared the US to a paper tiger, which is torn to shreds bit by bit 'so that onlookers can see that it is not a tiger but paper'.[74] He saw Iran and the US as in a 'psychological war', the objective of which is to 'crush the morale of the other side', and he judged Iran's spirit of solidarity and defiance as unparallelled:[75]

In the past eight or ten years we have seen the height of this legend. But, in my opinion, these days are the climax.

By the end of 1987 the Western naval presence in the Gulf appeared more durable than might earlier have been expected. No major direct clashes between Iran and the US had taken place. Relations between Iran and the Gulf states had improved after their plunge in the middle of the year, but the US presence was still (privately) welcomed by the latter. Iran had substituted fervour for the war with popular defiance against any peace imposed by outside powers. The Security Council was stymied on its next move and diplomacy was at a standstill. The tanker war had proved a diversion in so far as Iraq was unable to interdict Iran's oil exports despite occasional spectacular operations such as the attack on Larak in the southern Gulf on 22 December. Iran had not managed to insulate the war from the international community or to get what it deemed a 'fair' hearing for its case in international bodies. The very style of its government and the tone of its rhetoric seemed to feed fears that any concessions given to it would be pocketed without being reciprocated, and become the basis for still further claims. Revolutionary Iran was the object of curiosity, dismay and occasionally alarm in the West, but whatever else it did, it did not inspire confidence among governments inside or outside the region. The Iranian leadership would not have been surprised or sorry to hear this: theirs was a revolution for the people, for the nations, not for governments. Inevitably, however modulated its acts, Iran's pose and rhetoric was at cross purposes with its diplomacy.

Without going full circle, Iran–US relations have evolved on both sides. The demands of the war have been at the root of the movement on Iran's part, while strategic interests have provided the motive, and the war the opportunity, for the US overture. Ironically, while the war is the central concern of the Islamic authorities, and the need for victory or at least apparent victory is indispensable for the continuing vitality and possibly the legitimacy of the revolution, for the US the war is a potential danger but primarily a day-to-day irritant. For the US, there can be no question of aiding an Iranian military victory in the hope of achieving a better strategic relationship; containment will have to continue to co-exist with cultivation. This difference in perspective and priorities has not prevented some attenuated contacts but it does limit the scope for a complete normalization of relations. The contacts have revealed a regime in Tehran able to adapt, to trim its ideology to its needs, to seek more room for manoeuvre. It reflects both confidence at home and near-desperation about the state of the war. The channel to the US had brought some limited returns but not enough to make a decisive difference to the prosecution of the war. And as long as priorities differed Iran would seek assistance for its major concern from another quarter.

Relations with the USSR

The formal view of the Iranian Government was that the superpowers were to all intents and purposes the same: equally exploitative and arrogant in their relations with the 'oppressed' nations, lacking in any spiritual values, and essentially in collusion vis-à-vis the world's masses. If the US, because of its support of the Shah, was seen as the primary threat to the Islamic republic, the potential threat of the USSR, proximate, atheist, and traditionally cynically opportunistic, could not be discounted either. The new leaders in Tehran were at one in believing that Iran would do well to minimize its contacts with the superpowers to avoid becoming ensnared in their disputes or dependent on them. The policy was to seek something close to a 'negative equilibrium', excluding both from positions of influence rather than attempting to balance concessions to one with concessions to the other.

The roughly equal distaste for the superpowers was not to be reflected in policy. Some elements in Iran distrusted the United States and its assumed local allies – liberals, secularists, nationalists, intellectuals, etc. –

and the cultural threat they posed to a clerically-run country more than they did the cruder Soviet threat. In any case, in order to speed up the revolution the radicals, with the connivance and encouragement of the clerics, systematically used the bogey of the 'US Satan' to deepen the revolution and exclude the 'moderates' from its ranks. The resulting hostage crisis and its aftermath led to the weakening of links not only with the United States but also with Western Europe. By the time the war began, Iran was already more dependent upon the Eastern bloc for trade and transit of its goods to the West.

Phase (i).   It was thus scarcely surprising that in the first phase of the war (1980–82) the Soviet–Iranian relationship reflected this. On the Soviet side, the war saw an intensified effort to reduce Iran's suspicions and to demonstrate Soviet good faith. The Soviet authorities forewarned Iran of the impending attack, offered to supply it directly with arms, cut off direct supplies of arms (new orders) to Iraq, supplied Iran with jet fuel, and gave Tehran assurances about their joint frontier to enable the deployment of Iranian troops westwards.[76]

Iran did not exactly encourage this Soviet orientation but it was aware of it. It refused to buy or rather request *direct* arms purchases or deliveries. But it swiftly became reliant on arms from Soviet clients, including Syria and Libya, and from Eastern bloc sources such as North Korea, which may have been acting as Soviet proxies or laundering stops.[77] At the same time, trade, mainly barter, with the Soviet bloc increased substantially. The Iranian Communist party – the Tudeh – was allowed to function unimpeded, while 'Western' parties were banned. The attitude toward the Tudeh was indicative of Iran's relations with the Soviet Union. As long as the USSR (and the Tudeh) were seen as supportive of the Islamic republic, it was allowed to function. This was despite the perception of many, and articulated by Hashemi Rafsanjani, that 'they are inspired from abroad; they are practically Russians'.[78] Iranian commentaries continued to exhibit considerable distrust of Soviet motives. A good illustration is the comment by one J. Sa'adat in 'Independence is the essence of the Islamic revolution'.[79] He argued that the superpowers were exploitative, wanted to dominate, and were often in collusion, but that they were also in competition, and that it was wise to use this competition for Iran's ends, that is, to achieve independence. Thus, Iran ought to accept the USSR's proffered hand of friendship but be under no illusions about Moscow's basic aims. By force of circumstances, Iran's relations with the superpowers thus saw a distinct tilt towards the USSR, manifested in relative restraint on the issue of Afghanistan, a distinct tolerance for the Tudeh and moderation in comments about the USSR. At the same time, its closest relations in the region were with the states closest to the USSR – Syria and Libya.

Phase (ii).   If the first stages of the war had seen an Iran unwilling to consider concessions or compromise with the United States, and confident of its own ability to prevail through the use of existing stocks of arms and by promoting the value of self-reliance, it was also the case that Tehran accepted the Soviet Union as the lesser threat, and pragmatically reduced the areas of dispute with it. The second phase of the relationship opened in mid-1982 with Iran's decision to take the war into Iraq after the expulsion of Iraqi forces from its own territory, and to overthrow the Ba'thist regime in Baghdad. The Soviet Union could not countenance the defeat of a nominal ally, nor was it keen to see the extension of Iranian/Islamic power in the region. But above all Moscow did not want an Iranian invasion of Iraq to provide the US with an excuse to intervene militarily in the Gulf, or to gain access to bases in the name of defending its regional allies. To prevent this, Moscow warned Iran against such a policy, and shifted from its earlier stance of 'neutrality' to a resumption of direct arms supplies to Iraq. By the autumn of 1982 Soviet-supplied *Frog* SSMs were landing on towns in western Iran, causing civilian casualties, and by the end of the following year, longer-range *Scud-B*s were made available to Iraq.

Rumours circulated that the price for these arms deliveries had included the release of Iraqi Communists from jail.[80] The Iranian leaders evidently reasoned by analogy that the freedom of the Tudeh in Iran must also be worth something to Moscow, and promptly banned the party (which had criticized the continuation of the war) and imprisoned its leadership. In April 1983, Iran chose to act on the information provided by Britain and the US (mentioned above) and moved against Soviet agents in Iran, expelling eighteen Soviet diplomats for espionage and trying the Tudeh leadership under the same charge. Confident that it could prosecute the war on its own without reliance on either superpower, Iran persisted in the war, which under the Pasdar consisted largely of human wave assaults by volunteer Basij forces. The Soviet shift only served to confirm the Iranians' view that the superpowers shared a common fear of the Islamic republic, in other words, Islam, and that they were working in collusion. Iran began to amplify its criticisms of the Soviet role in Afghanistan, which had been relatively restrained.

It was no accident that the Islamic authorities allowed demonstrations by Afghan refugees outside the Soviet embassy in Tehran, and rejected Soviet protests, noting that 'abundant Soviet political and military aid to Iraq' had been responsible for 'bringing many (Iranian) towns under Iraqi artillery fire'.[81] A radio commentary asked whether there had not been a link between the Iraqi attack on Iran and the Soviet interest in weakening Iran in order to prevent it assisting the Afghan resistance movement.[82] Other comments equated the superpowers, and singled out the relationship between the war, the weakening of Iran and the issue of Afghanistan: 'The Soviet hostility towards the Islamic revolution which it regards as a threat to its imperialist entity in the occupied Islamic republic (i.e. Afghanistan) is nothing new'.[83] The Soviet response was to turn up the volume of its criticisms of the clerical regime, noting its horrible record of bloodshed, and its reactionary policies that smacked of 'Islamic despotism'. The Soviet Union began to interpret Iranian criticisms as a sign of a drift towards the West.[84] Other Soviet comments emphasized the interest in an independent Iran, recalled the possibility of establishing good economic relations, and accused Iran of deliberately blocking a peace settlement.[85] At the end of 1983 the USSR supported a Security Council resolution calling for a ceasefire in the war.

Phase (iii).   By early 1984 there was a period of relative truce; nine months of vituperation had advanced neither side. Iran was still pursuing the war, handicapped, by its own choice, by poor relations with both superpowers. It had become increasingly clear, however, to the leadership in Tehran that a military victory would prove elusive without access to weapons systems to offset those available to Iraq. Furthermore, while the alienation of the United States had led to an arms embargo that was now beginning to be felt in Tehran, the decision to take the war into Iraq had resulted in the transfer of sophisticated weapons systems by the USSR to Iraq. Clearly the time had come for a reconsideration of Iran's principles in light of its war needs.

The upshot was a new moderation on the part of Tehran. Rafsanjani was conciliatory: he told the Soviet ambassador, V.K. Baldyrov, that in the light of the common policies of anti-imperialism of the two countries, in Lebanon for example, 'we do not expect the USSR . . . to pour its missiles on our civilian population'. He was also quoted as saying rather plaintively: 'If the Soviet Union will not co-operate with us in our struggle against imperialism, at least it should not be a participant in aggressions launched on us'.[86] A month later, he warned the USSR that the supply of missiles to Iraq was inconsistent with the aim of good-neighbourly relations: 'If you do not want this (current) hostility turned into a clash in the future, then stop what you are doing . . . We want good-neighbourly relations, but you are lying'.[87] The Foreign Minister harped on the same theme.[88] In June, a senior Foreign Ministry official was dispatched to Moscow to discuss the principal obstacle to improved ties: arms supplies to Iraq.[89] He met Gromyko and some progress was apparently made. Rafsanjani now sought to decouple the subject of improved relations from the war:[90]

> The issue is not connected to the war . . . We have our relations with the Soviets, we have commercial dealings with each other. We have many dealings and meetings with each other. We do not wish relations with the USSR to become darkened, neither do they. Of course, we protest the sale of arms by the USSR to Iraq; we protest about Afghanistan. There are other similar issues; but we should try to improve our relations and solve these problems.

The change in tone did not herald an immediate improvement in relations: Iran was still highly critical of the Soviet failure to condemn

Iraq's use of chemical weapons, of the continuous feeding 'of Iraq's arsenals with the latest of the art in weaponry' and of the number of Soviet advisers allegedly in Iraq.[91] Criticism equating the two super-powers and accusing them of collusion in trying to save Saddam Hussein continued. Indeed, one Iranian newspaper commented that 'Saddam Hussein goes to war with Soviet arms and Western strategy.'[92]

What had changed was Iran's belief that it could dictate the nature of the relationship, and a new willingness to seek to cultivate the USSR, despite differences on the war and Afghanistan. As Rafsanjani said in February 1985: 'We are inclined to have good relations with the Soviet Union'.[93] Iran was now prepared to separate the issue of the war and political differences from the question of overall relations; the former were no longer to dictate the entire relationship nor was their solution to be the precondition for any relationship. This shift was significant. It led to a more subtle, less ideological stand that now sought to imply trade-offs in the relationship, and to obtain, if not a cut in arms supplies to Iraq, an equivalence in indirect supplies to Iran. In short, by 1985 Iran no longer attempted as a matter of principle to sever the arms link between Moscow and Baghdad, rather it conceded its reality and now sought to gain some access itself. As we have noted above, by this time some 50 per cent of Iran's arms inventory came from Eastern bloc sources, and had the advantage of being relatively robust, inexpensive and easy to assimilate – all points in their favour in fighting a basically infantry war with unskilled manpower. Access to Soviet arms was becoming important.[94]

By early 1985, agreement had been reached to revive the joint economic commissions and to pursue economic and commercial activity unlinked to the state of political relations. Iranian officials, such as Deputy Foreign Minister Sheikoleslamzadeh, hinted that they hoped to achieve a scaling down of arms to Iraq or at least an indirect supply of arms to Iran, possibly from Syria and Libya.[95] By May 1985 Prime Minister Musavi detected a change: 'In our relations with the USSR, we sense a realistic approach on their part'. This presumably reflected the trend identified by Rafsanjani in February – a reduction in arms supplies to Iraq.[96] Whether real or imagined, it spurred Iran to make encouraging noises in the direction of the Soviet authorities despite the acknowledged existence of two outstanding major issues: arms supplies and Afghanistan.[97] On the latter, it was indicative of the shift in the balance of the relationship, that it was now the USSR that brought up the question of Iran's support for the Afghan 'rebels' whenever Iran raised the question of Soviet arms supplies to Iraq.[98] While Soviet communiqués took Iran to task for continuing a 'senseless' war, Iranian commentaries pointed to the discrepancy between Soviet talk and actions: 'They keep talking about a meaningless war while on the other hand arming the Aflaqite regime with more weapons'.[99] Another referred to the 'duality' of the Soviet position which sought to supply arms to Iraq and pretended that it was exercising restraint in exporting sophisticated weapons which could aggravate the war.[100]

Whether the new realism stemmed from Iran or the Soviet Union is debatable. What *was* clear was that the USSR was now in the position of supplying arms directly to Iraq and simultaneously indirectly – if it wished – to Iran. It could turn the arms tap on and off to either party, thus demonstrating its relevance to the warring parties and its influence to the other Gulf states.

At the same time, it had succeeded in decoupling its overall relationship with Iran, as an important neighbour, from its policy in the Gulf war. The Iranians had been forced to admit that they could not afford to make bilateral relations conditional on the war situation without losing even more. Thus, when the Soviet Union withdrew its economic advisers on the grounds that they were endangered by the war, the Iranians saw this as a pretext and a means of destabilizing the Tehran regime, which needed their assistance, particularly in power-generation in the summer.[101]

Indeed, the Soviet authorities were not averse to taking a tough line. In March 1985, a *Pravda* article, no doubt reflecting a belief that Iran had burned its bridges to both superpowers and lacked any great room for manoeuvre, called Iran's tendency to equate the two superpowers 'absurd and insulting', referred to its assistance to Afghan 'counter-revolutionaries' in training centres at Mashhad and concluded:[102]

> The Soviet Union is not indifferent to the Iranian authorities' policy with respect to Afghanistan, which is our friend. Likewise, we cannot ignore that anti-Soviet attacks have become more frequent in Tehran, and we cannot fail to draw appropriate conclusions from these facts.

At the end of May 1985, the Soviet-based 'National Voice of Iran' called for the first time for the overthrow of the Islamic republic.[103] And Soviet statements angrily continued to shrug off responsibility for the scale of damage in the war, as in the war of the cities which largely consisted of the use of Soviet equipment by both sides.[104] For their part, the Soviet authorities, whose primary concern in the war remained the United States, accused Washington of supplying arms to Iran to keep the war going and to provide a pretext to intervene.[105] (From the viewpoint of superpower rivalry rather than Iran–Soviet relations, Soviet arms supplies to both parties in the war may be seen as a preclusive measure to pre-empt any moves by the US.)

While Soviet official statements became progressively more critical of Iran's unwillingness to end the war, and endorsed Iraq's willingness to do so, Moscow showed no sign of wanting to choose definitively between the two antagonists. Nor did it show any sign of reducing its economic relationship with Tehran. The exchange of delegations increased; an agreement was reached in principle in August 1986 on the resumption of gas sales through IGAT-1 to the Soviet Union and culminated in February 1987 in the first visit of the Iranian Foreign Minister to Moscow since the revolution.[106]

Soviet suspicions about Iran's Afghanistan policies, and disquiet about the escalation and intensification of the war, did not interfere with the pace of these contacts, or inhibit Soviet officials from scolding their counterparts. The Soviet authorities' reluctance to jeopardize their contacts with the Islamic regime stemmed as much from hopes of future influence, possibly post-war when Iran would need access to new weapons sources, as from suspicions of US policies and machinations (which may have been intensified in the wake of Irangate).[107] But differences continued to rankle on both sides. Foreign Minister Velayati's comment that 'Iran will not agree to Soviet domination over it' was called 'unnecessary' and it was clear that the Foreign Minister's visit was characterized by continuing differences on the war.[108]

By the beginning of 1987 various considerations were coming together to dictate a more activist Soviet policy in the Iran–Iraq war. The revelations about US overtures towards Iran, however unsuccessful, were a reminder that there was no automaticity or inevitability about hostile relations between Washington and Tehran; Afghanistan might well serve as the excuse for an eventual, probably *de facto*, rapprochement. In the war too, Iran's renewed pressure on Basra in late 1986–early 1987 served notice that an eventual Iranian breakthrough (however remote a possibility) could confront the USSR with embarrassing and difficult choices. So far it had avoided making any definitive commitments and had sidestepped these choices. It did not want to support Iraq at the price of alienating Iran or vice versa; it did not want to cultivate the Arab states of the Gulf at the price of antagonizing Iran, nor did it seek to support Iran if this meant weakening its improved and evolving ties with the US. Nevertheless, the balancing act which had lost it little had also, so far, not gained it much either. Besides being painful, the straddling act was in danger – in early 1987 – of being ignored, for the USSR was offered the opportunity to enter the Gulf's diplomacy legitimately in response to Kuwait's invitation to extend its naval and diplomatic support to its harassed shipping. With limited naval resources the USSR accepted the invitation, apparently initially with greater alacrity than the US. In so doing it served notice of a willingness to enter the diplomacy of the Gulf, however limited its actual resources, and however complicated the balancing act that would ensue.

The Soviet decision did not signify a new element in its relations with Iran, but underlined an old one that the Islamic republic, with its self-absorption, would ignore at its peril: as a superpower, the USSR dealt on a much larger chessboard than Iran. However important its bilateral relations with Iran, these were never the most important consideration for the USSR, which focused instinctively on relations with the US first and foremost. This aspect of Soviet diplomacy became increasingly evident in its policy toward Iran and the war throughout 1987. At one and the same time it highlighted Iran's importance *and* the limitations on Iran's capacity to influence or manoeuvre at the summit of international relations.

As the United States became more involved in the Gulf in the course of 1987 through the reflagging operation (discussed above), which had as one announced motive the blocking of Soviet influence in the region, the Iran–Iraq war became more focused on the waterway itself. Spent after two land offensives, Iran responded to Iraq's internationalization of the war by retaliatory attacks in the Gulf. Tehran saw Kuwait's invitation to the superpowers as a deliberate Iraqi-sponsored strategy to involve outside powers in the war, to prevent Iraq's otherwise imminent defeat.

It therefore saw the willingness of the superpowers to dive in as proof of their similarity, their opportunism and their propensity for collusion. Iranian leaders and media did not mince their words about this state of affairs.

As the war became an object of superpower competition and involvement, Iran also found it had fewer cards to play. Lacking much prospect of striking a bargain with a newly inflamed United States, its leaders sought, as a prudent insurance policy, an improved relationship with the USSR. For Iran such a relationship held out the promise of a) increasing its room for manoeuvre with the US; b) weakening the prospect for superpower collusion at its expense; and c) reducing Soviet arms, and possibly commitment, to Iraq over time. Specifically with regard to the war, Iran's relations with the USSR became focused in 1987 on blocking diplomatic pressures from the United Nations and the West, and gaining an ally in diplomacy to reduce its general isolation and to help in articulating its views sympathetically. In exchange for such limited support Iran offered limited compensation: a posture predominantly anti-Western in rhetoric and action; a toning down of criticism of the Soviet position in Afghanistan (and possibly more); and improved commercial relations, holding out the prospect of reasonable 'good-neighbourly' bilateral relations in the future.

Far from being identical, Iranian and Soviet interests in the Gulf merely came to overlap to a degree in 1987. The common denominator stemmed from the mutual opposition to the Western, and in particular the American, military presence. This was an adequate basis for a finite, circumscribed tactical partnership, but hardly a basis for much more. Above all, it was limited as much by the inherent broader scope of Soviet interests and ambitions as by any failure on the part of the Islamic republic. At best, it meant that Iran could only buy time with its diplomacy with the USSR, and that this revived connection could not serve as a substitute for basic strategic decisions about the war. To contrast the emphases and to show the divergence between the positions of Iran and the USSR we shall examine the diplomacy of each in turn.

The improvement in political relations with the USSR came only gradually. Iranian leaders and media persisted in seeing the superpowers as two sides of the same coin – essentially interchangeable. In this view they were reinforced by the revelation in May 1987 that the USSR had agreed to reflag Kuwaiti tankers. A Foreign Ministry spokesman criticized Soviet Foreign Minister Shevardnadze's comment that 'only a political solution' is possible, saying that the USSR was seeking to increase its influence in the region; Rafsanjani equated the two superpowers and accused them of collusion, while the newspaper *Ettela'at* said it was regrettable that the USSR had involved itself in hostile plots against Iran.[109] Sometimes this criticism was more forthright: the Commander of the Pasdaran, Reza'i, suggested that perhaps the USSR had been behind the Iraqi attack on the *USS Stark* (in May) to rupture the links between Iran and the West. A radio commentary accused the USSR of 'inundating Iraq with its military and economic aid', while *Resala'at* suggested that the USSR had chosen the wrong side and must change this as they were now facing defeat.[110] In general Iran was sceptical about Soviet intentions, insisting, for example, during the visit of Yuli Vorontsov, the Soviet Deputy Foreign Minister, in June, on the rights of the regional states to assure the security of the Gulf.[111] Besides equating the superpowers and accusing them of conspiracy, Iran sometimes adopted an injured tone asking, as Rafsanjani did in May, how the USSR could support a dictatorial aggressive regime like Ba'thist Iraq and not Iran, 'a great anti-imperialist revolution'.[112]

A basis for an improvement in relations was provided by their joint opposition to the build-up of US forces in the region. For it became apparent that the US had decided to accompany the decision to put its flag on 12 Kuwaiti tankers with the provision of a naval convoy in their defence. This necessitated a heavy build-up of US military forces (by September the US had some 40 ships in the region in contrast to the USSR's 6). Starting in June when the US decision was announced, Soviet opposition was noted with gratification by Iran. Iranian comments now differentiated between the two superpowers, noting the USSR's 'change of mind'.[113] The concrete manifestation of the convergence of the two positions came with the Soviet declaration on 3 July calling for a withdrawal of foreign ships from the area together with a cessation of attacks on commercial shipping,[114] which was immediately welcomed enthusiastically by Iran's leaders. The Prime Minister called it a 'constructive proposal', the Foreign Ministry welcomed it as 'positive' and Rafsanjani said it was 'very progressive and no one can oppose it'. . . 'The Russians have the honour of being the forerunners in ensuring peace in the region'.[115]

This formulation that stressed the need for the withdrawal of 'foreign forces' from the Gulf, that pointed to this naval presence as the primary threat to the peace, and that emphasized, after the passage of Security

Council Resolution 598 on 20 July that these forces were in contravention of Article 5 of that resolution (namely the need to refrain from acts likely to aggravate the situation), became the basis for subsequent Iran–Soviet joint communiqués. In a further visit to Iran by Vorontsov in August the formulation figured prominently; it was repeated by the Prime Minister in September, in Foreign Minister Velayati's meeting with his Soviet counterpart in New York, and again when Vorontsov visited Tehran in November and the Iranian ambassador in Moscow met Gromyko in December.[116]

It seemed at times that the very fragility of the improvement in relations necessitated a tight grasp on this area of common ground. For even as the two states emphasized their common stance, the USSR invariably at the same meeting also called for a rapid end to the war (implicitly admonishing Iran), and it was by no means certain that the Soviet position on 'foreign forces' was unconditional; a certain ambiguity underlay the Soviet position (as we shall see) suggesting that perhaps this, too, was negotiable with the US.

Nevertheless the US decision to commit forces on a large scale to the Gulf region did provide for a tactical convergence of Soviet–Iranian interests. Iran benefited from this in a concrete manner, insofar as Soviet diplomacy became more solicitous of Tehran's position in the diplomacy of the war. Without discounting the Soviet Union's own priorities or 'hidden agenda', it was notable that it went to considerable pains to put the most constructive interpretation possible on Iran's international behaviour. For example, Soviet spokesmen emphasized that Iran had not rejected Resolution 598, and depicted it as showing flexibility and being prepared to co-operate with the Secretary General.[117] The Soviet authorities hinted to the Arab states that if Iran had rejected the resolution, they would have been a great deal tougher. And to push the Iranians they intimated directly that the passage of a second resolution was still perfectly conceivable.[118] However, by their diplomacy of demurring on the need for a quick follow-up mandatory resolution on the heels of SC 598, they undoubtedly helped Iran wriggle free from international pressures. In so doing they have chosen despite – or because of – their support for a rapid end to the war, to emphasize diplomacy more than the threat of an embargo, whose effectiveness they profess to doubt. On a very contentious issue separating Iran and Iraq in the diplomacy of the war, namely, the sequence in which a ceasefire and a commission of inquiry on the responsibility for the war are instituted, the Soviet Union has taken a neutral position, saying that these should be done 'simultaneously and quickly'.[119] This attitude has not been acceptable to Iraq which saw Soviet footdragging as 'indulgent' of the Iranian position.[120] Iran has reason to be satisfied even if the results stemmed less from the fruits of its own diplomacy than as benefits spilling over from superpower rivalry.

An area in which Iran was a moving force was in trade relations with
the Soviet Union. What concerns us here is the degree to which this was
seen as relevant to Iran's war needs and therefore acted upon. Already in
mid-1986 there was the possibility that the Soviet Union might become
an important outlet for Iranian oil exports endangered by heavy Iraqi air
attacks. Similar considerations again came to the fore in 1987, when these
attacks and the threat of an arms embargo (possibly combined with a naval
blockade and trade embargo) revived interest in diversifying trade outlets
and routes. The quickest way to do this was overland, and the most
natural partner was the USSR. However, the Iranian leaders were not
clear as to the impact an intensified trade relationship would have on
political relations with the USSR and on the two states' respective
leverage on each other.

At times it was depicted as a consequence of US pressure on Iran, as in
Musavi's comment: 'When the USA threatens our waterways in the
Persian Gulf, we have to seek other routes'; at other times the
reorientation was attributed to geography, as in Rafsanjani's comment in
August: 'I believe that the future of bilateral relations are bright because
both are neighbours and have a common border of 2,000 kilometres'.[121]
Consistently the scope for, and the pace of, development of bilateral
relations have been either deliberately exaggerated or misjudged. For
example, a report in August insisted that a political decision had been
made to convert a gas pipeline (IGAT-1, in disuse since 1980) to an oil
pipeline leading to the USSR to serve as an outlet for Iran's oil exports; it
expected completion in three months. This pipeline with a capacity of
700,000 b/d was routed to Baku and thence to the Black Sea; it was to be
replaced (reportedly) in due course by a new pipeline, while it reverted to
gas.[122]

In fact, neither of these projects had moved beyond the stage of
discussions by the end of the year. (Indeed Iranian officials had by that
time reopened official discussions about the possibility of laying a pipeline
across Turkey.) The explanations for these miscalculations lie not only in
the complexity of negotiations or the high price of the projects involved,
but in the mixed political motives behind them. On the one hand, Iran
finds it in its interest to publicize the option of getting closer to the USSR
in every way, as a means of deterring excessive pressure on it from the
US. On the other hand, in dealing with the USSR, it appears often to
misread its own bargaining position, and to see itself less as the *demandeur*
than as a neighbour engaging in a mutually profitable enterprise.
Rafsanjani seems to be doing both simultaneously in the following
statement:[123]

> . . . we could benefit from Soviet transit routes, roads, railroads and ports for
> our oil and gas. And they could obtain advantages in return . . . For instance
> we could construct a railroad leading from the Soviet border to the Persian
> Gulf or the Gulf of Oman.

Whatever the explanation (and this does not deny that the USSR, which is extremely hard-headed in money matters, may also misjudge the respective positions, and demand too high a price), by the end of year only limited progress had been made. An air-link was resumed, a shipping route in the Caspian agreed, and agreement completed on the exchange of 100,000 b/d of Iranian crude oil for oil products from the USSR.[124]

Granted that Iran has found it in its interest to improve its relations with the USSR, including in the commercial domain, what does it offer the USSR in return, and how (if at all) has the view of the leadership towards the USSR evolved? What President Khamenei characterized as a 'strategic' tie, Prime Minister Musavi referred to in more sober terms:[125]

> The Russians have adopted a much more realistic stand on the revolution and on the war than the West . . . The Soviet Union knows that it cannot exert too much pressure on us.

Rafsanjani characterized the relationship as a pragmatic *modus vivendi* in which Iran objects to Soviet arms supplies to Iraq and the Soviet Union protest against Iran's aid to the Afghans: 'These two problems remain, but they are much less important because we have stopped criticizing each other about them'.[126] Elsewhere he described an explicit attempt by the Soviet Union to link the two issues:[127]

> The Russians tell us frankly that because we support the Afghans they give support to Iraq. If we stopped helping Afghanistan the Russians would be prepared to cut their arms supplies to Iraq. However, we remain loyal to our principles.

If this is an accurate characterization of the Soviet position (and it certainly represents the style of Soviet activities) the question that suggests itself is whether Iran has in fact already tacitly accepted this trade-off, for it has been evident that it was less active in Afghanistan in 1987 than in earlier years. And if the explanation lies elsewhere, under what conditions would the Soviet linkage appear more attractive to Iran's leaders in the prosecution of their war with Iraq? In either case despite Iran's attempt to increase its margin for manoeuvre, by dangling the possibility of 'friendship' treaties and revised 'defence' pacts before the Soviet Union, so far the latter has not bitten.[128] And Iranian officials appear at times to be under no illusions about the tenuous and conditional nature of their influence on the USSR, and the priority in Soviet policies. As one realist observed after the Reagan–Gorbachev summit in Washington in December:[129]

> It seems that the Soviets did not give in to the US pressures. We should thank them for this. Of course they have their own calculations. [But given their technical and economic requirements], they do not want to make the Americans very angry.

The USSR's 'own calculations' included three sets of unequal concerns revolving around Iran, the Arab states and the overall strategic relationship with the United States. Although bilateral relations with Iran are very important, Soviet standing in the region as a whole and the entire complex of issues in Soviet–American relations, including the balance of relative advantage and the scope for co-operative relations, all figure in Soviet calculations. Soviet policy toward Iran and the war with Iraq is thus comprised of several distinct but inter-related elements which inevitably include Soviet global interests, Soviet aims in Afghanistan, and Soviet bilateral relations with an important neighbour. Soviet policy on the specific issue of the war is thus intended to serve several purposes at once – or is at least framed with the aim of not exacerbating or harming other interests. For example, the Soviet preoccupation with its role and status as a superpower entails a highly competitive approach, but at the same time moderates that policy so that US critics cannot seize on it as an excuse for freezing relations. Any desire to cultivate Iran cannot be such as to interfere with the openings that the conflict may give to Soviet diplomacy in the Gulf. Besides being difficult to implement, such a policy is bound at times appear inconsistent, or worse, insincere. For it must speak to several audiences often in several tongues.

Soviet policy in the war has been aimed at three sets of interests and major audiences which we shall examine in turn, starting with our principal concern, Iran. Despite a strong – even obsessive – traditional concern about relations with adjacent states which is evident in attempts to improve relations with the Islamic republic, the USSR has not treated its militant neighbour with 'kid gloves', or hidden its dislike of the regime. Indirect criticism is indicative, since its provenance is generally no secret:[130]

> ... Soviet people do not hide their concern about the injustice of the reactionaries ruling Iran, the suppression of Iran's patriots and the unjust, war-mongering anti-Communism under the false slogan of saving Islam.

Soviet–Iranian meetings are invariably characterized as 'frank and businesslike'. Even when on a relatively high level, as in the visit of the Iranian Foreign Minister to Moscow in February 1987, no attempt was made to disguise differences. Gromyko told Velayati:

> Our assessment of that war and your view of it do not coincide ... Common sense suggests that primary attention should be focused on the future and not the past – on putting an end to the war ... The only ones who gain from the continuation of military conflict are the imperialist forces for whom this war is profitable.

Nor are differences on Afghanistan, where Iran aids the *Mojahedin* ignored. The Soviet Union reminds Iran of its 'full responsibility for the fact that its territory is being used for armed warfare against the

Democratic Republic of Afghanistan . . .'.[131]

The Soviet authorities have not been shy about warning Iran about attacks on their shipping through 'memoranda', but generally have been restrained and (in contrast to the US) have taken a low military profile in the Gulf, insisting that their loan of three tankers to Kuwait was a 'purely commercial' operation.[132] At the same time, the USSR has always been acutely sensitive to any suggestion that there is any similarity or comparability in the behaviour of the superpowers, reacting quickly to any such canard in the Iranian press.[133] It also reminded Iranians of the period in 1980 when they were under a Western embargo, and it was the USSR that stepped forward and 'placed its transit routes at the disposal of Iran'.[134]

The situation changed as the US entered the Gulf in force. A Soviet statement of 3 July called for a withdrawal of 'all warships that have no relation to the region . . . as quickly as possible', coupling this with a call for a cessation of activities (presumably by Iran and Iraq) 'that could pose a threat to international shipping'.[135] This was interpreted by Iran as a conciliatory gesture making it easier for both states, despite their differences, to attribute the primary responsibility for the deterioration in the region to the US. Iran's Deputy Foreign Minister Larijani (in Moscow in mid-July) could not escape a stern lecture from Gromyko on the war, but the Soviet authorities also played up their desire to 'achieve a positive settlement of the problems having to do with the Persian Gulf' and both sides shared the view that the US naval presence was exacerbating the situation, while the USSR expressly 'condemned' these actions.[136]

With the beginnings of a US–Iran confrontation, the tendency to attribute specific strategic aims to US policy came to the fore. Indicative of Soviet mistrust (rather than purely propagandist), and of Soviet thinking as well, was an article in *Literaturnaya Gazeta*, arguing that US pressure on Iran was intended as a means of returning 'to that country so as to be able to use it as a bridgehead against the USSR'. Similarly, it argued that US pressure on Afghanistan was intended to result in the use of Afghanistan 'as a backdoor' to Iran.[137]

The temptation to score points off the US bilaterally became irresistible as well. Deputy Minister Vorontsov told Iran's ambassador Heyrani-Nobari that the US, having failed to infiltrate Iran domestically, was now seeking to exert pressure on it externally. Soviet statements after Iran–US clashes labelled the US acts as 'armed aggression' and stated that the US was now 'a participant in the military conflict', implying (as did Iranian statements) that it thereby had forfeited any legitimacy as a peacemaker.[138]

Despite the convergence of Iran and the USSR on opposition to the US presence in the Gulf, there was little in the way of real warmth in the relationship. In mid-July Iran quickly returned a Soviet military transport

plane with its soldiers/passengers that had been forced to land in Iran.
The USSR took a neutral position in September on the question of
whether a commission of inquiry on responsibility for the war should
precede a ceasefire. Soviet diplomacy helped Iran stall for time and put
counterproposals to the Security Council Resolution 598 that some
Western states believed was not subject to further negotiation. There was
not yet any sign of a clear swap between the two on the question of their
respective support for each other's opponent. In December the Soviet
Union in protesting about an attack on its consultate in Isfahan by
Afghans in Iran who were opposed to Soviet policy, claimed that they
sought to harm relations.[139]

Soviet policy towards Iran has been only one factor in Soviet
calculations in the war. Soviet attitudes have been less those of a state
desperately anxious to improve ties with an important neighbour than of a
power secure in the knowledge that it has the whip hand and that it is
dealing with a *demandeur*. It has thus been relatively dismissive in
reporting developments in bilateral trade, and well aware of the attempts
of the Iranians to break out of their limited room for manoeuvre
(especially with the US) by 'playing the Soviet card'. However, the USSR
must consider Iran's possible role in any settlement of the Afghanistan
question including its capacity to play the 'spoiler'. It must also weigh the
extent to which its severity or coldness might lead to a more even-handed
hostility towards the superpowers in the future than has been the case
since 1979.[140] It must also consider the possibility of an eventual
rapprochement between Iran and the US. Soviet policy in the Gulf war
should therefore be seen as a derivative of Soviet policy towards the wider
region, in which Iran figures most prominently. There is no policy
towards the Gulf war distinct from this, and such a policy is bound to be a
subset of policies towards individual states. Inevitably because of the
strategic importance of Iran, and the value that the USSR attaches to
keeping it anti-Western, or to put it differently, denying the US access –
especially strategic access – to it, the USSR cannot be expected to see
approaches to ending the Iran–Iraq war other than in terms of the net
outcome for its standing in Tehran. Seen from this standpoint, Soviet
reluctance to alienate Iran is comprehensible.

Soviet policy toward Islamic Iran in the Gulf war has evolved, coming
closer to Iran, and avoiding any major crises. It is not evident that it can
do so for much longer. Iran's continuation of the war creates problems for
the USSR, in terms of possible benefits that might be extracted from it by
the US (such as access to bases in the Arabian peninsula on a permanent
basis) and of the negative effects of an Iranian victory in the region for
fundamentalism and the regional balance (as well as on Soviet credibility
as an ally in the Arab world). It risks forcing choices that the USSR would
prefer to avoid. The only opportunities it provides are in the Arab Gulf
states where the USSR has posed as a 'protector'. Additional benefits

might be the weakening of both belligerents and their likely dependence on the USSR in the future. But these are likely to happen anyway and do not need additional years of conflict. Nor can they be measured against the risks of the war for the enhancement of the strategic position of the major Soviet preoccupation and its principal rival for status and power – the United States.

The USSR has used the Gulf war to open up channels to the Gulf states with which it has no diplomatic relations. Soviet interest in these 'moderate' states is a new factor changing somewhat the emphasis and calculus in Soviet policy. Now in some diplomatic questions the value of Iran may have to be weighed against the value of *all* the Arab states of the Gulf; and the decision is not as self-evident as was a straight choice between Iran and Iraq. Moscow has sought to reassure the Gulf Arabs about its relations with Iran. Like Syria, it has argued that these ties are not only not incompatible with good ties with the Gulf states, but, because of their value as a restraining factor in Iran's policies, should even be considered as indispensable. The alacrity with which the Soviet authorities, despite their limited naval means, accepted Kuwait's invitation, and the diplomatic support extended to Kuwait against Iranian threats and actions,[141] were doubtless intended as models, the advantages of which should be clear to other states. At the same time, the Soviet Union has been quite clear as to where *its* primary adversary was located. It has sought to contrast its own clear policies on the war with those of the US, which covertly armed Iran in 1985–6 and which was now allegedly planning to regain its position in Iran to use it as a US bridgehead, as in the past when it had been used 'for staging operations against the Arab countries'.[142]

Soviet policy towards Iran in the Gulf war has been shaped with one eye always on competition with the US. This has meant that Iran has been able to benefit to some extent from the inability of the superpowers to align their policies to move to a joint position to end the war. It has also given it a margin for manoeuvre in exploiting the respective anxieties of the superpowers about each other's capacity to entrench themselves in Tehran while excluding the other. At the same time, because there is a significant overlap in their positions on the Gulf war itself (as opposed to the question of respective influence in Iran), and because relations between them are in a state of transition in many dimensions, the Gulf war has been a period of experimentation and strategic dialogue between *les deux grands* themselves to the exclusion of the local states. This fact has tempered Soviet policy and also altered the strategic calculation, diluting somewhat, and potentially importantly, Soviet policy toward Iran.

The Soviet authorities have sought during the Gulf war to emphasize three related themes to the United States:[143]

(i) The unacceptability of a major US military presence in the region, which aggravates the situation and whose withdrawal is the precondition for any progress in co-operation on the war. (Together with this is the leitmotiv of the legitimacy of Soviet interests, given the proximity of the region to the southern frontier of the USSR).

(ii) The need for joint or collective, rather than unilateral, efforts to settle the problem, together with an emphasis on past Soviet suggestions on assuring the flow of oil and guaranteeing the freedom of navigation in the context of the Indian Ocean – and by extension now the Gulf and the Strait of Hormuz. This theme has been complemented in 1987 by stress on the need for an approach through the United Nations, including a UN naval force and the revival of the Military Staff Committee of the Security Council.

(iii) Their willingness to consider a joint/co-operative, or collective, approach to issues, in which they are included as full partners, as the new model for dealing with regional conflicts. In arguing that such conflicts are rarely 'zero-sum' (i.e. a loss for one superpower rarely automatically translates into a gain for the other) they are dangling the carrot of 'good behaviour' in front of the US, as the price of being included in a settlement, that is, having their interests and presence formally acknowledged.

So far the United States has not risen to the bait. Nevertheless, there is an active debate both about the nature of evolving Soviet foreign policy and the necessity, if not indispensability, of 'including' the USSR, either because it 'cannot' be excluded, or because this approach to regional conflicts promises to defuse regional troublespots and reduce the likelihood of superpower clashes. For our purposes what is critical is the extent to which this approach is acted upon in the future, allowing US–Soviet co-operation over the head of Tehran and at its expense. What can be said is that by the end of 1987 this prospect still looked a distant one in the Gulf. The extraordinary strategic importance of the region – in particular Iran – and consequently the stakes involved, made uncertain and open-ended co-operative policies too hazardous a diplomatic undertaking. The Gulf was not a good place to start such experiments.

A critical choice would present itself to Moscow if the Western countries offered to associate the USSR with a settlement and formally to acknowledge its interest. Would it be prepared then to co-operate in tough measures against Tehran at the cost of its future relations with Iran? And would its relations with the US, and the gratitude of the Arab states of the Gulf, count for more? In posing these questions one can see that Soviet relations with Iran are subject to much more than strictly bilateral considerations, and may become more so in the future.

By the end of 1987 Iran was still at war with Iraq, the superpowers had not yet moved jointly to pass a second resolution imposing an arms embargo on Iran (as the recalcitrant party), and Iran still maintained passable relations with the USSR. How far could this be judged a success and how far (if it was) was it attributable to Iran's skilful diplomacy? As we have seen, as superpower competition became more pronounced in the war in 1987, the interests of Iran and the USSR converged on a narrow, specific but not unimportant point, namely the withdrawal of the naval vessels of the US and its allies from the Gulf, prior to any other consideration. On this and only this, Iranian–Soviet interests overlapped. The USSR still insisted on Kuwait's right to be left alone and supported its sovereignty and independence; still called on Iran at every opportunity to end the 'senseless bloodletting'; still deplored Iran's policy in Afghanistan, its domestic policies and its attempts to export the revolution to the Islamic world.[144] Even on the issue of the withdrawal of foreign naval forces from the Gulf, Iran and the USSR did not see exactly eye to eye, for while Iran sought a *total* withdrawal of these vessels (as an affront to the strongest local state), the USSR sought a withdrawal of the navies of Western countries, and offered as a substitute a multilateral presence, that is, a UN naval force authorized by the Security Council, implicitly bringing itself into the picture directly.

Nor were the differences between the USSR and the US on the issue of naval forces as insurmountable as they may have appeared. By the end of 1987 the US was already keen to reduce its naval presence in the Gulf, and there was no reason why a 'reconfiguration' of these forces might not accommodate the Soviet's insistence on a UN naval presence. The Soviet Union in turn was beginning to move closer to the US, opening up the possibility of a superpower compromise at Iran's expense. Thus in mid-December Soviet officials were underlining the utility of a UN naval force not only to substitute for a predominantly Western presence, but also as a useful means of implementing the compulsory measures that would follow from a second Security Council resolution. They argued that the USSR did not consider the creation of these naval forces a *precondition* for an embargo. They noted that the US was now studying their proposal for a UN naval force, and welcomed this development but denied that the US consideration of their proposal *ipso facto* committed them to an embargo.[145]

This is not to argue that US–Soviet co-operation in the Gulf is imminent, but rather that it is closer than it may sometimes appear, and contingent on the policies of the superpowers, not the regional states. By late 1987 there had been a considerable narrowing of differences, although the competitive dimensions of relations persist and are likely to do so. This gives third powers some room for manoeuvre, but in an improved climate of superpower relations and direct dialogue, the scope for this is limited.

By late 1987 Iran had gained a breathing spell without solving any of its principal problems. Some progress had been registered in bilateral relations with the USSR, but not much; economic relations remained minimal, less than a tenth of those existing in 1980 ($1 billion). Iran had not succeeded in de-internationalizing the war and the USSR did not share its view on this, wanting to be involved rather than excluded. Iran's determination to continue the war left open the possibility that in the face of a new Iranian threat to the Iraqi lines, the superpowers would be driven together to bridge the small gap that now separates them on the war.

Islamic Iran has proved neither inept nor unrealistic in its diplomacy with the superpowers. It has shown a capacity to adapt and learn from its mistakes – avoidable mistakes, to be sure, stemming from rigid applications of its own rhetoric, literal interpretations of its ideology. As the war has come to dominate the diplomacy of the Islamic republic, a greater premium has come to be given to flexibility. Iran now seeks to avoid any repetition of the period in 1984 where it was stuck in a hole of its own making, with poor relations with both superpowers simultaneously and few outlets. To get out of that impasse its leaders accepted that they could not stop Soviet arms to Iraq and concentrated instead on limiting them, while gaining access to arms for Iran itself. They used with limited success the US interest in contacts to foster fears of an impending post-Khomeini power vacuum in order to gain some access to US arms. While dangling the bait of a possibly friendly (but in any case anti-Communist) Iran in front of Washington, the Iranians kept their channels open to the USSR. Sometimes they argued that the West was seeking to impair these relations by exaggerating the Soviet military threat.[146] At other times without accepting a direct *quid pro quo* on Afghanistan, the Iranian leaders hinted that their position on Afghanistan had evolved (and could further evolve) as a result of Soviet policies in the area of Iran's principal interest.[147]

Conclusions

Revolutionary Islamic Iran's view of the world is a North/South rather than an East/West perspective. It sees the superpowers as similar and as the quintessential oppressors, seeking to impose themselves on the rest of the world. As one Tehran commentary observed: 'Both Moscow and Washington wish to dominate the Middle East, each pursuing its own particular policy'.[148] Another aspect of this view has been the belief in the centrality of the mission of the Islamic republic, its vital importance to the superpowers and the threat that it poses to their interests, and hence their collusion in wishing to weaken it. This conveniently feeds a conspiratorial view of the world, while making of Iran a martyr nation being punished for its resistance. Comments such as those of Ayatollah Montazeri, Khomeini's successor, are illustrative of this view:[149]

Today any blow that is dealt at this fledgling republic emanates either from

Western imperialism, the US . . . or from the East by means of such advanced weapons as the MIG, Soviet missiles . . .

It has been a basic part of Islamic Iran's ethos that its role is to lead the oppressed masses in combat against these arrogant powers, to help expose their impotence, and to cut them down to size. The other face of this role, the opposite of militancy, has been the belief that all relations with the superpowers are bound to be culturally contaminating, inherently unequal, and relations of dominance and subservience, preferably to be avoided altogether or at least scaled down. The experience of the past seven years and the dictates of the war have seen some evolution in this view. The belief that 'Neither East nor West' constituted a policy rather than a slogan has evaporated. Iran still rejects the East/West matrix, or the suggestion that to be anti-Western implies a pro-Eastern orientation. Its leaders still believe that ideally the weaker states should minimize their contacts with the oppressors. But the evolution in policy suggests a distinct learning process. Iran found its antagonization of both the US and the USSR in 1983–4 unduly restricting in its prosecution of the war, and it learned that the continued alienation of the US reduced its leverage in bargaining with the USSR, and unduly narrowed its margin for manoeuvre. It also found that self-sufficiency, however admirable a value in the abstract and a useful rationalization of its situation, could not be of paramount importance, and that the winning of the war and the acquisition of arms must take priority in the event of a conflict between theory and practical needs.

In rejecting the common exclusion of the two superpowers as unduly restricting its flexibility, Iran sought to enter into contacts with them, but in equilibrium. In the process it was obliged to accept that it could not dictate to them; rather it had to accept their terms. For example, it could not insist on the severence of arms to Iraq; it could only hope to compete for equivalent supplies. It had to accept a formula of 'agreeing to disagree' with Moscow. It could and did play on its own presumed strategic centrality. Rafsanjani, in 1983, pointedly said that he doubted that the USSR 'with whom we have a 2,000 kilometre border' would want 'to go so far as to completely lose a neighbouring country like Iran'.[150] Iranian officials are aware of their nuisance value on Afghanistan, and can turn the volume up and down on this issue, and exchange hints about a linkage between their policies on it and Soviet policies in the Gulf war. They can also hint at a drift toward the West to get Soviet attention. In their less formal dialogue with the US too, they have embraced power-politics with a vengeance, providing tantalizing glimpses of pragmatism, and hints of common concerns and a joint interest in containing the USSR. They want recognition of the revolution, arms supplies, and the possibility of a normalization of relations, if only to improve their leverage with other parties.

Iran has joined in and even led a game of three-sided manoeuvring in which each of the actors has different but not always opposing goals. Islamic Iran's policies have adapted to its practical needs, especially those of its primary foreign policy concern – the war. But the adaptation has not been completely unprincipled; Tehran has still refused to compromise on its opposition to Soviet policies in Afghanistan, although at times it may have waxed strangely silent about them.

How much success has Iran had in its policies with the superpowers? Some, no doubt. Its leadership is resourceful and has played its hand with skill, but it may well have overplayed it. Revolutionary Iran may have misjudged its own centrality to world politics. While the superpowers are in competition over the scope of their respective future influence in the Gulf and in Tehran, they are in substantial agreement on the fact that they do not wish to see Islamic Iran win the war, and in avoiding their own manipulation by regional states. Their primary difference at present is on how to bring an end to the war that does not jeopardize their interests in Tehran now and in the future. This gives Tehran some, but not much, room for manoeuvre. The revelations of its manipulation of first US suspicions of the USSR, and possibly also Moscow's of the United States,[151] does little to encourage faith in the good judgement, let alone good faith, of its leaders in the superpowers' capitals. By embracing power-politics so wholeheartedly, and bargaining so cynically, the Islamic authorities have gained little in the coin of influence, arms, or change in the policy of the superpowers. Iran may well have been too clever by half.

12

The Reckoning

Iraq at war

In examining the Iran–Iraq war from the perspective of Iraqi politics, two sets of conclusions emerge, stemming from two different sets of questions about the relationship between political structure and war. On the one hand, these concern the attempt to discover the ways in which the particular character of the Iraqi state has determined the principal features of the war by setting its initial goals, organizing the instruments for its prosecution and laying down the conditions for its termination. On the other hand, after a conflict of over seven years' duration, it is equally important to enquire about the degree to which the organization of such a war effort, as well as the unforeseen consequences of the fighting, have affected the fabric of the state itself and thus the political system which dominates it. In both cases, the conclusions drawn are contingent upon a series of observations regarding the nature of the Iraqi state. The latter are obviously coloured by the historical, geographical and cultural specificities of the communities encompassed by the modern state of Iraq. Nevertheless, the endeavour to bring these communities and traditions within a form of collective organization such as the territorial state is common not only to other parts of the Middle East but also to much of the Third World. In this regard, one may legitimately ask whether some of the conclusions concerning the relationship between state and war might have a comparative validity beyond the specific case of Iraq.

The study of Iraqi politics has revealed a significant dualism between an indigenous tradition of political behaviour and an extraneous tradition implicit in the state framework within which politics are conducted. Although the two traditions in many senses contradict one another, the appropriation of the state by a group of men deriving their strength from the primordialism of local politics has demanded that they pay attention to the logic of territorial statehood. Instrumentally, this has been of considerable benefit to the extension of their power, since it has provided them with an unparalleled degree of control over a fragmented society. The machinery of the state has, therefore, been adapted to serve these ends. More problematic has been the attempt to disguise this particularism by constructing a myth that would convince their subjects of the legitimacy of the state itself and thus induce the collective loyalty appropriate to the acknowledgement of such legitimacy. Inevitably, therefore, the effort to rule Iraq by one set of norms while seeking to justify that domination by recourse to a set of norms bearing little resemblance to political reality, has produced considerable tensions within the system. These were apparent in the Ba'th Party long before its adherents seized power in 1968. After that year, they became increasingly salient, as the leaders of the party sought to use it as a vehicle for the definition and domination of the state.

Two responses developed as a means of coping with the tensions that emerged. The first, ensuring the immediate security of the conspiratorial inner circle of leadership, was the close attention paid to the instruments of coercion available to those who controlled the state. The use of force to eliminate any significant opposition based on alternative views about the proper ends of politics, or on competing collective loyalties, has been a characteristic feature of Iraqi politics. It has not removed the tensions inherent in the conflict between society and state, but it has severely reduced the capacity of those who would challenge the Ba'thist regime's definition of the state. In doing so, however, it has both perpetuated itself as an appropriate, and perhaps the only possible, means of acting to achieve political ends, and reinforced the trend towards autocratic control. This, the second response to the strain involved in exploiting the state for the benefit of traditionally based power, seeks to overcome the disruptive consequences of the duality of Iraqi politics. By transforming the institutions of the state, and incidentally the Ba'th as well, into the servants of an absolute ruler, it is hoped that the dangers and contradictions of institutional autonomy in such a setting will be avoided. Having established his primacy in this sphere, the autocrat can then, on his own terms, project his own person as the embodiment of the collective ideals that define the state. These two features, of private control and public myth, have been evident in Saddam Hussein's seemingly inexorable rise to a position of primacy in Iraq.

However, this process has, if anything, reinforced the dual nature of the Iraqi state. Nowhere has this become more apparent than in the commitment of that state to war. The personalization of politics involved in the assertion of autocratic control has shaped Saddam Hussein's perception of the organization and utility of the instruments of state power. These are to be the means by which his personal power is amplified, both domestically and beyond the territorial confines of the Iraqi state itself. Considerations of precisely this nature led to the establishment in 1980 of the National Assembly, which was to act as the echo chamber of his views and the institutional representation of the state-wide extent of his authority. Similarly, the expansion and modernization of the Iraqi armed forces was to little purpose unless they could be used in a decisive demonstration of his power. Their deployment in the service of the rights of the state, expressed in the language of territorial sovereignty, would increase the identification of Saddam Hussein's leadership with the interests of the state. It would also disguise the fact that he had arbitrarily surrendered some of those rights to Iran in 1975 without reference to the collectivity presumed to underlie the Iraqi state itself. There was thus a double sense in which war was to be a public means of realizing private ends. The public means were to be determined by the structure and idiom of statehood, whereas the private ends stemmed from a persistent cultural tradition which interpreted politics as the service of a powerful individual.

The same set of assumptions as those which determined Saddam Hussein's view of Iraqi politics and its imperatives, appear to have underpinned his perception of Iran, and indeed of much of the region. Revolutionary Iran was seen as an enfeebled autocracy, whose leader appeared to be dismantling the instruments of coercion necessary for the maintenance of his power. Under this interpretation, the Iranian leadership lacked the resources to prevent the inevitable internal and external challenges thrown up by social rejection of the new regime. In addition, precisely because it was assumed that they could have no alternative power base, the leaders would be only too willing to make a deal with Iraq. This would give them time to reconstruct their power base, whilst considerably enhancing that of Saddam Hussein. In such a calculation of perceived advantage and opportunity, the utility of force, about which there were in any case few inhibitions, became more marked. The demonstrative war was to be limited and brief. It was to be devastating largely in its symbolic repercussions, rather than in the amount of damage it would cause.

From this perspective, the rapid termination of the war was predicated on two factors: the military prowess of the Iraqi armed forces and the mirror-image nature of the Iranian regime. Since both were intimately bound up with Saddam Hussein's perception of his own power within Iraq, they could not be gainsaid. Nor is it likely that his colleagues within the inner circle would have felt inclined to contradict him, since they shared a common approach to politics. As subsequent events demonstrated, neither premise proved to be correct and Saddam Hussein discovered that he had committed his state to a very different kind of war. Nevertheless, despite the increase in the intensity of effort required for its prosecution, the war has failed significantly to alter his views either on the proper conduct of politics or on the nature of the Iraqi state. On the contrary, the defensive war upon which Iraq is now engaged has been used by Saddam Hussein to strengthen his personal identification with the state in symbolic terms, and to tighten his personal control over the organs of state power. Thus, the war has witnessed, and in some senses permitted, a determined entrenchment of his autocracy.

However, at the same time, the conditions of the war have made the survival of that autocracy dependent as never before on a relatively competent military defence of the state. The armed forces are no longer simply the extension of Saddam Hussein's personal power domestically and in the region. The nature of the Iranian war effort and its war aims has compelled them to become the principal means whereby the survival not only of Saddam Hussein, but also of Iraq as a Sunni-dominated or Ba'thist state and possibly as a territorial entity, can be assured. The spectrum of interests clustered behind the protective shelter of the Iraqi armed forces, and the latter's awareness of the domestic conditions they require to fulfil their well-defined, externally-oriented role, create the basis for a rather different relationship with Saddam Hussein from that of the simple subordination which he is still exerting himself to maintain. He has been determined to foster the illusion that defence of his leadership and defence of the state are inseparable. This is a contingent and not a necessary connection, however, and the possibility therefore arises that the fortunes of the war may make it seem that there is a contradiction between the two. The Iranians have done their best to create this impression, but hitherto the mistrust with which they are regarded by those in Iraq who are in a position to put this proposition to the test has overridden all other considerations. Nevertheless, it remains the case that such a separation is not only possible conceptually but may have been facilitated by the effects of the war.

It is in this respect that the perennial vulnerability of Saddam Hussein's autocracy becomes apparent. The duality of politics in Iraq has meant that the mass appeals of the leader, the personality cult, the creation of mass organizations, the apparent attention, in short, that he has paid to the collective foundations of the state count for little in a balance of power where decisive advantage goes to those who can successfully organize a minimum of selective force in the service of a closed conspiracy. The absence of any institutional foundations for power has allowed Saddam Hussein to use the pretext of the war to tighten his personal direction of politics. It has also required that he should do so, and thereby points to the fact that he is unable to transform present gains into future assets. The evident discontinuity between personal power and state power, and their uneven rates of development, suggest that the war, while it has strengthened Saddam Hussein in the short term, may have weakened his regime in the long run. It has not, in sum, altered the bases of politics in Iraq.

The sense of beleaguered solidarity in facing up to the ordeal represented by the war cannot be channelled into political support for the state in the absence of some form of participation beyond military service at the front. Nor can the considerable growth of that most symbolic instrument of state power – the armed forces – be seen as contributing to the strengthening of the state itself whilst it is maintained primarily as an instrument for the defence of the regime. The war may have caused it, or rather elements within it, to see their role, and thus their relationship to the regime, in a rather different, and possibly antagonistic, light. However, this is more likely to develop into a familiar pattern of military conspiracy, leading to the attempted armed seizure of power, than into a consistent advocacy of the prerequisites for a strong and stable Iraqi state. In so doing, the conspirators may opportunistically exploit such sentiments among the officer corps. However, the tenacity of the old methods as a basis for political thought and action seems likely to prevail over any revulsion at their consequences caused by the experience of war.

A corollary of the observation that war reflects in many important respects the nature of the society and state that wages it, is the view that the nature of the state and of the society must mediate the political effects of war. In the case of Iraq, as elsewhere in the Third World, it is the dual or divided nature of the state which acts as the central means of transmission for these impulses. The war between Iraq and Iran has highlighted this duality both in its causes and in its effects. In so doing, it both illustrates and increases the instability of a polity where two conflicting traditions are in operation: that of the particularistic and communally based assertion of personal power and that of the territorially based collectivity underlying the nation state. The appropriation of the latter and its instruments by the former has created a distinctive and uncompromising context for regional conflict. Once this is transformed into war, the effect has been to narrow still further the central core of power, whilst increasing the need to mobilize ever larger numbers of the subject population, through the myths and instruments believed appropriate. The result has been to widen the gap between the illusion and the reality of the state, creating expectations which cannot be fulfilled and necessitating further recourse to coercive methods. The mixture of strength and vulnerability which this denotes indicates the persistence of a cycle of instability and domestic violence which seems set to perpetuate both the duality of the state and the disruptive effects of its relations with similarly constituted states. This is the legacy with which not just Saddam Hussein, but also Iraq itself, is faced. It represents a challenge to their security which will not end with the ending of the war.

Iran at war

The war, which followed hard on the heels of the revolution, was a direct outgrowth from it. Self-absorbed and utterly confident, revolutionary Iran provoked a war which it imprudently failed to prepare for, but, once embarked on, embraced with characteristic zeal. It defined it as a clash of supreme metaphysical values rather than national wills.

The 'imposed war' came to exemplify many facets of the revolution –

its sense of moral rectitude, its universal spiritual mission and its belief in the power of faith and commitment. As it continued, it came also to reflect the tenacious unyielding nature of the Islamic republic which prided itself on its unique moral rectitude, and accepted losses as acceptable adjuncts to the process of self-reliance and spiritual purgation on which it had launched itself. According to this view, established ways were defunct, compromise debilitating, and will-power and sacrifice sufficient for Iran to prevail. In making the war the test of everything, the Iranian leadership in effect staked the future of the Islamic republic, not to mention their own political future, on its outcome.

The consequence of this general attitude was to drive an otherwise cautious set of neighbours and interested powers into what could, with justice, be termed defensive opposition. By the end of 1984 the price of this was seen in Tehran as being too high. Iraq had not turned out as fragile, nor its Shi'a population as suggestible, as Iranian clerics had suspected. Iran sought to show the Gulf states that its relations with Syria demonstrated a new-found pragmatism. But even a form of working arrangement with some of these states could not be expected to survive an Iranian victory. Furthermore, Iran had become a new *genus* of threat for its neighbours: not military *per se* nor even an exemplary model for their dissidents, but rather a state with the power of subversion, and with a mission for creating disorder.

Starting from the premise that a 'negative equilibrium' in which neither superpower secured any influence in Iran was preferable to a 'positive' one (characteristic of Mohammad Reza Shah's Iran), the Islamic leaders had found that their free hand had also turned out to be an empty one. So Iran shifted and tried to play off the superpowers against each other, secure in the knowledge of its strategic importance. It sought to use their rivalry and mutual suspicion to its own ends – increasingly, and almost exclusively, the winning of the war. In this, it had by 1987 been only partially successful. The superpowers had written off the Islamic regime as neither dependable nor admirable, although both rather reluctantly accepted it as a fact. Each sought in its own fashion to contain the revolution without conceding any advantages to the other. At the same time, both, for overriding reasons stemming from their own relationship and responsibilities, had become increasingly distrustful of possible inadvertent confrontations generated by regional entanglements. By 1988 Iran had indeed achieved a balance between the superpowers insofar as they both treated it with suspicion and caution. But this gave it no practical leverage in the war nor understanding for its cause in their capitals.

The regime that rejected the need for arms in the prosecution of the war (arguing that the costs of the US connection were too onerous in terms of Iran's fledgling independence) has spent most of the years since the resolution of the hostage crisis in 1981 scouring the world for compatible weapons systems. The change is not one of outlook but of relative priorities and is a metaphor for Islamic Iran at war. From a refusal to believe that arms are necessary in the conduct of war, it is but a short step to rejecting the need for military professionalism altogether. Thence it is even easier to convince oneself (or one's impressionable constituency) that the old forms of warfare are corrupt and perverse, and do not take into account the spirit of the new Islamic man. By 1984, however, Iran had painfully learned that zeal was not a substitute for arms and that a willingness to accept high casualties did not guarantee results on the battlefield.

Iran's military conduct of the war has been restrained except in the profligate use of manpower and the escalation of hostilities, not through widening or intensifying them but through *prolonging* them. Whether through multiple/limited or grand final offensives, a decisive military result has proved tantalizingly and frustratingly elusive. Iran's search for a winning formula has alternated between reliance on a military break-through and hope that cumulative pressure will lead to the political collapse of its foe. There are few grounds for such an expectation (although Iraqi collapse through sheer exhaustion is conceivable), but this is a question of relative commitment. Despite Iran's inflation of the stakes, there is an asymmetry between its interests in the war and those of Iraq, which are quite literally vital. Meaningful victory was in its grasp in mid-1982 but, intoxicated by a combination of military momentum, revolutionary hubris and the chimera of a region ripe for proselytizing, Iran failed to seize it. Since then only an unholy faith in miracles has nurtured the Iranians in battle.

The Iranian revolutionaries refused to accept the premises of their predecessor regime that the nation needed a military able to deter external enemies and defend its frontiers. They insisted that the military had served an internal role in repressing the regime's enemies and fostering a climate of dependence on foreign, primarily Western, powers. The new leaders therefore wished to disband the armed forces and substitute reliable Islamic warriors motivated by faith, organized into a militia, and dependent on no-one but themselves. A citizen army, a nation in arms, a country of '20 million soldiers', became the slogans, while the reality remained a refusal (after November 1979) responsibly to consider the nation's manifold defence needs. The war, when it came, served a variety of purposes among which the theme of an infant republic, embattled and alone, became part of the revolution's folklore, assuming with the passage of time a mythological quality and epic stature. The reality was more prosaic. Citizen armies are not very good at deterring border incursions; voluntarily dismantling defence capabilities can sometimes send the wrong message to aggrieved neighbours.

Another notable casualty of the war has been Islamic Iran's sense of moral superiority. The war has tested some of its assumptions, confirming some and finding others wanting. While discipline, self-reliance and commitment can go a long way in war, they cannot replace weapons, planning and professionalism. A willingness to cultivate moral virtues and eschew compromise, however commendable in theory, cannot be any good in practice if the result is the antagonization of the superpowers and most (and possibly all) of one's neighbours. In making the achievement of prime goals more difficult, such postures are self-defeating. Iran's diplomacy since 1984 has been consecrated almost exclusively to the theme of reassurance, to the repair of damage caused by its own rhetorical or actual excesses.

The proposition that Iran's Islamic revolution has universal validity, at least in the Islamic world, has proved increasingly dubious. The Shi'a in Iraq have not been as responsive as Khomeini had hoped. Nor are the Shi'a in Lebanon experiencing a spontaneous or undivided surge towards Khomeinism. For the Shi'a in the Gulf states, cultural differences, as well as those of national interests, have proved a barrier to the 'new Shi'a commonwealth'. The export of the revolution as a voluntary model, and not by the sword, has been a constant refrain in Tehran in recent years. Despite reiteration, the distinction is not always clear in practice, in part because the war obscures Iran's professions of peaceful intent, in part because its past acts have not been reassuring, and in part because militant elements within the regime do not necessarily agree with this formulation. The size and power of Iran and the uncertainty of its future political orientation do not allow its smaller neighbours much margin for error; hence its attempts at reassurance have met with mixed success.

Islamic Iran's assumption that the world could be re-invented, history undone or reversed, and the bygone era of an 'Islamic community' reconstituted anew, complete with a new Islamic man, an Islamic way of warfare, etc. in place of the changes wrought by science and a world of nation-states, was the most central assumption and the one most based on faith. The past eight years of war do not make it any more tenable. Iran has used nationalism and religious fervour to motivate its troops in the war and its populace at home, and its declarations, particularly in the Gulf, have an imperial or at least nationalist ring to them. Its ability to show pragmatism in its relations with the United States, Israel, Turkey, Pakistan, and the USSR, suggests a cynicism to some and, with its tortured ideological justifications, an acceptance of *raison d'état* to others. Whether interpreted as reassuring or as a 'sellout', the evolution of Iran's policy gives little hint of its earlier ideological professions.

The life of the revolutionary system and the length of the war have been virtually coterminous; by December 1987 Islamic Iran had been in existence for 106 months and at war for 88. In historical memory as well as in contemporary politics, they have become virtually indistinguishable, their fates interdependent and linked. The centrality of the war to the political life of the Islamic republic needs no emphasis; increasingly it has displaced all other politics and loomed large over its future.

As a revolutionary society, Iran has enjoyed many advantages in the prosecution of a long war,[1] – an 'awake' population, an ethic of sacrifice and social and civil co-operation, and a self-image and historical-cultural consciousness that embrace suffering, exertion and renewal. And the revolution was 'born lucky', inheriting a near tripling of oil prices as a result of the turmoil it created. Shi'ism, an effective wielder of symbols and a powerful mobilizer of groups in opposition, was given its chance to perform as the doctrine of an established government. Its legitimacy was effectively challenged by no-one.

The onset of the war gave the regime the sort of cause that was necessary to revitalize the flagging revolution, and precisely the yardstick by which they wanted the revolution to be judged. It quickly institutional-ized a state of crisis, enforcing unity, chilling debate and criticism, generally freezing the political process as well as key posts (witness the continuity among the Prime Minister, Foreign Minister, President, and Speaker), and distorting political and economic life. The artificial freezing process was evident in the postponing of contentious issues in the name of unity, in the decisions not made (with high costs later on), in the stilling of debate on first-order questions, and in the tendency for sloganeering to prevail over the arts of persuasion and compromise. The war which has distorted the allocation of resources has also created interest groups which have gained from it. The Supreme Defence Council has functioned as a super-cabinet for the past seven years. The Revolutionary Guards are virtually a law unto themselves; expanded in number and mission, they may resist disbandment and seek to retain the 'perks' of war. As for the professionals, rehabilitated by the war and vindicated in their scepticism about the value of ill-considered offensives, they embody many of the values that the Islamic authorities had sought to discard. The bazaar, so necessary to the economy, has been amply (some may say excessively) rewarded. The conservative, often landed, clerics have resisted moves toward a socialization of land ownership, or an appropriation and redistribution of property by the government. Others insist that the revolution remains incomplete. The newly enfranchised, restive, 'oppressed' classes have given much in the name of the revolution and have been identified as its true sons. For the moment, they act as a brake against any excessive flexibility on the part of the government. In the future, it is their commitment which could lead to disappointment and fury.

The war has acted as a unifying social force, creating a relatively natural focus for consensus. Yet the unity is illusory, for it papers over some of the submerged and postponed issues such as the course the revolution ought to follow in the future, the price it should be prepared to pay for its values, and most directly how and to whose benefit resources should be allocated in peacetime. The failure to address these questions or to encourage a process that can at least accommodate variations in approaches to these issues, is likely to have a high cost in political terms later on.

The qualities necessary for war – sacrifice, self-denial, group cohesion, resourcefulness and commitment – are not necessarily those needed for a healthy stable society in peacetime. Nor is the resilience achieved under war conditions transferable or transmutable to political flexibility under less exceptional conditions. The postponement or avoidance of issues due to the pressures of war may inculcate habits of compromise and discipline, or it may build up pressures leading to political disruptions. Decisions *not* made as a result of the war have costs, most visibly but not exclusively in the economic realm, as surely as those consciously taken.

The war has distorted the economy and society and a serious challenge will be how to redress the balance in a normal period. The task will not be made easier by the fact that the Islamic authorities have found the mobilization of society, the propagation of the myth of being surrounded by an 'ocean of satanic forces', the use of inflexible ideology and appeals to a willingness to suffer, indispensable *and* congenial. The type of heroic politics in which appeals to the memory of the martyrs and the Prophet, and a stoical willingness to suffer, prevail, will be difficult to use in normal times. How will the clerical regime manage to demobilize its faithful, if any there be, after the war?[2] The spirit of Shi'ism as an opposition doctrine does not sit well with its new role as a legitimator of government.

The regime has depicted the war as a necessary staging post on the road to self-realization and self-reliance, and there is no doubt that here necessity has been the mother of invention. Iran has shown resilience and resourcefulness in the conduct of the war, using initiative and improvization on the work-bench as well as on the battlefield. But the economic costs of the war are not the only (even the principal) costs involved.[3]

Revolutionary Iran's self-image as the solitary morally upright challenger of a corrupt and oppressive order quickly became tansformed into quasi-reality. Its war with Iraq confirmed it in its view of confronting a hostile world – of being ranged against an extensive international conspiracy bent on its destruction. Drawing deep upon its reserves of commitment, fortitude and self-reliance, Islamic Iran has managed to sustain a war for the better part of a decade almost singlehanded, against a broad coalition, with few willing to wish it well, let alone lend it a hand. Its brilliant improvization on the battlefield, its resourcefulness in adapting available technology to its specific needs, have been matched by considerable virtuosity in diplomacy under adverse conditions. It has managed to keep channels open to some European states, to cultivate some of the Arab states of the Gulf, to co-exist with its pro-Western neighbouring states (Turkey and Pakistan), and to some extent to exploit US–USSR rivalry. It has obtained arms from many sources, including China and North Korea. It has kept the initiative, has rarely been manipulated or exploited, and has given its own population a sense of pride in its government's refusal to be dictated to or intimidated. Its adaptability suggests pragmatism and shrewd realism.

But none of this undoubted talent and ingenuity, tactical skill, perseverance and sense of moral rectitude has been at the service of a strategy. There is a sense of futility, a lack of perspective, a neglect of relative values hanging over the experiment or enterprise. Like the use of dedicated but untrained and poorly equipped young men on the battlefield, (which recalls the phrase describing the Charge of the Light Brigade: 'C'est magnifique, mais ce n'est pas la guerre'), Iran's overall strategy scarcely does justice to so much valour. The tendency to want to score propaganda or debating points, and to keep the masses at home happy, seems to prevail, at the cost of a careful explanation of Iran's international position. In the war itself the lack of strategy is clear in the mismatch between aims and capabilities. Even less excusable is the failure, once the war was clearly going to be a lengthy one, to plan accordingly. To take but two striking illustrations: the failure to look seriously for other sources of aircraft once relations with the US were clearly destined to be poor; and the failure, despite endless talk, to build alternative pipelines bypassing the Gulf. Both of these suggest an unwillingness, or inability, to plan strategically or over the medium term. Sloganeering and improvization were no substitutes for war planning, but the impression remains that the process of forging a new nation in war was more important for the Islamic authorities than devising an economical means of assuring victory.

Towards the future

By investing the war with far greater stakes than it inherently possessed, Khomeini miscalculated badly. It is true that the stirring eschatological rhetoric of revenge and redemption served to fire an already restive nation. But an Iraqi attack beaten back and with retribution exacted, was within Iran's capabilities and indeed within its grasp by mid-1982. Yet the world view that saw the invasion as a war against Islam, brooking no compromise and demanding as punishment the overthrow of a neighbouring regime, misjudged international reactions as well as Iran's means. Unable to muster the military capability to overthrow the enemy or to bring about its change through internal revolt, Iran was destined to fight a long, arduous and costly war, which in historical perspective appeared arcane and senseless. In demanding the removal of Saddam Hussein, Khomeini put too high a value on his, and his nation's, foe and too little value on the lives of his countrymen. The chance to obtain an honourable peace with victory eluded him (like so many others in history) when, in the elation of success in 1982, he chose to carry on the war and to snatch stalemate from the jaws of victory.

After seven years the momentum of the war is not yet exhausted. However, in the past year there has been a marked change in the tempo of the war, domestic politics in Iran and (to the extent that they can be discerned) what might be called psychological expectations. Within Iran there has been a quickening of the pace of domestic politics, as if the war was in its last phase and the domestic decks needed to be cleared for action. The Islamic Republican Party has been dissolved, conscription broadened, an anti-profiteering campaign initiated, a financial jihad proclaimed, a new will for Khomeini submitted. An uncharacteristic decision by Khomeini (in January 1988) to side with the more reformist-radical (socialist) factions identified with Musavi and Rafsanjani against the more traditionalist group associated with the Council of Guardians, suggests a desire to break the domestic log-jam that has built up in a system characterized by political immobilism rather than consensus. The sense of urgency is unmistakable and derives as much from the pressures of the war as it does from anticipation of Khomeini's imminent demise.

In the war itself the past year has seen an acceleration of trends associated with its internationalization; the United Nations is now seized of the matter; the superpowers are in varying degree involved; detachments from the fleets of five European nations are nearby; and various Arab fora have become more involved. As if to signal a new phase in the conflict after seven years of war, the two antagonists finally broke off diplomatic relations in October 1987. The Iran–Iraq war has truly become the Gulf war. And if it has not yet become a war between Persians and Arabs this is due to persistent divisions among the Arab states and the structure of Gulf politics. Neither of the superpowers and none of the regional states, without exception, wants an Iranian victory and most have conspired in some manner to prevent it. The Security Council, which was so dilatory at the outset of the war, in truth only bestirred itself with the prospect of an Iranian victory.

Iran appeared no closer to devising a winning strategy now than earlier. Breakthrough on the battlefield appeared as remote as ever, a political upset in Iraq was possible but scarcely something to base a strategy upon, and a diplomatic solution through negotiations appeared harder the more blood and treasure was invested in the war. Increasingly the war looked as if it would be decided, if at all, by the relative weakness of the two adversaries, the victor being the one that collapsed last. The Islamic republic that so prided itself on self-reliance as a virtue, had gradually found that this was now an inevitability not a matter of choice. And the war that had by now served its purpose, would not go away.

By the end of 1987, although the war was no closer to a settlement, the outlines of an eventual peace were dimly discernible. An Iranian military victory now looked more improbable than at earlier times. Saddam Hussein seemed to have weathered the storm; Iraq's will had not been broken and it appeared less likely to collapse. In Iran the will for war continued somewhat diminished, but the means to achieve victory declined more precipitously. If Iran could not win the war or gain a peace consistent with its domestic needs, perhaps it could just let the war wind down?

Some observers see in the intersection of Khomeini's inevitable demise and the unsettled problems of the Islamic republic, grounds for hope. They believe that inevitably a mellowing process, which has already started, will accelerate, leading to greater flexibility. This would be manifested as regards the war by a willingness to end it by letting it die down tacitly rather than formally (e.g. by extending the intervals between offensives, reducing the propaganda etc.) and by de-emphasizing Iran's revolutionary message, reducing its external claims and entanglements, and concentrating on its domestic needs including reconstruction, which could serve as a new crusade. For this school of thought, none of the problems in habituating the Iranian populace to peace, or in de-ideologizing it on a case by case basis, or in substituting 'Islam in one country' for the Islamic republic's erstwhile universal claims, loom large. They foresee Iran as a republic in which Islam will continue to play a major role but in which Iranian national interests will be a dominant consideration, allowing, for example, a more pragmatic foreign policy characterized by an 'open door' as suggested by Khomeini in 1984 and 1985.

A second school of thought puts rather more emphasis on the difficulties of honourable extrication from the war and on the effect such a stalemate – in effect at best a disguised defeat – would have on the legitimacy of the entire edifice of the Islamic republic. This school is more sceptical of the ability of the leadership – the high priests of the war – to shrug off its manifold consequences. They foresee an Iran post-Khomeini that is less motivated to launch major offensives or sustain the war at previous levels, but also – lacking Khomeini's authority – less able to make a formal withdrawal or peace. Khomeini's less well-equipped successors will inherit a war and its consequences, an ill-defined political system, a high birth rate, and a host of economic and social problems. A cold peace will require a standing army which will have to be re-equipped.

This second view also sees economic pressures as conducive towards moderation, doubting that material gratification can be permanently deferred in favour of a heavy diet of ideological sustenance. But they see the path from crusades to 'normalcy' as uncertain, uneven and full of surprises. Above all, this view emphasizes the relationship between the appeal of the Islamic republic as a model for other states and its foreign policy; the inextricable bond between the moral authority and legitimacy of the Islamic republic on the one hand and its claims, struggles and exertions on behalf of other Muslim states on the other. They foresee the move from a universal to a national mission as hazardous for the Islamic republic and a course unlikely to be adopted without internal dissension. Above all, they see the Islamic republic dependent, in the final analysis, on a hard core of militant supporters – the true believers in the Imam's message, who with their families have paid in blood for it. It is this constituency that they foresee as the most fractious and difficult to placate by a return to more mundane goals.

Both views of Iran's future share a belief that Islamic Iran will endure, that it has put down roots and is here to stay, but they differ on its future course and content. While the one sees no insuperable difficulty in the transition to a less militantly ideological quasi-nationalist state, the other is more sceptical that this transition can be effected without a significant, if not devastating, loss of authority and unity. If the former foresees a relatively peaceful evolutionary succession, the latter anticipates a bloodier, more disruptive one not devoid of future international crises.

A source of cohesion while it is pursued, the war will be a disintegrative force as it limps toward its inglorious end. Criticism muffled by the need for unity, elemental patriotism and deference to the memory of the martyrs, will be amplified. Politics suspended by the war will be resumed and the delayed shock and horror of the conflict may truly come home.

A flood-tide of recrimination and criticism can be expected as various players jockey for power and seek to blame each other for errors, and to assign elsewhere responsibility for unpopular decisions. A split leadership will reflect a fragmented society. Khomeini's principal if not sole legacy will have been a war that was unwinnable on the terms in which he defined it, and extrication from which was beyond the capacity of the Islamic regime as currently constituted. The people who had sought to link the validation of the regime to the outcome of the war had gambled and failed; those who had brought on the war could not be the ones to end it without repudiating their own handiwork. Questions about the cost and conduct of the war and the definition of war aims, will be raised for the first time. The failure to grasp peace with honour in 1982 will be debated.[4]

Peace in the post-Khomeini period will have no arbiter, and politics few signposts. War has instilled in society a certain discipline, a degree of social consensus, otherwise lacking. Contentious and vital issues such as the proper content of social and economic policy for the Islamic republic, or its appropriate foreign orientation, will be no nearer to agreement. The urgent needs of the war have displaced the imperative to address the problem of political immaturity, and skewed the process by which decisions can be made, undergirded by a true consensus. The problems of peace will therefore be at least as difficult as those of the war, and, because of it, much less easy to acknowledge or resolve.

Whatever the outcome of the war and the fate of the Islamic republic, Iran's revolutionary message – of Islam as a mobilizing and legitimating force – has entered the mainstream of Middle East politics, and is likely to stay. But this did not need a war; Iran had already achieved it with its revolution. Whatever the future of the Islamic republic, there can be no disagreement on the degree to which the war has shaped its language and institutions and conditioned its influence abroad and also how much it will continue to condition and constrain its future course at home.

Notes

Chapter 1 Introduction

1 For the relevant citations from Clausewitz, see Shahram Chubin, 'La Conduite des Opérations Militaires', *Politique Etrangère*, 2 (1987), pp. 303–17.
2 Sun Tzu, *The Art of War* (tr. Samuel Griffiths) (New York: Oxford University Press, 1963). See p. vi in Liddell Hart's introduction, and pp. 72–6.

Chapter 2 Iraq and the Origins of the Iran–Iraq War

1 H. Batatu, *The Old Social Classes and the Revolutionary Movements of Iraq* (Princeton: Princeton University Press, 1978), pp. 1073–93.
2 A. Baram, 'Culture in the service of Wataniyya: the treatment of Mesopotamian-inspired art in Ba'thi Iraq', *Asian and African Studies*, 17 (1983), pp. 265–9.
3 See Saddam Hussein's comments of 8 September 1982, quoted in C.M. Helms, *Iraq: Eastern Flank of the Arab World* (Washington, D.C.: Brookings Institution, 1984), p. 114.
4 BBC Summary of World Broadcasts, Middle East, 2 July 1980 (A/7–9); see also A. Baram, 'The June 1980 Elections to the National Assembly in Iraq: an experiment in controlled democracy', *Orient*, (September 1981), pp. 391–412.
5 BBC/SWB/ME, 19 July 1979 (A/2–3); BBC/SWB/ME 15 April 1980 (A/1–4).
6 A. Abbas, 'The Iraqi Armed Forces, past and present', in CARDRI, *Saddam's Iraq – Revolution or Reaction?* (London: Zed Books, 1986), pp. 216–18.
7 J.S. Wagner, 'Iraq', in R.A. Gabriel (ed.), *Fighting Armies: Antagonists in the Middle East* (Westport, Conn.: Greenwood Press, 1983), p. 75.
8 Ibid., p. 72; W. Seth Carus, 'Defense Planning in Iraq', in S.G. Neumann (ed.), *Defense Planning in Less-Industrialized States* (Lexington , Mass.: D.C. Heath and Co., 1984), pp. 36–8.
9 Batatu, *Old Social Classes*, pp. 1093–4; Helms, *Iraq*, pp. 42–5.
10 M. Khadduri, *Socialist Iraq: A Study in Iraqi Politics Since 1968* (Washington, D.C.: The Middle East Institute, 1978), pp. 57–61.
11 W.O. Staudenmeier, 'Commentary: Defense Planning in Iraq', in Neumann, *Defense Planning*, p. 59.
12 D. McDowall, *The Kurds* (London: Minority Rights Group Report 23, 1985), pp. 22–3.
13 Saddam Hussein's speech to the National Assembly, 17 September 1980, abrogating the 1975 agreement, BBC/SWB/ME, 19 September 1980 (A/1–7).

14 BBC/SWB/ME, 30 December 1980 (A/5); see also General Adnan Khayrallah's press
   conference in BBC/SWB/ME, 27 September 1980 (A/6–8).
15 BBC/SWB/ME, 24 July 1980 (A/16).
16 See Saddam Hussein's speech at Nineveh on 15 April 1980, BBC/SWB/ME, 18 April
   1980 (A/1–4); also the speech of Adnan Khayrallah on 8 January 1979, BBC/SWB/ME,
   10 January 1979 (A/1).
17 BBC/SWB/ME, 8 February 1979 (A/5).
18 C. Mallat, 'Aux origines de la guerre Iran–Irak: l'axe Najaf-Téhéran', *Les Cahiers de
   l'Orient* (1986/3), pp. 126–34.
19 *Al-Ahram*, 5 August 1979.
20 BBC/SWB/ME, 19 January 1979 (A/8), 27 June 1979 (A/2–3), 18 June 1980 (A/1);
   Al-Thawra, 12 June 1979, 13 June 1979, 11 October 1979.
21 See Ayatollah Montazeri's sermon of 19 October 1979, BBC/SWB/ME, 22 October
   1979 (A/1).
22 BBC/SWB/ME, 4 April 1980 (A/3–4), 11 April 1980 (A/1–3); *International Herald
   Tribune*, 7 April 1980; *The Guardian*, 9 April 1980.
23 *Al-Thawra*, 14 June 1979; BBC/SWB/ME, 4 October 1979 (A/1–2), 12 February
   1980 (A/1–4), 28 February 1980 (A/8), 18 April 1980 (A/1–4).
24 It has been suggested that this view was considerably reinforced by the senior Iranian
   military and political exiles who visited Iraq during 1980, *Foreign Report*, 24 September
   1980.
25 BBC/SWB/ME, 24 July 1980 (A/12).
26 Ibid. and BBC/SWB/ME, 6 September 1980 (A/1–2).
27 BBC/SWB/ME, 12 September 1980 (A/7), 17 September 1980 (A/1–2).
28 BBC/SWB/ME, 19 September 1980 (A/4–5).
29 As the Minister of Foreign Affairs, Sa'dun Hammadi, stated in October 1981: 'Iran
   used its military to annex half of the Shatt al-Arab and to occupy some strategic areas
   along the land border ... The heart of the problem is how to maintain a balance
   between the two sides of the Arabian Gulf, how to end the longstanding tendency of
   the bigger and stronger side to try to dominate the other side'. Quoted in A.C. Turner,
   'Nationalism and Religion: Iran and Iraq at War', in J. Brown and W. Snyder (eds), *The
   Regionalization of Warfare* (New Brunswick: Transaction Books, 1985), p. 152.
30 BBC/SWB/ME, 27 September 1980 (A/4–6).
31 BBC/SWB/ME, 27 September 1980 (A/8).
32 BBC/SWB/ME, 24 July 1980 (A/12).

Chapter 3 Iran and the Politics of the War

1 See Geoffrey Blainey, *The Causes of War* (New York: The Free Press, 1972). The
   correlation between revolutions and wars is striking on pp. 70–1, 72 *et passim*.
2 Raymond Aron, *Clausewitz: Philosopher of War* (London: Routledge and Kegan Paul,
   1983), pp. 232.
3 Ibid., pp. 381, 386.
4 Jonathan R. Adelman, *Revolution, Armies and War: A Political History* (Boulder, Col.:
   Lynne Rienner, 1985), pp. 5, 204. For a discussion of how social and political factors
   influence military affairs, see John Ellis, *Armies in Revolution* (London: Oxford
   University Press, 1974).

5   See Dankwart Rustow, 'Political Ends and Military Means in the Late Ottoman and Post-Ottoman Middle East', in V.J. Parry and M.E. Yapp (eds), *War, Technology and Society in the Middle East* (London: Oxford University Press, 1975), pp. 386–99. (See also Yapp's 'Introduction', p. 26.)

6   See M.E. Yapp, 'The Modernization of Middle Eastern Armies: A Comparative View', in Parry and Yapp, *War, Technology and Society*, p. 351.

7   *The Economist*'s article 'Getting Rusty' was illustrative of the view of Iran's state of military preparedness, *The Economist*, 18 August 1979, pp. 52–3.

8   William F. Hickman, 'Ravaged and Reborn: The Iranian Army 1982' (Washington, D.C.: Brookings Institution, 1983) (Staff Paper), pp. 17–18.

9   *A Review of the Imposed War* (Tehran: Ministry of Foreign Affairs (Legal Department), February 1983), pp. 79–84, 122.

10 Bani Sadr (1 Ashura speech), 19 November 1980, in Foreign Broadcast Information Service VIII, I–4, 20 November 1980.

11 President Ali Khamenei, Chairman, Supreme Defence Council, Tehran: Home Service, 25 July 1985, BBC/SWB/ME, 27 July 1985 (A/1-2).

12 Gary Sick, *All Fall Down: America's Encounter with Iran*, (New York: Random House, 1985), p. 245.

13 *A Review of the Imposed War*, p. 84. For a general discussion, see Masih Muhajeri, *Islamic Revolution: Future Path of Nations* (Tehran: Jihad-e Sazandegi (2nd ed.), 1983).

14 Prime Minister Rajai subsequently explained the cause of the war as Iraq's fear of the Islamic republic and the threat it posed to the existing regime in Baghdad. The war was designed, in his view, to suppress the revolutionary system before the threat was realized. Tehran: Home Service, 9 October 1980, in FBIS VIII, I 4–5, 18 October 1980.

15 *Kayhan*, 30 Farvardin 1359 (19 April 1980).

16 Bani Sadr, *L'Espérance Trahie* (Paris: Papyrus Editions, 1982) quoted in Shaul Bakhash, *The Reign of the Ayatollahs* (New York: Basic Books, 1984) pp. 118–19. (This is the best book on post-revolutionary Iran.) Updated edition, London: Unwin Paperbacks, 1986.

17 *New York Times*, 5 January 1980 ('Maktabi' roughly translates as 'religiously committed').

18 Tehran: Home Service, 2 September, in *FBIS* VIII, I 3–4, 3 September 1980.

19 Interview with Bani Sadr, Tehran: Home Service, 6 September, in *FBIS* VIII, I 6–10, 8 September 1980.

20 See Parry and Yapp, *War, Technology and Society*, pp. 29, 437.

21 Bani Sadr, *Le Monde*, 18 November 1979.

22 See Sick, *All Fall Down*, pp. 311–15, and Alton Fyre, *International Herald Tribune*, 21 November 1986.

23 Speech at Shiraz air base, May 1981, quoted in Sepehr Zabih, *Iran since the Revolution*, (London: Croom Helm, 1982) p. 131.

24 As he put it in an open letter to Khomeini in October 1980, text in *International Herald Tribune*, 19 January 1981; *Iran Times*, 12 December 1980.

25 *Financial Times*, 17 March 1981.

26 Hashemi Rafsanjani, 20 October, in *FBIS* VIII, I 4, 27 October 1980, *Le Monde*, 24 October 1980.

27 Mansour Farhang, an adviser to Bani Sadr, in *Christian Science Monitor*, 16 December 1980.

28 Khomeini's Address to the Nation, Tehran: Home Service, 30 September 1980, in BBC/SWB/ME, 2 October 1980 (A/3–6).

29   Khomeini, Home Service, 20 October 1980, in *FBIS* VIII, I–1, 21 October 1980.

30   Khomeini's Id al-Fitr speech, Tehran: Home Service, 1 July 1984, in *FBIS* VIII, I–1, 2 July 1984.

31   See Khomeini's Id al-Fitr Speech, Tehran: Home Service, 20 June 1985, in BBC/SWB/ME, 22 June 1985 (A/3–4).

32   Address to Friday Imams, Tehran: Home Service, 14 December 1983, in *FBIS* VIII, I–2, 15 December 1983; and Tehran: Home Service, 31 December 1984, in *FBIS* VIII, I–1, 2 January 1985.

33   Hossein Musavi, Address to Conference of Iraqi Islamic Cadres, Tehran: Home Service, 24 November 1984, *FBIS* VIII, I–5, 26 November 1984; Tehran: Home Service, 5 June 1985, in BBC/SWB/ME, 7 June 1985 (A/1).

34   Sun Tsu, *The Art of War*, pp. 64 *et passim*.

35   Khomeini, Tehran: Home Service, 30 September 1980, in BBC/SWB/ME, 2 October 1980 (A/3–6).

36   Khomeini, Id al-Fitr speech, 20 June 1985, in BBC/SWB/ME, 22 June 1985 (A/3–4).

37   Tehran: Home Service, 20 June 1985, in BBC/SWB/ME, 22 June 1985 (A/3–4); Tehran: Home Service, 9 October 1980, in FBIS VIII, 1–6, 10 October 1980; Tehran: Home Service, 20 October 1980, in *FBIS* VIII, I 4–5, 21 October 1980.

38   Tehran: Home Service, 9 March 1982, in *FBIS* VIII, I–1, 10 March 1982.

39   Khomeini, 14 August 1987 in *FBIS* V. S–34, 17 August 1987.

40   Khomeini's address on the Prophet's birthday, Tehran: Home Service, 10 November 1987, in BBC/SWB/ME, 12 November 1987 (A/14–16).

41   Ayatollah Montazeri, Tehran: Home Service, 26 June 1986, in BBC/SWB/ME, 27 June 1986 (A/2).

42   Tehran: Home Service, 8 October 1980, in *FBIS* VIII, I 8–10, 10 October 1980.

43   Rafsanjani Press Conference, 13 October 1980, in *FBIS* VIII, I 25–26, 14 October 1980.

44   Interview with Eric Rouleau, *Le Monde*, 1 January 1981.

45   Musavi to the Revolutionary Guards, Tehran: Home Service, 7 January 1985, in *FBIS* VIII, I–4, 8 January 1985.

46   Tehran: Home Service, 6 February 1985, in *FBIS* VIII, II–7, 7 February 1985.

47   Interview in magazine *Sorush*, Islamic Republic News Agency (IRNA), 27 November 1982, in BBC/SWB/ME, 30 November 1982 (A/9), with Colonel B. Suleimaz, Deputy Commander of the 21st Division: 'We are going to write our own (military) manuals, with absolutely new tactics that the American, British and French can study at their staff colleges', *New York Times*, 8 April 1982.

48   President Khamenei, Tehran, in English Service, 31 May 1984, in *FBIS* VIII, I–I, 31 May 1984; Tehran: Home Service, 12 July 1986, in BBC/SWB/ME, 15 July 1986 (A/2–3). For similar comments by Khomeini after Majnoon, see Tehran: Domestic Service, 4 March 1984, in *FBIS* VIII, I–2, 5 March 1984.

49   Tehran: Home Service, 31 May 1986, in BBC/SWB/ME, 3 June 1986 (A/2).

50   Morteza Reza'i: Tehran: International Service, 13 December 1980, *FBIS* VIII, I 16–17, 15 December 1980.

51   Mohsen Rafiqdust, Interview, *L'Express*, 24 October 1986, p. 9.

52   Ellis, *Armies in Revolution*, p. 250.

53   Interview of Mostafa Chamran, *Kayhan*, in Persian, 30 November, in *FBIS* VIII, I 3–4, 11 December 1980.

54   Khomeini on IRGC day, Tehran: Home Service, 22 May 1982, in *FBIS* VIII, I 2–3, 28 May 1982; President Khamenei, Tehran: Home Service, 29 November 1984, in *FBIS* VIII, I 1–2, 30 November 1984.

55 Rafsanjani, 26 November 1985, in BBC/SWB/ME, 29 November 1985 (A/9); Musavi, Tehran, 1 April 1986, in BBC/SWB/ME, 3 April 1986 (A/1–2).

56 *The Military Balance* (London: International Institute for Strategic Studies, 1980–1 and 1986–7).

57 Currently by General Zahir-Nezhad and Colonel Shirazi, neither of whom appears to hold any command position any longer.

58 Tehran: Home Service, 17 September 1985, in BBC/SWB/ME, 18 September 1985(i). For the cabinet review, see BBC/SWB/ME, 20 September 1985 (A/11).

59 Tehran: Home Service, 23 March 1986, in BBC/SWB/ME, 25 March 1986 (A/3).

60 For Khomeini's weak attempt at reassurance, see Tehran: Home Service, 23 December 1985, in BBC/SWB/ME, 30 December 1985 (A/2–3). For Montazeri's comments, see *Tehran Times*, 21 December 1983, in *FBIS* VIII, I 6–7, 9 February 1984.

61 IRNA in English, 19 September 1985, in BBC/SWB/ME, 23 September 1985 (A/10).

62 See Shahram Chubin, *The Iran–Iraq War: Expectations, Conduct, Implications*, (Washington, D.C.: Department of Defense [Net Assessment] 1986) and Hickman, 'Ravaged and Reborn'. Ephraim Karsh, 'The Iran–Iraq War: A Military Analysis', Adelphi Paper No. 220 (London: International Institute for Strategic Studies, 1987).

63 Khomeini on Martyrs Day, 7 February 1985, in *FBIS* VIII, I–I, 8 February 1985.

64 This phrase was attributed to an Iranian official who referred to Iran's lack of interest in reclaiming its child prisoners of war. It is quoted in Flora Lewis, *International Herald Tribune*, 27 April 1984.

65 See especially the report of the letter from Colonel Sayyid Shirazi to Colonel Salimi, Minister of Defence, in July, Hazhir Teimouran, *The Times*, 25 September 1984. See also Jean Gueyras' report in *Le Monde*, 5–6 August 1984; and the reports of Amir Taheri in *The Sunday Times*, 1 April, 29 April, and 10 June 1984; and *International Herald Tribune*, 11 April 1984. See also *Le Matin*, 6 June 1984; David Ottoway, *International Herald Tribune*, 23–24 June 1984; Richard Halloran, *International Herald Tribune*, 5 July 1984.

66 Rafsanjani to IRGC Commanders, Tehran: Home Service, 30 November 1984, in *FBIS* VIII, I/2–3, 30 November 1984.

67 See the report by Elaine Sciolino, *International Herald Tribune*, 6 July 1987.

68 War Support Supreme Council, Tehran: Home Service, 12 and 13 November 1987, in BBC/SWB/ME, 16 November 1987 (A/3–5).

69 Rafsanjani, Tehran: Home Service, 13 November 1987 in BBC/SWB/ME, 17 November 1987 (A/1–5). See also President Khamenei's comments on the need for adequate forces at the front for 'continuous operations . . . to bring the issue to a just conclusion'. Friday Sermon, 20 November 1987, in BBC/SWB/ME, 23 November 1987 (A/1).

70 Morteza Reza'i, Tehran: Home Service, 22 September 1987, in *FBIS*/NES–87–186. pp. 47–50, 25 September 1987.

71 Khomeini, Persian Home Service, 30 September 1980, in BBC/SWB/ME, 2 October 1980 (A/3–4); Khomeini, IRGC Day, Tehran: Home Service, 27 May 1982, in *FBIS* VIII, I–2, 28 May 1982; Rafsanjani, Tehran: Home Service, 15 March 1983, in BBC/SWB/ME, 17 March 1983 (A/1).

72 Rafsanjani, Tehran: Home Serice, 6 February 1983, in *FBIS* VII, I–1, 7 February 1983; and Rafsanjani to Military Officers, 24 November 1984, in *FBIS* VIII, I–2, 27 November 1984.

73 Rafsanjani in an interview with *Jeune Afrique*, 23 September 1987, pp. 11–17.
74 Mohsen Rafiqdust, Interview with *Asahi Shimbun*, *FBIS* VIII, South Asia Annex, 21 November 1984.

Chapter 4   Iraqi Politics and War Strategies

1   A.H. Cordesman, 'Lessons of the Iran–Iraq War: The First Round', *Armed Forces Journal International* (April 1982) pp. 32–47. *International Herald Tribune*, 3 October 1980; *The Observer*, 5 October 1980.
2   A. Ayalon, 'The Iraqi–Iranian War', in C. Legum, H. Shaked and D. Dishon (eds), *Middle East Contemporary Survey IV 1979–80* (London: Holmes and Meier, 1980) pp. 18–22.
3   BBC/SWB/ME, 20 October 1980 (A/6–8); *Foreign Report*, 12 November 1980.
4   *Al-Anba'*, 14 October 1980.
5   *Keesings Contemporary Archives XXVII* (1981), p. 3015.
6   *Al-Thawra*, 22 October 1980; *Al-Jumhuriyya*, 4 January 1981.
7   BBC/SWB/ME, 17 March 1981 (A/9–10).
8   BBC/SWB/ME, 23 January 1981 (A/8–9); *Al-Thawra*, 22 October 1980.
9   BBC/SWB/ME, 6 November 1980 (A/5–10).
10 See Saddam Hussein's news conference of 20 July 1980 in BBC/SWB/ME, 24 July 1980 (A/12).
11 BBC/SWB/ME, 16 December 1980 (A/1–3) and 23 January 1981 (A/8–9).
12 BBC/SWB/ME, 6 November 1980 (A/5–10).
13 BBC/SWB/ME, 17 February 1981 (A/10–11).
14 BBC/SWB/ME, 22 June 1982 (A/1–11).
15 *Al-Watan al-Arabi*, 6 November 1981; *Middle East Reporter*, 28 February 1985.
16 BBC/SWB/ME, 14 April 1982 (A/1–3); Saddam Hussein, *Fourth Message to the Iranian People* (Baghdad, Dar al-Ma'mum, 1985), p. 13.
17 BBC/SWB/ME, 7 September 1987 (A/3–4).
18 BBC/SWB/ME, 2 June 1982 (A/7), and see the statement issued by the RCC in Saddam Hussein's absence BBC/SWB/ME, 11 June 1982 (A/19–20).
19 *Al-Siyasa*, 2 August 1985.
20 *The Guardian*, 13 September 1986.
21 *International Herald Tribune*, 17 November 1982.
22 See Saddam Hussein's interview of 6 February 1983 in Saddam Hussein, *Two Letters to the Iranian People* (Baghdad, Dar al-Ma'mun, 1983), pp. 98–103. See also the comments by an Iraqi Major-General of Engineers about the 'quiet war' Iraq had been waging for some time against Iran, BBC/SWB/ME, 13 September 1982 (A/4); and M. Heller, D. Tamari, Z. Eytan, *The Middle East Military Balance 1984* (Tel-Aviv, ICSS, Tel-Aviv University, 1984), pp. 239–40.
23 BBC/SWB/ME, 1 September 1982 (A/2).
24 *Al-Watan*, 4 November 1982.
25 *The Daily Telegraph*, 8 March 1984; *The Sunday Times*, 13 January 1985; *Al-Watan al-Arabi*, 8 February 1985. See also W.O. Staudenmeier, 'Iran–Iraq (1980–)', in R.E. Harkavy and S.G. Neumann (eds), *The Lessons of Recent Wars in the Third World*, Vol. I (Lexington, Mass.: D.C. Heath and Co., 1985), p. 225.
26 BBC/SWB/ME, 1 February 1983 (A/3–6).
27 BBC/SWB/ME, 14 April 1983 (A/7–8).

28   *International Herald Tribune*, 6 March and 12 March 1984, 23–24 March and 27 March 1985; *Middle East Reporter*, 15 March and 22 March 1986.

29   Saddam Hussein's statement in *Press Release*, (London: Embassy of Iraq, 16 September 1986); see also Tariq Aziz's comment, FBIS/MEA, 25 November 1986 (E1–4).

30   *The Daily Telegraph*, 21 March 1985; *International Herald Tribune*, 13 June 1985.

31   Saddam Hussein, *Two Letters*, pp. 53–4.

32   Ibid., pp. 16–17.

33   *Al-Thawra*, 4 September 1983.

34   *Al-Jumhuriyya*, 8 November 1983; *International Herald Tribune*, 25–26 October 1986.

35   *Al-Jumhuriyya*, 26 March 1985; *The Daily Telegraph*, 21 March 1985; FBIS/MEA, 6 January 1986 (E 3–4).

36   *International Herald Tribune*, 15 July 1982; *The Daily Telegraph*, 11 October 1983.

37   *The Guardian*, 2 April 1985.

38   *The Sunday Times*, 11 January 1987.

39   *The Daily Telegraph*, 14 January 1987; *The Times*, 26 January 1987 and 3 February 1987; *The Guardian*, 13 February 1987; BBC/SWB/ME, 14 January 1982(i).

40   *The Observer*, 1 February 1987.

41   See Saddam Hussein's 'Letter to the Iranian People' of 21 January 1987, in BBC/SWB/ME, 23 January 1987 (A/1–2).

42   BBC/SWB/ME, 20 February 1987 (A/2–3). *The Times*, 19 February 1987.

43   *Khaleej Times*, 18 August 1985; *The Guardian*, 2 April 1985.

44   *The Economist*, 23 August 1986; *Jane's Defence Weekly*, 16 August 1986; *The Financial Times*, 26 November 1986.

45   *International Herald Tribune*, 1 August and 25–26 October 1986.

46   *Al-Qadisiyya*, 21 April 1986.

47   *The Guardian*, 19 March 1985.

48   Saddam Hussein, *Two Letters*, pp. 20, 101–3.

49   *The Washington Post*, 4 March 1986.

50   *Al-Anba'*, 24 May 1986.

51   *Middle East Reporter*, 7 May 1986; FBIS/MEA/DR, 13 May 1986 (E 1–2).

52   See Saddam Hussein's revealing remark that 'Our victory over the Iranian enemy will be achieved soon, and they will suffer a decisive defeat' on accepting delivery of five Super-Etendards, plus Exocets, from France. *The Daily Telegraph*, 11 October 1983.

53   *The Sunday Times*, 17 August 1986.

54   *International Herald Tribune*, 23 February 1987.

55   BBC/SWB/ME, 25 September 1987 (A/11).

56   BBC/SWB/ME, 24 April 1987 (A/12–13).

57   *The Financial Times*, 20 August 1987; BBC/SWB/ME, 11 August 1987(i) and 20 August 1987(i). For further discussion of this issue see Chapter 10 below.

58   BBC/SWB/ME, 8 September 1987 (A/6–7).

59   BBC/SWB/ME, 31 August 1987 (A/11–13).

60   *The Guardian*, 14 October, 31 October, 9 November and 3 December 1987.

61   *Al-Siyasa*, 2 August 1985.

62   *International Herald Tribune*, 13 June 1985.

Chapter 5   Iran: War and Society

 1   See Robert Suro's report, *New York Times*, 25 January 1987.

 2   J.F.C. Fuller, *The Conduct of War 1789–1961*, (London: Methuen, 1972) pp. 208–9 (see also pp. 26–37).

3   Adelman, *Revolution, Armies and War*, pp. 7–9.

4   As Robert Fisk, a sensitive reporter on the region and occasional visitor to Iran, acutely phrased it, *The Times*, 10 June 1985.

5   Islamic Republic News Agency in English, 22 August 1986, in BBC/SWB/ME, 25 August 1986 (A/4).

6   *The Economist*, 11 October 1986, pp. 43–4.

7   See Robert Fisk, *The Times*, 14 April 1982 and *The Times* (editorial), 1 October 1980.

8   On the war's impact on domestic politics consult *inter alia*: Eric Rouleau, *Le Monde*, 7 January, 22–23 July 1981; *The Economist*, 19 September 1981, p. 63; *The Times*, 22 January 1982; *The Financial Times*, 21 May, 23 November 1982; R.W. Apple, *International Herald Tribune*, 22 November 1982; R. Dowden, *The Times*, 22 February and 17 December 1983.

9   See especially Eric Hooglund, 'The Gulf War and the Islamic Republic', *MERIP Reports*, July/September 1984, and Tony Allaway, *The Times*, 16 June 1981.

10 See Shaul Bakhash's informed and perceptive comments, *The Times*, 14 February 1985.

11 See the 'Letter from Iran' written by a special correspondent, an Iranian woman, *The Times*, 22 January 1982.

12 See Khomeini's comments, Tehran: Home Service, 26 August 1984, in *FBIS* VIII, I 1–2, 27 August 1984; see also Khomeini's comments, 2 August 1983, Montazeri's comments on the 'real owner of the revolution', Tehran: Home Service, 20 November 1984, *FBIS* VIII, I–4, 21 November 1984; and especially Khomeini, Tehran: Home Service, 11 February 1985, in *FBIS* VIII, I 1–2, 12 February 1985.

13 Tehran: Home Service, 9 November 1986, in BBC/SWB/ME, 11 November 1986 (A/2). Compare with statements made in 1980 quoted above.

14 For a discussion, see Bakhash, *The Reign of the Ayatollahs*, p. 232 *et passim*.

15 For reports that it is not a political issue domestically, see Claude van England in *Christian Science Monitor*, 13 April 1984; *The Economist*, 28 April 1984, pp. 15–16 and 25 August 1984, pp. 35–6. However, already by Spring 1984 there were *some* signs of clerical dissatisfaction with the war, see *The Economist*, 9 June 1984, p. 44.

16 See *International Herald Tribune*, 30 August 1984, and citations in section below.

17 For these themes, see IRNA in English, 29 August 1986 in BBC/SWB/ME, 2 September 1986 (A/3–4). See also *Le Monde*, 3 December 1985.

18 See Rafsanjani's comments, Tehran: Home Service, 10 June 1986, BBC/SWB/ME, 12 June 1986 (A/5).

19 Rafsanjani Press Conference, Tehran: Home Service, 8 February 1985, in *FBIS* VIII, I 2–3, 8 February 1985.

20 See D.J. Allan, *The Daily Telegraph*, 19 June 1985; A. Frachon, *Le Monde*, 25 February 1987.

21 Prime Minister Musavi, 5 December 1985, BBC/SWB/ME, 7 December 1985 (A/3), Tehran: Home Service, BBC/SWB/ME, 3 April 1986 (A/1–2).

22 Prime Minister Musavi, Tehran: Home Service, 11 October 1987, BBC/SWB/ME, 13 October 1987 (A/1–2).

23 These are my own observations on the effects of the war on several middle-class Iranians who might have been expected to react differently to the stringencies of war. Personal interviews, 1980–87.

24 For a report on Iran's relative openness, see *The Economist*, 13 April 1985. For a discussion of the Friday sermon, see Robert Fisk, *The Times*, 31 January 1987. An example of the skills involved are seen in the issue of US arms supplies to Iran in November 1986. (Rafsanjani's first description of it was seen to stand up to

examination in detail, while the White House's statements went through various versions, ultimately, after attempted cover-ups, coming out very close to that of Rafsanjani.)

25   For example, see Jean Gueyras, *Le Monde*, 17 May 1985.

26   See the excellent article of A. Frachon, *Le Monde*, 25 February 1987.

27   Quoted by Robert Suro, *The New York Times*, 25 January 1987.

28   Quoted by Edward Cody, *International Herald Tribune*, 26 August 1987.

29   Rafsanjani interview with *Ettelaat* 23 July. Paris, Agence France Press, 7 August 1987, in *FBIS* V, 7 August 1987, S–4. See also *The Independent*, 8 August 1987; *The Times*, 13 August 1987.

30   Interview, *Tehran Times* in Persian, 30 August 1987, p. 19 in *FBIS*, V, 87–174, 9 September 1987.

31   See Richard Dowden, 'In the Terror of Tehran', *New York Review of Books*, 2 February 1984, pp. 8–12.

32   See Appendix 4 for details of the Iranian armed forces.

33   See *The Times* (editorial), 1 July 1982. See also Cheryl Benard and Zalmay Khalilzad, *The Government of God: Iran's Islamic Republic*, (New York: Columbia University Press, 1984).

34   See *The Economist*, 11 February 1984, and the summary of the UN report by Galina Pohl, *Journal de Genève*, 12 February 1987.

35   See BBC/SWB/ME, 16 October 1985 (A/9), and 20 December 1985 (A/2).

36   See Dilip Hiro, *The Guardian Weekly*, 16 March 1986. For a sympathetic treatment of the Islamic republic, see the same author's *Iran Under the Ayatollahs*, (London: Routledge and Kegan Paul, 1985).

37   *The Guardian Weekly*, 16 March 1986.

38   *International Herald Tribune*, 28 April 1986, and BBC/SWB/ME, 6 June 1986(i).

39   Viz: Rafsanjani's comment after the recapture of Mehran in June that this 'proved the falsity of the views of those who believed that there could be no military solution to the war'. IRNA in English, 16 July, BBC/SWB/ME, 17 July 1986 (A/9). See also *Le Monde* (editorial), 5 August 1986.

40   BBC/SWB/ME, 3 June 1986 (A/2–3).

41   The Council consisted of the Speaker of the Majles, the Prime Minister, the President, the Guards Corps Commander, the Head of the Basij, the Chairman of Joint Staff, the Head of the Islamic Property Organization and the Chairman of the Supreme Judicial Council. See BBC/SWB/ME, 24 June 1986 (A/5–6).

42   See Rafsanjani, Tehran: Home Service, 13 November 1987, in BBC/SWB/ME, 17 November 1987 (A/1–5); and Khamenei, Home Service, 16 November 1987, in BBC/SWB/ME, 18 November 1987 (A/1–3).

43   See Khamenei's comments. Tehran: Home Service, 11 January 1988, in BBC/SWB/ME, 13 January 1988 (A/4).

44   See Tehran: Home Service, 1 July 1987, in BBC/SWB/ME, 3 July 1987 (A/4); and Tehran: Home Service, 6 July 1987, in BBC/SWB/ME, 8 July 1987 (A/8).

45   Tehran: Home Service, 9 December 1987, in BBC/SWB/ME, 11 December 1987 (A/1). Volunteers are required to spend five periods of three months duration at the front, less than those conscripted.

46   Tehran: Home Service, 5 January 1988, in BBC/SWB/ME, 6 January 1988 (A/6); see also *Le Monde* 17–18 January 1988.

47   Reza'i, summarizing the year's political and military gains, Tehran: Home Service, 27 November 1987, in BBC/SWB/ME, 2 December 1987 (A/2–6).

48   Reza'i speech 31 May 1986, Tehran: Home Service, BBC/SWB/ME, 3 June 1986
     (A/2). John Cushman Jr. reported from Tehran that the Pasdaran were in charge of the
     general strategy of total mobilization of the economy behind the war effort. *International
     Herald Tribune*, 31 August 1987.

49   See the Report of the UN Commission on Human Rights, *Tribune de Genève*, 12
     February 1987.

50   See Khomeini's Message, Tehran: Home Service, 11 February 1985, in *FBIS* VIII, I
     1–2, 12 February 1985, and *Le Monde*, 13 February 1985; Tehran: Home Service, 10
     December 1985, in BBC/SWB/ME, 12 December 1985 (A/1).

51   Robert Fisk, *The Times*, 14 April 1982. See also Fisk's article 'Nation with a Death
     Wish', *The Times*, 7 March 1986.

52   For a report on the dramatization of Iranian offensives in mock-battles and military
     movements as 'street theatre', see *The Times*, 28 October 1985.

53   *The Times*, 7 March 1986.

54   *The Times*, 7 March 1986. At the start of the war, an Iranian pilot released from jail in
     Tehran said: 'I am fighting for Iran not Khomeini', *International Herald Tribune*, 10
     October 1980. The regular military can be said to share this sentiment.

55   Khomeini on the anniversary of the birth of Imam 'Ali, Tehran: Home Service, 24
     March 1986, in BBC/SWB/ME, 26 March 1986 (A/5–7).

56   See, *inter alia*, *Le Monde*, 13 March and 2 May 1985; *The Observer*, 24 March 1985; *The
     Guardian*, 7 May 1985; Amir Taheri, *International Herald Tribune*, 3 June 1985; *The
     Economist*, 4 May, pp. 42, 45 and 22 June 1985; Claude Van England, *Christian Science
     Monitor*, 11 June 1985; *The Sunday Times*, 16 June 1985.

57   I have made an attempt to analyse this decision in Shahram Chubin, 'Reflections on the
     Gulf War', *Survival*, July/August 1986, pp. 306–21. The regime was shaken not only
     by the criticisms but by riots in southern Tehran, an area of the 'oppressed'. It
     mobilized counter-demonstrations and sought to improve air defences.

58   See Jean Gueyras, *Le Monde*, 8–9 February 1987.

59   For similar comments, see Bani Sadr, who called the war 'a political necessity' for the
     regime, *International Herald Tribune*, 4 September 1982; and Ali Reza Nobari, on the
     same lines, *International Herald Tribune*, 29 December 1981.

60   These figures come from the latest census published in the autumn of 1986. See
     BBC/SWB/ME, 11 November 1986 (A/4). See Shahram Chubin, 'The Blast of War',
     International Herald Tribune, 6–7 December 1986.

Chapter 6   The Impact of the War on Iraqi Politics

1   O. Bengio, 'Saddam Hussein's Quest for Power and Survival', *Asian and African Studies*
    15 (1981), pp. 326–8; A. Baram, 'Saddam Hussein: A Political Profile', *Jerusalem
    Quarterly* 17 (1980), pp. 115–25.

2   A. Baram, 'The June 1980 Elections to the National Assembly in Iraq', *Orient*,
    September 1981, pp. 391–4.

3   BBC/SWB/ME, 6 November 1980 (A/7–8); *Al-Watan al-Arabi*, 6 November 1981.
    The early use of the term 'Qadisiyya' to describe the war was an obvious attempt to
    draw on the power of the memory of the Arab Islamic armies' defeat of the Persians at
    Qadisiyya in 635 AD – a site now in modern Iraq.

4   Staudenmeier, 'Commentary: Defense Planning in Iraq', pp. 53–5. In addition to Izzat
    Ibrahim al-Duri (Deputy Chairman of the RCC), General Adnan Khayrallah Tulfah

(Minister of Defence), Taha Ramadhan (Commander of the Popular Army), Tariq Aziz (Minister of Foreign Affairs), and until 1987 Sa'dun Shakir (Minister of the Interior), it also appears to include General Abd al-Jawad Dhannoun (Chief of the General Staff), General Shanshal (Presidential Adviser on Military Affairs), Ali Hassan al-Majid (Director General of Public Security), and Latif Nussayyif al-Jasim (Minister of Information and Culture).

5   *The Washington Post*, 23 November 1982.

6   *Middle East Economic Digest*, 9 August 1986; *Le Monde*, 15 October 1986.

7   BBC/SWB/ME, 11 June 1982 (A/19–20).

8   BBC/SWB/ME, 14 June 1982 (A/23–4).

9   BBC/SWB/ME, 13 November 1982 (A/6–10).

10 BBC/SWB/ME, 29 June 1982 (A/4–5) and 30 June 1982 (A/1–2).

11 O. Bengio, 'Iraq', in C. Legum et al. (eds), *Middle East Contemporary Survey VII, 1982/1983*, (London: Holmes and Meier, 1985) pp. 562–3.

12 *Al-Watan al-Arabi*, 6 November 1981.

13 BBC/SWB/ME, 16 July 1987 (A/10–12).

14 Reportedly, when asked why he had not yet visited Egypt, Saddam Hussein replied that he was prevented from doing so 'by the domestic situation, where there are always some people plotting against me'. *Middle East Reporter*, 25 July 1985.

15 Saddam Hussein's first cousin Adnan Khayrallah Tulfah, had been Minister of Defence and Deputy Chairman of the RCC since 1979. The new measures included the appointment of Ali Hassan al-Majid (a cousin of Saddam Hussein and Director General of Public Security) to the Regional Command of the Ba'th, and of Fadil al-Barrak al-Takriti (Director of Intelligence) to reserve membership of the Regional Command. *Middle East Economic Digest*, 12 July 1986. Takrit is the town north-west of Baghdad from which Saddam Hussein and many of those around him come.

16 FBIS/MEA, 14 July 1986 (E1); *Middle East Reporter*, 12 July 1986.

17 See, for instance, the dismissal of Saddam Hussein's three half-brothers in the autumn of 1983 – Barzan Ibrahim al-Takriti (Director of Intelligence), Wathban al-Takriti (Governor of Takrit) and Sebbawi al-Takriti (Deputy Chief of Police). The reasons for their dismissal appear to lie in their implicit challenge to Saddam Hussein and in particular family rivalries, rather than in any attempted coup d'état. *Keesings Contemporary Archives XXX* (1984), p. 32689; *The Financial Times*, 9 December 1983.

18 J.S. Wagner, 'Iraq', in R.H. Gabriel (ed.), *Fighting Armies: Antagonists in the Middle East* (Westport, Conn.: Greenwood Press, 1983), p. 75; BBC/SWB/ME, 6 February 1980 (A/10).

19 IISS, *Military Balance 1987–8*, p. 100; *The Financial Times*, 9 December 1983; Bengio, 'Saddam Hussein's Quest', pp. 335–6.

20 *Middle East Reporter*, 6 September 1986.

21 Mallat, 'Aux origines de la guerre Iran–Irak', p. 130.

22 BBC/SWB/ME, 19 July 1979 (A/2–3).

23 A. Baram, 'Culture in the Service of Wataniyya: the Treatment of Mesopotamian-inspired Art in Ba'thi Iraq', *Asian and African Studies* 17 (1983), pp. 265-73, 296.

24 See Saddam Hussein's speech of 8 February 1980 in BBC/SWB/ME, 12 February 1980 (A/1–4) and his speech of 1 May 1980, in BBC/SWB/ME, 5 May 1980 (A/8–9).

25 See Saddam Hussein's interview of 6 February 1983 in Hussein, *Two Letters*, pp. 101–3. BBC/SWB/ME, 12 July 1982 (A/1) and 13 November 1982 (A/10).

26 *Al-Thawra*, 23 August 1986; BBC/SWB/ME, 2 August 1983 (A/1–2) and 9 September 1983 (A/1–2); FBIS/MEA, 10 December 1986 (E1).

27 BBC/SWB/ME, 14 July 1982 (A/1).
28 *Keesings Contemporary Archives XXXI* (1985), p. 33495.
29 BBC/SWB/ME, 31 August 1987 (A/11–13).
30 BBC/SWB/ME, 13 November 1982 (A/7–10) and 30 August 1983 (A/1–2).
31 Bengio, 'Iraq', pp. 565–6; *The Guardian*, 11 May 1984.
32 *The Independent*, 31 December 1986.
33 BBC/SWB/ME, 16 July 1987 (A/10–12).
34 FBIS/MEA, 17 March 1986 (E1).
35 *Al-Hawadith*, 28 October 1985.
36 *Foreign Report*, 12 November 1980; O. Bengio, 'Shi'is and Politics in Ba'thi Iraq', *Middle East Studies*, 21/1 (January 1985), pp. 5–6.
37 P. Martin, 'Le clergé chiite en Irak hier et aujourd'hui', *Maghreb Machrek*, 115 (1987), pp. 41–3.
38 Batatu, *The Old Social Classes*, pp. 983–5.
39 Mallat, 'Aux origines de la guerre Iran–Irak', pp. 126–34.
40 Bengio, 'Shi'is and Politics', pp. 8–11; *International Herald Tribune*, 7 April 1980; BBC/SWB/ME, 11 April 1980 (A/1–3).
41 BBC/SWB/ME, 13 November 1982 (A/8–10).
42 Bengio, 'Shi'is and Politics', p. 8. *Frankfurter Allgemeine Zeitung*, 7 August 1986.
43 *Keesings Contemporary Archives XXVIII* (1982), p. 31851.
44 *Al-Qadisiyya*, 24 July 1984.
45 *Keesings Contemporary Archives XXVIII* (1982), p. 31851 and *XXX* (1984), p. 32688; *The Guardian*, 28 June 1983; *Middle East Reporter*, 9 March 1985.
46 BBC/SWB/ME, 3 August 1982 (A/4); *The Guardian*, 14 December 1984.
47 *The Observer*, 10 May 1987.
48 BBC/SWB/ME, 14 January 1986 (A/7–8); *The Observer*, 11 January 1987.
49 Bengio, 'Iraq', pp. 577–9.
50 *Al-Anwar*, 19 May 1987. The Shu'ubiyya was a movement which arose in the first century of the Islamic Empire to challenge the Arabs' domination of that empire. It was largely based in the Persian-speaking provinces.
51 BBC/SWB/ME, 9 July 1986 (A/10); *The Guardian*, 11 January 1986.
52 *Middle East Reporter*, 19 September 1985.
53 McDowall, *The Kurds*, pp. 7–9.
54 BBC/SWB/ME, 27 February 1982 (A/1–2).
55 *The Guardian*, 30 July 1983; McDowall, *The Kurds*, p. 24.
56 *International Herald Tribune*, 28 March 1984; *The Times*, 1 March 1985.
57 Saddam Hussein admitted in 1983 that the number of Kurdish deserters was 48,000, McDowall, *The Kurds*, p. 24; BBC/SWB/ME, 14 February 1983 (A/9–10); *The Guardian*, 24 May 1984 and 14 February 1985; *Middle East Reporter*, 30 January 1986.
58 McDowall, *The Kurds*, pp. 24–5; *The Guardian*, 19 January 1984; *International Herald Tribune*, 31 July 1984.
59 *The Independent*, 21 April 1987; *The Guardian*, 2 May 1987.
60 *The Times*, 5 June and 21 August 1986; *The Financial Times*, 7 January 1986.
61 Interview with Amin Noshirwan, Secretary General of the PUK, *Le Monde*, 16 April 1987.
62 *The Financial Times*, 4 September 1987.
63 BBC/SWB/ME, 30 November 1987 (A/6).
64 BBC/SWB/ME, 23 March 1979 (A/16), 16 September 1981 (A/8) and 14 July 1982 (A/1).

65 H. Batatu, 'State Capitalism in Iraq: A Comment', *MERIP*, 142, September/October 1986, p. 11.
66 BBC/SWB/ME, 13 August 1979 (A/4), and 31 August 1979 (A/3); *Frankfurter Allgemeine Zeitung*, 7 August 1986.
67 BBC/SWB/ME, 1 January 1982 (A/1), 21 December 1982 (A/7) and 18 July 1985 (A/3–18).
68 BBC/SWB/ME, 19 June 1981 (A/5–6) and 1 January 1982 (A/1).
69 *The Financial Times*, 14 July 1981; J. Townsend, 'The Economic and Political Impact of the War', in M.S. El-Azhary (ed.), *The Iran–Iraq War*, (London: Croom Helm, 1984), pp. 58–9.
70 *Middle East Reporter*, 6 September 1986.
71 BBC/SWB/ME, 8 January 1983 (A/5–7).
72 *Middle East Reporter*, 13 September 1986; BBC/SWB/ME, 26 August 1981 (A/8–9).
73 *The Guardian*, 6 January 1984; *Middle East Reporter*, 27 May and 3 June 1986.
74 *The Financial Times*, 9 December 1983; BBC/SWB/ME, 30 August 1983 (A/1–2), 20 October 1983 (A/1) and 26 October 1983 (A/6).
75 *The Financial Times*, 9 December 1983.
76 Bengio, 'Iraq', pp. 567–8.
77 *Keesings Contemporary Archives XXXI* (1985), p. 33497; FBIS/MEA, 20 August 1986 (E2).
78 *The Financial Times*, 7 May 1985; *Middle East Economic Digest*, 10 August 1985, 19 April 1986 and 27 June 1986. It was reported that some of the Iraqi Government's apparent military successes in Kurdistan in 1986 had been due to the simple expedient of paying local Kurdish chieftains £1.5 million for the capture of each mountain. *The Financial Times*, 28 May 1986.
79 *Middle East Reporter*, 17 July 1986.
80 This calculation was made by Dr Abbas al-Nasrawi, and published in the Lebanese daily *Al-Safir. Middle East Reporter*, 13 September 1986.
81 R. Springborg, 'Infitah, Agrarian Transformation and Elite Consolidation in Contemporary Iraq', *Middle East Journal*, 40/1 (Winter 1986) pp. 44–6. Issam al-Khafaji, 'State incubation of Iraqi capitalism', *MERIP*,, 142, September/October 1986, pp. 6–7.
82 Springborg, 'Infitah', p. 37.
83 Ibid., pp. 40–2.
84 BBC/SWB/ME, 12 June 1987 (A/5) and 16 July 1987 (A/8–10).
85 FBIS/MEA, 21 January 1986 (E3); al-Khafaji, 'State incubation', p. 9; Batatu, *The Old Social Classes*, pp. 47–9.
86 Al-Khafaji, 'State incubation', p. 4.
87 FBIS/MEA, 24 June 1986 (E1).
88 *Middle East Reporter*, 3 October 1986.
89 Khadduri, *Socialist Iraq*, pp. 51–63.
90 Wagner, 'Iraq', p. 76; BBC/SWB/ME, 10 January 1979 (A/1).
91 Wagner, 'Iraq', p. 72; Abbas, 'The Iraqi Armed Forces', pp. 215–17.
92 Carus, 'Defense Planning', pp. 37–8.
93 *Foreign Report*, 12 November 1980; Saddam Hussein interview of 6 February 1983 in Hussein, *Two Letters*, pp. 98–105; BBC/SWB/ME, 7 September 1987 (A/3–4).
94 Bengio, 'Iraq', pp. 584–5; *Le Monde*, 30 July 1982; Heller et al., *The Middle East Military Balance 1983*, pp. 308–10.
95 Hussein, *Two Letters*, p. 106; BBC/SWB/ME, 27 July 1982 (A/12), 30 June 1983 (A/10), 2 July 1983 (A/1), 9 September 1983 (A/2).

96 *Middle East Reporter*, 4 April 1985; BBC/SWB/ME, 20 March 1985 (A/9).
97 BBC/SWB/ME, 12 November 1983 (A/2).
98 FBIS/MEA, 6 January 1986 (E1).
99 *Foreign Report*, 6 October 1983; *Keesings Contemporary Archives XXXI* (1985), p. 33496; *Le Monde*, 6 April 1984.
100 *The Sunday Times*, 23 February 1986; *The Guardian*, 11 January 1986.
101 FBIS/MEA, 2 April 1986 (E1–2).
102 Cordesman, 'Lessons of the Iran–Iraq War', p. 42; Wagner, 'Iraq', p. 78; *The Washington Post*, 4 March 1986.
103 *Al-Anba'*, 24 May 1986.
104 *Middle East Economic Digest*, 9 August 1986.
105 FBIS/MEA, 15 August 1986 (E2).
106 *Le Monde*, 15 October 1986; FBIS/MEA, 9 September 1986 (E1).
107 FBIS/MEA, 29 July 1986 (E1) and 1 October 1986 (E1).
108 *Al-Thawra*, 20 November 1986 quoted in FBIS/MEA, 21 November 1986 (E2–4).
109 BBC/SWB/ME, 9 September 1983 (A/1–2).
110 Such a development is hinted at in the interesting article on the role of the 'Mosul' faction within the regime, *Le Monde*, 15 October 1986.

Chapter 7   Iran: The War and the Economy

1 Prime Minister Musavi's submission of the 1367 (1988–9) budget to the Majles, Tehran: Home Service, 28 December 1987, in BBC/SWB/ME, 12 January 1988 (A1/1–6).
2 Eric Rouleau, *Le Monde*, 22 July 1981.
3 Hashemi Rafsanjani, Comments, 22 October 1982, see BBC/SWB/ME, 25 October 1982 (A/3).
4 Some like Rafsanjani spoke of only 10 per cent of Iran's resources and currency reserves being devoted to the war, see his speech of 22 October 1982 in BBC/SWB/ME, 25 October 1982 (A/3). More representative is Behzad Nabavi (Minister of Heavy Industries) who mentioned one-sixth of the budget, see BBC/SWB/ME, 25 February 1981 (A/2).
5 Hashemi Rafsanjani is a typical but not a sole example, 14 December 1984, *FBIS* VIII, I–1, 15 December 1984. See also *Tehran Times*, 30 November 1983.
6 For example Rafsanjani's comment: 'We should prepare to end the war as soon as possible with victory'. In July 1986, alluding to low oil prices, he said: 'We have decided to accelerate our policy'.
7 The figures are only recalled here as indicative, for they represent statistics by Iran's Plan Organization intended as a basis for claims for war reparations from Iraq. *Middle East Economic Digest*, 27 September 1986. An earlier figure for the period September 1980–March 1983 totalled $163.7 billion, with damages to the oil sector $54 billion, agriculture $41 billion, industry $8 billion. *Ettela'at*, 23 June 1984, in *FBIS* VIII, I–4, 27 June 1984.
8 *Kayhan Weekly* (London), 5 November 1987, p. 8.
9 Hashemi Rafsanjani, Tehran, IRNA in English, 1 February 1985, in *FBIS* VIII, I–4, 7 February 1985.
10 See International Institute for Strategic Studies, *The Military Balance*, 1980–81 through to 1987–8 issues. (London: ISSS, annual).

11   See the *New York Times* report by Elaine Sciolino in *International Herald Tribune*, 26 November 1986.

12   See Rafsanjani, *Journal de Genève*, 8–9 November 1986 and *Jomhuri-ye Eslami*, 18 July 1987.

13   See *The Financial Times, 3 July 1984* (see also *Le Monde*, 10 July 1984), and *The Financial Times* (Iran Survey), 1 April 1985.

14   See Prime Minister Hossein Musavi's comments in the Parliament (*Majles*) debate of 5 August. War costs for 1984/85 were estimated at 42 per cent of the budget, at 1,117,000 million rials as against 381,000 million rials in 1979/80. See BBC/SWB/ME, 14 August 1984. In the draft budget 1985/86, the direct allocation to the war was $4.35 billion, as against $8.54 billion for war-related costs. See Tehran IRNA in English, 27 November 1984, in *FBIS* VIII, I–1, 28 November 1984.

15   See Rafsanjani's interview, *The Observer*, 1 May 1987. He repeated the figure of $3 billion as the cost of the war in the preceding year (i.e. ending March 1987) in *Ettela'at*, 23 July in *FBIS* V, 7 August 1987, S–4. For background see Tehran: Home Service, 19 March 1985 in BBC/SWB/ME, 21 March 1985 (A/1) and *Middle East Economic Digest*, 7 December 1985.

16   They are tentative and must be treated with caution for they do not correlate well with oil revenues, and also do not include war-related expenditures.

17   Tehran: Home Service, 27 August 1987, in BBC/SWB/ME, 29 August 1987 (A/8).

18   See *The Economist*, 5 September 1987, p. 80.

19   See the discussion by the IRGC Minister Rafiqdust with others, Tehran: Home Service, 27 August 1987, in BBC/SWB/ME, 29 August 1987 (A/2–6).

20   Rafiqdust, Tehran: Home Service, 12 October 1987, in BBC/SWB/ME,14 October 1987 (A/4). Rafiqdust and Commander of the IRGC, Reza'i, on Tehran: Home Service discussion, 7/8 November 1987, in BBC/SWB/ME, 10 November 1987 (A/14–16).

21   Brigadier-General Jalali, Tehran: Home Service, 28 August 1987, in BBC/SWB/ME, 1 September 1987 (A/6), Reza'i, IRNA in English, 10 October 1987, in BBC/SWB/ME, 12 October 1987 (A/1). Prime Minister Musavi's submission of the general budget, Tehran: Home Service, 28 December 1987, in BBC/SWB/ME, 12 January 1988 (A/1–6).

22   See *Middle East Economic Digest*, 1 April 1983, p. 13 and 6 April 1984, p. 19; *The Times*, 20 December 1983.

23   *The Economist*, 8 September 1984, pp. 71–2.

24   *Middle East Economic Digest*, 18 January 1985, p. 16 (according to the Interior Minister, Nateg Nouri).

25   See *The Times*, 15 February 1985.

26   D. Saleh Ispahani, 'The Iranian Economy since the Revolution', in Shireen Hunter (ed.), *Internal Developments in Iran*, (Washington, D.C.: Georgetown CSIS, 1985) p. 47.

27   *The Times*, 3 December 1983.

28   *The Financial Times* (Iran Survey), 1 April 1985.

29   Khomeini, Tehran: Home Service, 17 October 1982, in BBC/SWB/ME, 19 October 1982 (A/3).

30   Prime Minister Musavi's speech on the Economy, 7 November 1982, in BBC/SWB/ME, 10 November 1982 (A/13–18).

31 See *International Herald Tribune*, 18 December 1983.
32 Khomeini Message, Tehran: Home Service, 11 February 1985, in *FBIS* VIII, I 1–2, 12 February 1985.
33 Khomeini, Tehran: Home Service, 30 August 1986, in BBC/SWB/ME, 2 September 1986 (A/1–2).
34 IRNA in English, 5 December 1985, in BBC/SWB/ME, 7 December 1985 (A/3).
35 Speech to Friday Imams, Tehran: Home Service, 17 June 1986, in BBC/SWB/ME, 19 June 1986 (A/2).
36 The Plan and Budget Organization allocated credit of $1.35 billion for this purpose, Radio Tehran reported citing IRNA. See *FBIS* V, 13 April 1987, p. ii.
37 For a representative sample see Commentary on Tehran radio on 'Inflation and Economic Terrorism', 28 June 1987, in BBC/SWB/ME, 1 July 1987 (A/9–11). Commentary on the Government's duty regarding inflation, Tehran: Home Service, 30 June 1987, in BBC/SWB/ME, 3 Julky 1987 (A/5–6); and Ayatollah Montazeri's criticism of 'Profiteers' and 'Hoarders', Tehran: Home Service, 9 July 1987, in BBC/SWB/ME, 11 July 1987 (A/1–2). For a general discussion from Tehran see Edward Cody, *International Herald Tribune*, 20 August 1987.
38 Musavi, 24 June 1986, in BBC/SWB/ME, 26 June 1986 (A/1–5).
39 Tehran Radio Commentary, Home Service, 8 January 1985, *FBIS* VIII, I 4, 9 January 1985.
40 *International Herald Tribune*, 1 July 1984.
41 Ahmed Nasir, *Far Eastern Economic Review*, 30 October 1986, pp. 36–7.
42 Such policies as support for the rial. See Wolfgang Leutenschlager (psd.), 'The Effects of an Over-valued Exchange Rate on the Iranian Economy 1979–84', *International Journal of Middle East Studies*, 18/1 (February 1986) pp. 36–49. For a discussion of the bazaaris in politics and the economy, see *Iran Press Digest*, 3/12, 22 May 1984, pp. 13–19.
43 Bijan Mossavar Rahmani and Fereydoun Fesharaki, 'Oil Dependence and Mega-projects', Supplement to *Middle East Economic Survey*, XXVI, No. 19, 21 February 1983.
44 On this early period, see Shaul Bakhash, 'The Politics of Oil and Revolution in Iran' (Staff Paper), (Washington, D.C.: Brookings Institution, 1982).
45 See *The Financial Times*, 3 July 1984; *Le Monde*, 10 July 1984.
46 *The Times*, 15 February 1985.
47 Report to the Majles by Prime Minister Musavi, 1 December 1985, in BBC/SWB/ME, 10 December 1985 (A/1–6). See also *Middle East Economic Digest*, 21 December 1985, p. 52.
48 Tehran: Home Service, 3 October 1985, in BBC/SWB/ME, 5 October 1985 (A/2).
49 This was announced on 22 December 1985, by Prime Minister Musavi, and by Tehran in English, 26 December 1985, in BBC/SWB/ME, 31 December 1985 (A/5–8, i).
50 *International Management*, 20 December 1985.
51 See the report carried in the *International Herald Tribune*, 28 July 1986. See also *The Economist*, 9 August 1986, p. 56, which reports that Iran's oil income in the first six months of 1986 was 60 per cent lower than in the first half of 1985.
52 See *Le Monde*, 13, 14 August 1986; *International Herald Tribune*, 3 August 1986.
53 *The Economist*, 23 August 1986, pp. 41–2.
54 Baghdad, Voice of the Arab Masses, 16 July 1986, in BBC/SWB/ME, 18 July 1986 (A/2–4).
55 Rafsanjani, Tehran in Arabic and IRNA in English, 23 April 1986, in BBC/SWB/ME, 25 April 1986 (A/8–9).

56 For press reports, see *The Financial Times*, 8 June 1986; *The Times*, 8 May, 11 June 1986; *International Herald Tribune*, 28 May, 12 August 1986; *New York Times*, 26 October 1986; *The Economist*, 11 October 1986, pp. 43–44; *The Times*, 21 November 1986; *Le Monde*, 28 November 1986.

57 See *Middle East Economic Digest*, 27 September 1986, p. 41 and *The Economist*, 18 October 1986, pp. 54–5.

58 See Bakhash, 'The Politics of Oil'.

Chapter 8   Iraq and the Region

1 O. Bengio and U. Dann, 'Iraq', in C. Legum et al. (eds), *Middle East Contemporary Survey III*, (London: Holmes and Meier, 1980) pp. 572–3.

2 *Al-Ahram*, 7 August 1979.

3 Helms, *Iraq: Eastern Flank of the Arab World*, pp. 180–2; *Al-Thawra*, 20 September 1979 and 24 September 1979.

4 BBC/SWB/ME, 31 July 1979 (A/10–11). See Saddam Hussein's address to the Republican Guards on 6 February 1979, BBC/SWB/ME, 8 February 1979 (A/5); also Saddam Hussein's 'Pan-Arab Declaration' of February 1980, BBC/SWB/ME, 12 February 1980 (A/1–4).

5 *The Times*, 9 April 1980; BBC/SWB/ME, 18 April 1980 (A/1–4) and 24 July 1980 (A/16).

6 G. Nonneman, *Iraq, the Gulf States and the War*, (London: Ithaca Press, 1986) pp. 21–3.

7 *Saddam Hussein Press Conference on 10 November 1980*, (London: Press Office of the Embassy of Iraq, n.d.).

8 In many respects, this message is aimed as much at a domestic as at a regional audience. See Saddam Hussein's address to the – largely Shi'i – inhabitants of Najaf Governorate, telling them of their common Arab identity, in the face of Persian aggression, BBC/SWB/ME, 12 July 1982 (A/1).

9 BBC/SWB/ME, 30 August 1983 (A/1–2).

10 BBC/SWB/ME, 11 November 1987 (A/4–5).

11 BBC/SWB/ME, 3 December 1987 (A/3).

12 C. Tripp, 'Iraq – Ambitions Checked', *Survival* (November/December 1986) p. 504.

13 *The Financial Times*, 28 May 1983; *The Sunday Times*, 29 May 1983; *Middle East Reporter*, 4 August 1983.

14 *The Times*, 18 October 1984, 21 August 1986 and 5 March 1987; *The Guardian*, 18 October 1984; *Keesings Contemporary Archives* XXXI (1985), pp. 33497–8.

15 BBC/SWB/ME, 16 February 1979 (A/2).

16 BBC/SWB/ME, 2 April 1979 (A/6).

17 *Saddam Hussein's Press Conference of 10 November 1980*.

18 BBC/SWB/ME, 30 September 1980 (A/13).

19 BBC/SWB/ME, 25 June 1981 (A/4–6) and 6 October 1981 (A/12).

20 BBC/SWB/ME, 10 November 1981 (A/1–2).

21 BBC/SWB/ME, 27 June 1985 (A/5) and 20 February 1986 (A/6).

22 *The Daily Telegraph*, 12 November 1982; *Jane's Defence Weekly*, 16 August 1986.

23 BBC/SWB/ME, 24 December 1985 (A/5–6).

24 BBC/SWB/ME, 5 January 1983 (A/6). Interview with Saddam Hussein of 25 August 1982.

25 *Saddam Hussein Press Conference of 10 November 1980.*

26 Quoted in Helms, *Iraq: Eastern Flank of the Arab World*, p. 114.

27 R. King, *The Iran–Iraq War: the Political Implications*, Adelphi Paper 219 (London: International Institute for Strategic Studies, 1987), p. 43.

28 *Al-Anba'*, 27 April 1983; *The Guardian*, 19 March 1985.

29 This was emphasized at every opportunity by the Iraqi authorities – especially when inducting members of the one million-strong Egyptian community living in Iraq into the ranks of the Popular Army, BBC/SWB/ME, 6 February 1982 (A/3–4), and 8 February 1982 (A/11–12).

30 *Middle East Reporter*, 27 May 1986 and 3 June 1986; BBC/SWB/ME, 16 July 1985 (A/6).

31 *The Financial Times*, 10 February 1983; *Middle East Reporter*, 10 February 1983.

32 *The Guardian*, 19 March 1985.

33 *Al-Majalis*, 13 July 1985; BBC/SWB/ME, 29 June 1985 (A/3–4).

34 BBC/SWB/ME, 18 July 1985 (A/3–4).

35 BBC/SWB/ME, 12 November 1985 (A/11).

36 BBC/SWB/ME, 12 November 1987 (A/9–11) and 13 November 1987 (A/1–3).

37 BBC/SWB/ME, 11 November 1987 (A/9).

38 D. Dishon and B. Maddy-Weitzman, 'Inter-Arab Relations', in C. Legum et al. (eds), *Middle East Contemporary Survey IV 1979–1980*, (London: Holmes and Meier, 1981) pp. 203–5.

39 See Hafez al-Assad's speech of 8 March 1982, BBC/SWB/ME, 9 March 1982 (A/9–13).

40 S. Chubin, 'Soviet Arms and the Gulf War', *International Defense Review*, June 1987; *International Herald Tribune*, 20 April 1982 and 25 May 1982.

41 See Saddam Hussein's speech to the National Assembly of 12 April 1982, BBC/SWB/ME, 14 April 1982 (A/1–3).

42 *Middle East Reporter*, 21 July 1983.

43 BBC/SWB/ME, 18 July 1985 (A/6–7).

44 BBC/SWB/ME, 12 August 1985 (A/1–5).

45 BBC/SWB/ME, 28 March 1986 (A/4).

46 BBC/SWB/ME, 31 March 1986 (A/7).

47 BBC/SWB/ME, 1 January 1987 (A/18).

48 BBC/SWB/ME, 8 January 1987 (A/2–4).

49 BBC/SWB/ME, 8 January 1983 (A/5–7) and 18 July 1985 (A/3–8).

50 BBC/SWB/ME, 11 June 1982 (A/19–20).

51 Tariq Aziz, *Iraq–Iran Conflict: Questions and Discussions*, tr. Naji al-Hadithi (London: Third World Centre for Research and Publishing, 1981) pp. 81–4.

52 BBC/SWB/ME, 3 April 1987 (A/1–4).

53 BBC/SWB/ME, 9 April 1987 (A/2–4).

54 BBC/SWB/ME, 10 August 1985 (A/3).

55 BBC/SWB/ME, 1 November 1985 (i), 26 November 1985 (i), 7 February 1986 (A/1).

56 *Al-Thawra*, 20 July 1986.

57 BBC/SWB/ME, 11 May 1987 (A/7–8) and 8 July 1987 (A/13).

58 BBC/SWB/ME, 13 May 1987 (i) and 23 May 1987 (A/3).

59 BBC/SWB/ME, 27 July 1987 (A/8–10).

60 BBC/SWB/ME, 11 November 1987 (A/5).

61 BBC/SWB/ME, 12 November 1987 (A/9–11).

62 BBC/SWB/ME, 23 November 1987 (i) and 2 December 1987 (i).

63   BBC/SWB/ME, 13 November 1987 (A/1–3).

64   *Al-Watan al-Arabi*, 17 May 1983.

65   *International Herald Tribune*, 5/6 March 1983; *Middle East Reporter*, 18 February 1983.

66   In 1982 the plane carrying the Algerian Minister of Foreign Affairs from Baghdad to Tehran on a mediation mission was shot down. Considerable mystery still surrounds this incident, but it is possible that it was an illustration of this determination.

67   BBC/SWB/ME, 28 March 1987 (A/7–8).

68   BBC/SWB/ME, 18 July 1985 (A/3–8).

69   BBC/SWB/ME, 10 September 1985 (A/3) and 28 September 1985 (i).

70   BBC/SWB/ME, 31 July 1985 (A/5–6).

71   *Al-Sharq al-Awsat*, 20 May 1985; BBC/SWB/ME, 12 July 1985 (A/1–2), 30 August 1985 (i), 5 September 1985 (A/1) and 12 December 1985 (i).

72   King, *Iran–Iraq War*, pp. 17–18, 33; *Middle East Economic Digest*, 29 March 1986 and 19 April 1986; *Gulf News*, 16 August 1985.

73   *Middle East Economic Digest*, 10 August 1985 and 19 April 1986; *Middle East Reporter*, 27 June 1986, 22 August 1986 and 23 October 1987.

74   Nonneman, *Iraq, the Gulf States and the War*, pp. 40–41, 68–9; *Al-Thawra*, 20 September 1979.

75   For example, the persistent Iraqi attempts to pressure Kuwait into leasing Bubiyan Island have slackened, as has the tone of recrimination in Saddam Hussein's comments about the contributions of the lower Gulf states. Ibid., pp. 41, 59, 69–71.

76   It was significant that the first systematic and successful Iraqi bombing of Kharg Island coincided with the Arab Summit at Casablanca, where the leaders of sixteen Arab states came out in strong support for Iraq and in vehement condemnation of Iran for spurning all peace offers. It also came just before the opening of the half a million barrel per day Iraqi oil pipeline to Yanbu on Saudi Arabia's Red Sea coast. BBC/SWB/ME, 12 August 1985 (A/1–5) and 1 October 1985 (i); *Gulf News*, 16 August 1985.

77   BBC/SWB/ME, 27 February 1986 (i).

78   *Al-Thawra*, 29 March 1987.

79   BBC/SWB/ME, 20 March 1987 (A/6–7).

80   BBC/SWB/ME, 7 March 1986 (i).

81   BBC/SWB/ME, 13 August 1987 (A/3).

82   BBC/SWB/ME, 27 August 1987 (A/3–5) and 28 August 1987 (A/2–3).

83   *International Herald Tribune*, 10 September 1987.

84   BBC/SWB/ME, 11 November 1987 (A/4–9).

Chapter 9   Iran and the Region

1   Tehran: Home Service, 6 November 1987, in BBC/SWB/ME, 9 November 1987 (A/8–9).

2   For a discussion along these lines in the Saudi case, see Françoise Chipaux, *Le Monde*, 8 January 1988. See also Robert Fisk, *The Times*, 13 August 1987.

3   Khomeini, 24 March, in BBC/SWB/ME, 27 March 1986 (A/5–7).

4   IRNA in English, 8 December, in BBC/SWB/ME, 9 December 1985 (A/1).

5   For a comparison of the foreign policy of the Shah and the Islamic Republic, see Shahram Chubin, 'The Foreign Policy of the Islamic Republic of Iran', in *Negotiations in Asia*, (Geneva: Centre for Applied International Negotiations, 1984) and 'The Islamic Republic's Foreign Policy in the Gulf', in Martin Kramer (ed.), *Shi'ism*,

Resistance and Revolution, (Boulder, Colo: Westview Press, 1987) pp. 159–72.

6 See the following figures derived from James A. Bill, 'Resurgent Islam in the Persian Gulf', *Foreign Affairs*, 1984.

Illegal immigration and inaccurate census statistics in the Gulf states bedevil all attempts to calculate exact numbers, or to assess the breakdown in ethnic, religious or sectarian terms. The numbers of migrants have steadily decreased with the recession. The table below, first published in 1984, may therefore somewhat overestimate present population levels.

'Total populations' includes immigrants (legal and illegal) plus citizens from each state.

Country	Total Population (in thousands)	Citizen Population (in thousands)	Number of Shi'a (in thousands)	Percentage of Shi'a Citizens
Qatar	255	70	11	16
Oman	950	700	28	4
UAE	1,100	250	45	18
Kuwait	1,370	570	137	24
Bahrain	360	240	168	70
Saudi Arabia	8,500	5,500	440	8
Iraq	14,400	13,500	8,100	60
Iran	42,000	40,000	36,800	92
Totals	69,935	60,830	45,729	75

See also Joseph Kostiner, 'Shi'i Unrest in the Gulf', in Kramer, *Shi'ism, Resistance and Revolution*, pp. 173–88.

7 See *The Economist*, 9 January 1982, pp. 45–6; *Le Monde*, 9 February 1982; J. Fitchett, *International Herald Tribune*, 27–28 March 1982.

8 *Journal de Genève*, 4 February 1982; *Middle East Economic Digest*, 9 April 1982, pp. 18–19 (Rafsanjani's comment was made on 26 March 1982).

9 See *Le Monde* 14, 26 May 1982; *The Financial Times*, 14, 17 May 1982.

10 Rafsanjani, 26 May, in *FBIS* VIII, I–1, 1 June 1982.

11 Khomeini, 21 June 1982, in *FBIS* VIII, I 1–3, 22 June 1982.

12 See his comments, 25 July 1982, in BBC/SWB/ME, 27 July 1982 (A/1).

13 Patrick Seale, *The Observer*, 18 July 1982.

14 See Eric Rouleau's reports, 'Who Threatens the Gulf States?', *Le Monde*, 11, 12, 13, 14 May 1982.

15 See Saudi Radio commentary by Jasim Abd al-Aziz al-Jasir, Riyadh: Home Service, 10 November 1982, in BBC/SWB/ME, 12 November 1982 (A/6).

16 Rafsanjani, Tehran in Arabic, 26 November 1982, in BBC/SWB/ME, 29 November 1982 (A/1).

17 Khomeini, Tehran: Home Service, 16 August 1983, in *FBIS* VIII, I–1, 17 August 1983.

18 Khomeini, Tehran: Home Service, 2 August 1983, in *FBIS* VIII, I–1, 3 August 1983.

19 Velayati, Tehran: Home Service, 2 August 1983, in *FBIS* VIII, I–2, 3 August 1983.

20   Colonel Sayyad Shirazi, interview in *La Repubblica* (Rome), 21 February 1984, in *FBIS* VIII, I 1–4, 24 February 1984.

21   See Rafsanjani, Tehran: Home Service, 4 March 1984, in *FBIS* VIII, I–5, 5 March 1984.

22   Rafsanjani, Home Service, 18 May 1984, in *FBIS* VIII, I 5–6, 21 May 1984.

23   See J. Fitchett, *International Herald Tribune*, 13 April 1984 and D. Lamb, 26 March 1984.

24   See *Kayhan*, 21 May 1984, in *FBIS* VIII, I–1, 21 May 1984; *Jomhuri-ye Eslami*, 22 May 1984, in *FBIS* VIII, I–4, 24 May 1984. At the same time, Prime Minister Musavi was publicly suggesting that some of the Gulf states had changed their ways.

25   Text of Foreign Ministry protest note, Tehran: Home Service, 6 June 1984, in *FBIS* VIII, I–1, 7 June 1984.

26   See reference in Commentary, Tehran Radio, 11 June 1984, in *FBIS* VIII, I 6–7, 12 June 1984.

27   *Jomhuri-ye Eslami*, 5 July 1984, in *FBIS* VIII, I 4–5, 26 July 1984.

28   Hossein Ardebili, 8 August 1984, in *FBIS* VIII (South Asian Annex), 15 August 1984.

29   Rafsanjani, Tehran: Home Service, 17 August 1984, in *FBIS* VIII, I–1, 20 August 1984.

30   President Khamenei, 26 November 1984, in *FBIS* VIII, I–1, 27 November 1984.

31   Tehran commentary on the GCC Meeting, in Arabic, 27 November 1984, in *FBIS* VIII, I 5–6, 30 November 1984.

32   See, for example, Foreign Minister Velayati's statement, Tehran: Home Service, 27 May 1985, in BBC/SWB/ME, 29 May 1985 (A/1); and Tehran in Arabic, 21 July 1985, in BBC/SWB/ME, 24 July 1985 (A/7–8).

33   Radio Commentary (Advice to the GCC Summit), Tehran in Arabic, 2 November 1984, BBC/SWB/ME, 4 November 1984 (A/3).

34   See *Middle East Economic Digest*, 29 June 1985, p. 10.

35   Rafsanjani, Tehran: Home Service, 3 October 1985, in BBC/SWB/ME, 5 October 1985 (A/2).

36   Gerald Seib and Barbara Rosewicz, *Wall Street Journal*, 9 December 1985.

37   See IRNA in English, 8 December 1985, in BBC/SWB/ME, 9 December 1985 (A/1); Riyadh, Home Service, 10 December 1985, in BBC/SWB/ME, 12 December 1985 (A/3–4).

38   Iranian commentaries regularly allude to differences among the attitudes of the Gulf states and the close ties with the UAE. See, for example, Tehran: Home Service, 10 December 1985, in BBC/SWB/ME, 11 December 1985 (A/3).

39   Tehran: Home Service, 16 November 1985, in BBC/SWB/ME, 18 November 1985 (A/5): *Jomhuri-ye Eslami*, Tehran Radio in Arabic, 10 November 1985, in BBC/SWB/ME, 12 November 1985 (A/4); Tehran Commentary, Home Service, 28 November 1985, in BBC/SWB/ME, 30 November 1985 (A/4).

40   Prime Minister Musavi to the *Tehran Times*, 10 December 1985, in BBC/SWB/ME, 11 December 1985 (i).

41   One scholar argued that this was already the case in 1983. Adeed Dawisha, 'Iran's Mullahs and the Arab Masses', *Washington Quarterly* 6/3 (Summer 1983), pp. 162–8. The argument is weakened when three years later the same author writes that there are 'growing indications' that the 'clarion call of the Islamic revolution . . . no longer has the impact it once had'. *International Herald Tribune*, 26 November 1986.

42   IRNA in English, 28 December 1985, in BBC/SWB/ME, 31 December 1985 (A/9).

43   Rafsanjani, Tehran in Arabic, 21 February 1986, in BBC/SWB/ME, 24 February 1986 (A/9).

44 Kuwait, ME/8192/i, 25 February 1986, Kuwait News Agency, in BBC/SWB/ME, 25 February 1986 (A/7); Tehran in Arabic, 2 March 1986, in BBC/SWB/ME, 5 March 1986 (A/15–16); Rafsanjani, interview, Tehran: Home Service, 20 March 1986, in BBC/SWB/ME, 22 March 1986 (A/2–3).

45 Kuwait: Home Service, 3 July 1986, in BBC/SWB/ME, 5 July 1986 (A/1–2).

46 GCC Ministerial Council, BBC/SWB/ME, 5 March 1986 (i); Iranian Foreign Ministry comment, 4 March 1986, in BBC/SWB/ME, 6 March 1986; Tehran: Home Service, Commentary, 4 March 1986, in BBC/SWB/ME, 7 March 1986 (A/8).

47 Iran's comment on GCC Statement, 7 March 1986, in BBC/SWB/ME, 10 March 1986 (A/7–8); Tehran: Home Service, 6 November 1986, in BBC/SWB/ME, 8 November 1986 (A/5); Tehran in English, 13 November 1986, in BBC/SWB/ME, 15 November 1986 (A/3).

48 GCC Ministerial Council, Saudi Press Agency in Arabic, 30 June 1986, in BBC/SWB/ME, 2 July 1986 (A/1–2). Iran's response was to assert its interest in the security of the region and the necessity for 'punishing the aggressor'. See Tehran: Home Service, 1 July 1986, in BBC/SWB/ME, 3 July 1986 (A/8–9); Commentary, 3 July 1986, in BBC/SWB/ME, 4 July 1986 (A/2–3).

49 GCC Ministerial Council Session, 27 August 1986, in BBC/SWB/ME, 29 August 1986 (A/8–9).

50 See International Herald Tribune, 28 October 1986; Le Monde, 7 November 1986; The Financial Times, 3 November 1986; Final Statement of GCC Summit, 5 November 1986, in BBC/SWB/ME, 6 November 1986 (A/10–12).

51 Rafsanjani, Tehran: Home Service, 31 July 1986, in BBC/SWB/ME, 2 August 1986 (A/1–2).

52 Rafsanjani, interview on the war, Tehran TV, 28 August 1986, in BBC/SWB/ME, 1 September 1986 (A/2).

53 Montazeri, Tehran: Home Service, 10 March 1986, in BBC/SWB/ME, 12 March 1986 (A/2). See Rafsanjani's interview in Pasdar-e Eslam, Tehran, 27 July, in BBC/SWB/ME, 29 July 1986 (A/2–3).

54 See for example Khamenei, Tehran: Home Service, 22 August 1986, in BBC/SWB/ME, 25 August 1986 (A/3–4).

55 According to Lloyds List, 80 of the ships in 1986 were petrol tankers or cargo vessels. See Journal de Genève, 10 January 1987.

56 See Robin Lustig, The Observer, 26 July 1987.

57 Tehran: Home Service, 22 April 1987, in BBC/SWB/ME, 27 April 1987 (A/10).

58 Rome, 2 July 1987, in BBC/SWB/ME, 4 July 1987 (A/10). See also The Financial Times, 1 June 1987; Le Monde, 2 June 1987; and Jean Gueyras, Le Monde, 17 July 1987.

59 Musavi Khoini'a, Tehran: Home Service, 2 July 1987, in BBC/SWB/ME, 4 July 1987 (A/7–9).

60 Riyadh: Home Service, 29 June 1987, in BBC/SWB/ME, 1 July 1987 (A/17–18).

61 See Andrew Gowers, The Financial Times, 4 August 1987.

62 Le Monde, 8 September 1987.

63 International Herald Tribune, 5 October 1987.

64 For reports see Le Monde, 16 October 1987; International Herald Tribune, 22 October 1987.

65 International Herald Tribune, 5–6 December 1987.

66 Musavi, Tehran: Home Service, 18 October 1987, in BBC/SWB/ME, 20 October 1987 (A/7). There were good reasons for making this point. By the end of 1987, the year when foreign navies in the Gulf were supposed to have contributed to the safety of navigation, attacks on commercial vessels numbered 165, more than the total for all the

preceding six years of the war combined. For the first time Iranian attacks outnumbered those of Iraq by 85:80. See the report in *Neue Zürcher Zeitung*, 28 December 1987.

67   Tehran: Home Service, 23 October 1987, in BBC/SWB/ME, 27 October 1987 (A/1–7); see also *Le Monde*, 25–26 October 1987.

68   For one of several sources, see President Khamenei, Tehran: Home Service, 30 May 1987, in BBC/SWB/ME, 1 June 1987 (A/7).

69   Rafsanjani, Tehran: Home Service, (Excerpt from Friday Sermon) 15 January 1988, in BBC/SWB/ME, 18 January 1988 (A/4).

70   See his interview with *Die Welt*, 10 August 1987, in *FBIS* V, Nes–87–154, S–2–4, 11 August 1987.

71   Tehran TV, 9 November 1987, in BBC/SWB/ME, 11 November 1987 (A/11–12).

72   See Saudi Press Agency in Arabic, 29 December 1987, in BBC/SWB/ME, 31 December 1987 (A/3). See also the articles by Françoise Chipaux, *Le Monde*, 27–28, 29, 31 December 1987.

73   Quoted in Patrick Bishop and Simon O'Dwyer, *The Sunday Telegraph*, 23 January 1987. A not dissimilar view is found in 'If Iran wins', *The Economist*, 24 January 1987, pp. 14–15.

74   For an analysis of Iran's view of the war, see Shahram Chubin, 'Iran's View of the War'.
     Paper presented at the *Regional Implications of the Gulf War Conference*, Amman, Jordan (IISS: University of Jordan), June 1986.

75   For details of the agreement, see: *Middle East Economic Digest*, 16 April 1982, p. 2 and 23 April 1982, p. 3; Edward Lody, *International Herald Tribune*, 5 May 1982; Tom Friedman, *International Herald Tribune*, 20 April 1982; R. Fisk, *The Times*, 19 April 1982; *The Financial Times* (editorial), 21 April 1982; *The Economist*, 17 April 1982, pp. 54–5.

76   I have discussed this extensively in 'Soviet Arms and the Gulf War', *International Defense Review*, June (6), 1987. See also Tom Friedman, *New York Times*, 25 May 1982; David Ottoway, *International Herald Tribune*, 30 December 1983.

77   Foreign Minister Velayati, Tehran: Home Service, 31 March, in *FBIS* VIII, I–1, 1 April 1983.

78   See Fuad Ajami, *The Vanished Imam: Musa Sadr* (Ithaca (NY): Cornell University Press, 1986).

79   Khomeini, Tehran: Home Service, 21 March, in *FBIS* V, 7–8, 24 March 1980.

80   See John Waterbury, *International Herald Tribune*, 16 November 1982.

81   Mohsen Rafiqdust, IRGC Minister, Tehran: Home Service, interview, 19 October 1986, in BBC/SWB/ME, 17 October 1986 (A/2–3).

82   Hafez al-Assad interview, in *Al-Qabas*, Damascus: Home Service, 24 January 1987, in BBC/SWB/ME, 27 January 1987 (A/5). See also *The Financial Times*, 8 July 1982.

83   The number of Iranian soldiers in Lebanon is not known and figures vary, perhaps due to fluctuations in actual numbers. Patrick Cockburn, *The Financial Times*, 23 June 1982, put the number at 2,100. Other figures vary from Robert Fisk, *The Times*, 15 August 1984, 500, to Scott Macleod's, 350, in *New York Review of Books*, 'A Dangerous Occupation', 16 August 1984, p. 47; and David Ottoway, 1,000–1,500, in *International Herald Tribune*, 30 December 1983.

84   See his interview in *Le Monde*, 16 February 1984.

85   See especially *Tehran Times*, 16 February 1984; Nora Boustany, *International Herald Tribune*, 20 July 1987; and Jim Muir, *The Sunday Times*, 13 December 1987. One

report claimed that Iran provides students with grants and military training, putting the number of recipients at 70,000. Voice of Lebanon, 29 October 1987, in BBC/SWB/ME, 31 October 1987 (A/10).

86   This was well put by Anthony Lewis when in Damascus in 'The View from Syria'; 'Syrians do not so much support Iran as oppose Iraq', *New York Times*, 14 May 1984.

87   Quoted by David Ottoway, *International Herald Tribune*, 10 January 1984.

88   INA in Arabic, 28 June 1986, in BBC/SWB/ME, 30 June 1986 (A/2–3).

89   See, for example, the communiqué after the visit of the Syrian Prime Minister to Tehran, Tehran: Home Service, 4 December 1985, in BBC/SWB/ME, 5 December 1985 (A/1–3).

90   Iran has endorsed these principles frequently. See, for example, the Iran–Syria–Libya meeting of Foreign Ministers communiqué, Damascus: Home Service, 23 December 1985, in BBC/SWB/ME, 24 December 1985 (A/2).

91   *Tehran Times*, 16 February 1984. See also David Ottoway, *International Herald Tribune*, 30 December 1983, and note 75 above.

92   *Middle East Economic Digest*, 20 April 1984, p. 40.

93   *The Economist*, 3 May 1986, pp. 51–2, and Jonathan Randel, *International Herald Tribune*, 10 June 1986.

94   For the text of the agreement, see BBC/SWB/ME, 22 July 1986 (A/1–2).

95   *The Economist*, 14 March 1987, pp. 55–6; *The Times*, 27, 28 April 1987; *The Financial Times*, 5 May 1987.

96   *International Herald Tribune*, 18–19 July 1987.

97   Shiam Bhatia, *The Observer*, 1 November 1987; *The Economist*, 26 September 1987, p. 65.

98   For example, Syrian Vice-President Abd al-Halim Khaddam, Damascus: Home Service, 20 December 1987, in BBC/SWB/ME, 23 December 1987 (A/2).

99   See especially *The Times*, 7 August 1987; see also *Le Monde* (editorial) 8 August 1987; and Françoise Chipaux, *Le Monde*, 27 October 1987.

100 For the communiqué of the summit see *Le Monde*, 13 November 1987; see also *Le Monde*, 14 November 1987; *The Economist*, 14 November 1987, p. 15. For Syrian assurances to Iran before the summit see Syrian Prime Minister Abdel Ra'uf al-Kasm, Damascus, Dispatch 20 October 1987, in BBC/SWB/ME, 22 October 1987 (A/4).

101 Robin Lustig, *The Observer*, 28 September 1986, 23 November 1986; John Kifner, *International Herald Tribune*, 1 January 1987; Lucien George, *Le Monde*, 10 March 1987; Françoise Chipaux, *Le Monde*, 25 October 1986; and *The Economist*, 28 February 1987, pp. 46–7.

102 See Lucien George, *Le Monde*, 30 June 1987; *Le Monde*, 3, 8, July 1987; Jim Muir, *The Sunday Times*, 12 July 1987.

103 Rafsanjani, Tehran: Home Service, 26 June 1987, in BBC/SWB/ME, 27 June 1987 (i).

104 Commentary, Damascus: Home Service, 31 October 1987, in BBC/SWB/ME, 3 November 1987 (A/6–7). Prevention of a 'fabricated' Arab–Iranian conflict is called a 'primary aim' in a later commentary: Damascus, Home Service, 30 December 1987, in BBC/SWB/ME, 1 January 1988 (A/5).

105 See the comment of Taha Ramadhan, Iraqi Deputy Prime Minister, in an interview with the *Jordan Times*, Amman: Home Service in English, 11 November 1987, in BBC/SWB/ME, 12 November 1987 (A/9).

106 See, for example, Robin Wright, *The Sunday Times*, 3 June 1984.

Chapter 10   Iraq and the Superpowers

1   *Al-Jumhuriyya*, 5 September 1987.
2   J.M. Abdulghani, *Iraq and Iran: the Years of Crisis* (London: Croom Helm, 1984), pp. 160–65.
3   See, for example, Saddam Hussein's 'Pan-Arab Declaration' of February 1980, BBC/SWB/ME, 12 February 1980 (A/1–4).
4   *Al-Watan*, 3 February 1979; BBC/SWB/ME, 3 April 1979 (A/6–7).
5   BBC/SWB/ME, 16 February 1979 (A/2).
6   *Al-Sharq al-Awsat*, 30 September 1980.
7   BBC/SWB/ME, 20 July 1981 (A/1–5).
8   BBC/SWB/ME, 19 September 1980 (A/1–7).
9   FBIS/MEA, 17 March 1981 (E1).
10 O. Bengio, 'Iraq', in C. Legum et al. (eds), *Middle East Contemporary Survey V 1980–1981*, (London: Holmes and Meier, 1982) pp. 591–3.
11 King, *Iran–Iraq War*, pp. 49–50.
12 *The Guardian*, 17 December 1985; *International Herald Tribune*, 17 February 1985.
13 Nonneman, *Iraq, the Gulf States and the War*, pp. 11–12.
14 *The Guardian*, 27 September 1982; *The Daily Telegraph*, 11 January 1983.
15 BBC/SWB/ME, 10 April 1987 (A/5–6) and 11 April 1987 (A/7–8).
16 Quoted in Bengio, 'Iraq', *Middle East Contemporary Survey VII 1982–1983*, p. 588.
17 BBC/SWB/ME, 5 January 1983 (A/6).
18 Ibid. ·
19 *Middle East Reporter*, 18 February 1983.
20 King, *Irah–Iraq War*, pp. 55–6.
21 *The Sunday Times*, 17 March 1985; *The Times*, 16 February 1986.
22 *Kul al-Arab*, 4 April 1986; see also Taha Ramadhan's comments in FBIS/MEA, 20 January 1987 (E2); *International Herald Tribune*, 7 May 1987.
23 *The Financial Times*, 25 April 1984; *The Guardian*, 3 July 1984.
24 *Middle East Reporter*, 18 February 1983 and 16 January 1987; *Keesings Contemporary Archives XXXI* (1985), p. 33497.
25 *International Herald Tribune*, 6 March 1983; *Middle East Economic Digest*, 10 August 1985 and 29 March 1986; *Middle East Reporter*, 27 June 1986.
26 *International Herald Tribune*, 17 November 1982; *Al-Watan*, 8 March 1983; *Al-Thawra*, 20 July 1983.
27 BBC/SWB/ME, 8 January 1982 (A/9).
28 BBC/SWB/ME, 22 June 1982 (A/1–11).
29 *Al-Tadammun*, 15 November 1986. For a useful survey of successive UN resolutions since 1980, see King, *Iran–Iraq War*, Appendix I, pp. 70–72.
30 See Saddam Hussein's five 'Open Letters to the Iranian People', published by Dar al-Ma'mun, Baghdad between 1983 and 1986. See also Iraq's 4-point proposal to the UN Security Council, FBIS/MEA, 4 September 1986 (E1).
31 King, *Iran–Iraq War*, pp. 51–2.
32 *Al-Thawra*, 29 March 1987.
33 BBC/SWB/ME, 18 June 1987 (A/11–12).
34 BBC/SWB/ME, 28 January 1987 (A/5–6).
35 BBC/SWB/ME, 10 April 1987 (A/6), 11 April 1987 (A/7–8), 30 April 1987 (A/1), 19 June 1987 (i).
36 BBC/SWB/ME, 28 February 1987)A/5), 12 May 1987 (i).

37 BBC/SWB/ME, 20 May 1987 (A/1).
38 BBC/SWB/ME, 29 May 1987 (A/10).
39 BBC/SWB/ME, 6 July 1987 (i).
40 BBC/SWB/ME, 24 April 1987 (A/12–13).
41 BBC/SWB/ME, 20 July 1987 (A/1–7).
42 See Adnan Khayrallah's comments on the 'Irangate' revelations. These were in many respects moderate in their criticism of the United States. He argued that the United States was quite naturally concerned with the balance of power in the Middle East, of which Iraq formed an important part. Consequently, it would cease selling arms to Iran. BBC/SWB/ME, 6 January 1987 (A/3–5).
43 BBC/SWB/ME, 22 July 1987 (i) and 24 July 1987 (A/10–11).
44 BBC/SWB/ME, 27 July 1987 (A/6–8) and 4 August 1987 (A/12).
45 BBC/SWB/ME, 15 August 1987 (A/1–2), 20 August 1987 (A/1–3), 1 September 1987 (A/1–3), 16 September 1987 (A/1–2) and 29 September 1987 (A/11–12).
46 BBC/SWB/ME, 1 August 1987 (i).
47 Article in *Al-Thawra*, quoted in BBC/SWB/ME, 22 August 1987 (A/4–5); see also BBC/SWB/ME, 21 September 1987 (A/5).
48 BBC/SWB/ME, 7 September 1987 (A/7).
49 BBC/SWB/ME, 8 September 1987 (i), 31 October 1987 (A/5); *The Guardian*, 31 October 1987.
50 BBC/SWB/ME, 8 September 1987 (A/6–7).
51 The most recent of the 'Open Letters' setting out the principles which Iraq insists are the only acceptable basis for a just and lasting peace, published by Dar al Ma'mun, Baghdad.
52 BBC/SWB/ME, 20 July 1987 (A/1–7).
53 *Al-Siyasa*, 12 October 1987; *Al-Thawra*, 19 September 1987.
54 BBC/SWB/ME, 9 July 1987 (A/4–6).
55 BBC/SWB/ME, 9 July 1987 (A/4–6).

Chapter 11   Iran and the Superpowers

1 For an early summary, see M.S. El-Azhary, 'The Attitudes of the Superpowers towards the Gulf War', *International Affairs*, 59/4 (Autumn 1983), pp. 609–20.
2 A good summary of the rationale is found in Henry Kissinger's article, 'Pressure Points in the Gulf', *Washington Post*, 5 February 1985.
3 For a discussion of Iran's view of the superpowers, see Richard Cottam, 'Iran's Perception of the Superpowers', in Barry M. Rosen (ed.), *Iran since the Revolution: Internal Dynamics, Regional Conflicts and the Superpowers*, (New York: Social Science Monographs: Columbia University Press, 1985) pp. 133–47.
4 Khomeini, Tehran: Home Service, 9 September 1984, in *FBIS* VIII, II, 10 September 1984.
5 See, for example, Khomeini, 10 February 1986, in BBC/SWB/ME, 12 February 1986 (A/9); Tehran Radio Commentary, Home Service, 25 September 1986, in BBC/SWB/ME, 27 September 1986 (A/1–2).
6 See *Aviation Week and Space Technology*, 29 September 1980, p. 27; 6 October 1980, p. 21; 3 November 1980; 24 November 1980, p. 66.
7 See Defence Minister Musa Namjou's comments, *The Daily Telegraph*, 21 September 1981.

8   See the relevant references in Chapters 3 and 5; see also *Aviation Week and Space Technology*, 3 November 1980; *The Times*, 8 October 1980; *Le Monde*, 6 October 1982.

9   US policy-makers have been well aware of this dilemma. For an authoritative report, see Leslie Gelb, *New York Times*, 19 September 1982; Joe Craft, *International Herald Tribune*, 15 April 1982; Cord Mayer, *Richmond Times Dispatch*, 9 April 1982; *International Herald Tribune* (*Washington Post* edn), 25 May 1982.

10 This was Secretary of State Alexander Haig's formulation in his important statement of the US position on 26 May 1982 at the Chicago Council on Foreign Relations. See *Department of State Bulletin*, July 1982, pp. 44–7; *Le Monde*, 28 May 1982; *The Financial Times*, 28 May 1982.

11 See Defense Secretary Weinberger's speech to the Foreign Policy Association, New York, reported in *Middle East Economic Digest*, 28 May 1982, p. 10.

12 *Le Monde*, 18–19 July 1982.

13 See *Le Monde*, 3, 6 April 1982, and Tehran in Arabic, 17 December 1982, in BBC/SWB/ME, 20 December 1982 (A/4–5).

14 See *Le Monde*, 31 January–1 February 1982; *International Herald Tribune*, 6 April 1982; C. Cordrry, *Baltimore Sun*, 15 July 1982; Michael Getler, *Washington Post*, 15 July 1982.

15 President Ali Khamenei's comments, *New York Times*, 3 November 1984.

16 *Le Monde*, 9 February 1983.

17 On Iran's position, see Rafsanjani's comments in October, in *Tehran Times*, 12 October 1983; *Kuwait Times*, 17 October 1983; see also *Middle East Economic Digest*, 29 July 1983, p. 8; 7 October 1983, p. 3.

18 For the US, see Secretary of State Shultz's comments on 'blackmail', *New York Times*, 18 October 1983; *Washington Post*, 18 October 1983; *The Financial Times*, 19 October 1983. On the task force, see *The Times*, 13 October 1983; President Reagan said on 20 October: 'The free world would not stand by and allow anyone to close the strait of Hormuz and the Persian Gulf'.

19 See Michael Getler, *Washington Post*, 24 October 1983: some normalization of trade had been reported with repayment of debts and trade through third parties reaching $1 billion. See *International Herald Tribune*, 14 April, 26 December 1983.

20 See Secretary Shultz's interview in *US News and World Report*, 12 March 1984, pp. 27–9; Joe Stork and Martha Wenger, 'US Ready to Intervene', *MERIP Reports*, July/September 1984, pp. 44–8.

21 See *Boston Globe*, 17 May 1984; *Washington Post*, 18 May 1984; Bernard Gwertzman, *New York Times*, 24 May 1984; J. Harsch, *Christian Science Monitor*, 1 June 1984.

22 D. Oberdorfer, *Washington Post*, 24 February 1984; *The Financial Times*, 8 March 1984; *New York Times*, 18, 31 May 1984.

23 *New York Times*, 12 June 1984. See also 'Developments in the Persian Gulf June 1984', *Hearings*, House Committee on Foreign Affairs (Subcommittee on Europe and Middle East), 98th Congress, 2nd Session, 11 June 1984 (USGPO: 1984).

24 C. Cordrry, *Baltimore Sun*, 1 June 1984.

25 On 'Operation Staunch', see Shultz's criticism of Britain in *The Times*, 2 April 1984; *Philadelphia Inquirer*, 22 April 1984; *New York Times*, 26 April 1984; J. Goshko, *Washington Post*, 6 August 1984; *Washington Times*, 7 August 1984; *Wall Street Journal*, 28 March 1984.

26 See, for example, *International Herald Tribune*, 17 July and 2–3, 5 August 1985.

27 B. Gwertzman, *International Herald Tribune*, 22 March 1985; *International Herald Tribune*, 3 April 1985; *Le Monde*, 4 April 1985.

28   Peggy Riley, *The Observer*, 31 March 1985.
29   See *The Times*, 21 November 1986; *Le Monde*, 10 December 1986.
30   *Le Monde*, 15 November 1986; *International Herald Tribune*, 19 November 1986.
31   For an analysis of this problem at the beginning of the war, see Shahram Chubin, *Security in the Persian Gulf: The Role of the Outside Powers* (London: Gower for the IISS, 1982).
32   See D. Ottoway, *International Herald Tribune*, 18 November 1986.
33   See the comments of the influential *Abrar* newspaper, 31 March 1986, in BBC/SWB/ME, 2 April 1986 (A/1–2); and Foreign Minister Velayati, BBC/SWB/ME, 16 May 1986 (i).
34   See Shahram Chubin, *International Herald Tribune*, 6–7 December 1986.
35   The figures are the official ones. See *International Herald Tribune*, 22–23 November 1986; Iran's denial in *International Herald Tribune*, 25 November 1986. Other sources put the number of TOW at 10,000. See *Le Monde*, 30 November–1 December 1986.
36   Patrick Seale reports Israel's arms sales during 1980–86 totalling $5 billion. *The Observer*, 23 November 1986. For an earlier analysis, see Shahram Chubin 'Israel and the Gulf War', *International Defense Review*, March 1985, pp. 303–4.
37   *International Herald Tribune*, 20–21 December 1986; *Le Monde*, 17 December 1986; *New York Times*, 23 November 1986. See also *International Herald Tribune*, 13 January 1987.
38   See the report in *The Observer*, 3 May 1987, and *International Herald Tribune*, 20 January 1987.
39   See Iran's Foreign Ministry condemnation of this assistance on 17 December 1986, in BBC/SWB/ME, 19 December 1986 (A/2); and Rafsanjani's comments on 19 December 1986 in BBC/SWB/ME, 22 December 1986 (A/4–5).
40   See *International Herald Tribune*, 21 November 1986; Loren Jenkins, *International Herald Tribune*, 28 January 1987; *International Herald Tribune*, 23 February 1987; *Le Monde*, 21 February 1987; *The Times*, 30 January 1987.
41   Rafsanjani's comments, *Le Monde*, 26 November, 30 November–1 December 1986 and 19 December 1986, in BBC/SWB/ME, 23 December 1986 (A/3–4).
42   See *International Herald Tribune* 15–16, 21 November 1986; *Le Monde*, 22, 23–24 November 1986; *The Times*, 21 November 1986.
43   Khomeini's message on Martyrs Day, 6 February 1987, in BBC/SWB/ME, 6 February 1987 (A/9).
44   See Rafsanjani, 28 January 1987 Press Conference, in BBC/SWB/ME, 29 January 1987 (A/7–13); *The Times*, 29 January 1987; *Le Monde*, 22 April 1987; *International Herald Tribune*, 21 April 1987.
45   See Shultz in *International Herald Tribune*, 29 January 1987; 27 March 1987; 6 April 1987; Weinberger in *Le Monde*, 24 March 1987; on China's arms sales, *International Herald Tribune*, 3 March 1987.
46   See *Sunday Times*, 1 March 1987; *International Herald Tribune*, 3 and 22 April 1987.
47   See Shultz's testimony to the Committee on Foreign Affairs of the House of Representatives, US Congress, 8 December 1986 (Press Release); *Le Monde*, 8 January 1987; *International Herald Tribune*, 8 January 1987. For a report favouring this approach, see James A. Philips, 'The Continuing Need for a US Opening to Iran', *The Heritage Foundation* (Backgrounder), 5 March 1987.
48   Rafsanjani, Tehran: Home Service, 7 November 1986, in BBC/SWB/ME, 10 November 1986 (A/2–3); Khomeini, Tehran: Home Service, 20 November 1986, in BBC/SWB/ME, 21 November 1986 (A/1–3).

49 Rafsanjani, excerpt from sermon at Tehran University, Tehran: Home Service, 19 December 1986, in BBC/SWB/ME, 23 December 1986 (A/3–4).

50 President Reagan, quoted in *The New York Times* (Sunday edition), 31 May 1987.

51 President Reagan's address to the nation, 13 November 1986, 'US Initiative to Iran', US Department of State, Bureau of Public Affairs, No. 890.

52 The confusion in US policy was both deliberate and unintended. Where it demonstrated real ignorance was in attempting to depict Iran rather than Iraq as the threat to freedom of navigation. A yet more basic failure was to consider the implications of the naval presence in terms of the hostilities on the ground. Reassurance of the Gulf states against intimidation by Iran was valuable in itself, but the naval deployments, which were depicted as having a decisive effect on the war, could at best play only a marginal role.

53 See Richard Armitage, Assistant-Secretary of Defense, *The Economist*, 20 June 1987, p. 39.

54 *International Herald Tribune*, 15 June 1987.

55 *The Economist*, 5 September 1987, p. 13.

56 A trade embargo was finally imposed in November 1987.

57 *Wall Street Journal* (editorial), 20 October 1987.

58 *The Independent* (editorial), 20 October 1987; for a similar discussion see also *The Financial Times* (editorial), 20 October 1987.

59 See Rafsanjani statement IRNA in English, 6 September 1987, in BBC/SWB/ME, 8 September 1987 (A/2–4), see also *Le Monde*, 21 and 22 August 1987 and Patrick Seale, *The Observer*, 23 August 1987.

60 See the report by Elaine Sciolino, *International Herald Tribune*, 3 November 1987.

61 Rafsanjani, Tehran: Home Service, 22 May 1987, in BBC/SWB/ME, 25 May 1987 (A/1).

62 Rafsanjani, Tehran: Home Service, 4 November 1987, in BBC/SWB/ME, 6 November 1987 (A/5).

63 For Khamenei's comment see Tehran: Home Service, 29 May 1987, in BBC/SWB/ME, 30 May 1987 (A/4–5); for representative comment see Tehran: Home Service, 9 August 1987, in BBC/SWB/ME, 11 August 1987 (A/13–14).

64 Tehran: Home Service, 28 August 1987, in BBC/SWB/ME, 31 August 1987 (A/5).

65 Tehran: Home Service, 6 September 1987, in BBC/SWB/ME, 8 September 1987 (A/1–2).

66 Tehran: Home Service, 26 June 1987, in *FBIS*–NES–87–123, p. S–1. 26 June 1987.

67 See Khamenei, Tehran: Home Service, 29 May 1987, in BBC/SWB/ME, 1 June 1987 (A/2–7).

68 See Rafsanjani, Tehran: Home Service, 30 September 1987, in BBC/SWB/ME, 2 October 1987 (A/10–11); *Le Monde*, 2 October 1987; see also Rafsanjani, Tehran: Home Service, 2 October 1987, in BBC/SWB/ME, 3 October 1987 (i).

69 See *Le Monde*, 11-12 October 1987 and *International Herald Tribune*, 10–11 October 1987.

70 Tehran: Home Service, 26 June 1987, in *FBIS*–NES–87–123, V, p. S–1, 26 June 1987.

71 Tehran: Home Service (excerpt from a sermon) 23 October 1987, in BBC/SWB/ME, 26 October 1987 (A/1–7) (emphasis added).

72 For the volunteers see Head of the Basij (Mobilization) forces, Hojjat-el-Eslam Mohammed Ali Rahmani in *Ettela'at*, 4 October 1987, in BBC/SWB/ME, 6 October 1987. On the demonstrations see *International Herald Tribune*, 5 November 1987.

73 Harvey Morris, *The Independent*, 4 November 1987.

74 Tehran: Home Service (sermon extract), 13 November 1987, in BBC/SWB/ME, 17 November 1987 (A/3).

75 Tehran: Home Service (excerpt from sermon), 27 November 1987, in BBC/SWB/ME, 30 November 1987 (A/2–3).

76 See Chubin, *Security in the Persian Gulf* and 'Soviet Gains in the Middle East', *International Security* 6/4 (Spring 1982) pp. 122–52. Specifically on the Soviet arms offer, see Eric Rouleau, *Le Monde*, 9 October 1980; on Soviet reassurances about the border, *Le Point*, 27 October 1980; on Iranian requests for an end to Soviet arms to Iraq, *FBIS* VIII, I–I, 18 November 1980. Soviet press commentaries of the period reflected the tilt.

77 See Shahram Chubin, 'Hedging in the Gulf: Soviets Arm Both Sides', *International Defense Review*, 20/6 (June 1987), pp. 731–5.

78 *Iran Times*, 26 March 1982.

79 *Kayhan*, 1 January 1981. See also *FBIS* VIII, I–I–9, 8 January 1981.

80 See Liz Thurgood, *The Guardian*, 6 October 1982.

81 Velayati, BBC/SWB/ME, 3 January 1983.

82 'Soviet Stance Against Iran', Tehran Radio International in Turkish, 19 January 1983, in *FBIS* VIII, 14, 21 January 1983.

83 See Tehran in Arabic, 30 April 1983, in BBC/SWB/ME, 3 May 1983 (A/2–3); and Tehran in Turkish, 27 March 1983, in BBC/SWB/ME, 31 March 1983 (A/1–2).

84 R. Ullyanovskiy, *Literary Gazette*, 22 June 1983, in BBC/SWB/SU, 29 June 1983 (A4/1–7).

85 See *Pravda*, 5 August 1983, and *Krasnaya Zvezda*, 7 December 1983.

86 Tehran: Home Service, 18 January 1984, in *FBIS* VIII, I–I, 18 January 1984. See also *Tehran Times*, 19 January 1984.

87 Tehran: Home Service, 26 February 1984, in *FBIS* VIII, I–2, 27 February 1984.

88 Velayati, 9 February 1984, *FBIS* VIII, I–2, 9 February 1984.

89 See *The Financial Times*, 25 June 1984; *The Times*, 7 June 1984; *Le Monde*, 4 July 1984.

90 Rafsanjani, 11 June 1984, in *FBIS* VIII, I–3, 12 June 1984.

91 See Prime Minister Musavi's comments, 11 March 1984, in *FBIS* VIII, I–2, 12 March 1984; 19 March, in *FBIS* VIII, I–7, 20 March 1984; and Minister of the Pasdar (IRGC), Mohsen Rafiqdust, Tehran, IRNA in English, 28 September, in *FBIS* VIII, I–3, 1 October 1984, and in *Jomhuri-ye Eslami*, 23 September, in *FBIS* VIII, I–2, 5 October 1984.

92 *Kayhan* (editorial, 'Collusion of US and USSR cannot save Saddam Hussein'), 21 July 1984, in *FBIS* VIII, I 4–5, 3 August 1984.

93 Press Conference, 7 February in *Middle East Economic Digest*, 15 February 1985, p. 12. Foreign Minister Velayati characterized relations between Iran and the USSR as normal: 'They are exactly what relations between two neighbors should be', *New York Times*, 4 October 1984.

94 For reports of pressures on Iran, see John Kifner, *International Herald Tribune*, 26 July 1984. For reports of indirect supplies, see Jack Anderson, *Washington Post*, 4 August 1984.

95 See 'Iran: A Survey', *Financial Times*, 1 April 1985. For a report that arms from these sources, approved by the USSR, reached Iran, see *Foreign Report*, 26 September 1985.

96 Tehran: Home Service, 13 May 1985, in BBC/SWB/ME, 15 May 1985 (A/1).

97 See Rafsanjani, 18 June 1985, in BBC/SWB/ME, 18 June 1985 (i) and 22 June 1985 (i). —

98 See *Le Monde*, 7–8 April 1985; *Middle East Economic Digest*, 12 April 1985.

99 Tehran: Home Service, 7 December, in BBC/SWB/ME, 10 December 1985 (A/4–5). See also Tehran, 17 December, in BBC/SWB/ME, 19 December 1985 (i).

100 *Kayhan Al-Arabi*, Tehran in Arabic, 30 December 1985, in BBC/SWB/ME, 1 January 1986 (A/14–15).

101 See *Le Monde*, 18 July 1985.

102 *Pravda*, 6 March 1985, in *Current Digest of the Soviet Press* XXXVII/10, 3 April 1985, pp. 8–9.

103 National Voice of Iran (Baku) in Persian, 29 May 1985, in BBC/SWB/ME, 1 June 1985 (A/4–5).

104 See *Le Monde*, 7–8 April 1985.

105 See *Pravda*, 5 August 1983, and *Krasnaya Zvezda*, 15 January 1984.

106 See Bhodan Nahayto, 'Moscow and Tehran: Cultivating Mutual Relations Without Budging on Political Differences', Radio Liberty Report, No. 47/87 (3 February 1987).

107 See *Pravda*, 9 January 1987, 1/1–6.

108 See A. Seregin, *Izvestia*, 7 December 1986; *Izvestia*, 15 February 1987, 1/1–6; *Pravda*, 15 February 1987, 4/1–5.

109 See Tehran commentary on Shevardnadze, and Rafsanjani, Tehran: Home Service, 7 May 1987, in BBC/SWB/ME, 9 May 1987 (A/1–2); *Ettela'at*, Tehran: Home Service, 11 May in BBC/SWB/ME, 13 May 1987 (A/1–2).

110 Reza'i quoted on Tehran, IRNA in English, 24 June 1987, in *FBIS* NES–87–123, V, S–I, 24 June 1987; Tehran: Home Service, 28 May 1987, in BBC/SWB/ME, 30 May 1987 (A/6–7); *Resala'at*, 15 June 1987 reported in Tehran: Home Service, 14, 15 June 1987, in BBC/SWB/ME, 17 June 1987 (A/3–4).

111 See Tehran: Home Service, 14, 15 June 1987, in BBC/SWB/ME, 16 June 1987 (i) and 17 June 1987 (A/1).

112 See Tehran: Home Service, 13 May 1987, in BBC/SWB/ME, 15 May 1987 (A/6–7).

113 Tehran radio commentary, Home Service, 17 June 1987, in BBC/SWB/ME, 19 June 1987 (A/9); Rafsanjani, Tehran: Home Service, 20 June 1987, in BBC/SWB/ME, 22 June 1987 (A/4–5).

114 *Tass* statement carried in *Pravda*, 4 July 1987, translated in *Current Digest of the Soviet Press* (hereafter cited as *CDSP*), XXXIX/27 (5 August 1987) p. 13.

115 Musavi, Tehran: Home Service, 5 July 1987, in BBC/SWB/ME, 7 July 1987 (A/1–2); Deputy Foreign Minister Larijani with Soviet Ambassador Boldyrev, Tehran: Home Service, 4 July 1987, in BBC/SWB/ME, 6 July 1987 (i). Rafsanjani, Tehran: Home Service, 9 July 1987, in BBC/SWB/ME, 11 July 1987 (A/8). See also *Le Monde*, 19–20 July 1987.

116 Tehran: Home Service, 3 August 1987, in BBC/SWB/ME, 5 August 1987 (A/5–7); Musavi, Tehran: Home Service, 20 September 1987, in *FBIS*–NES–87–182, 21 September 1987, p. 34; Tehran: Home Service, 21 September 1987, in BBC/SWB/ME, 22 September 1987 (A/1); Tehran and Moscow (Tass), 31 October, 1 November, in BBC/SWB/ME, 3 November 1987 (A/2–4); Tehran: Home Service, 5 December 1987, in BBC/SWB/ME, 7 December 1987 (A/5).

117 'Dark Clouds above the Gulf', *Pravda*, 16 August 1987, in BBC/SWB/SU, 18 August 1987 (A4/1–2); *Al Anba*, Kuwait News Agency 20 August 1987, in BBC/SWB/ME, 21 August 1987 (i).

118 Shevardnadze told Velayati ambiguously 'we believe that events should not necessitate

another resolution', Tehran: Home Service, in BBC/SWB/ME, 22 September 1987 (A/1); Soviet roving ambassador Mikhael Sytenko referred to Iran's flexibility, Gulf News Agency dispatch (Baghdad) 16 December, in BBC/SWB/ME, 18 December 1987 (A/1); Gromyko to Iranian ambassador Heyrani-Nobari, *Tass* 4 December, in BBC/SWB/SU, 7 December 1987 (A4/1).

119 Shavardnadze, speech to United Nations General Assembly, *Tass* 23 September, in BBC/SWB/SU, 25 September 1987 (A1/1–7).

120 See Tariq Aziz (Iraqi Deputy Prime Minister) Paris, Radio Monte Carlo (in Arabic) 21 September 1987, in *FBIS–NES–87–187*, 28 September 1987, p. 25; Taha Yassin Ramadhan (1st Deputy Prime Minister) in *Al Ittihad*, Abu Dhabi (in Arabic) 12 September, in *FBIS–NES–87–177*, 14 September 1987, pp. 12–13; *Al-Jumhuriyya*, 5 September, in BBC/SWB/ME, 7 September 1987 (A/7); *Le Monde*, 30 October 1987.

121 Musavi, Tehran: Home Service, 17 December 1987, in BBC/SWB/ME, 18 December 1987 (A/3); Rafsanjani interview *Tehran Times*, IRNA in English 29 August, in BBC/SWB/ME, 31 August 1987 (A/6–8).

122 See Tehran: Home Service, 12 August 1987, in BBC/SWB/ME, 14 August 1987 (A/8), and 18 August 1987 (A1/1); *Le Monde*, 11 August 1987.

123 Hashemi Rafsanjani, interview *Jeune Afrique*, 23 September 1987, pp. 11–17, in *FBIS–NES–87–188*, 29 September 1987, Annex 1–7.

124 Tehran: Home Service, 7 October 1987, in BBC/SWB/ME, 9 October 1987 (i); Tehran: Home Service, 17 October 1987, in BBC/SWB/ME, 20 October 1987 (A/11).

125 Khamenei, Tehran, IRNA in English, 27 October, in BBC/SWB/ME, 29 October 1987 (A/1); Musavi, interview with *Interviu* (Spanish magazine) in Tehran: Home Service, 15 October 1987, in BBC/SWB/ME, 16 October 1987 (A/3–8).

126 Rafsanjani, *Jeune Afrique*, 23 September 1987, in *FBIS–NES–87–188*, 29 September 1987.

127 Rafsanjani, interview with *Die Welt*, 10 August in *FBIS–NES–87–154* p. S–2, 11 August 1987.

128 See Rafsanjani's hints reported in *Iran Press Digest* VI/45 (24 November 1987); *Le Monde*, 21 November 1987. Rafsanjani's visit to the USSR did not materialize in 1987.

129 Rafsanjani interview with *Kayhan*, 15 December 1987, IRNA in English 15 December, in BBC/SWB/ME, 17 Deember 1987 (A/1–2).

130 Radio Peace and Progress in Persian, 28 April, in BBC/SWB/SU, 1 May 1987 (A4/4–5).

131 *Pravda*, 14 February 1987, in *CDSP* XXXI/7 (18 March 1987) pp. 15–16.

132 Tass called the attack on a Soviet ship a 'bandit attack', 8 May, in BBC/SWB/SU, 13 May 1987 (i); A. Karalov, 'Fabrications and Facts', *Izvestia*, 1 May in *CDSP* XXXIX/18 (3 June 1987), p. 14.

133 See the commentary by Igor Sheftunov in Persian, Moscow 31 May in response to *Jomhuri-ye Eslami* criticisms, in BBC/SWB/SU, 11 June 1987 (A4/21).

134 See the Soviet reminder that when the West placed Iran under an embargo the USSR made its transit routes available, Moscow in Persian, 14 June in BBC/SWB/SU, 20 June 1987 (A4/3).

135 *Pravda*, 4 July 1987, *CDSP* XXXIX/27 (5 August 1987) p. 13.

136 *Pravda*, 18 July 1987, *CDSP* XXXIX/29 (19 August 1987) p. 13.

137 Igor Belayev in *Literaturnaya Gazeta* 30 September 1987, in BBC/SWB/SU, 1

October 1987 (A4/1–2).

138   Vorontsov, Tehran: Home Service, 15 October 1987, in BBC/SWB/SU, 19 October 1987 (A4/5); *Tass*, 19 October (*Pravda*, 20 October) in BBC/SWB/SU, 21 October 1987 (A4/1–3); Gennady Gerasimov (Foreign Ministry spokesman), *Tass*, 20 October, in BBC/SWB/SU, 23 October 1987 (A1/1).

139   See Radio Moscow in Persian, 27 December, in BBC/SWB/SU, 29 December 1987 (A4/6–7).

140   For an earlier discussion noting the absence of balance in practice see Shahram Chubin, 'The USSR and Iran', *Foreign Affairs* 61/4 (April 1983) pp. 921–49.

141   See, for example, Radio Peace and Progress in Arabic and Persian of 7 June which blamed Iran for continuing the war and pressuring Kuwait, in BBC/SWB/SU, 8 June 1987 (A4/11). In response to an Iranian missile attack on Kuwait's port, *Izvestia* commented: 'Such attacks against a sovereign state not involved in the conflict, no matter who originates them, are unacceptable'. 18 October in *CDSP* XXXIX/42 (18 November 1987), p. 19. For direct criticism of Iran reaffirming support for Kuwait's sovereignty, see *Tass*, 24 October, in BBC/SWB/SU, 26 October 1987. For an explanation of the Soviet rationale for ties with Iran see Vladimir Vinogradov (Foreign Minister of the RSFSR) Moscow in Arabic, 22 October in BBC/SWB/SU, 27 October 1987 (A4/1); Gorbachev's message to the Emir of Kuwait, *Tass*, 31 October, in BBC/SWB/ME, 2 November 1987 (A/3).

142   Alexsey Zlatorunskiy commentary, 'Window on the Arab World', Moscow in Arabic, 29 October, in BBC/SWB/SU, 10 November 1987 (A1/2).

143   Since Soviet statements on this subject are numerous and the issue is only of tangential concern to our discussion I have included only a sample of salient references.

a) For comments on the withdrawal of US forces as a precondition: Vladimir Peresda, 'Fist Over the Gulf', *Pravda*, 26 March in *CDSP* XXXIX/12 (22 April 1987) p. 11. V. Gan, 'Dangerous Pretensions', *Pravda*, 2 June and Vikenty Matveyev, 'What are they trying to achieve?', *Izvestia* in *CDSP* XXXIX/22 (1 July 1987) p. 12. One comment was typical: 'Washington has usurped the role of protector in the Persian Gulf area, which lies thousands of miles away from American coasts, . . . [The USSR] cannot be indifferent to the state of affairs in the Persian Gulf, a region located not too far from its southern frontiers.' Commentary Yuriy Soltan, Moscow, world service in English, 20 June, in BBC/SWB/SU, 26 June 1987 (A4/5–6); *Tass* and *Izvestia*, 28 July in BBC/SWB/SU, 30 July 1987 (A4/1–2).

b) On the relationship between earlier Soviet proposals on the Indian Ocean (going back in fact to Brezhnev's proposal in New Delhi in December 1980) and the need for co-operative acts to guarantee freedom of navigation etc. see Vladimir Petrovsky (Deputy Foreign Minister), *Izvestia*, 28 April in BBC/SWB/SU, 6 May 1987 (A4/1–2), *Tass* (*Pravda*, 19 May) offered Soviet readiness to help in any 'constructive efforts' to end the war, including within the UN, in BBC/SWB/SU, 20 May 1987 (A4/1–3); Soviet official statement, *Pravda*, 27 May in *CDSP* XXXIX/21 (24 June 1987) p. 11; Pavel Demchenko, 'Cruisers, Tankers and the Road to Peace', *Pravda*, 12 June in *CDSP* XXXIX/24 (15 July 1987) p. 12; *Tass* (in Russian and English), 26 May in BBC/SWB/SU, 1 June 1987 (A1/3); Viktor Ivanov, Moscow 28 May in BBC/SWB/SU, 2 June 1987 (A4/3); V. Petrovsky, *Moscow News* Interview, 3 June in BBC/SWB/SU, 5 June 1987 (A4/1–2); Alexandr Bovin, 'The Gulf', *Izvestia*, 31 July in *CDSP* XXXIX/31 (2 September 1987) pp. 1–2; Gerasimov, 9 August in *CDSP* XXXIX/32 (9 September 1987) p. 17. On the reactivation of the Military Staff

Committee see the Soviet briefing, *Izvestia*, 14 October in *CSDP* XXXIX/41 (11 November 1987); Vladimir Peresda, *Pravda*, 20 October in *CDSP* XXXIX/42 (18 November 1987) p. 19. For Soviet comments at the UN see *Tass*, 23 October in BBC/SWB/SU, 26 October 1987 (A1/12–13). Gorbachev message to Emir of Kuwait, *Tass*, 31 October in BBC/SWB/ME, 2 November 1987 (A/3); Gerasimov, Moscow: Home Service, 17 December, in BBC/SWB/SU, 22 December 1987 (A1/10).

c) On a new approach to regional conflicts see General Secretary Gorbachev's message to President Reagan which noted that the prerequisite for ending the war was joint USSR–US actions in the Security Council of the UN, *Tass*, 21 July (*Izvestia*, 23 July) in *CDSP* XXXIX/29 (19 August 1987) p. 12; Gerasimov arguing for a joint approach observed: 'This is one regional conflict which proves that the US view of the world as one of Soviet–American confrontation is wrong'. *Tass*, 7 August in BBC/SWB/SU, 10 August 1987 (A1/9–10); Gorbachev amplified his view in a subsequent speech:

> The permanent members of the Security Council could become guarantors of regional security. They could, for their part, assume an obligation not to use force or the threat of force, and to renounce a demonstrative military presence. This is because such a practice is one factor fanning regional conflicts.

'Reality and the Guarantees of a Secure World', *Pravda* and *Izvestia*, 17 September in BBC/SWB/SU, 17 September 1987 (A1/1–9). The theme is repeated in Foreign Minister Shevardnadze's UN speech, *Tass* 23 September; Gorbachev raised the issue of US unilateral actions outside of the UN and their compatibility with Resolution S.C. 598 with Secretary Shultz, see *Tass*, 23 October in BBC/SWB/SU, 26 October 1987 (A1/6). See also John Walcott, *Wall Street Journal*, 2 November 1987.

144 To take but one example of each in sequence: *Tass*, Foreign Ministry spokesman, 24 October in BBC/SWB/SU, 26 October 1987 (i), Shevardnadze told Velayati in a 'thorough and frank exchange of views' and 'businesslike atmosphere' of Soviet hostility toward the war, see *Tass*, 21 September in BBC/SWB/SU, 22 September 1987 (A1/2); on Afghanistan Soviet anxieties about possible co-ordination between Iran and the US are in evidence in an article in *Literaturnaya Gazeta*, 24 December in *FBIS* 111 (USSR International Affairs) 24 December 1986, A1; on export of the revolution see the Soviet commentary by Konstantin Kapitanov in *Literaturnaya Gazeta*, 9 December, in BBC/SWB/SU, 14 December 1987 (A4/3–4); on Iran's policies see the criticism through Radio Peace and Progress, in Persian, 11 June in BBC/SWB/SU, 20 June 1987 (A4/4).

145 See G. Gerasimov, Moscow: Home Service, 17 December 1987 in BBC/SWB/SU, 22 December 1987 (AI/10); V. Petrovsky (Soviet Deputy Foreign Minister) on Soviet TV, 22 December in BBC/SWB/SU, 24 December 1987 (A1/1–2); Gerasimov, *Tass*, 29 December in BBC/SWB/SU, 31 December 1987 (A1/7–8).

146 See Rafsanjani's comments, Tehran: Home Service, 13 March, in BBC/SWB/ME, 14 and 16 March 1987 (i) and 16 March 1987 (A/4–5).

147 For example, Rafsanjani's comment to the Soviet Ambassador in Tehran, Tehran: Home Service, 30 January 1988 in BBC/SWB/ME, 2 February 1988 (A/3).

148 Tehran: Home Service, 22 July 1985, in BBC/SWB/ME, 31 July 1985 (A/7–9).

149 Tehran: Home Service, 6 July 1985, in BBC/SWB/ME, 9 July 1985 (A/6).

150 *Jomhure-ye Eslami*, 27 May 1983; *Middle East Economic Digest*, 10 June 1983, p. 16.

151 See Rafsanjani's comments, BBC/SWB/ME, 14 March 1987 (i); and Tehran: Home Service, 13 March 1987, BBC/SWB/ME, 16 March 1987 (A/4–5).

Chapter 12   The Reckoning

1   The advantages are not peculiar to Islamic Iran but to all revolutions. The first modern revolution in France ended the limits on warfare by liberating and involving the energies of an entire nation. This new broadly based power made up in commitment what it lost in professionalism, that is, it lost the aura of power but gained it in tangible ways, leading to an underestimation of it at first glance. At the same time, the involvement of the nation in war tended to make it more absolute. Clausewitz's comments on revolutionary France have a striking resonance in application to the very different revolutionary Iran.

> Looking at the situation in the conventional manner, people at first expected to have to deal only with a seriously weakened French army, but in 1793 a force appeared that beggared all imagination. Suddenly war again became the business of the people – a people of thirty millions, all of whom considered themselves to be citizens ... The people became a participant in war; instead of governments and armies as heretofore, the full weight of a nation was thrown into the balance. The resources now available for use surpassed all conventional limits; nothing now impeded the vigor with which war could be waged, and consequently the opponents of France faced the utmost peril.

What Clausewitz calls the 'juggernaut of war', based on the entire strength of a people, changed the 'vigour' with which war was waged.

> It took on an entirely different character, or rather closely approached its true character, its absolute perfection ... Various factors powerfully increased that vigor: the vastness of available resources, the ample field of opportunity, and the depth of feeling generally aroused. The sole aim of war was to overthrow the opponent. Not until he was prostrate was it considered possible to pause and try to reconcile the opposing interests. War untrammelled by any conventioned restraints had broken loose in all its elemental fury. This was due to the people's new share in these great affairs of state; and their participation, in turn, resulted partly from the impact that the Revolution had on the internal conditions of every state and partly from the danger that France posed to everyone.

Howard and Paret, *Clausewitz: On War* (Book 8), pp. 592–3.

2   As J.F.C. Fuller wrote: 'the conscript armies of the Revolution had one crucial defect which, politically, annulled one and all of [their advantages]. This was the difficulty for a conscripted nation – that is, a nation in arms – a nation fed on violent propaganda, to make an enduring peace'. *The Conduct of War*, pp. 36–7.

3   Leaders like Hashemi Rafsanjani insist that the war is affordable: 'We fight cheaply. We don't spend massively on the war', *The Observer*, 10 May 1987. This is true in a narrow financial sense but is otherwise delusory.

4   There are already some signs of this in Iran in the 'open letters' sent to Khomeini or secretly circulated, which address both the conduct of the war and its aims. Generally the war has been a subject off-limits, beyond the ambit of public debate, but just as unity grows with every glimpse of victory, restiveness increases with signs of stagnation and failure. The regime will be hamstrung in the politics of peace-making both by the constituency wanting to end the war and other powerful groups taking a maximal position on it. Without a victory the politics of the peace, it is clear, will be no easier to manage.

Appendix 1
Iraq: Political and Military Chronology

POLITICAL CHRONOLOGY

1979
July Saddam Hussein becomes President, Chairman of the Revolutionary Command Council and Commander in Chief of the Armed Forces

August Purges and executions of senior figures in the RCC, Ba'th Party Regional Command and Cabinet

1980
April Assassination attempt on Tariq Aziz

Execution of Ayatollah Baqr al-Sadr

Membership of Shi'i-based Al-Da'wa party made punishable by death

Beginning of mass deportation of Iraqi residents of Iranian origin to Iran

June General elections for National Assembly

September Invasion of Iran

November Iraqi opposition fronts form in Iran and Syria: formed of secular opposition, Iraqi Communist party, Kurdish nationalist parties and, eventually, Al-Da'wa

1981

1982
April Syria halts transit of Iraqi oil through Banias pipeline

Saddam Hussein's first public call for austerity

Serious unrest in Kurdistan

June RCC, meeting in absence of Saddam Hussein, agrees to cease-fire terms (rejected by Iran)

9th Regional Congress of Ba'th Party: reassertion of Saddam Hussein's complete control

Reshuffle and dismissals from RCC, Regional Command of Ba'th and Cabinet

November   Supreme Council for the Islamic Revolution in Iraq established in Tehran as umbrella organization for Islamic opposition groups. Chairman: Hojjat al-Eslam Sayyid Muhammad Baqir al-Hakim

1983
June   Beginning of campaign to solicit private donations to war effort

1984
October   General elections for National Assembly

1985

1986
July   Extraordinary Congress of the Ba'th Party Regional Command. Saddam Hussein tightens control. Dismissals and reshuffles in RCC, Ba'th Party Regional Command and Cabinet

1987

MILITARY CHRONOLOGY

1980
June–August   Border clashes
4 September   Iranian shelling of Khanaqin and Mandali
9–10 September   Iraq claims to 'liberate' two pockets of territory between Qasr-e Shirin and Naft-e Shah
17 September   Iraq abrogates 1975 Algiers agreement and declares it will exercise full sovereignty over the Shatt al-Arab
22 September   Iraq invades Iran and bombs Iranian airfields
October   Iraq declares a cease-fire; Iran rejects it
    Iraq captures Khorramshahr
November   Iraq fails to take Susangird

1981
June   Iraq offers Ramadhan cease-fire; Iran rejects it
September   Iraqi forces pushed back across Karun River and break off siege of Abadan

1982
March   Iraqi forces obliged to withdraw from Shush/Dezful area
April   Saddam Hussein announces Iraq would withdraw from all Iranian territory if it could be assured that this would end the war
    Iraq bombs Kharg Island

May   Iraqi forces driven out of Khorramshahr
June   Iraq announces withdrawal from Iranian territory, but some pockets remain in Iraqi hands
August   Iraq announces maritime exclusion zone in the Gulf
Iraq attacks Kharg Island
September   Iraqi planes attack ships in maritime exclusion zone
November   Iraqi territory occupied in Musian area
December   Iraqi missiles fired at Dezful

1983
March   Iraq bombs Nowruz oil field in Gulf
April   Iraqi missile attacks on Dezful
July   Iraqi forces driven out of Haj Umran in Iraqi Kurdistan
Iraqi forces driven out of Mehran
October   Iraqi forces driven out of territory east of Panjwin in Iraqi Kurdistan

1984
February   Iraqi forces driven out of Majnoon islands
March   Beginning of series of Iraqi attacks on shipping in Gulf

1985
March   Iraq bombs Ahwaz: beginning of 'war of the cities'
Iraqi air attacks on Tehran
June   Iraq declares end to war of the cities
August   Iraq launches series of air raids on Kharg Island
November   Iraq bombs industrial targets in Iran

1986
January   Iraq bombs Ghanaveh oil installations
February   Iraqi forces driven out of Fao peninsula
March   UN Secretary General reports confirmation of use by Iraq of chemical weapons
July   Iraqi air raids on Iranian cities and industrial targets
August   Iraqi air raid on Sirri oil terminal
September   Iraqi air raid on Lavan oil terminal
November   Iraqi air raid on Larak oil terminal

1987
January   Iraqi air raids on Iranian cities
February   Iraq calls a halt to raids on cities
August   Iraq resumes air raids on industrial targets, then on Iranian oil terminals and on shipping

Appendix 2
Iraq: Armed Forces 1980–87

Force Category	1980	1987
TOTAL REGULAR ARMED FORCES	242,250	850,000 (a)
LAND FORCES		
Regular Army		
Active	200,000	805,000
Reserves	250,000	230,000
People's Army	250,000	500,000
Divisions		
Armoured	4	5
Mechanized	4	3
Infantry	4	10
Special Forces	0	2
Republican Guard	1	1
Reserve, People's Army, Volunteer	—	8
Major Equipment		
Main Battle Tanks	2,500	4,800
Armoured Fighting Vehicles	2,000	3,800
Major Artillery	1,000	5,200
AIR FORCE		
Manpower	38,000	40,000
Combat aircraft	335	400–500
Combat helicopters	40	100–180
Total helicopters	250	360–400
Surface to Air Missile Batteries	28	75

Force Category	1980	1987
NAVY		
Manpower	4,250	5,000
Frigates	1	2
Corvettes	0	6
Missile Patrol Craft	12	10
Other Patrol Craft	25	12
Minesweepers	8	7
Landing craft and other ships	4	8

(a)   It must be borne in mind that this figure, like all the other figures in this table, is an approximation. Even before the war with Iran, the Iraqi Government was not very forthcoming about the details of its armed forces. During the war it has become understandably more reticent, except when this serves the needs of propaganda. This factor, combined with the attrition of eight years of war, means that one must approach tables such as the one above with due caution. It has been adapted from various editions of the IISS *Military Balance* and from Anthony H. Cordesman, *The Iran–Iraq War and Western Security 1984–1987* (London: Jane's Publishing Co. for RUSI, 1987).

Appendix 3
Iran: Political and Military Chronology

POLITICAL CHRONOLOGY

1979
February Revolutionary forces take over government

April Large-scale fighting between Kurds and Azeris, many deaths

May Khuzestan Arabs in street marches calling for autonomy fight with government troops in Khorramshahr

August Government announces cancellation of $9 billion in US arms ordered by previous regime

August/September Heavy fighting between government and Kurdish population

November 4 Iranian students storm and occupy US embassy in Tehran

November 5 Iran cancels 1957 Treaty of Military Co-operation with US

November 9 US halts shipment of $300 m. worth of spare parts purchased by Iran

December 2 New Islamic Constitution approved in referendum

December 14 Tehran radio announces Iraqi forces enter Iranian territory but repulsed

December 22 State of emergency declared in Baluchestan in face of local rebellion against central government

1980
July 20 Islamic Assembly elects Hashemi Rafsanjani as Speaker

July 21–29 Over 70 army and air force officers arrested for plotting to overthrow government; 30 of them executed immediately, 21 others in August

September 20 President Bani Sadr orders call-up of military reservists to defend 'the integrity of the country'

1981
January 1 Mobilization of the Oppressed (Basij) merged with Islamic Revolution Guards Corps (Pasdaran)

September 12 Morteza Rez'ai appointed Commander of IRGC

October 1 Brigadier Zahirnejad appointed Chief of Joint Staff of armed forces and Colonel Ali Sayid Shirazi appointed commander of the ground forces

1982

March 15   Khomeini urges depoliticization of army and IRGC – 'if armed forces personnel become involved in any party, such an army must be considered finished'

July 18   Tudeh (Communist) Party paper *Ettehad-e Mardom* banned for 'clear opposition' to Islam

October 30   IRGC announces intention to organize naval units

November 16   Following Ayatollah Montazeri's suggestion about need for active presence by clergy at battlefront, 350 clerics from Qom dispatched to front

1983

July 19   In address to Council of Experts Khomeini warns that continuing discord among clergy is harming revolution and calls for unity

November 28   Majles approves bill turning the Construction Crusade into formal government ministry

1984

May 22   IRGC Commander Reza'i announces Pasdaran naval units now operational

July 22   West German Foreign Minister, first senior diplomat from West in Tehran since revolution, is also first to detect moderates in Iran and observes that Iran wishes to re-establish contacts with West

August 28   Khomeini urges bigger role for bazaar merchants in running economy

November   Khomeini calls for an 'open door' in foreign relations

1985

March/April   Signs of war weariness and discontent evident in demonstrations in various towns

April 29   Alliance between two major opposition groups – Mojaheddin and Kurdish Democratic Party – breaks down

November 23   Ayatollah Hossein Montazeri selected by Council of Experts as Khomeini's successor

1986

March 5   Khomeini refers to possibility of women assisting directly in war (IRGC training for women reported on March 12)

June 12   Rafsanjani admits existence of 'two relatively powerful factions' in politics, but observes that while they have different approaches to problems they do not disagree on main issue – support for Islamic republic

July 10   Rafsanjani says Iran's conditions for ending war remain unchanged but that Iran would modify and reduce them if an Islamic regime were to come to power in Iraq

July 16   Khomeini appoints Colonel Sayid Shirazi and IRGC Minister Rafiqdust to Supreme Defence Council for duration of war

September 2   Khomeini warns critics of government to be realistic and limit criticism for 'the issue is not the government but the Islamic republic'

October 1   Musavi says conduct of war unaffected by oil price slump and decline in foreign exchange, nevertheless this is 'the year of the great test'

October 6   Rafsanjani announces petrol rationing, notes improvement in morale and says that those who wish to end war (by compromise) must consider whether they would gain any reparations or obtain return of Iranian nationals expelled by Iraq without a victory

October 9   Power and fuel shortages announced by energy ministry which calls for conservation by consumers

October 30   Rafsanjani says that after war 'We hope that . . . the armed forces of the Islamic Republic of Iran will become a source of security for the countries of the region'

October 30   Musavi refers to results of first census in 10 years which show a population of over 48 million, 11 million of which has been added since revolution. Of those aged over 6, employment is calculated to be 28% and literacy 62%

November 4   On 7th anniversary of seizure of US embassy, Ayatollah Montazeri in Qom says that 'unity between wings inside Iranian regime is lacking'

November 9   Khomeini announces: 'the Republic . . . has been stabilized and is not dependent on any one person'

1987

April 7   IRNA reports Rafsanjani as saying that Iran will resume normal relations with US after it is sure it does not pose a threat to Islamic republic

June 2   IRP officially dissolved. Rafsanjani says it is no longer needed and party polarization could lead to discord and damage national unity

June 14   Rafsanjani elected Speaker of Majles for eighth one-year term

July 8   Tehran reports conscription to begin for IRGC

October 2   Iran and Iraq break off diplomatic relations

November 12   Khomeini refers to new stage in war in which Iran's strategy is to be 'continuation of operations with repeated blows to deprive the enemy of respite'

November 16   Khamenei explains that new strategy is based on involving all groups and classes in war effort in total mobilization

MILITARY CHRONOLOGY

1979
May   Border clashes in Kurdish areas
October 30   Iraq demands revision of Algiers accord of 1975 regulating border

1980
January/September   Border clashes; hostile propaganda; mutual accusations of subversion and terrorism
September 17   Iraq denounces Algiers accord
September 22–26   Iraq launches offensive into Iran together with air strikes; Iran retaliates in Shatt al-Arab
October 24   Iraq captures Khorramshahr after subjecting it to massive bombardment
November   Iraqi shelling of Khuzestan
December 25   Opening of third front in Kurdistan

1981
January   Iranian counterattack at Susangird unsuccessful
September/December   Successful Iranian counter-offensives recapturing much territory including Abadan, Bostan, and Gilan-e Gharb

1982
March   Iran recaptures territory threatening strategically important town of Dezful
April 29–May 24   Iranian counterattacks succeed in recapturing Khorramshahr which because of destruction is renamed Khunin-shahr (or city of blood)
June 30   Iraqi forces retreat from remaining positions on Iranian territory
July 13   Iran rejects Security Council resolution appealing for ceasefire, and orders advance on Baghdad to 'rid the Iraqi people of the Ba'th'
August 15   Iraq declares a 'total exclusion zone' around Iran's oil terminal at Kharg island
November   After Iranian human wave offensive checked, front stabilizes into species of trench warfare

1983
February 9 and April 13   Iranian offensives
March   Iraq attacks Iran's oil platforms causing damage and leakage

April–November   Repeated costly and inconclusive Iranian human wave attacks on Kurdish northern front and central region near Mehran

1984

February 15–March 30   After diversionary attacks in north, Iran launches major offensives on central and southern fronts to cut Baghdad–Basra road. While this is unsuccessful, Iran makes some progress in marshy oil-rich Majnoon region. Iran accuses Iraq of using chemical weapons – subsequently confirmed

Iran for first time begins to shell Basra (indicating diminished confidence in spontaneous support of its Shi'a population for Islamic republic)

Iraq announces new policy of attacking Kharg island and tankers serving Iran to internationalize war and bring pressure to bear on Iran

April 26–May 25   Tanker war intensifies with some 70 ships hit – mainly by Iraqi planes

June 5   Iran's attempt to put pressure on Gulf states to rein in Iraq backfires when it loses an F-5 aircraft to Saudi air force

September–October   Minor engagements on ground

1985

March   After pause of a year Iran launches another offensive, this time in Howeiza marsh region, which proves costly and fruitless

Start of 'war of the cities' with Iran exchanging artillery and missile attacks against Basra and occasionally Baghdad, as against Iraq's intensive and deep aerial bombardment of several Iranian cities including Tehran and Isfahan. This intensifies between May 26 and June 15. Ends with help of UN Secretary-General

June/July   Iran announces new strategy of limited offensives designed to tie down Iraqi forces and wear them down along entire length of front through a form of actual and psychological attrition

July 14   Iran declares that any ship transporting contraband or arms to Iraq through the Gulf will be subject to interdiction and the goods confiscated by Iranian naval patrols

August/September   Iraq launches first intensive air attacks on Kharg island

1986

February   Iran launches night-time offensive against abandoned oil port of Fao and succeeds in capturing and holding it. First unequivocal case of advance at front by Iranian forces in over 4 years; renews hope in feasibility of eventual military victory

May 17   Iraq launches counterattack and captures Mehran only to lose it again in July

August–December   Iraq launches series of air attacks on Iranian economic infrastructure including oil installations (Kharg), refineries (Tehran, Tabriz, Isfahan), pumping stations (Ghanaveh), and power generating plants. These attacks range from those reaching deep inland to those covering for first time Iran's shuttle operation in southern Gulf at Sirri and Lavan. Iran launches ground operation against Iraq's installation in north at Kirkuk

December 24   Iran launches major offensive against Basra with little effect

1987

January 9   Iran's Kerbala 5 offensive opposite Basra, heavy fighting, some advances by Iranian troops. US sources estimate 10,000 Iraqis killed and wounded since December 24 as against 20,000 Iranians. At same time Iran launches Kerbala 6 in central sector of front

January 17–25   Iraq bombs Tehran for first time in two years, and other cities including Qom, Tabriz, Isfahan and Dezful. Iran fires missiles at Basra and Khanaqin

January 25   Rafsanjani in speech to Majles urges Arab states to withdraw support from Iraq and says Iran has no interest in widening war to other Gulf states

February/April   Resumption of war of cities, with heavy bombardment of civilian centres by Iraq resulting, according to Iranian reports, in 15,000 casualties. Iraq unable to dislodge Iran from positions acquired near Basra and suffers heavy loss of aircraft in campaign (45 in 3 months)

April 15   Iran's Foreign Ministry spokesman warns Kuwait that it would be a 'very dangerous situation' if Kuwait leased tankers to outside powers

May 25   Iranian authorities distinguish between land war which they will continue 'until victory' and 'tanker war' which they are prepared to halt if Iraq is restrained from attacking Iran's oil assets

May 31   Foreign Minister Velayati reiterates warnings to US and USSR not to intervene in Gulf

June 15   President Reagan defends his policy in Gulf saying that if the US did not protect shipping in region the USSR would intervene.

June 20   Iraq resumes tanker war after lull of a month. Iran continues land operations in Kurdish areas and accuses Iraq of using chemical weapons and resorting to scorched-earth policy in Iraqi Kurdistan

July 20   UN Security Council approves Resolution 598 calling for ceasefire and withdrawal of forces. Text is attempt at balance between demands of two parties, with clear implication that non-compliance will lead to passage of second resolution containing sanctions and having mandatory force under Chapter VII of UN Charter

July 22   US starts convoying tankers flying US flag

August/September Amid signs of intensified Soviet diplomatic activity, Iran focuses with Moscow on presence of foreign fleets in Gulf as main precondition for further diplomatic progress on war. Iran refuses to give unequivocal or unconditional response to Security Council Resolution 598, telling UN Secretary-General its precondition for acceptance is identification and condemnation of aggressor in war by impartial international panel; pending this Iran offers possibility of *de facto* ceasefire. Secretary-General continues his consultations amid signs that both USSR and China are less than keen about a second resolution

November 11 Iran condemns Arab League Emergency Summit as sell-out of Palestinians. No discussion of Arab states severing diplomatic relations. Syria's acceptance of communiqué critical of Iran does not indicate any reversal of alliances

November 12 Khomeini refers to new stage in war ushering in new military strategy by Iran in which emphasis is put less on size of offensives than on their continuation and repetition to increase pressure on Iraq and 'to deprive the enemy of respite'

November 13/16 New strategy amplified by Rafsanjani and Khamenei who refer to need for more complete mobilization, rotation of groups at front and start of a financial jihad

Appendix 4
Iranian Forces: 1980–86

Force Category	1980	1986
TOTAL ACTIVE MILITARY MANPOWER SUITABLE FOR COMBAT	240,000	1,250,000
LAND FORCES		
Regular Army Manpower		
Active	150,000	350,000–355,000
Reservce	400,000+	NA
Revolutionary Guards/		200,000–300,000
Basij/People's Army (a)		70,000–100,000
Hezbollahi (Home Guard)		2,500,000
Division Equivalents		
Armoured (Divisions/Brigades)	6+4	?
Mechanized	3	3–4? (b)
Infantry and Mountain	3	9–12/1 (b)
Special Forces/airborne	—	0/2
Pasdaran/People's Militia	—	9?/?
Major Combat Equipment		
Main Battle Tanks	1,740	900–1,250
Other Armoured Fighting Vehicles	1,075	1,190–2,000
Major Artillery	1,000+	1,000–1,360
AIR FORCES		
Air Force Manpower	70,000	35,000
Combat Aircraft	445	80–105 (c)
Combat Helicopters	500	50?
Total Helicopters	750	150–370
Surface to Air Missile Batteries (d)	—	12

Force Category	1980	1986
NAVY		
Navy Manpower	26,000	20,000
Destroyers	3 (e)	3 (e)
Frigates	4 (f)	4 (f)
Corvettes (g)	4	2–4
Missile Patrol Craft	9 (h)	3–8 (h)
Other Patrol Craft and Gunboats	—	83
Mine warfare vessels	—	5
Hovercraft	14	10
Landing craft and Ships	—	17
Maritime Patrol Aircraft	6 P–3F	2 P–3F

(a)   Manpower estimates are uncertain. The core of the Iranian land forces seems to total about 200,000 regular army, 200,000 long-term conscripts, and 250,000 Revolutionary Guards. Iran, however, can rapidly build up its manpower and can rotate massive numbers of men from its civil economy. The Basij Mostaz'afin is the principal volunteer base of the forces, nearly half of which are now Revolutionary Guards, and which total about 1,250,000 men. Virtually all villages, urban units, etc. have a Basij unit which both conducts paramilitary training and raises money. About 422,000 Iranians reach conscription age every year, and Iran introduced military training for all secondary students in March 1986. Nearly 3 million Iranians have now received Basij training.

(b)   Estimates differ sharply. The current IISS estimate is based on the Shah's force structure and shows 7 mechanized divisions with 3 brigades each and a total of 9 armoured and 18 mechanized battalions. Also 2 special forces divisions, 1 airborne brigade, and 8 division-sized Revolutionary Guard formations organized in battalions. The actual unit structure is in almost total flux.

(c)   Includes 35–50 F–4D/E, 17–50 F–SE/F, 10–14 F–14A, and 3 RF–4E. Large numbers of additional combat aircraft are in storage due to lack of parts. Some Argentine A–4s and Chinese or North Korean F–6s and F–7s may be in delivery. The number of AH–1J attack helicopters still operational is unknown.

(d)   The number of operational SAM units on each side is unknown. Many of Iran's 12 Hawk batteries are not operational.

(e)   3 equipped with Standard Arm SSMs. One Battle-class and two Sumner-class in reserve. 4 Lupo-class Italian-made frigates on order.

(f)   Equipped with Sea Killer SSM.

(g)   6 Wadi-class Italian-made 650-ton corvettes on order.

(h)   Equipped with Harpoon surface to surface missiles.

Adapted from various editions of IISS, *Military Balance*, JCSS, *The Middle East Military Balance*, work by Drew Middleton for *The New York Times* and Anthony Cordesman, *The Iran–Iraq War and Western Security 1984–1987* (London: Jane's Publishing Co. for RUSI, 1987).

Bibliography

Books

Abdulghani, J.M., *Iraq and Iran: the Years of Crisis*, London: Croom Helm, 1984.

Adelman, Jonathan, *Revolution, Armies and War: A Political History*, Boulder, Colo.: Lynne Rienner, 1985.

Afkhami, Gholam R., *The Iranian Revolution: Thanatos on a National Scale*, Washington, DC: The Middle East Institute, 1985.

Afshar, Haleh (ed.), *Iran: A Revolution in Turmoil*, New York: State University Press, 1985.

Ajami, Fuad, *The Vanished Imam*, Ithaca: Cornell University Press, 1986.

Amin, S., *Irak et Syrie 1960–1980*, Paris: Editions de Minuit, 1982.

Amin, S.H., *The Iran–Iraq War: Legal Implications*, London: Butterworth, 1982.

Amnesty International, *Report and Recommendation – Iraq*, London: Amnesty International, 1983.

Armitage, M.J. and Mason, R.A., *Air Power in the Nuclear Age, 1945–84: Theory and Practice*, London: Macmillan (2nd edition), 1985.

Aziz, T., *On the Iraqi-Iranian Conflict*, London: Iraqi Cultural Centre, 1981.

——, (tr. N. al-Hadithi), *The Iraq–Iran Conflict: Questions and Discussion*, London: Third World Centre for Research and Publishing, 1981.

Bakhash, Shaul, *The Reign of the Ayatollahs*, New York: Basic Books, 1984; London: Tauris, 1985 and Counterpoint, 1986.

Batatu, H., *The Old Social Classes and the Revolutionary Movements of Iraq*, Princeton: Princeton University Press, 1978.

Benard, Cheryl and Khalilzad, Zalmay, *The Government of God: Iran's Islamic Republic*, New York: Columbia University Press, 1984.

Ben-Dor, G., *State, Society and Military Elites in the Middle East*, Tel-Aviv: Tel-Aviv University Press, 1984.

Brown, J. and Snyder, W.P., *The Regionalization of Warfare*, New Brunswick: Transaction Books, 1985.

C.A.R.D.R.I., *Saddam's Iraq – Revolution or Reaction?*, London: Zed Books, 1986.

Clausewitz, Carl von, *On War*, (Edited–translated Michael Howard and Peter Paret), Princeton: Princeton University Press, 1984.

Cole, Juan R.I. and Keddie, R. Nikki (eds), *Shi'ism and Social Protest*, New Haven: Yale University Press, 1986.

Cordesman, A.H., *The Gulf and the Search for Strategic Stability*, Boulder, Colo: Westview Press, 1984.

——, *The Iran–Iraq War and Western Security 1984–1987*, London: Jane's Publishing Co. for RUSI, 1987.

Cottam, Richard, *Nationalism in Iran*, Pittsburgh: University of Pittsburgh, 1979.

Dann, U., *Foundations of the Ba'th Regime in Iraq 1968–73*, Tel-Aviv: Tel-Aviv University Press, 1974.

Dawisha, Adeed (ed.), *Islam in Foreign Policy*, London: Cambridge University Press for Royal Institute of International Affairs, 1983.

Dessouki, A.E.H. (ed.), *The Iraq–Iran War*, Princeton: Princeton University Press, 1981.

Devlin, J.F., *The Ba'th Party: A History from its Origin to 1966*, Stanford: Stanford University Press, 1976.

El-Hajj, A., *L'Irak nouveau et le problème kurde*, Paris: Les Editions Khayat, 1977.

El-Azhari, M.S. (ed.), *The Iran–Iraq War: An Historical, Economic and Political Analysis*, London: Croom Helm for CAGS, University of Exeter and CAGS, University of Basra, 1984.

Ellis, John, *Armies in Revolution*, London: Oxford University Press, 1974.

Enayat, Hamid, *Modern Islamic Political Thought*, Austin: University of Texas Press, 1982.

Fuller, J.F.C., *The Conduct of War 1789–1961*, London: Methuen, 1972.

Gabriel, R.A. (ed.), *Fighting Armies: Antagonists in the Middle East*, Westport, Conn.: Greenwood Press, 1983.

Guerreau, A., *L'Irak: développement et contradictions*, Paris: Sycamore, 1978.

Hammadi, S. (ed.), *Studies in Arab Nationalism and Unity* (Arabic), Beirut: Centre of Arab Unity Studies, 1984.

Heller, C. (ed.), *The Military as an Agent of Social Change*, Mexico: Collegio de Mexico, 1981.

Heller, M.A., *The Iran–Iraq War: Implications for Third Parties* (JCSS Paper No. 23, January 1984), Tel-Aviv: Tel-Aviv University Press, 1984.

Heller, M.A., Tamari, D., and Eytan, Z., *The Middle East Military Balance 1983, 1984, 1985*, Tel-Aviv: JCSS, Tel-Aviv University Press, 1983–5.

Helms, C.M., *Iraq: Eastern Flank of the Arab World*, Washington, DC; Brookings Institution, 1984.

Hiro, Dilip, *Iran Under the Ayatollahs*, London: Routledge, Kegan Paul, 1985.

Hünseler, P., *Der Irak und sein Konflikt mit Iran*, Bonn: Europa–Union, 1982.

Hussein, Saddam, *Message to the Fourth Corps Commander*, Baghdad: Dar al-Ma'mun, 1982.

——, *Speech on Army Day: the 59th Anniversary of the Founding of the Iraqi Army*, Baghdad: Dar al-Ma'mun, 1982.

——, *Iraq Addresses the Islamic World on the Conflict With Iran*, Baghdad: Dar al-Tarjama wa'l-Nashr bi'l-Lughat al-'Ajnabiyya, 1983.

——, *Iraq and International Politics* (Arabic), Baghdad: Dar al-Hurriya, 1981.

——, *Iraqi Policies in Perspective*, Baghdad: Dar al-Ma'mun, 1981.

——, *Discours prononcé au Congrès international de Solidarité avec le peuple irakien*, Baghdad: Dar al-Ma'mun, 1981.

——, *Letters to the Iranian People 1–4*, Baghdad: Dar al-Ma'mun, 1983–5.

Ismael, T., *Iraq and Iran: the Roots of Conflict*, Syracuse: Syracuse University Press, 1982.

Islamic Republic of Iran, *War Against Revolution: A Study of The Iraqi Regime's Aggression Against Iran*, Tehran: June 1981.

——, *A Review of the Imposed War*, Tehran: Ministry of Foreign Affairs (Legal Dept), 1983.

——, *The Imposed War: Defence vs. Aggression*, Tehran: Supreme Defence Council [War Information Headquarters]. Vol. 1, February 1983; Vol. 2, April 1984; Vol. 3, September 1985.

——, *The Displaced People in the War Iraq Imposed on Iran*, Tehran: Ministry of Islamic Guidance, April 1982.

——, *Our Tyrannized Cities: Statistical Survey of Aggressions of the Ba'thist Regime of Iraq Against Iranian Cities and Residential Areas*, Tehran: Supreme Defence Council [War Information Headquarters], 1983.

Jawad, S., *Iraq and the Kurdish Question*, London: Ithaca Press, 1981.

Kanovsky, E., *Iran–Iraq War: its Economic Implications*, Tel-Aviv: Shiloah Centre, Tel-Aviv University, 1983.

Kelidar, A., *Iraq: the Search for Stability*, London: I.S.C., 1975.

Khadduri, M., *Socialist Iraq*, Washington DC: Middle East Institute, 1978.

King, R., *The Iran–Iraq War: the Political Implications*, Adelphi Paper 219, London: International Institute for Strategic Studies, 1987.

Knorr, Klaus (ed.), *Historical Dimensions of National Security Problems*, Lawrence: University of Kansas Press, 1976.

Kodmani, B. (ed.), *Quelle sécurité pour le Golfe?*, Paris: I.F.R.I., 1984.

Kolodziej, E.A. and Harkavy, R.E. (eds), *Security Policies of Developing Countries*, Lexington, Mass.: Lexington Books, 1982.

Korany, B. and Dessouki, A.E.H. (eds), *The Foreign Policies of Arab States*, Boulder, Colo.: Westview Press, 1984.

Kramer, Martin (ed.), *Shi'ism, Resistance and Revolution*, Boulder, Col.: Westview, 1987.

Legum, C., Shaked, H., and Dishon, D. (eds), *The Middle East Contemporary Survey*
III–VII 1978–83, London: Holmes and Meier, 1980–84.

Litwak, R., *Sources of Interstate Conflict: Security in the Persian Gulf 2*, London: Gower for I.I.S.S. 1981.

Lloyds Bank, *Iraq: Annual Report 1985*, London: Lloyds Bank Group, 1985.

McDowell, D., *The Kurds*, M.R.G. Report 23, London: Minority Rights Group, 1985.

McLaurin, R.D., Peretz, D., and Snider, L.W. (eds), *Middle East Foreign Policy*, London: Praeger, 1982.

Mahrad, A., *Der Iran–Irak Konflikt*, Frankfurt am Main: Peter Land, 1985.

Marr, P., *The History of Modern Iraq*, Boulder, Colo.: Westview, 1985.

Martin, L.G., *The Unstable Gulf: Threats from Within*, Lexington, Mass.: Lexington Books, 1984.

Ministry of Culture (Iraq), *The Condemnation* (Arabic), Baghdad: Ministry of Culture, 1984.

——, *International Peace Efforts to End the War* (Arabic), Baghdad: Ministry of Culture, 1984.

Ministry of Foreign Affairs (Iraq), *The Iraqi–Iranian Dispute: Facts and Allegations*, Baghdad: Ministry of Foreign Affairs, 1981.

——, *The Iraqi–Iranian Conflict: a Documentary Dossier*, Baghdad: Ministry of Foreign Affairs, 1981.

Ministry of Guidance (Iraq), *Selections from the Iraq–Iran Dispute*, Baghdad: Ministry of Culture, 1983.

Mottahedeh, Roy, *The Mantle of the Prophet: Religion and Politics in Iran*, London: Chatto and Windus, 1986.

Neumann, S.G. (ed.), *Defense Planning in Less-Industrialised States*, Lexington, Mass.: D.C. Heath and Co., 1984.

Neumann, S.G. and Harkavy, R.E. (eds), *The Lessons of Recent Wars in the Third World*, Volumes I and II, Lexington, Mass.: D.C. Heath and Co., 1985, 1987.

Niblock, T. (ed.), *Iraq: the Contemporary State*, London: Croom Helm, 1982.

Nonneman, G., *Iraq, the Gulf States and the War*, London: Ithaca Press, 1986.

Nyrop, R. (ed.), *Iraq – a Country Study*, Washington, DC: American University Press, 1979.

Parry, V.J., and Yapp, M.E. (eds), *War, Technology and Society in the Middle East*, Oxford: Oxford University Press, 1979.

Piscatori, James P.(ed.), *Islam in the Political Process*, London: Cambridge University Press for Royal Institute of International Affairs, 1986.

Ramazani, R.K., *Revolutionary Iran: Challenge and Response in the Middle East*, Baltimore: Johns Hopkins University Press, 1986.

Rosen, Barry M. (ed.), *Iran Since the Revolution*, Social Science Monographs, New York: Brooklyn College, 1985.

Sader, M., *Le développement industriel de l'Irak*, Beirut: C.E.R.M.O.C., 1983.

Samarbakhsh, A.G., *Socialisme en Irak et en Syrie*, Paris: Anthropos, 1980.

Shariati, Ali, *What is to be Done: The Enlightened Thinkers and an Islamic Renaissance* (edited by Farhang Rajaee), Houston, Texas: Institute for Research and Islamic Studies, 1986.

Sick, Gary, *All Fall Down: America's Tragic Encounter with Iran*, New York: Random House, 1985.

Stein, G. and Steinbach, U. (eds), *The Contemporary Middle Eastern Scene*, Opladen: Leske and Budrich, 1979.

Sun Tzu, *The Art of War* (edited and translated by Samuel Griffith), New York: Oxford University Press, 1963.

Taheri, Amir, *The Spirit of Allah: Khomeini and the Islamic Revolution*, London: Hutchinson, 1985.

——, *Holy Terror: The Inside Story of Islamic Terrorism*, London: Sphere, 1986.

Tahir–Kehli, S. and Ayubi, S., *The Iran–Iraq War: New Weapons, Old Conflicts*, New York: Praeger, 1983.

Tchamran, Mustapha, *La révolution islamique et la guerre imposée*, Tehran: Ministry of Islamic Affairs, 1982.

Westwood, J.N., *The History of Middle East Wars*, London: Hamlyn Publishing, 1984.

Yodfat, Aryeh, H., *The Soviet Union and Revolutionary Iran*, London: Croom Helm, 1984.

Articles

Akhavi, Shahroukh, 'Elite Factionalism in the Islamic Republic of Iran', *The Middle East Journal*, 41/2, Spring 1987.

——, 'The Ideology and Praxis of Shi'ism in the Iranian Revolution', *Comparative Studies in History and Society*, V/25, April 1983.

Al-Khafaji, I., 'State Incubation of Iraqi Capitalism', *M.E.R.I.P. Report 142*, Sept./Oct. 1986.

Alaolmolk, Nozar, 'The New Iranian Left', *The Middle East Journal*, 41/2, Spring 1987.

Arjomand, Said Amir, 'Iran's Islamic Revolution in Comparative Perspective', *World Politics*, XXXVIII/3, April 1986.

Baram, A., 'Saddam Hussein: a Political Profile', *Jerusalem Quarterly*, 17, 1980.

——, 'The June 1980 Elections to the National Assembly in Iraq: An Experiment in Controlled Democracy', *Orient*, 22, 1981.

——, 'Culture in the Service of Wataniyya', *Asian and African Studies*, 17, 1983.

——, 'Qawmiyya and Wataniyya in Ba'thi Iraq', *Middle Eastern Studies*, 19/2, 1983.

——, 'Mesopotamian Identity in Ba'thi Iraq', *Middle Eastern Studies*, 19/4, 1983.

Batatu, H., 'Class Analysis and Iraqi Society', *Arab Studies Quarterly*, 1, 1979.

——, 'Iraq's Underground Shi'i Movements', *Middle East Journal*, 35, 1981,

——, 'State and Capitalism in Iraq', *M.E.R.I.P. Report*, 142, Sept./Oct. 1986.

Bengio, O., 'Saddam Husayn's Quest for Power and Survival', *Asian and African Studies*, 15, 1981.

——, 'Shi'i and Politics in Ba'thi Iraq', *Middle Eastern Studies*, 21/1, 1985.

Bill, James, 'Resurgent Islam in the Persian Gulf', *Foreign Affairs*, 63/1, Fall 1984.

Braun, Ursula, 'The Iran–Iraq War: its Regional and International Dynamics' (mimeo), April 1987.

Chabry, L., 'L'Irak et l'émergence de nouveaux rapports politiques interarabes', *Maghreb-Machrek*, 88, 1980.

Chubin, S., 'The Foreign Policy of the Islamic Republic of Iran', in *Negotiations in Asia*, Geneva: Centre for International Negotiations, 1984.

——, 'Israel and the Iran–Iraq War', *International Defense Review*, 3, 1985.

——, 'Iran's View of the War', Paper presented to Conference on *Regional Impact of Gulf War* (IISS/University of Jordan), Amman, June 1986.

——, 'Reflections on the Gulf War', *Survival*, July/August 1986.

——, 'Hedging in the Gulf: Soviets Arm Both Sides', *International Defense Review*, 20/6, June 1987.

——, 'The Conduct of Military Operations', *Politique Etrangère*, 2, 1987.

——, 'Iran and its Neighbours: The Impact of the Gulf War', *Conflict Studies*, 204, 1987.

Cohen, Eliot, 'Distant Battles: Modern War in the Third World', *International Security*, 10/4, Spring 1986.

Cordesman, A., 'Lessons of the Iran–Iraq War', Parts I and II, *Armed Forces Journal International*, April, June 1982.

Cottam, Richard, 'Regional Implications of the Gulf War: Iran, Motives behind Foreign Policy', *Survival*, November/December 1986.

Dann, U., 'The Kurdish National Movement in Iraq', *Jerusalem Quarterly*, 9, 1978.

Dawisha, A., 'Iraq and the Arab World: the Gulf War and After', *The World Today*, May 1981.

——, 'Iran's Mullahs and the Arab Masses', *Washington Quarterly*, 6/3, Summer 1986.

Farhang, Mansour, 'The Iran–Iraq War: The Feud, the Tragedy and the Spoils', *World Policy Journal*, Fall 1985.

Farley, J., 'The Gulf War and the Littoral States', *The World Today*, July 1984.

Farouk-Sluglett, M., 'Socialist Iraq 1963–1978: Towards a Reappraisal', *Orient*, 23, 1982.

Farouk-Sluglett, M., Sluglett, P. and Stork, J., 'Not Quite Armageddon', *M.E.R.I.P. Report*, 125–6, July/Sept. 1984.

Gennaoui, J., 'L'Irak en guerre au Moyen-Orient', *Projet*, 151, 1981.

George, Alan, 'Iraq Tips the Scales', *Defence*, December 1984.

Haim, S., 'Shi'ite Clerics and Politics: Some Recent Tendencies in Iraq', *Israel Oriental Studies*, 10, 1980.

Hamm, Manfred R., 'Deterrence, Chemical Warfare, and Arms Control', *Orbis*, 29/1, Spring 1985.

Harkavy, Robert E., 'The Lessons of Recent Wars: A Comparative Perspective', *The Third World Quarterly*, 6/4, October 1984.

Helms, C.M., 'The Iraqi Dilemma: Political Objectives versus Military Strategy', *Brookings General Series Reprint*, 398, 1983.

Hiro, D., 'Chronicle of the Gulf War', *M.E.R.I.P. Report*, 125–6, July/Sept. 1984.

Hunter, S., 'After the Ayatollah', *Foreign Policy*, 66, Spring 1987.

Iftekhari, Kajal, 'Les Kurdes dans la Guerre Iran–Irak', *L'Afrique et l'Asie Modernes*, 148, Spring 1986.

Ja'fer, M., 'The Gulf War as the Extinction of Politics', *Khamsin 12: The Gulf War*, 1986.

Jansen, G., 'The Gulf War: the Contest Continues', *Third World Quarterly*, October 1984.

Johansen, Robert C. and Renner, Michael G., 'Limiting Conflict in the Gulf', *Third World Quarterly*, 7/4, October 1985.

King, Ralph, 'Impact of the Iran–Iraq War on Gulf Security', Conference on *Regional Implications of Gulf War* (IISS/University of Jordan), Amman, June 1986 (mimeo).

Kolodziej, E.A. and Harkavy, R., 'Developing States and the International Security System', *Journal of International Affairs*, 34, 1980.

Lewis, Bernard, 'Islamic Revolution', *New York Review of Books*, 21 January 1988.

Mallat, C., 'Aux origines de la guerre Irak–Iran: l'axe Najaf-Téhéran', *Les Cahiers de l'Orient*, 3, 1986.

Mansur, A.K., 'The Military Balance in the Persian Gulf: Who will guard the Gulf States from their Guardians?', *Armed Forces Journal International*, 118, 1980.

Martin, P., 'Le clergé chiite en Irak hier et aujourd'hui', *Maghreb Machrek*, 115, 1987.

Najmabadi, Afsaneh, 'Iran's Turn to Islam: From Modernism to a Moral Order', *The Middle East Journal*, 41/2, Spring 1987.

O'Ballance, E., 'The Iraqi-Iranian War: The First Round', *Parameters*, 11, March 1981.

Rondot, P., 'L'Irak; une puissance régionale en devenir', *Politique Etrangère*, 45, 1980.

——, 'Irak gegen Iran: Krieg ohne Entscheidung?', *Europa Archiv*, 36, 1981.

Rosser-Owen, David, 'The Gulf War', *Defence Today International*, Winter 1984.

——, 'The Iran–Iraq War', *Defence*, December 1984.

Sick, Gary, 'Iran's Quest for Superpower Status', *Foreign Affairs*, 64/4, Spring 1987.

Sirriyeh, H., 'Development of the Iraqi–Iranian Dispute 1847–1975', *Journal of Contemporary History*, 20/3, 1985.

Springborg, R., 'Infitah, Agrarian Transformation and Elite Consolidation in Contemporary Iraq', *Middle East Journal*, 40/1, 1986.

Strika, V., 'L'inizio delle ostilità tra Iraq e Iran secondo le fonti irachene', *Oriente Moderno*, 62, 1982.

Tripp, C., 'Iraq – Ambitions Checked', *Survival*, November/December 1986.

——, 'La guerre Irak–Iran: l'impossible retour au statu quo ante', *Les Cahiers de l'Orient*, 3, 1986.

Western European Union, Assembly, 'Consequences of the Gulf War', Paris: WEU (Report on Behalf of General Affairs Committee), Document 994, 30th Ordinary Session: Second Part, 12 November 1984.

Wright, C., 'Iraq: New Power in the Middle East', *Foreign Affairs*, 58, 1979/80.

——, 'Implications of the Iraq–Iran War', *Foreign Affairs*, 59, 1980/81.

——, 'Religion and Strategy in the Iraq–Iran War', *Third World Quarterly*, 7/4 October, 1985.

Index

Hussein, President Saddam, 7, 8, 10,
15–17, 23–30, 49, 51, 53–60, 63–7,
passim, 80, 83–98, 100–3, 105–22
passim, 136, 139–57, 161, 164, 168,
172, 183, 186, 188–202 *passim*, 206,
224, 242–5 *passim*, 251, 252
Hussein, Riyadh Ibrahim, 89

ideology, 1, 3, 6, 7, 9–10, 16–17, 21, 31, 34,
36, 38–9, 143, 145, 147, 189, 203–6
passim, 213, 219, 238–9, 246–8 *passim*
see also Iran; Iraq
IGAT–1, 226, 230
Indian Ocean, 204, 236, 288n.143
inflation, 110, 124, 126, 132
internationalization of war, 3, 8, 9, 48, 52,
63, 66, 155, 160, 173–7, 196, 214,
216, 227–9, 233, 252 *see also* Gulf;
shipping; tanker war
Iran, 1, 2, 6–7, 16, 22–52, 68–83, 100–2,
105–6, 123–38, 149–50, 158–87, 195,
196, 199, 201–40, 245–55
and Gulf states, 2, 9, 51, 135, 153,
158–79, 185, 187, 196, 219, 246,
250, 276n.38
and Kuwait, 156, 160, 161, 163, 168,
170–1, 174–7 *passim*, 246
and Saudi Arabia, 73, 136, 156, 165, 167,
169, 172–3, 175–6, 178, 210
and Soviet Union, 2, 9, 197, 204–5,
220–38, 246, 248, 250
and Syria, 2, 151, 152, 159, 179–86, 208
and US, 2, 9, 36–7, 66, 149, 167, 176,
177, 196, 198, 204–21, 226, 227,
234, 239, 246, 248, 250
conduct of war, 2, 3, 7–12, 32, 36–51
passim, 68–70, 74–7 *passim*, 87, 126,
155, 160, 162, 167, 174, 196, 222,
227, 247, 254, 299–302
economy, 63–4, 66–7, 70, 75, 123–38
ideology, 2, 3, 6, 7, 9–10, 31, 32, 35, 36,
38–42 *passim*, 46, 51, 72, 78–9,
81–2, 124, 132, 158–9, 161–3,
167–8, 181, 203–6 *passim*, 213, 219,
238–9, 246–8, 250
military, 6, 7, 9, 33–7 *passim*, 43–9, 51,
60, 206, 207, 247, 249, 253, 303–5
oil, 63, 66–7, 123–7, 134–8, 155, 166,
168, 171–4 *passim*, 196, 214
opposition, 34, 46, 62, 69–71, 79–83
politics, 37, 52, 56, 59, 60, 62, 69–78,
249–52, 254, 290n.4, 296–9
revolution, 6–7, 31–2, 34–5, 39, 40, 42,
44, 49, 51, 68–70, 124, 131, 150,

162, 167, 170, 181, 203, 206, 207,
211, 212, 218–19, 249
war aims, 1, 3, 8–10, 38–40, 49–52, 58,
70, 79–80, 83, 89–91, 161, 202
Irangate, 174, 197, 211–13, 215, 226,
281n.42
Iranians overseas, 162, 274n.6
Iraq, 2, 6, 13–30, 33, 34, 50–1, 53–67, 81,
84–122, 139–57, 162, 180, 182,
188–202, 209, 210, 241–5
and Arab world, 10, 16–17, 25, 28,
139–41, 143–57
and Gulf states, 2, 3, 139, 140, 152–7,
163
and Kuwait, 152, 154, 163, 170–1
and Soviet Union, 2, 9, 188–92 *passim*,
194, 197–9, 221–4, 227–9 *passim*,
231, 238
and Syria, 139, 147–52, 185
and US, 2, 9, 66, 189–91, 193–4, 197,
200, 208–10 *passim*, 212
conduct of war, 2, 3, 8, 23–5, 28–30,
54–6, 58–67, 118, 134–7, 154–6
passim, 160, 168, 171–3, 196, 209,
214–15, 219, 292–3
economy, 108–14, 180
ideology, 9, 10, 16–17, 21, 84, 94–6, 145
military, 9, 10, 18–22 *passim*, 114–20,
122, 140, 242–5, 294–5
oil, 110, 137, 148, 154, 174, 179–80 *see
also* pipelines
opposition, 9, 21, 25, 54–5, 89–92,
100–8, 148, 242
politics, 3, 6, 7, 13–22, 53, 55–7, 84–108,
120–2, 241–5, 291–2
war aims, 8, 13, 29, 55, 57, 58, 60, 64, 67,
87, 89, 190, 201, 258n.14
Irfani, Minister of Economy, 128
Isfahan, 62, 137, 234
Islam, 5, 7, 9, 32, 33, 35, 38–43 *passim*, 50,
70, 73, 79, 81–2, 103, 131, 132, 146,
150, 156, 158–62 *passim*, 165, 179–81,
185, 206, 211, 222, 232, 251, 253, 254
Islamic Conference Organization, 174
Islamic Jihad, 163, 182, 208, 210
Islamic Liberation Movement, 70, 82
Islamic Republican Party, 37, 69–70, 207,
252
Israel, 6, 9, 10, 16, 21, 22, 139, 143–5,
148–50 *passim*, 152, 159, 161, 181,
183, 184, 186, 212, 213, 248
Italy, 215

al-Jaish al-Sha'bi *see* Popular/People's
Army

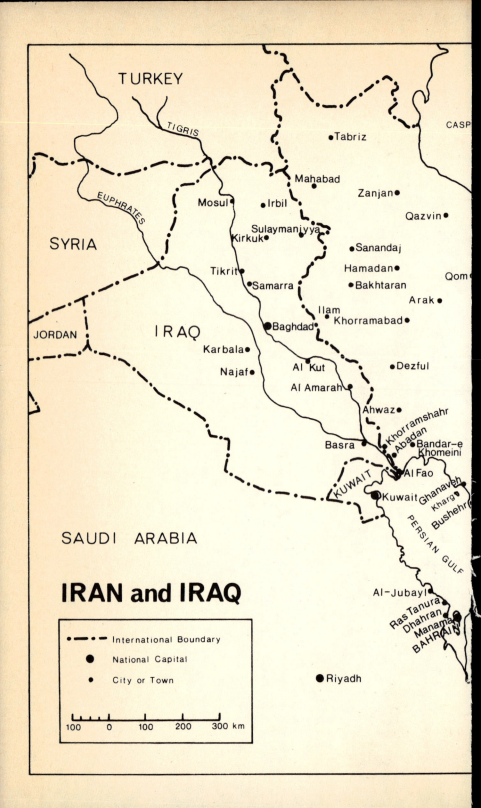

Jones-Quartey, K. A. B. "Anglo-African Journals and Journalists in the 19th and early 20th Centuries", *Transactions of the Historical Society of Ghana*, 4, 1959, pp. 47–56.

"Thought and Expression in the Gold Coast Press 1874–1930", *Universitas* (Legon, Ghana), 3, 1958, pp. 72–75.

"Sierra Leone's Role in the Development of Ghana 1820–1930", *Sierra Leone Studies*, New Series, No. 10, June 1958.

"The Institutions of Public Opinion in a Rapidly Changing Africa" in *Conference on Representative Government and National Progress*, Ibadan, 1959, pp. 2–3.

"A Note on J. Mensah Sarbah and J. E. Casely Hayford, Ghanaian Leaders, Politicians and Journalists 1864–1930", *Sierra Leone Studies*, New Series, No. 14, Dec. 1960, pp. 57–62.

"Sierra Leone and Ghana, 19th Century Pioneers in West African Journalism", *Sierra Leone Studies*, Dec. 1957, pp. 230–244.

Levy-Strauss, C. "Social Structure" in *Anthropology Today* (ed. Krober, A. L.).

Lewis, L. J. "Problems in British Colonial Territories", *Year Book of Education*, 1956, pp. 555–563.

"The Social and Cultural problems of urbanisation for the individual and the family", *Rural Life*, Vol. 5, No. 2, 1964.

"Technical Change and the Curriculum", *Year Book of Education*, 1958, pp. 421–425.

"The Challenge of Education in Tropical Areas", *The Modern Churchman*, Vol. 9, No. 1, October 1965.

Little, K. "The Study of Social Change in British West Africa", *Africa*, 1953, Vol. 28, No. 4.

"The Role of Voluntary Associations in West African Urbanisation", *American Anthropologist*, Vol. 59, pp. 579–596.

Lochner, N. "Anton Wilheim Amo, A Ghana Scholar in 18th Century Germany", *Transactions of the Historical Society*, Ghana, 3, 1957, pp. 169–179.

Lynch, H. "The Matirie Pastorate Controversy and Cultural Ethnocentrism in Sierra Leone 1871–1874", *Journal of African History*, 5, 3, 1964, pp. 395–413.

Mair, L. "How small-scale societies change", in *Penguin Survey of the Social Sciences* (1966).

"African Chiefs Today" (The Luggard Memorial Lecture for 1958) in *Africa*, July 1958, pp. 200 ff.

Martin, E. C. "Early Educational Experiment on the Gold Coast", *Journal of the Royal African Society*, Vol. 23.

Mayhew, A. "A Comparative Survey of Educational Aims and Methods in British India and British Tropical Africa", *Africa*, 6, 1963, pp. 172–186.

Mercier, P. "The Evolution of Senegalese Elites", *International Social Science Bulletin*, 8 (3), 1956, pp. 445 ff.

Meyerowitz, E. L. R. "Concepts of the soul among the Akan of the Gold Coast", *Africa*, 21, 1, January 1951, pp. 24–31.

Nesiah, K. "British Impact on Education in Ceylon", *Year Book of Education*, 1958, pp. 121–122.

Newbury, C. W. "North African Trade in the 19th Century", *Journal of African History*, 1964, pp. 244–245.

Nicol, D. "West Africa's First Institution of Higher Education", *Sierra Leone Journal of Education*, Vol. 1 (1), April, 1966.

Nicol, A. "West Indians in West Africa", *Sierra Leone Studies*, New Series, 13, June 1960, pp. 14–23.

Ormsby-Gore, W. "Education in the British Dependencies of Tropical Africa", *Year Book of Education*, 1932, pp. 764 ff.

Perraton, H. D. "British Attitudes towards East and West Africa 1888–1914", *Race*, 8 (3), January 1967.

Read, M. "Africans and their schools", *British Commonwealth Affairs*, No. 8, 1953.
"Education in Africa: Its Pattern and Role in Social Change", *Annals of the American Academy of Political and Social Science*, 298, March 1955, p. 173.

Rhodie, S. "The Gold Coast Aborigines Abroad", *Journal of African History*, 6, 3, 1965.

Richards, A. I. "Economic and social factors affecting the education of African girls in territories under British influence", *UNESCO*, Meeting of Experts on Education (Cotonou/4/May 24, June 2, 1960).

Scott, H. S. "The Development of the Education of the African in Relation to Western Contact", *Year Book of Education*, 1938, pp. 693 ff.

St. Clair Drake. "Social Change and Social Problems in Contemporary Africa" in *The United States and Africa* (ed. by Goldschmidt, New York, 1963).

Swanzy, H. "A Trading Family in the 19th Century Gold Coast (the Swanzys)", *Transactions of the Gold Coast and Togoland Historical Society*, 2, 1956, pp. 87–120.

Tardits, C. "The notion of the elite and urban social survey in Africa", *UNESCO* (1956), pp. 492–495.

Thompson, E. W. "Christian Education in British West Africa", *Church Missionary Review*, Vol. 75, 1924, pp. 6–17.

Tiryakian, E. A. "The Prestige Evaluation of Occupations in an Underdeveloped Country (the Philippines)", *American Journal of Sociology*, 1958, 63, pp. 390–399.

Ward, W. E. F. "Education in the Colonies" in *New Fabian Colonial Essays* (ed. by Creech Jones, A., London, 1959, Ch. 8).

Wilkie, A. W. "An attempt to conserve the work of the Basel Missions on the Gold Coast", *International Review of the Missions*, 1920, pp. 94–96.

Wolfson, F. "British Relations with the Gold Coast 1843–1880", *British Institute of Historical Research*, 24, 70, 1951, pp. 182–186.

Wright, F. "System of Education in the Gold Coast Colony" in *Board of Education Special Reports on Educational Subjects* (London, 1905).

Xydias, N. "Prestige of Occupations" in *Social implications of Industrialisation and Urbanisation in Africa South of the Sahara*", *UNESCO*, 1956, pp. 458–469.

Others

(i) Mfantsipim Log Book (1892–1903).

(ii) "A Friend of Africa", *Hints on Education Printed for School Masters in the Gold Coast Colony*, printed in 1876 by W. J. Johnson, 121 Fleet Street, London, E.C. (By an anonymous author.)

(iii) Hague Archives. Letters and Despatches to and from the Dutch West Indian Company—15/2/1743, 1/7/1745.

(iv) *Educational Record* (1822), Vol. XVIII, p. 21. (Monitorial Schools and their successors).

(v) Educational Exposition (March 1853).

(vi) Minutes of Conference (Methodist), 1836, Vol. 8.

(vii) "African Education—A Study of Educational Policy and Practice in British Tropical Africa", produced on behalf of the Nuffield Foundation and the Colonial Office (1953).

(viii) *Comparative Educational Review*, Vol. 4, No. 3, 1961, pp. 136–139. (Article by F. Schneider).

(ix) *The International Review of Missions*, Vol. 15, No. 59.

(x) Gold Coast Education Ordinance.

(xi) "The Roman Catholic Tradition in Education", *Year Book of 1938.*

(xii) "The Nature and Determinants of Social Status", *Year Book of Education*, London, 1953.

(xiii) "The Emerging African Middle Class in Southern Africa", Colonial Review IX, No. 5, March 1956.

(xiv) "Social Learning and Interaction", *Current Sociology*, Vol. 14, No. 3, 1966 (Chapter 4).

(xv) The British Government Report—The Settlements on the West Coast of Africa (1863).

C. *Secondary Sources*

Adamson, J. W. *English Education, 1789–1902* (Cambridge, 1965).

Ahuma, S. R. B. Attoh. *Memoirs of West African Celebrities, 1700–1850* (Liverpool, 1905).
The Gold Coast Nation and National Consciousness (Liverpool, 1911; 2nd edition, with a new introduction by Professor J. C. de Graft-Johnson, Frank Cass, London, 1971).

Ainslie, R. *The Press in Africa* (London, 1966).

Anene, J. C. *Southern Nigeria in Transition 1885–1906* (London, 1966).

Apter, D. *The Gold Coast in Transition* (Princeton, 1955).

Astley, T. *A New Collection of Voyages and Travels* (London, 1743–47; reprinted Frank Cass, London, 1968, 4 vols.).

Ayandele, E. A. *The Missionary Impact on Modern Nigeria, 1824–1914: a political and social analysis* (London, 1966).

Baldridge, C. *White Africans and Black (Sketches and Impressions of Fourteen Months in Africa)* (New York, 1929).

Baldwin, T. W. *William Shakespeare's Petty School* (Urbana, 1943).

Bales, R. F. and Parsons T. *Family, Socialisation and Interaction Process* (London, 1955).

Barnard, H. C. *A History of English Education from 1760 to 1944* (London, 1952).

Bartels, F. L. *The Roots of Ghana Methodism* (Cambridge, 1965).

Beattie, J. *Other Cultures: aims, methods and achievements in social anthropology* (London, 1964).

Beetham, T. A. *Christianity and the New Africa* (London, 1967).

Benedict, R. *Patterns of Culture* (London, 1945).

Birchenough, C. *History of Elementary Education in England and Wales from 1800 to the Present Day* (London, 1927).

Blake, J. W. *Europeans in West Africa 1450–1560* (London, 1942, 2 Vols.).

Boeke, J. H. *Economics and Economic Policy in Dual Societies* (New York, 1953).

Body, A. H. *John Wesley and Education* (London, 1936).

Bourret, F. M. *Ghana—Road to Independence 1919–1957* (London, 1960).

Bowdich, T. E. *A Mission from Cape Castle to Ashantee* (London, 1819; 3rd edition, with a new introduction by W. E. F. Ward, Frank Cass, London, 1966).

Bradshaw, H. L. *Hints to Teachers* (translated into Luganda by Ebisanira Abaigiriza) (London, 1928).

Brasio, A. *Monumenta Missionaria Africana* (Lisbon, 1952).

Brenna, T. Cooney, and others. *Social Change in South West Wales* (London, 1954).

Brokensha, D. *Social Change at Larteh, Ghana* (Oxford, 1966).

Brooking, R. *Nucleus of a Grammar of the Fanti Language with a Vocabulary* (Cape Coast, 1843).

Buell, R. L. *The Native Problem in Africa* (New York, 1928; reprinted Frank Cass, London, 1965, 2 vols.).

Burns, A. *Colour Prejudice* (London 1948).

Burr, N. R. *Education in New Jersey 1630–1871* (Princeton, 1942).

Busia, K. A. *The Position of the Chief in the Modern Political System of Ashanti* (Oxford, 1951; reprinted Frank Cass, London, 1968).
Purposeful Education for Africa (London, 1964). *Democracy in Africa* (London, 1967).

Buxton, C. (ed.) *Memoirs of Sir T. F. Buxton* (London, 1852).

Buxton, T. F. *Committee of the House of Commons* (London, 1837).
The African Slave Trade and its Remedy (London, 1839; 1840; reprinted Frank Cass, London, 1967).

Cardinal, A. W. *A Bibliography of the Gold Coast 1496–1931* (Accra, 1931).

Cannell. *A Concise Fanti-English Dictionary* (London, 1886).

Chinoy, E. *Sociological Perspective—basic concepts and their application* (New York, 1954).

Claridge, W. Walton. *A History of the Gold Coast and Ashanti from the earliest times to the commencement of the twentieth century* (London, 1915; 2nd edition, with a new introduction by W. E. F. Ward, Frank Cass, London, 1964).

Collier, K. G. *The Social Purposes of Education* (London, 1959).

Cowan, L. G. (ed.). *Education and Nation-building in Africa* (New York, 1965).

Crooks, J. J. *History of the Colony of Sierra Leone* (Dublin, 1903).
Records relating to the Gold Coast Settlements from 1750 to 1874 (Dublin, 1923).

Cruickshank, B. *Eighteen Years on the Gold Coast of Africa* (London, 1853; 2nd edition, with a new introduction by Dr. K. A. Busia, Frank Cass, London, 1966).

Danquah, J. B. *Gold Coast Akan Laws and Customs* (London, 1928).
The Akan Doctrine of God. A Fragment of Gold Coast Ethics and Religion (London, 1944; 2nd edition, with a new introduction by the Rev. K. A. Dickson, Frank Cass, London, 1968).

Davey, C. J. *The Methodist Story* (London, 1955).

Davies, K. G. *The Royal African Company* (London, 1957).

de Graft Johnson, J. W. *Towards Nationhood in West Africa* (London 1928; 2nd edition, with a new introduction by F. K. Drah, Frank Cass, London, 1970).

Dennis, J. S. *Christian Missions and Social Progress* (London, 1899).

Dent, H. C. *A New Order in English Education* (London, 1942).
Change in English Education: a historical survey (London, 1952).

Du Bois, W. E. B. *The Suppression of the African Slave Trade to the U.S.A. 1638–1870* (Massachusetts, 1916).
The World and Africa—an inquiry into the part which Africa has played in world history (New York, 1947).

Dupuis, J. *Journal of a Residence in Ashantee* (London, 1824; 2nd edition, with a new introduction by W. E. F. Ward, Frank Cass, London, 1966).

Durkheim, E. *Moral Education—a Study in the Theory of the Application of the Sociology of Education* (Glencoe, 1961).

Evans-Pritchard, E. E. *The Position of Women in Primitive Societies and Other Essays in Social Anthropology* (London, 1965).

Fage, J. D. *Introduction to the History of West Africa* (London, 1959).

Ferguson, G. E. *Report on Mission to Atabubu* (London, 1898).

Findlay, G. G., and N. W. Holdsworth. *The History of the Wesleyan Methodist Missionary Society* (London, 1922, 2 Vols.).

Fortes, M., and G. Dieterlen. *African Systems of Thought* (Oxford, 1965).

Foster, P. J. *Education and Social Change in Ghana* (London, 1965).

Fraenkel, M. *Tribe and Class in Monrovia* (Oxford, 1964).

Freeman, Rev. Thomas Birch. *Journal of Various Visits to the Kingdoms of Ashanti, Aku and Dahomi* (London, 1840–43; 2nd ed. 1844; 3rd edition, with a new introduction by Professor Harrison M. Wright, Frank Cass, London, 1968).

Gellner, E. A. *Thought and Change* (Suffolk, 1959).

Gisborne, T. *An Inquiry into the Duties of the Female Sex* (London, 1786).
An Inquiry into the Duties of Men in the Higher and Middle Classes of Society in Great Britain (London, 1795).

Grey, H. G. *The Colonial Policy of Lord John Russell's Administration*, Vol. 2 (London, 1853).

Groves, C. P. *The Planting of Christianity in Africa* (London, 1948).

Guggisberg, F. G., and A. G. Frazer. *The Future of the Negro* (London, 1929).

Hailey, M. *The Future of Colonial Peoples* (Oxford, 1942: London, 1943).
An African Survey—a study of problems arising in Africa south of the Sahara (London, 1938; revised 1956).

Hallingey, J. T. F. *Methodism in West Africa* (London, 1907).

Hayford, C. M. *West Africa and Christianity* (London, 1901).

Hayford. J. E. Casely. *Gold Coast Native Institutions* (London, 1903; reprinted Frank Cass, London, 1970).
The Truth about the West African Land Question (London, 1913; 2nd edition, with a new introduction by Professor E. U. Essien-Udom, Frank Cass, London, 1971).

Herskovits, M. J. *The Human Factor in Changing Africa* (New York, 1962).

Hill, P. *The Gold Coast Farmer* (*A Preliminary Survey*), (Oxford, 1956).

Hilliard, F. H. *A Short History of Education in British West Africa* (Edinburgh, 1957).

Hodgkin, T. *Nationalism in Colonial Africa* (London, 1956).

Horton, J. A. B. *West African Countries and Peoples* (London, 1868).

Letters on the Political Condition of the Gold Coast (London, 1870; 2nd edition, with a new introduction by Professor E. A. Ayandele, Frank Cass, London, 1970).

Hutton, W. *John Wesley* (London, 1927).

Isaacs, S. S. *Psychological Aspects of Child Development* (London, 1950).

Jahoda, G. *White Man* (Oxford, 1961).

Jones, C. A. *New Fabian Colonial Essays* (London, 1959).

Jones, M. G. *The Charity School Movement* (London, 1938; reprinted Frank Cass, London, 1964).

Kardiner, A. *The Individual and his Society* (New York, 1939).

Kay, Joseph. *The Education of the Poor in England and Europe* (London, 1846).

The Condition and Education of Poor Children in English and German Towns (London, 1853).

Kay-Shuttleworth, J. P. *Social Conditions and Education of the People in England*, Vol. 1 (London, 1853).

Four Periods of Public Education as reviewed in 1832, 1839, 1846, 1862 (London, 1862).

The earliest British document on education for the coloured races (Pretoria, 1862).

Kemp, D. *Nine Years on the Gold Coast* (London, 1898).

Kepe, W. *The Education of Children* (London, 1588).

Kerstiens, T. *The New Elite in Asia and Africa: A Comparative Study of Indonesia and Ghana* (New York, 1966).

Kilson, M. *Political Change in a West African State—a study of the modernisation process in Sierra Leone* (Massachusetts 1966).

Kimble, D. *A Political History of Ghana 1850–1928* (Oxford, 1963).

Kingsley, Mary. *Travels in West Africa* (London, 1897; 1900; 3rd edition, with a new introduction by Dr. John E. Flint, Frank Cass, London, 1965).

West African Studies (London, 1899; 1901; 3rd edition, with a new introduction by Dr. John E. Flint, Frank Cass, London, 1964).

Kuper, Leo. *An African Bourgeoisie: Race, Class and Politics in Southern Africa* (New Haven, 1965).

Lawrence, A. W. *Trade Castles and Forts of West Africa* (London, 1963).

Leith-Ross, S. *African Women* (London, 1938).

Lewis, L. J. *Education and Political Independence in Africa* (Edinburgh, 1962).

Lipset, M. *The First New Nation* (New York, 1963).

Little, K. *West African Urbanisation* (Cambridge, 1965).

Lloyd, P. C. *Africa in Social Change* (London, 1967).

Lockwood, D. *The Blackcoated Worker* (London, 1958).

Macartney, W. M. *Dr. Aggrey, 1875–1927* (London, 1949).

McCully, B. T. *English Education and the Origins of Indian Nationalism* (New York, 1940).

Maclure, J. S. *Educational Documents, England and Wales, 1816–1963* (London, 1965).

MacRae, D. G. *Ideology and Society* (London, 1961).

McWilliam, H. O. A. *The Development of Education in Ghana: An Outline* (London, 1959).

Mair, Lucy. *An African People in the Twentieth Century* (London, 1934).
    Education in the British Colonies (United Kingdom, Ministry of Information, Reference Division, 1944).
    Welfare in the British Colonies (London, 1944).
    New Nations (London, 1963).

Marris, P. *Family and Social Change in an African City* (London, 1961).

Martin, E. C. *The British West African Settlements 1750–1821: a study in local administration* (London, 1927).

Maunier, R. *The Sociology of Colonies—an introduction to the study of race contact* (translated and edited by E. O. Lormer, London, 1949).

Metcalfe, G. E. *George Maclean of the Gold Coast, the life and times of George Maclean 1801–1847* (London, 1962).

Meyer, A. *An Educational History of the Western World* (New York, 1965).

Meyerowitz, E. L. R. *The Divine Kingship of Ghana and Ancient Egypt* (London, 1960).

Misra, B. B. *The Indian Middle Class* (London, 1961).

Moore, W. E. *Social Change* (New Jersey, 1963).
    Order and Change: essays in comparative sociology (New York, 1967).

Morel, E. D. *Affairs of West Africa* (London, 1902; 2nd edition, with a new introduction by Kenneth Dike Nworah, Frank Cass, London, 1968).

Morrell, W. P. *British Colonial Policy in the Age of Peel and Russell* (Oxford, 1930; reprinted Frank Cass, London, 1966).

Murray, A. V. *The School in the Bush. A Critical Study of the Theory and Practice of Native Education in Africa* (London, 1929; 1938; reprinted Frank Cass, London, 1967).

Newbury, C. W. *British Policy Towards West Africa—Select Documents, 1786–1874* (Oxford, 1965).

Ogilvie, J. N. *Our Empire's Debt to Missions* (London, 1924).

Oliver, R. *Sir Harry Johnston and the Scramble for Africa* (London, 1957).

Parsons, T. *Essays in Sociological Theory* (Glencoe, 1954).

Rattray, R. S. *Ashanti Law and Constitution* (Oxford, 1929). *Religion and Art in Ashanti* (Oxford, 1927).

The Tribes of the Ashanti Hinterland (Oxford, 1932).

Read, M. H. *Education and Social Change in Tropical Areas* (London, 1955).

Reindorf, C. C. *History of the Gold Coast and Ashantee* (Basel, 1895).

Rich, R. W. *The Training of Teachers in England and Wales during the Nineteenth Century* (London, 1950).

Robinson, Ronald, and J. Gallagher. *Africa and the Victorians —the Official Mind of Imperialism* (London, 1965).

Rottman, W. J. *The Educational Work of the Basel Missions on the Gold Coast* (London, HMSO, 1905).

Salmon, D. *Joseph Lancaster* (London, 1904).

Salmon, L. M. *The Newspaper and the Historian* (Oxford, 1923).

Sampson, M. J. *Gold Coast Men of Affairs* (London, 1937).

Sarbah, J. M. *Fanti Customary Laws* (London, 1897; 1904; 3rd edition, with a new introduction by Professor Hollis R. Lynch, Frank Cass, London, 1968).

Fanti National Constitution (London, 1906; 2nd edition, with a new introduction by Professor Hollis R. Lynch, Frank Cass, London, 1968).

Scanlon, D. G. *Church, State and Education in Africa* (New York, 1966).

Sloan, R., and H. Kitchen. *The Educated African—a country by country survey of educational development in Africa* (London, 1962).

Smith, E. W. *Aggrey of Africa—A Study in Black and White* (London, 1929).

Smith, F. *A History of English Elementary Education 1760–1802* (London, 1931).

Smith, Noel. *The Presbyterian Church of Ghana, 1835–1960: A Younger Church in a Changing Society* (Ghana: Oxford, 1967).

Smythe, H. H., and M. M. Smythe. *The New Nigerian Elite* (Stanford, 1960).

Sommerlad, E. L. *The Press in Developing Countries* (Sydney, 1966).

Southall, I. *Social Change in Modern Africa* (Oxford, 1961).

Southon, A. E. *Gold Coast Methodism—The First Hundred Years* (Cape Coast, 1935).

Stevens, A. *The History of the Religious Movement of the 18th Century called Methodism* (London, 1878).

Thomspon, T. *An Account of Two Missionary Voyages* (London, 1758; reprinted with an introduction and notes by the S.P.C.K., London, 1937).

Tildsley, A. *A remarkable work achieved by Rev. Dr. M. C. Hayford* (London, 1926).

Trevelyan, G. M. *English Social History* (London, 1944). *British History in the 19th Century* (London, 1931).

Trimmer, Mrs. *Reflections upon the Education of Children in Charity Schools* (London, 1792).

Tylleman, E. *Guinea* (Copenhagen, 1697).

Wallerstein, I. M. *The Road to Independence* (New York, 1959).

Ward, W. E. F. *Education in the Colonies* (London, 1959). *A History of the Gold Coast* (London, 1948).

Wartenberg, J. S. *Sao Jorge d'Elmina, Premier West African Settlement* (Stockwell, 1951).

Watson, Foster. *The English Grammar Schools to 1660* (Cambridge, 1908; reprinted Frank Cass, London, 1968).

Watts, I. *An essay towards the encouragement of Charity Schools* (*Works*, Vol. 4, 1728).

Weiler, H. N. *Education and Politics in Nigeria* (Rombach, 1964).

Wesley, J. *Works* (8 Vols.).

West, D. *The Life and Journals of the Rev. Daniel West* (London, 1857).

Wilson, G. and M. *The Analysis of Social Change* (Cambridge, 1945).

Wilson, J. L. *Western Africa: Its History, Conditions and Prospects* (New York, 1856).

Wiltgen, R. M. *Gold Coast Missionary History 1471–1880* (Illinois, 1956).

Williamson, S. G. *Akan Religion and the Christian Faith* (Ghana: Oxford, 1965).

Wise, C. *History of Education in British West Africa* (London, 1956).

Wyndham, H. A. *Atlantic and Slavery* (London, 1935; being reprinted Frank Cass, London).

Zollschan, G. K., and Walter Hirsch (eds.). *Explorations in Social Change* (London, 1964).

INDEX

213